EXAM CRAM 2

Designing and Implementing Databases with SQL Server 2000 Enterprise Edition

Thomas Moore

CERTIFICATION

MCAD/MCSE/MCDBA Designing and Implementing Databases with SQL Server 2000 Enterprise Edition Exam Cram 2 (Exam 70-229)

Copyright © 2005 by Que Publishing

International Standard Book Number: 0-7897-3106-1

Library of Congress Catalog Card Number: 2004118019

Printed in the United States of America

First Printing: June 2005

08 07 06 05   4 3 2 1

Trademarks

All terms mentioned in this book that are known to be trademarks or service marks have been appropriately capitalized. Que Publishing cannot attest to the accuracy of this information. Use of a term in this book should not be regarded as affecting the validity of any trademark or service mark.

Warning and Disclaimer

Every effort has been made to make this book as complete and as accurate as possible, but no warranty or fitness is implied. The information provided is on an "as is" basis. The author and the publisher shall have neither liability nor responsibility to any person or entity with respect to any loss or damages arising from the information contained in this book or from the use of the CD or programs accompanying it.

Bulk Sales

Que Publishing offers excellent discounts on this book when ordered in quantity for bulk purchases or special sales. For more information, please contact

> **U.S. Corporate and Government Sales**
> 1-800-382-3419
> corpsales@pearsontechgroup.com

For sales outside the U.S., please contact

> **International Sales**
> international@pearsoned.com

Publisher
Paul Boger

Executive Editor
Jeff Riley

Development Editor
Mark Renfrow

Managing Editor
Charlotte Clapp

Project Editor
Dan Knott

Copy Editor
Cheri Clark

Indexer
Erika Millen

Proofreader
Elizabeth Scott

Technical Editor
Randy Cornish

Publishing Coordinator
Pamalee Nelson

Multimedia Developer
Dan Scherf

Interior Designer
Gary Adair

Cover Designer
Anne Jones

Page Layout
Susan Geiselman

Que Certification • 800 East 96th Street • Indianapolis, Indiana 46240

A Note from Series Editor Ed Tittel

You know better than to trust your certification preparation to just anybody. That's why you, and more than 2 million others, have purchased an Exam Cram book. As Series Editor for the new and improved Exam Cram 2 Series, I have worked with the staff at Que Certification to ensure you won't be disappointed. That's why we've taken the world's best-selling certification product—a two-time finalist for "Best Study Guide" in CertCities' reader polls—and made it even better.

As a two-time finalist for the "Favorite Study Guide Author" award as selected by CertCities readers, I know the value of good books. You'll be impressed with Que Certification's stringent review process, which ensures the books are high quality, relevant, and technically accurate. Rest assured that several industry experts have reviewed this material, helping us deliver an excellent solution to your exam preparation needs.

Exam Cram 2 books also feature a preview edition of MeasureUp's powerful, full-featured test engine, which is trusted by certification students throughout the world.

As a 20-year-plus veteran of the computing industry and the original creator and editor of the Exam Cram Series, I've brought my IT experience to bear on these books. During my tenure at Novell from 1989 to 1994, I worked with and around its excellent education and certification department. At Novell, I witnessed the growth and development of the first really big, successful IT certification program—one that was to shape the industry forever afterward. This experience helped push my writing and teaching activities heavily in the certification direction. Since then, I've worked on nearly 100 certification related books, and I write about certification topics for numerous Web sites and for *Certification* magazine.

In 1996, while studying for various MCP exams, I became frustrated with the huge, unwieldy study guides that were the only preparation tools available. As an experienced IT professional and former instructor, I wanted "nothing but the facts" necessary to prepare for the exams. From this impetus, Exam Cram emerged: short, focused books that explain exam topics, detail exam skills and activities, and get IT professionals ready to take and pass their exams.

In 1997 when Exam Cram debuted, it quickly became the best-selling computer book series since "...*For Dummies*," and the best-selling certification book series ever. By maintaining an intense focus on subject matter, tracking errata and updates quickly, and following the certification market closely, Exam Cram established the dominant position in cert prep books.

You will not be disappointed in your decision to purchase this book. If you are, please contact me at etittel@jump.net. All suggestions, ideas, input, or constructive criticism are welcome!

Ed Tittel

I would like to dedicate this book to the people I work with. You tend to stretch your imagination further when you are surrounded by other creative individuals.

Eric – Jody – Kevin – Troy – Wes

May you never stop investigating new solutions to the problems you face.

About the Author

Thomas Moore (MCSE, MCSA, MCSD, MCDBA, MCT, CSE, CTT+) has been in the computer industry for more than 25 years. Thomas has a wide variety of expertise in all hardware environments and with most Microsoft Server products. "My first and lasting love," he says, "besides my wife and family, however, is programming." Thomas is comfortable in any programming language environment, achieving his MCSD and MCDBA certifications from their inception and recently completing his Microsoft CSE certification as a certified software engineer with Microsoft Business Solutions products. Over the past 18 years he has been working for various Microsoft partners and currently is an Intermediate Developer/Technical Consultant with Diamond Municipal Solutions (formerly Diamond Software) in Paris, Ontario, where he has been for the past three years. Thomas enjoys staying up-to-date, although, like most of us, he finds it a challenge to keep up with the pace of the industry.

Acknowledgments

There are always so many people to thank on any significant project like this one that it is difficult to cover everyone involved without the fear of missing an important cog. Rest assured that all the hundreds of individuals directly or indirectly involved in the project all deserve a portion of the recognition for its completion.

First off I must thank my wife, Joy, and children, Danny, Max, and Chelsea. As always, my family are the most deeply impacted when I decide to take on yet another of my "projects." The many hours that I spent typing away in the office were voluntarily given up by the people closest to me.

Next I would like to thank the editors. Randy Cornish, whom I have had the pleasure of working with on other projects, came through as expected. Randy, you have an eye for detail and you are as always the perfect technician. Cheri Clark proved to be an individual who performed above and beyond within the scope of her work. Cheri came through and managed to polish some of my most uncoordinated grammar.

I would also like to thank the individuals I work with day-to-day at Diamond Software. Each has provided indirectly to this manuscript. Those to whom I have dedicated this book and the others I work with every day make my life so much more rich and enjoyable. I truly look forward to going to work every day. Although R.B. I must admit I like to leave the place to go home too. :)

Finally, to the rest of the Que team. From the top down, the organization is professional, polished, and respected. I would like to thank Jeff Riley, the acquisitions editor, for coming up with the project in the first place. How many projects are good enough to have two development editors? Steve Rowe and Mark Renfrow were both a real pleasure to work with through the duration of the project, and Dan Knott, the project editor, really pulled things together and ensured that all the bases were covered.

It was fun, ladies and gentlemen; perhaps we should all do it again sometime?

Contents at a Glance

Table of Contents

We Want to Hear from You!

As the reader of this book, *you* are our most important critic and commentator. We value your opinion and want to know what we're doing right, what we could do better, what areas you'd like to see us publish in, and any other words of wisdom you're willing to pass our way.

As an executive editor for Que Publishing, I welcome your comments. You can email or write me directly to let me know what you did or didn't like about this book—as well as what we can do to make our books better.

Please note that I cannot help you with technical problems related to the topic of this book. We do have a User Services group, however, where I will forward specific technical questions related to the book.

When you write, please be sure to include this book's title and author as well as your name, email address, and phone number. I will carefully review your comments and share them with the author and editors who worked on the book.

Email: feedback@quepublishing.com

Mail: Jeff Riley
            Executive Editor
            Que Publishing
            800 East 96th Street
            Indianapolis, IN 46240 USA

For more information about this book or another Que Certification title, visit our website at www.examcram2.com. Type the ISBN (excluding hyphens) or the title of a book in the Search field to find the page you're looking for.

Introduction

So into the world of database development we plunge. The selection you have made of this *Exam Cram 2* series book will help you along your way to passing the 70-229 exam. You will find information within this book that will help ensure your success as you pursue this Microsoft exam and MCDBA certification.

This Introduction explains MCDBA certification in general and talks about how the *Exam Cram 2* series can help you prepare for the 70-229 exam. This Introduction discusses the basics of the MCDBA certification, including test-taking strategies. Chapters 1 through 10 are designed to remind you of everything you need to know to take and pass the exam. The two sample tests at the end of the book should give you a reasonably accurate assessment of your knowledge and, yes, we've provided the answers and their explanations. Along with the explanations, you will find some particularly useful links to more information on the topic. For each answer there is a reference to the chapter of the book that covers the topic, as well as a link to more information on the Microsoft MSDN site and another to SQL Server books online.

Read the book and understand the material, and you'll stand a very good chance of passing the test. Make use of the additional links to the other materials and points of reference, and that, along with actual product use, will put you in excellent shape to do well on the exam.

Exam Cram 2 books help you understand and appreciate the subjects and materials necessary to pass Microsoft certification exams. *Exam Cram 2* books are aimed strictly at test preparation and review. They do not teach you everything you need to know about a topic. Instead, we present and dissect the questions and problems we've found that you're likely to encounter on a test. We've worked to bring together as much information as possible about Microsoft certification exams.

The MCDBA certification will require you to know considerable information about the SQL Server product and its deployment with a network infrastructure. You must pass the two product-specific exams, 70-228 (SQL Administration) and 70-229 (SQL Implementation). You must also pass a networking exam dealing with Windows Server 2003 or Windows 2000 Server. Finally, you must select an elective to complete the certification. This could be a networking elective or programming elective, and there are numerous choices to select from. Again, consult the Microsoft website for more specific information.

Approximately 130,000 professionals have earned the MCDBA certification at the time this book was written. This would seem to indicate that even though the certification is challenging, it is most certainly attainable. The 70-229 exam is also one of the possible electives on the MCSD and MCSD.net certification paths.

About the Exam and Content Areas

The exam 70-229: Designing and Implementing Databases with Microsoft SQL Server 2000 Enterprise Edition includes a variety of content. For specifics on the exam, check the exam guide on the Microsoft website at this URL:

http://www.microsoft.com/learning/exams/70-229.asp

The broad topic areas covered by the exam include the following:

➤ *Developing a Logical Data Model*—Application of common database development theories to a database design project is initiated using common industry standards.

➤ *Implementing the Physical Database*—Turning the design into a reality within the SQL Server framework is the start toward SQL Server–specific implementation.

➤ *Retrieving and Modifying Data*—Getting the data in and out and manipulating the data to produce the results will be expected within the business solution.

➤ *Programming Business Logic*—Complex task will require procedure development and programming technique.

➤ *Tuning and Optimizing Data Access*—An application, once in place, will need to be analyzed and tweaked.

➤ *Designing a Database Security Plan*—Confidential data must be protected and access to areas of data controlled to prevent corruption.

Each of the task areas represents elements of a systems design from the outset of a project. The exam will be taking systems from a rough design through to the specifics of the implementation and then following up with fine-tuning of the application to improve performance and guarantee security.

How to Prepare for the Exam

The implementation exam is somewhat difficult to prepare for because it is very broad in scope. This is not an exam you can adequately prepare for by simply rote-memorizing terms and definitions. You need to be able to analyze a scenario and answer by combining various knowledge points from various topic areas. Successfully completing this exam requires a great deal of thought and analysis to properly choose the "best" solution from several "viable" solutions in many cases.

As stated and restated, this exam is best prepared for by doing. You must work with the databases and all the related objects to be comfortable with the material being addressed by the exam.

The only other recommendation we would give is to leave no stone unturned. You should be spending a considerable amount of time within SQL Server Books Online. This help facility is installed with the product, available from the Start menu, and it has a phenomenal amount of information. The other resource is www.microsoft.com. In particular, visit the MSDN library site. Within these two additional resources you'll find every answer to every question on the exam.

What This Book Will Do

This book is designed to be read as a pointer to the areas of knowledge you will be tested on. In other words, you might want to read the book one time just to get insight into how comprehensive your knowledge of this topic is. The book is also designed to be read shortly before you go for the actual test. We think you can use this book to get a sense of the underlying context of any topic in the chapters or to skim-read for Exam Alerts, bulleted points, summaries, and topic headings.

We have drawn on material from Microsoft's own listing of knowledge requirements, from other preparation guides, and from the exams themselves. We have also drawn from a battery of technical websites, as well as from our own experience with application development and the exam. Our aim is to walk you through the knowledge you will need. By reading this book, you will gain from the experience of real-world professional development.

What This Book Will Not Do

This book will *not* teach you everything you need to know about database development. The scope of the book is exam preparation. The book is intended to ramp you up and give you confidence heading into the exam. This book is also not intended as an introduction to database design and implementation. It reviews what you need to know before you take the test, with its fundamental purpose dedicated to reviewing the information needed on the Microsoft certification exam.

This book uses various teaching and memorization techniques to analyze the exam-related topics and to provide you with everything you will need to know to pass the test.

About the Book

We suggest that you read this book from front to back. You will not be wasting your time, because nothing we have written is a guess about an unknown exam. We have had to explain certain underlying information on such a regular basis that we have included those explanations here.

After you have read the book, you can brush up on a certain area by using the index or the table of contents to go straight to the topics and questions you want to reexamine. We have tried to use the headings and subheadings to provide outline information about each given topic. After you have been certified, we think you will find this book useful as a tightly focused reference and an essential foundation of information systems and controls auditing.

Each *Exam Cram 2* chapter follows a regular structure, and provides graphical cues about especially important or useful material. The structure of a typical chapter is as follows:

➤ *Opening hotlists*—Each chapter begins with lists of the terms you will need to understand and the concepts you will need to master before you can be fully conversant in the chapter's subject matter. We follow the hotlists with a few introductory paragraphs, setting the stage for the rest of the chapter.

➤ *Topical coverage*—After the opening hotlists, each chapter covers the topics related to the chapter's subject.

➤ *Exam Alerts*—Throughout the text, we highlight material most likely to appear on the exam by using a special Exam Alert that looks like this:

> This is what an Exam Alert looks like. An Exam Alert stresses concepts, terms, or best practices that will most likely appear in one or more certification exam questions. For that reason, we think any information presented in an Exam Alert is worthy of unusual attentiveness on your part.

Even if material is not flagged as an Exam Alert, *all* the content in this book is associated in some way with test-related material. What appears in the chapter content is critical knowledge.

➤ *Notes*—This book is an overall examination of database design and implementation. As such, we delve into many aspects of business systems. Where a body of knowledge is deeper than the scope of the book, we use notes to indicate areas of concern.

> Cramming for an exam will get you through a test, but it will not make you a competent database implementation professional. Although you can memorize just the facts you need to know in order to become certified, your daily work in the field will rapidly put you in water over your head if you do not know the underlying principles.

➤ *Tips*—We provide tips that will help you build a better foundation of knowledge or focus your attention on an important concept that reappears later in the book. Tips provide a helpful way to remind you of the context surrounding a particular area of a topic under discussion.

> Much of the performance of a database system comes out of a strong design. In contrast, a poor design will not perform well after it's implemented. Take the time during the initial stages of design to put together a sound foundation for the system.

➤ *Practice questions*—This section presents a short list of test questions related to the specific chapter topic. Following each question is an explanation of both correct and incorrect answers. The practice questions highlight the areas we found to be most important on the exam.

The bulk of the book follows this chapter structure, but we would like to point out a few other elements:

➤ *The Cram Sheet*—This appears as a tear-away sheet inside the front cover of this *Exam Cram 2* book. It is a valuable tool that represents a collection of the most difficult-to-remember facts and numbers we think you should memorize before taking the test. Remember, you can dump this information out of your head onto a piece of paper as soon as you enter the testing room. These are usually facts that we have found require brute-force memorization. You need to remember this information only long enough to write it down when you walk into the test room. Be advised that you will be asked to surrender all personal belongings other than pencils before you enter the exam room itself.

You might want to look at the Cram Sheet while in your car or in the lobby of the testing center just before you walk into the testing center. The Cram Sheet information is divided under headings, so you can review the appropriate parts just before each test.

➤ *Self-Assessment*—This is a quick look at your current status in preparing for the 70-229 Exam. This section contains some quick questions to ask yourself prior to diving into the book. Answer the questions honestly, and the advice given will allow you to make better use of your preparation time.

➤ *Glossary*—This is an extensive list of important terms used in this book.

Self-Assessment

Before you attempt to take the exam covered by this book, it is imperative that you know considerable information about SQL Server itself. Of course, this being a development exam, you must also be comfortable with the concepts of the language and its use. There is so much breadth to this exam that we felt it necessary to include a Self-Assessment within this book to help you evaluate your exam readiness. Within this portion of the book, let us take a look at what is needed to pass the exam and to achieve MCDBA certification. When you go through the actual Self-Assessment contained within this element of the book, you will have a good idea as to how far along you are toward readiness to take the exam.

Database Implementation and Administration as an MCDBA

To complete the MCDBA certification, you will have to be a very well-rounded, database-aware individual. This is perhaps the most meaningful of all Microsoft certifications and also the one that maps most closely to the everyday work environment found in the real world. With that said, you will also likely find this particular exam one of the most challenging to successfully complete.

The exam will require you to have knowledge about application development architecture and database design theories. Before you even consider anything about the actual SQL Server software, be ready for a significant portion of the exam to be testing you on design theories.

After considering the theory portion, remember that this is a Microsoft exam and it is focused around the SQL Server product. To pass the exam, you will need to know how the software interacts with both the hardware and the operating system. You will need to know how to configure the software, where to store the files and data, and how to organize the placement of all the individual elements.

You will find questions covering all SQL Server objects, including the appropriate creation and use of each object type. A business application has many supporting objects within the Database Management System over and above the data itself. You can expect a wide assortment of the objects to be throughout the questions on the certification exam.

You can get all the information you need from the material presented and the references to other resources given throughout the book. If you're willing to tackle the preparation process seriously and do what it takes to gain the necessary experience and knowledge, you can take and pass the exam. In fact, the *Exam Crams* and the companion *Exam Preps* are designed to make it as easy as possible for you to prepare for these exams, but prepare you must!

The Ideal MCDBA Database Developer Candidate

Just to give you some idea of what an ideal Database Development candidate is like, here is some relevant information about the background and experience such an individual should have (source: Preparation Guide for Exam 70-229, http://www.microsoft.com/learning/exams/70-229.asp):

➤ Experience in settings in which there are multiple database platforms (heterogeneous databases)

➤ Ability to integrate database security mechanisms with Windows Authentication

➤ Work in a client/server DBMS installations of sizes ranging from 50 to 5,000 users

➤ Use of SQL Server as a Back Office server for Internet/intranet websites

➤ Exposure to databases of all sizes ranging up to 2TB

➤ Ability to enable multiple instances of SQL Server on a single or multiple machines

Taking a closer look at the experience requirements, Microsoft explains that a candidate should have at least one year's experience implementing relational databases.

Put Yourself to the Test

The following questions and observations are designed to help you figure out how much work you'll face in pursuing the MCDBA certification and what kinds of resources you can consult on your quest. Be absolutely honest in your answers, or you'll end up wasting money on an exam you're not ready to take. There are no right or wrong answers to the following questions, only steps along the path to certification. Only you can decide when you are ready.

Two things should be clear from the outset, however:

➤ Even a modest background in logic will be helpful.

➤ Hands-on experience with designing, coding, testing, documenting, and fine-tuning on SQL Server tools used to handle complex database systems is an essential ingredient for success.

Educational Background

1. Were you strong in mathematics—in particular, algebra—in school? (Yes or No)

2. Do you enjoy solving logic puzzles? (Yes or No)

3. Have you taken any classes dealing with programming a computer in any language? (Yes or No)

   If you answered yes to any of the preceding three questions, you will likely be able to grasp most of the concepts presented that require the writing of SQL code.

   If you answered yes to all three, you will be very comfortable with most of the concepts dealing with logic and syntax.

   If you answered no to these first three questions, you may struggle with some of the development concepts and may want to do some preparatory reading or take a course to introduce you to some basic programming concepts.

   This site provides a good starting point for programming skills specific to SQL: http://www.w3schools.com/sql/sql_intro.asp.

   This Microsoft instructor–led course is an easy-to-understand look at programming for beginners: http://www.microsoft.com/learning/syllabi/en-us/2667Afinal.mspx.

4. Are you comfortable with databases and table relationships? (Yes or No)

5. Have you ever used Microsoft Access, dBASE, or any other database package? (Yes or No)

Database Development on SQL Server 2000

Terms you'll need to understand:

- ✓ Relational database
- ✓ SQL Server 2000 Enterprise Edition
- ✓ Enterprise Manager
- ✓ Query Analyzer
- ✓ Structured Query Language
- ✓ Stored procedure
- ✓ Books Online
- ✓ Transact-SQL (T-SQL)
- ✓ XML
- ✓ SQL Profiler
- ✓ Trigger
- ✓ Index
- ✓ User-defined function (UDF)
- ✓ View
- ✓ Roles

Techniques you'll need to master:

- ✓ Utilizing Books Online
- ✓ Tool and utility recognition
- ✓ SQL object definition and recognition

Introduction

This chapter serves two main purposes. The first purpose is to provide a bird's-eye view of Microsoft SQL Server 2000, the various programs installed with the product, and the basic concepts you should know before continuing in the book. The second is to provide an overview of relational databases and more specifically the handling of these databases by SQL Server 2000. Use this chapter to begin your preparation for passing the 70-229 exam; right from the start you will be gaining valuable tips through exam alerts. You must gain a complete understanding of SQL Server and its components, which of course include the databases and other objects of the database system.

Since the initial release of SQL Server, the product has come a long way in the handling of data systems both large and small. The product that was once considered sluggish and capable of handling only small to medium-sized systems is now among the leading products for database systems of any size. SQL Server's performance is on a par with, if not exceeding, that of all of its competitors. It is easy to see why it is being adopted more readily than any other data management product.

The Server and Its Components

SQL Server has many variations in its product line. These variations exist to handle every imaginable database system, from the smallest of personal architectures to large-scale data warehouses operating in multiserver environments. From the SQL Server–based MSDE to the Enterprise Edition running a Data Center, it is a truly versatile data-handling product. Following are some of the main reasons for the product's success:

➤Internet integration

➤Scalability and availability

➤Enterprise-level database features

➤Performance against TPC-C industry-standard benchmarks

➤ Ease of installation and deployment

➤Data warehousing

But these are more than just a few buzzwords used by Microsoft for marketing purposes. The SQL Server product falls neatly into line, filling the federated database servers can support the data storage requirements of the largest websites and enterprise systems. Partitioned views are covered fully in Chapter 4, "Advanced Physical Database Implementation."

Creating Your Own T-SQL Functions

You can extend the programmability of SQL Server by creating your own Transact-SQL (T-SQL) functions. T-SQL is an extension of the language defined by SQL standards and the basis for programming in SQL Server. A user-defined function can return either a scalar value or a table. User-defined functions (UDFs) are covered fully in Chapter 6, "Programming Business Logic."

Indexed Views

Indexed views can significantly improve the performance of an application when queries frequently perform certain joins or aggregations. An indexed view provides for a technique in which fast access to data is enabled (indexing) and associated with data display definitions (views), and where the resultset of the view is materialized and stored and indexed in the database. Indexed views are covered fully in Chapter 4.

New Data Types in SQL Server 2000

SQL Server 2000 introduces three new data types—`bigint`, `sql_variant`, and `table`—that are supported for variables and are the return types for user-defined functions. Data types are covered in full in Chapter 3, "Implementing the Physical Database."

INSTEAD OF and AFTER Triggers

`INSTEAD OF` triggers are executed in place of the triggering action (for example, `INSERT`, `UPDATE`, `DELETE`). They can also be defined on views, in which case they greatly extend the types of updates a view can support. `AFTER` triggers fire after the triggering action. SQL Server 2000 introduces the capability to specify which `AFTER` triggers fire first and last. Triggers are covered fully in Chapter 6.

Cascading Referential Integrity

Cascading actions enable you to control the actions SQL Server 2000 takes when deleting or changing data. If you attempt to update or delete a key to which existing foreign keys point, cascading actions will dictate the effects on the associated records. This is controlled by the new `ON DELETE` and `ON UPDATE` clauses in the `REFERENCES` clause of the `CREATE TABLE` and `ALTER TABLE` statements. Cascading referential integrity is covered fully in Chapter 3.

Collations

SQL Server 2000 includes support for most collations supported in earlier versions of SQL Server, and it introduces a new set of collations based on Windows collations. You can now specify collations at the database level or at the column level. Collations are covered fully later in this chapter.

Connecting to Multiple Instances of SQL Server

SQL Server 2000 supports running multiple instances of the relational database engine on the same computer. Each computer can run one instance of the relational database engine from SQL Server version 6.5 or 7.0, along with one or more instances of the database engine from SQL Server 2000.

Partitioned Views

SQL Server 2000 can partition tables horizontally across several servers, and define a distributed partitioned view on each member server so that it appears as if a full copy of the original table is stored on each server. Groups of servers running SQL Server that cooperate in this type of partitioning are called federations of servers. Partitioned views are covered fully in Chapter 4.

Other Relevant Exam Topics

This exam will of course cover traditional relational database concepts and features that have been historically present in the product. With this in mind, you need a solid knowledge of and hands-on experience with all facets of SQL Server 2000 database implementations before attempting the exam.

Expect to see many questions dealing with the designing of a database. Choosing the right number and makeup of the tables and other objects within a database will be probed from various perspectives on the exam. Like new features, these more traditional topics will represent another significant portion of the exam topic material.

SQL Server Product Implementation

The exam is geared for the Enterprise version of Microsoft SQL Server 2000 edition when it is used as a production database server. The Enterprise Edition supports all features available in SQL Server 2000 and scales to the performance levels required to support the largest websites and enterprise online transaction processing (OLTP) and data warehousing systems.

You can obtain 120-day evaluation versions of the product as a download from Microsoft's product download page, http://www.microsoft.com/sql/evaluation/ trial/2000.

The following hardware is the minimum needed to install the Enterprise version of SQL Server 2000:

➤ *Computer:*

    ➤ Intel or compatible

    ➤ Pentium 166MHz or higher

➤ *Memory:*

    ➤ 64MB minimum, 128MB or more recommended

➤ *Hard Disk Space:*

    ➤ SQL Server database components: 95–270MB, 250MB typical

    ➤ Analysis Services: 50MB minimum, 130MB typical

    ➤ English Query: 80MB

    ➤ Desktop Engine only: 44MB

    ➤ Books Online: 15MB

➤ *Monitor:*

    ➤ VGA or higher resolution

    ➤ 800×600 or higher resolution required for the SQL Server graphical tools

➤ *Other Peripherals:*

    ➤ CD-ROM drive

Product installation is pretty straightforward, though installing it correctly for use in a production environment will necessitate changing many of the defaults. To obtain the best installation in a production environment, you should review the SQL Server Administration topic within Books Online. Because this is a book on database implementation, administration concepts are out of our scope.

There are, however, a few more things you should know before you install SQL Server 2000 in a production environment. In most multi–SQL Server operations, the machine needs to participate in network security. An applications server, such as SQL Server, usually requires a large amount of resources exclusively available for its use. Also, appropriate permission sets need to be configured to ensure that sensitive data is not available where it shouldn't be. You seldom want SQL Server to share a machine with other applications, and certainly a SQL Server should never share a machine with a security server such as a Windows 2000, Windows 2003, or Windows NT Domain controller. Participating as a network user, with access to resources through a login ID, is an important aspect of SQL Server. The service accounts that make up the database and agent engines are assigned a domain user account that will have administrative rights over the machine where it is installed. Without this aspect the server is unable to send out email notifications. Once installed, the Enterprise Manager is the center of control for SQL Server. From this tool you can perform most activities needed to configure and maintain the server. Along with the Enterprise Manager, many other tools are installed. These tools have specific uses and provide intuitive means of accessing the SQL Server environment. A brief explanation of each tool is provided in the paragraphs that follow. Throughout the book, these tools will be used to aid in applying the implementation concepts. The short descriptions that follow will provide you with at least a point of initial discovery into their use.

SQL Server Tools

First off, SQL Server comes equipped with two additional broad-scale products that operate on top of the SQL Server database engine. *Analysis Services* and *English Query* provide support for data warehousing and plain language query, respectively. Analysis Services, formerly known as OLAP Services, provides for data warehouse cube storage and data mining capabilities used to find information in OLAP cubes and relational databases. English Query allows for the development of applications to allow users to ask questions from the data store using common English instead of traditional SQL statements. As mentioned previously, the Enterprise Manager is the primary administration tool for interacting with Microsoft SQL Server 2000. Using this tool, you can administer any server in the organization. The Enterprise Manager is an MMC snap-in tool that is installed along with the SQL Server client utilities. This is a good place to start exploring the contents of the server. Shown in Figure 1.1 is the Enterprise Manager with a set of SQL Servers registered. The right view pane has been set to Taskpad (from the View menu option, select Taskpad).

The installation of client tools provides many other tools, most of which are accessible from within the Enterprise Manager. Other tools can be accessed from the Windows, Programs menu in the Microsoft SQL Server menu group, as shown in Figure 1.2.

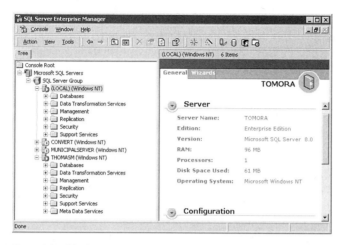

Figure 1.1 SQL Server 2000 Enterprise Manager.

Figure 1.2 The Microsoft SQL Server menu group.

By far, one of the most useful tools to be found for anyone trying to master Microsoft SQL Server 2000 is the complete reference guide available in Books Online. This thorough help system provides full coverage of the product with plenty of examples for coding assistance. It is generally regarded as one of the best help facilities of any of the Microsoft technical products, and it's mentioned here because of how much is actually inside.

NOTE

You will want to enable the use of personalized menus to gain the full use of the help facility. One facet of the help facility is the capability to mark favorites and maintain a list of topics you want to revisit, and this feature is not available if the option is not set within the taskbar properties.

Within Books Online, use the index pane to look up topics by key term or definition. The index pane is easy to use and links you to the most probable locations to get assistance. If you know an exact word or statement in SQL Server, you can look it up. You can find most any topic from this tab by typing a few letters of your topic. Of course, if that doesn't help, you can use the Search tab, but the main drawback of this tab is the number of matches that will be found for any given search. Use the Favorites tab as a means of saving topic links. If you find that your links are not being saved from session to session, it is likely that the personalized menu options have not been selected. To activate this option, right-click on the Windows taskbar and select Properties. There you will find the option to select, as shown in Figure 1.3.

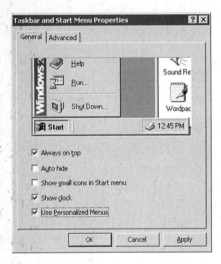

Figure 1.3 The Windows Taskbar and Start Menu Properties dialog.

The Client and Server Network utilities can be used to specify communication protocols and network libraries used in communications with the server. You may also use these tools to fine-tune some of the facets of communications such as configuring server aliasing or changing the default communications port. These two tools are used solely from the Windows menu system and cannot be accessed through the Enterprise Manager.

The Service Manager tool can be used to stop, pause, start, and monitor SQL Server services. This task can also be performed within the operating system's Services dialog or from within the Enterprise Manager. The Services drop-down list displays the services that can be controlled. These include the MSSQLServer Service, the Microsoft Search Service, the MSDTC Service, and the SQL Server Agent Service.

You can find some additional functionality in the Service Manager. Click the icon on the upper-left corner of the form and notice two menu items, Options and Connect. The Verify Service Control Action check box is checked by default. This controls whether an Are You Sure? dialog box appears when you stop a service. The Poll Interval determines how frequently Service Manager looks for the status of the services that are monitored. The default interval is 5 seconds. You also can set the default service icon viewed in the taskbar. It is recommended that you set this to the agent so that you can check the status of the service with a simple glance at the bottom of your screen.

The Query Analyzer is one of the primary tools used to create, test, and debug T-SQL commands and procedures. This tool is covered in depth in Chapter 7, "Tuning and Optimizing Analysis," and Chapter 8, "Designing for Optimized Data Access," because it has many useful benefits to the database implementer.

The Profiler is used to monitor and tune the server and its objects and applications. It is a versatile tool that can diagnose all activity on the server and aid in finding trouble spots in an application or performance bottlenecks in the system. This tool is discussed in depth in Chapter 7.

The Bulk Copy Program (BCP) and the ODBC Structured Query Language (OSQL) tools are command-line tools that can be used to execute commands against the server. Both tools, though seldom used, offer some advantages in particular circumstances. BCP can be used to populate databases with data. The main feature of the Bulk Copy Program is the capability to import or export data from text files to or from SQL Server tables. As the name suggests, the "Bulk" Copy Program is primarily used to shift large amounts of data from one place to another, so it is used only in this case. The rate at which the Bulk Copy Program transfers data from one place to another is about 2000 rows per second. The `BCP.exe` is stored in the `C:\Program Files\Microsoft SQL Server\MSSQL\Binn` folder and is run through the command prompt.

The OSQL tool provides the capability to execute T-SQL statements or batches from a server or workstation and view the results returned. The OSQL utility is similar to the Query Analyzer in that it executes batches of T-SQL code. The utility is run on the command line. Other than this, Query Analyzer and OSQL perform more or less the same function. OSQL's primary purpose is to allow the scheduling of operations via the operating system scheduler, SQL Server scheduler, or any other schedule application provided by a third party. Analysis Services and English Query are two additional programs that ship with SQL Server to provide some added functionality. Analysis Services is used to configure and utilize data warehouse cubes, and English Query provides simple language support. These tools are beyond the scope of this book and the exam. For this exam and consequently this book, we will focus on the tools that allow you to develop applications against SQL Server databases.

Program Execution

Because this exam is all about SQL coding against well-designed database systems, it is imperative that you understand how to code and execute SQL code. Executing SQL code can be achieved using various methods. The dialect of SQL code used by SQL Server is an extension on ANSI-SQL (the industry standard) known as *T-SQL*, or *Transact SQL*. T-SQL includes the entire implementation of the industry standard version as well as other commands that represent Microsoft's extension of the code. SQL Server 2000 supports the ANSI SQL-92 entry-level standard, but not the ANSI-92 intermediate-level standard. This is also true of SQL Server's primary competitors.

You can develop front-end applications with Visual Basic, Visual Basic .NET, Visual C, C#, Access, or the Internet, or in combination with other data and programming interfaces. Commands can be executed through ODBC or OLE-DB standard libraries connecting to the server from virtually any computer. Statements can be executed directly on the server using the Query Analyzer or OSQL. Commands are also executed within the context of Triggers, Stored Procedures, and user-defined functions.

With all of these different coding mechanisms, you will want to become intimately familiar with the Query Analyzer. This tool is the primary development environment for writing, testing, debugging, and executing T-SQL code.

The Query Analyzer

The Query Analyzer is shown in Figure 1.4. This tool is your primary tool for executing T-SQL code. As you write code for various implementations, you can use the Query Analyzer to initially enter the code; however, it is also a full development environment that has many qualities needed for code analysis and improvement.

SQL Query Analyzer is an interactive, graphical tool that enables the developer to write queries, execute multiple queries simultaneously, view results, analyze the query plan, and receive assistance to improve the query performance. The Analyzer screen is divided into three components. The object browser along the left side is handy for finding database object names and command syntax. On the right-hand side of the screen, you find the editing area on the top part. The bottom part, known as the Results pane, contains the output of your query, which is known as a *resultset*. The Query Analyzer in not used solely to execute T-SQL statements, but also to analyze them. Query Analyzer can report things such as how much time the queries took to run and how much time it took to read data from the hard disk. You can use tools built into the analyzer to diagnose the query, to redesign the query, and to achieve better performance. The Execution Plan options graphically display the data retrieval methods chosen by the query optimizer. If more intense scrutiny is required after designing and deploying your databases, the SQL Profiler would be used instead of the Query Analyzer. After you deploy an application and give access to users, you need to monitor how your server is functioning and make sure that it's working the way it was intended. Using the profiler, you can set up traces that monitor anything that happens to the server. These include knowing whether a login failed or succeeded, whether a query was executed, and other such events. Traces can be customized to monitor different angles of SQL Server at different times.

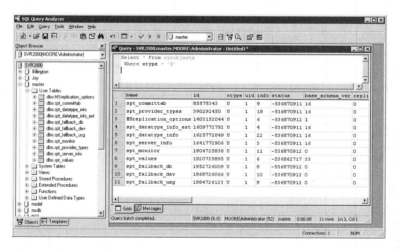

Figure 1.4   The Query Analyzer, your primary coding tool.

There is considerable exam content dealing with query optimization and the use of SQL Server tools to aid in optimization. We will delve into this content in detail in Chapter 7.

Each tool in one way or another will be seen on the exam. Often you will see the tool used as a misleading, incorrect answer. For this reason it is important to know what each tool is used for. To be properly prepared for the exam, you should try to use each tool and note its most appropriate implementation.

Other than the tools supplied with the product, SQL Server is made up of numerous objects. Each object has its own function on the server. Knowing how to work with each object is just as important as knowing how each tool is used.

SQL Server Objects

Objects are composed of two basic categories: *user objects* developed for use in a business application and *system objects* that the server itself uses to keep track of information on the server and help manage the server itself.

A first look after installation will reveal several databases that have already been created during the installation process. Two of these databases (Pubs and Northwind) are user databases used to provide implementation examples. The other databases created by the installation process are used by SQL Server to maintain the server. Pubs and Northwind are defined in the following list:

➤ *Pubs*—The Pubs database is a real-world example of a database serving as a learning tool. The Pubs database is a fictitious publisher's database containing publisher-specific tables and information such as authors and titles. The Pubs database may be dropped, because doing so does not affect the SQL Server environment whatsoever.

➤ *Northwind*—The Northwind database is the second sample database. It is preferred by many Microsoft Access users who are new to SQL Server because it is the same sample database that was provided for Microsoft Access.

The Northwind and Pubs configurations are poor examples of the configuration options to use in a live database. Don't use them as a measure for the options you need for your own database. Before selecting any option, know the impact of the option on the database and client connections, as well as any applications-required settings. Similarly, you will find that the settings of the system database are rather specialized and do not provide the typical settings used in a production database.

The system databases should not be deleted; doing so would be detrimental to the server. Master of the Server, the Master database, is crucial to the operations of SQL Server and should be considered to be as important as the most mission-critical database stored on the server. If it becomes damaged, the server ceases to function.

The Master Database

The Master database is provided to keep your instance of SQL Server functioning. This database records all the system information for an instance of SQL Server. The Master database contains all information that is global to the server, including logins, error messages, system configuration, and the list of other databases that exist on the server. The Master database helps in tracking the location of primary files in order to view other user databases.

The other system database that is almost equally critical is the *msdb database*. This database maintains information for the agent. If this database is damaged, most administrative tasks will be hampered.

The Msdb Database

The SQL Server Agent uses the msdb database to store information about the scheduling of alerts, the definition of jobs, and the recording of the server operators to be contacted when a particular event occurs on the server. Maintenance plans, backup jobs, scheduled data operations, and other administrative tasks are maintained within this database.

Another system database, perhaps less critical but still necessary for server operations, is the tempdb database. This database has no permanent storage file, but while the server is running, it is the most used.

The Tempdb Database

The tempdb database contains all temporarily created stored procedures and tables and is generally used as a work area by SQL Server. Tempdb is where tasks that require memory are performed, such as join and sort operations. The temporary tables and objects created in a SQL Server session are dropped after SQL Server is shut down. Tempdb never saves information permanently. By default, the size of the tempdb database automatically increases when needed and is restored to its default size (2.5MB) each time SQL Server is started.

Some of the system databases are used only during specific circumstances on the server. This is the case with the Model database. The Model is accessed only when another database is initialized for the first time.

The Model Database

The Model database stores a complete template for creating new databases. When you create a new database, SQL Server copies the contents of the

Model database into the new database you create. It is a good idea to populate the Model database with objects that are present in all of your other user databases. Common stored procedures, user-defined functions, and other resources can automatically be initialized with the creation of a new database.

You may not even recognize the existence of the final system database. The distribution database is seen only if replication is configured. This database is not generated upon installation but is created only when replication is configured.

The Distribution Database

The distribution database is used in the replication process. This database will store data temporarily when moving from a publishing system to the subscribers of the data. The data contained in the database would be transactions, snapshot jobs, synchronization status, and replication history information. Any server configured to participate either as a remote distribution server or as a combined Publisher/Distributor will have the distribution database.

Objects Within a Database

Many objects can be found within a database. Certain objects are present after database creation. These system-level objects are necessary for a database to function. The other objects are defined by the user as the physical structure of a database is assembled. The following list outlines the different database objects:

➤ *Table*—A table is the first thing you create in the database to facilitate data storage. Tables, like spreadsheets, are composed of rows and columns, usually referred to as fields and records in a database environment.

➤ *View*—A view is an object generally used in displaying a subset of data from a table. This can be used to ensure security or reduce data redundancy. A view is stored as a SQL query. You can assign permissions to a view to enable an administrator to forgo more granular permission assignments at the column level of a table.

➤ *User-defined function*—A user-defined function is a group of T-SQL statements that can be reused. Functions are subroutines used to encapsulate frequently performed logic. Any code that must perform the logic incorporated in a function can call the function rather than having to repeat all the function logic.

➤ *Stored procedure*—Stored procedures are collections of T-SQL statements that execute as a single unit. Stored procedures are stored on the server and can execute faster than queries at the client, without any extra overhead.

➤ *Trigger*—A trigger is a stored procedure that automatically executes at the invocation of INSERT, DELETE, or UPDATE. Triggers can be used to validate the data being entered and to enforce data integrity. They can also be used to alert users of changes to the data.

➤ *Database role*—A role is a collection of users and permissions. Users can be assigned to various database roles that determine what access they have to which database objects. Members of a role inherit the permissions associated with the role.

➤ *Database diagram*—Database diagrams are graphically created outlines of how your database is structured. Database diagrams show how tables, and the fields that compose the table, are related.

➤ *Constraint*—A constraint is an attribute that a column or table can take to restrict what users enter into your database.

➤ *Index*—An index is a database object that provides fast access to data in the rows of a table, based on key values. Indexes can also enforce uniqueness on the rows in a table. SQL Server supports clustered and nonclustered indexes. The primary key constraint of a table is automatically indexed.

➤ *User*—A database user is an individual who has a login on the server and has been given access to a database.

Each database object has its own properties that make it an important piece of the entire picture. This book looks deep into the SQL Server object structure and looks independently at each part of SQL Server from multiple perspectives.

A quick perusal of the SQL Enterprise Manager will show a number of other objects. These other objects serve various purposes, but for the most part they are used within the realm of server administration.

Other Objects Found on the Server

When moving data from one server to another, you can use various techniques, but in most instances Distributed Transaction Services (DTS) will be the preference for the import and export of data. If the process is repeated on an ongoing basis, a DTS definition can be saved and the correlated object is stored on the server.

A selection of objects is defined within the msdb database for use by the SQL Server Agent in the maintaining of the server. These objects are defined within the Management branch of the Enterprise Manager under the limb belonging to SQL Server Agent. Each of these objects is defined in the following list:

➤ *Operators*—An operator is an individual who can be contacted by the agent if need be for attention to a SQL Server condition. Contact can be made by email, network message, and/or pager.

➤ *Alerts*—Alerts represent the actions to be taken when something of interest occurs on the server. An alert will allow for a response to an error, a physical condition of the server, or an important alteration to data. The alert can then send an email, page an operator, or run a job to address the problem.

➤ *Jobs*—Jobs can be defined to perform one or more steps. The steps are T-SQL statements, operating-system commands, ActiveX scripting, and replication activities. The jobs can then be scheduled or left to be run on demand.

Another set of objects can be used in troubleshooting problems on the server. Also found in the Management branch, processes, server logs, and lock information can be quickly referenced to provide feedback on what the server is or has been doing. A short description of this set of objects follows:

➤ *Process Information*—Each process that is using server resources is tracked and logged. The information about these processes can be quickly identified. The types of information available include the ID of the process and 21 other attributes.

➤ *Locks by Process ID*—If a process ID is known, you can quickly find the resources locked by the process and the attributes associated with the lock.

➤ *Locks by Object*—If you desire information on what locks are in place for a given object, you can find that information under this limb.

➤ *SQL Server Logs*—The last seven detailed logs of server activity are maintained within the Enterprise Manager for quick reference.

Also within the Management branch can be found details about the maintenance plans currently defined for the server and the logical backup devices that are being utilized.

If a server has had replication enabled, you may have article objects defined. An *article* is data that is defined for replication. An article can be an entire table or a portion of the table as defined through the use of vertical or horizontal filters. An article could also be a partition of data, or a database object that is specified for replication. The article can be made up of a stored procedure, a view definition, the execution of a stored procedure, a view, an indexed view, or a user-defined function. Once defined, an article is made available by a publisher object and received by the subscriber objects.

Another set of objects found on the server includes those within the framework of the server "Security" branch. These objects define how a server can be accessed and by whom. The set of security objects includes the following:

➤ *Logins*—These objects will identify who can access the server.

➤ *Server Roles*—Server-based administrative groups indicate the level of administrative authority that a login has.

➤ *Linked Servers*—These items define an available OLE-DB data source.

➤ *Remote Servers*—This is a configuration definition that will allow a client to connect to one instance of SQL Server to execute a stored procedure on another instance of SQL Server without the need to establish another connection.

All in all, quite a wide variety of objects are held within the definitions maintained by the server. The system databases and tables store the object by definition, but these system objects do not store any production data. The data itself is stored within the user objects.

Types of Data

The main purpose, of course, for maintaining a SQL Server is to store data. All the previously discussed tools and objects simply make it easier to facilitate the main goal, data storage. Data maintained by the server falls into three main categories:

➤ Object definitions

➤ Metadata

➤ User application data

Object Definitions

We have discussed most of the actual object definitions themselves, and if you look into the master database, you can find the storage area for these definitions. Tables prefixed with "sys" store object definitions. There are many system tables, but the most commonly accessed and useful for development purposes are these:

➤ **Common System Tables in Every Database (Including Master)**

  ➤ *syscolumns*: Contains a row for every column in every table, for every view, and for each parameter in a stored procedure.

  ➤ *sysindexes*: Contains a row for each index and table in the database.

  ➤ *syscomments*: Contains entries for each view, rule, default, trigger, constraint, and stored procedure. The text column contains the original SQL definition statements.

  ➤ *sysobjects*: Contains a row for each object created within a database. In tempdb only, this table includes a row for each temporary object.

  ➤ *systypes*: Contains a row for each system-supplied data type and each user-defined data type.

  ➤ *sysusers*: Contains a row for each user or role in the database.

➤ **Common System Tables Additionally Found in Master Database Only**

  ➤ *syslogins*: Contains a row for each login.

  ➤ *sysmessages*: Contains a row for each system error or warning that can be displayed to the user.

  ➤ *sysdatabases*: Contains a row for each database on the server.

  ➤ *sysprocesses*: Holds information about processes running on the server.

  ➤ *sysremotelogins*: Contains a row for each remote user allowed to call remote stored procedures on the server.

  ➤ *sysservers*: Contains a row for each server that the current server can access as an OLE DB data source.

Don't ever delete any elements from the syscomments table. To hide or encrypt any definitions of objects, use the **WITH ENCRYPTION** clause during the creation of the object.

System tables can be queried like any other table, and in doing so you can obtain valuable information about the objects stored on a server. You can also develop applications that can aid in the development of data or for performing data conversions from one application to another.

Metadata

Metadata is arguably just another type of system data. Metadata differs in that it is statistical information, or data about data. Metadata describes the structure and meaning of data, as well as the structure and meaning of applications and processes. Metadata is abstract and has context.

Metadata study and storage is a major topic in itself and is beyond the context of the exam and consequently this book. If you would like more information on the topic, refer to Meta Data Services in SQL Server Books Online.

User Data

The most prevalent type of data stored on the server is, of course, user data. This is the data that makes up the information used in our business applications. Data is physically stored on the server inside large data files. Changes to the data first pass through log files before being placed by the server into these data files. These aspects are discussed further in Chapters 3 and 4.

Data in any form is stored on the server in one of a number of data types. Traditionally, data is divided into three basic categories: numeric, alphanumeric or character, and binary. Other data types exist, however, and several require special handling in applications and design considerations. Assigning a data type to an object defines four attributes of the object:

➤ The kind of data contained by the object

➤ The length of the data stored

➤ The precision of numeric data types

➤ The scale of numeric data types

In selecting an appropriate data type, you take into account the application, usage of the data, and future trends. In numeric data you must select a type that is large enough to store the data. In character data types you want to be careful not to waste storage unnecessarily by configuring the size of the data to be larger than necessary.

Numeric Data Types

Numeric data can be defined as one of the integer data types for whole-number storage or a type that accommodates decimal-point storage for real numbers. The bigint data type is an 8-byte integer type that is new to SQL Server 2000 and allows for the storage of very large integer numbers. Other integer data types support various smaller integers. The int data type uses 4 bytes of storage, the smallint data type uses 2 bytes, and the smallest integer data type, tinyint, uses only a single byte, supporting values from 0 through 255.

Decimal and numeric are functionally the same data type. They allow for the storage of a fixed precision and scale numeric data from $-10^{38}+1$ through $10^{38}-1$. Depending on the precision chosen, this data type uses from 5 to 17 bytes for the storage of values, as summarized in Table 1.1.

Table 1.1 Precision of Numeric Data	
Decimal and Numeric Storage Sizes	**Bytes**
1–9	5
10–19	9
20–28	13
29–38	17

Two data types are used for storage of monetary values: smallmoney and money. These values are stored with a scale of four decimal places. The smallmoney data type consumes 4 bytes and the money data type stores 8 bytes. Both currency data types use four decimal places.

Character Data Types

Character data types are subdivided into two categories depending on the byte size of the characters being stored. Traditionally, character data consumed 1 byte per character, allowing for 255 different characters. This standard was found to be inflexible and inadequate for working with international or extended character sets, so the Unicode standard was developed, in which each character uses 2 bytes of storage. This standard allows for approximately 64,000 different characters.

Each of these two data types has three variations for the storage of data: fixed-length, variable-length, and large character data. Non-Unicode data uses the char, varchar, and text data types, whereas Unicode data is stored in the nchar, nvarchar, and ntext types.

The char data type allows for the storage of fixed-length non-Unicode character data with lengths from 1 through 8,000. The varchar data type allows for the same sizes of data.

The primary difference between the two is that the varchar uses storage space more efficiently and uses only the space necessary to store the data value, regardless of the maximum size a variable has been configured to store. The nchar and nvarchar are essentially the Unicode implementation of char and varchar, and they allow for storage of up to 4,000 characters.

The text and ntext data types are used to store large variable-length character data. The text data type can store up to 2,147,483,647 characters, whereas ntext can store 1,073,741,823.

Binary Data Types

Several data types are used to store binary data. The smallest is the bit data type, which supports Boolean operations and stores values of 0 or 1 in a single storage bit. Other binary data types are used to store binary strings and are stored as hexadecimal values.

Binary data is stored using the binary, varbinary, and image data types. A column assigned the binary data type must have the same fixed length of up to 8KB. In a column assigned the varbinary data type, entries can vary in size. Columns of image data can be used to store variable-length binary data exceeding 8KB, such as Microsoft Word documents, Microsoft Excel spreadsheets, and images that include bitmaps and other graphic files.

Specialty Data Types

Many data types are used in special circumstances to store data that does not directly qualify as numeric, character, or binary. Data types are available to store time and date information, globally unique identifiers (GUIDs), cursors, and tables.

The T-SQL timestamp data type is not the same as the timestamp data type defined in the SQL-92 standard. The SQL-92 timestamp data type is equivalent to the T-SQL datetime data type.

Three data types support the storage of time and date information: datetime, smalldatetime, and timestamp. All three store dates and times, although the timestamp data type stores automatically generated binary values using 8 bytes of storage and is not used to store data.

Values with the datetime data type are stored as two 4-byte integers. The first 4 bytes store the number of days before or after the base date, which is January 1, 1900. The base date is the system reference date. Values for datetime earlier than January 1, 1753, are not permitted. The other 4 bytes store the time of day, represented as the number of milliseconds after midnight.

The smalldatetime data type stores dates and times of day with less precision than datetime. It stores them as two 2-byte integers. The first 2 bytes store the number of days after January 1, 1900. The other 2 bytes store the number of minutes since midnight. Dates range from January 1, 1900, through June 6, 2079.

The uniquidentifier data type stores a 16-byte data value known as a globally unique identifier. The GUID takes on the string format *xxxxxxxx-xxxx-xxxx-xxxx-xxxxxxxxxxxx*, in which each *x* is a hexadecimal digit. A GUID is long and obscure, but it has the advantage of being guaranteed to be unique throughout the world.

The sql_variant is a generic data type that stores values of various SQL Server–supported data types: except text, ntext, image, _timestamp, and sql_variant. It may be used in column definitions, as well as in parameters, variables, and return values of user-defined functions. A sql_variant can have a maximum length of 8,016 bytes.

The table data type is new to SQL Server in the 2000 release. It can be used to temporarily store a resultset for later use. The table data type is not used for defining column types within a structure; rather, it is used in functions, stored procedures, and batches.

The cursor data type is another data type that is used only in functions, stored procedures, and batches. Its primary purpose is to allow the storage of a pointer to a resultset. Attributes of a T-SQL server cursor, such as its scrolling behavior and the query used to build the resultset on which the cursor operates, are set up using a DECLARE CURSOR operation within the procedure.

User-Defined Data Types

User-defined data types are stored as database objects and are based on any of the system data types. User-defined data types can be used when several tables must store the same type of data in a column and you must ensure that these columns have exactly the same data type, length, and nullability.

Using these data types can help you create tables more quickly and can also help you control the data in a predictable manner. Often a user-defined data type is created in the Model database; it will then exist in all new user-defined databases created.

NOTE

A lot of the functions, statements, and system stored procedures that accepted **int** expressions for their parameters in the previous SQL Server versions have not been changed to support conversion of **bigint** expressions to those parameters. SQL Server only converts **bigint** to **int** when the **bigint** value is within the range of the **int** data type. A conversion error occurs at runtime if the **bigint** expression contains a value outside the range.

Although this is not a big exam topic, you may get a question or two in dealing with the selection of the most appropriate or most efficient data type. Use the byte sizes as presented previously to help you make the correct type determination.

Exam Prep Questions

1. You are the chief database administrator for a large manufacturing company. You need to install Microsoft SQL Server 2000 Enterprise for test purposes and have moderate storage capabilities. Which of the following systems suits your needs without requiring you to perform any alterations?

   ❑ A. Pentium 133, 256MB RAM, IE 5
   ❑ B. Pentium 200, 64MB RAM, IE 4
   ❑ C. Pentium 400, 128MB RAM, IE 3
   ❑ D. Pentium 400, 32MB RAM, IE 5

   Answer: B. To install SQL Server, you need a minimum of a Pentium 166, 64MB of RAM (though more is recommended), and Internet Explorer 4 or above. See the section "Installation Requirements" within SQL Server Books Online for more information.

2. You are the database administrator for a small private educational institution. You would like to use SQL Server 2000 as a gateway to various data sources that have been used for several applications. As a primary goal, you would like to get a copy of all data stored on the SQL Server 2000. What technologies could be used to solve this problem? (Select all that apply.)

   ❑ A. OLE-DB
   ❑ B. ANSI
   ❑ C. ISO
   ❑ D. ODBC
   ❑ E. Analysis Services
   ❑ F. SQL Profiler

   Answer: A, D. OLE-DB and ODBC are industry-standard technologies. They provide the standards for drivers that are supplied to allow data to be read from an underlying data source. ODBC (open database connectivity) is a mature interface supported by almost all database engines. OLE-DB is a set of driver APIs that has growing usage and allows for access to data in a generic form as well. See the section "Direct Execution" in SQL Server Books Online for more information.

3. A large shipping company uses a dual processor SQL Server to track load information for a fleet of transport vehicles that handle shipments throughout North America. The data being collected is shared with other vendors. This company requires a technology that will provide a data structure and formatting rules, and that will be easily transferable between applications. Which technology is best suited for this structure?

- ❏ A. HTML
- ❏ B. IIS
- ❏ C. XML
- ❏ D. Replication
- ❏ E. Triggers

Answer: C. XML, now supported through a number of new features, provides a mechanism in which the data can be transmitted from one application to the other while maintaining the data structure and other formatting provided by XML schemas and style sheets. For more information, refer to the section "XML Support," earlier in this chapter.

4. You are working on a database implementation in a production environment. You would like to perform analysis on the server hosting the database. You need to get detailed information on the types of queries being performed and the locking effects of all operations. Which tool should you use?

- ❏ A. Query Analyzer
- ❏ B. SQL Profiler
- ❏ C. Books Online
- ❏ D. Analysis Manager
- ❏ E. Enterprise Manager

Answer: B. To perform analysis of this type, you would use the Profiler to gather detailed server-wide information. The Query Analyzer is more appropriate to analyze and improve on the performance of singular queries, and the Analysis Manager is used to configure data warehousing. For more information see the section "Features of SQL Server 2000" within SQL Server Books Online.

Creating a Logical Data Model

Terms you'll need to understand:

✓ Entity Relationship Model
✓ Entity
✓ Kernel entity
✓ Associative entity
✓ Characteristic entity
✓ Attribute
✓ Identifier
✓ Dependency
✓ Primary key
✓ Foreign key
✓ Normalization
✓ Denormalization
✓ Normal forms
✓ Relationship
✓ Cardinality

Techniques you'll need to master:

✓ Entity Relationship Modeling
✓ Database normalization/denormalization
✓ Key and relationship definition

Introduction

Designing a logical data model is all about preparing for the physical data design. Whether physical elements end up being a simple database, a complex data warehouse, or some other data store, the ideas behind the logical design remain the same. In this stage of development, try not to gear any design to a specific physical structure. It is important to keep in mind that we are still just planning things out, and the decisions regarding the physical elements have yet to be made.

Even though the physical elements have yet to be determined, there is a definite correlation between what you see in the logical model and what will end up being present when the model takes on a physical form. There is almost a one-to-one mapping between the objects that we discuss in the logical stage of development and similar objects in the physical databases, tables, files, and other physical articles.

Though there are many data storage possibilities, the largest percentage of these will be databases—the storage mechanism of choice for most systems. Relational databases are databases in which data is organized into related objects. Each of the objects contained in a database is related to the others in some way.

Relational databases, based on the paper written by Dr. E. F. Codd in 1970, store sets of data in relations, called *tables*. The tables are often related to one another through dependencies, but this is not required. In all the time that has passed since then, the modeling of data structures has remained based on this concept.

Data Modeling and Logical Data Design

Most individuals in the technology arena understand the physical components of a database system. It is easy to recognize data in a columnar format from spreadsheets, tables, data files, and other common data storage techniques. In a structured data storage system, however, much planning goes into the makeup of the storage system before any physical forms are taken. Long before a combination of files containing records and fields along with tables containing rows and columns form a database, the data content is analyzed and a concept of the data, or *logical structure* is formed. This is an involved process that takes much practice before a database professional can become competent. *Logical modeling* is an integral part of database implementation. For this reason, logical data modeling encompasses many of the objectives of the exam.

It is difficult to discuss the data modeling exam objectives without looking at some of the physical elements in the database itself. This chapter mentions and defines some of the physical components of a database system. However, in this chapter our focus will be the logical design of the database. In most business problems the physical database itself would not be considered until a logical model had been drawn. For this reason, the physical elements mentioned in this chapter are discussed in full in Chapter 3, "Implementing the Physical Database," so we can concentrate here on drawing logical data models.

Logical data modeling in practice involves identifying important elements of data and recognizing how these elements interact. It is also important to be knowledgeable about the business process being analyzed. This knowledge will aid in determining data flows and processing required to pull meaningful information out of reams of raw data.

 For those heading down the path to becoming a database administrator, data modeling plays an important role in the MCDBA 70-229 Exam, but for those attempting the MCSD certification, similar information may be tested in the MCSD Exam 70-300 .NET Solutions Architecture Exam.

In designing a database, to meet a given business need, the logical data model most used is the *Entity Relationship Model*, or *ER Model*. In determining the ER model, you define the elements of data used in the business process and how they relate to each other. In looking at any logical implementation, you must understand the nature and use of the data. Knowing how the data is used helps you understand the relationships between the separate data elements.

Source documents, reports, and other samplings from an existing business process, together with information gathered through interviews, will assist in collecting data examples. With this information you can begin designing a data model in accordance with the current business situation. It is important that in gathering information, the data samples collected and drawn up be as complete as possible. Accompanying these data samples, full descriptions of all procedures that interact with the data would also be used as an aid to the development of a model.

Data Modeling

To develop a data model, various application architectures can be considered. During logical modeling, variations in implementations do not need to be known. In meeting a specific business need, the data needs to be modeled in a pristine fashion. If you have a tendency toward one implementation or another, you could hamper this design goal. It is best to design the model as a generic data model before taking that model into future phases. In subsequent stages of development, the database will take on its physical attributes and will be adjusted as applications take shape; yet these stages should not be stepped into prematurely. Focus first on the raw information as a base for the logical model.

 Relational database design modeling was first developed by the database engineer Charles Bachman, in 1960, and then in 1976, database design modeling became the ER Model by Peter Chen. An ER Model allows a database to be defined in a simple and organized manner. Other modeling techniques have come and gone over the years, but the ER Model is the preferred technique used by most experienced database developers.

Modeling with the ER Data Model

As mentioned previously, the ER data model is one of the most popular data models in use. An ER data model consists of three main components that are present in any model format: *entities*, *attributes*, and *relationships*.

➤ An *entity* is a discernible thing about which data is kept. In data modeling, entities can be closely compared to the physical element of a table in a database. An entity is a collection of related data elements or attributes and usually represents a major facet of the business problem. Supplier, product, employee, and order are all good examples of entities.

➤ *Attributes* are the characteristics given to an entity, such as `ProductNumber` and `FirstName`. Attributes of an entity represent a set of properties, each property being a data element within an entity. They will become the columns or fields in the physical database.

➤ *Relationships* show a logical link between two or more entities. Where two entities have a direct affiliation, a relationship is used to define the connection between the entities. A supplier entity may be related to orders; a product entity may be related to purchases. Relationships will normally establish constraints within the physical database.

Entities represent the primary elements of the ER Model. Each entity will represent a person, place, thing, or concept involved in a business process. It is usually easiest to determine the entities of a process by isolating the important players. When a customer places an order containing one or more products, the process utilizes at least three major entities: *customer*, *order*, and *product*.

An ER Model is drawn out using an *Entity Relationship Diagram (ERD)*. A rough diagram can be constructed using pencil and paper and a few simple shapes. For a more polished look a drawing tool is recommended, such as Microsoft Paint, or better yet a tool specifically used for the modeling process, such as Microsoft Visio. The actual tool used for drawing the diagram can vary, and you will find that different developers have their own preferences and reasons for preferring one tool over another. Most of the diagrams throughout this book have been developed using the two previously mentioned programs, along with SQL Server's own built-in tools. To illustrate the concepts of the ER modeling process, we will be using a fictional company, *Northwind Traders*. This company will be familiar to many Microsoft Access users and it is also supplied with SQL Server as a sample database.

Entity Selection

To begin the modeling process, you need to first isolate the entities required for the business process. A standard documentation technique is to draw entities as rectangular boxes with enough space to hold many attributes. An entity is the basic division of a database. In the logical design, entities are representative of the tables that will be present when the database development process moves into the physical design phase. Each entity exists as a separate individual data collection, unique from all the other entities.

Entities are generally the people, places, and things that make up a process. They can be qualified as one of three basic types: *kernel entities*, *associative entities*, and *characteristic entities*. These entity types are described further in the following list:

➤ A *kernel entity* exists on its own; it doesn't define or provide descriptive information for other entities. An example of a kernel entity would be a product listing in an inventory model. The information contained in each kernel entity of a table represents the heart of the database model.

➤ *Associative entities* are needed to allow multiple kernel entities to be tied together. In the inventory system, a sales entity would be needed to tie a customer kernel entity to the products they have purchased. This same sales entity could be tied to another kernel entity, such as salespeople.

➤ A *characteristic entity* provides additional information for a respective kernel or associative entity. Information contained in characteristic entities can be updated independently of the related entity. A product entity could have a characteristic parts entity. A given product could be made up of a number of parts. A part that becomes unavailable could affect the product's availability. Changes over time to parts information could be made more easily if a parts entity existed, instead of your having to make changes against the products kernel.

Some entities stand out within a process and are easily recognized, particularly those that represent people or organizations. Entities such as customer, supplier, employee, and shipper are all relatively easy to identify, whereas other entities are more difficult to identify. Careful thought about a business process will help flush them out. Let's look at the process used when a customer orders merchandise and use it as an example.

A customer will order products from one of our salespeople. The order is recorded on an invoice on which each line item represents the quantity of a single product ordered. Any products not currently in stock will be backordered. Ordering the needed products from the supplier will fill backorders. When an order is ready, the company can ship it to the customer using one of the available shipping methods. This simple process indicates that a few other entities are needed. Order, product, and order detail will be needed to fulfill the order process and track the data accordingly.

This process will allow for the initial sketch of entities to be drawn, as shown in Figure 2.1.

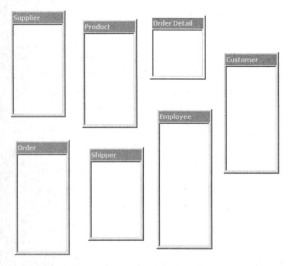

Figure 2.1   A rough draft of Northwind's entities.

With further knowledge of the business process, other entities may come to light. In the case of the Northwind process, products all fall into separate categories and the product categories are also tracked. This would require the addition of an additional entity, and the beginnings of the ER diagram would look similar to the example shown in Figure 2.2.

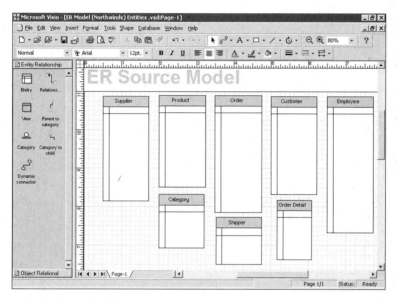

Figure 2.2 Northwind's entities in an ER Model.

Entity structuring accommodates the initial stages of database design. When you're designing an appropriate logical model, the data must be organized into these separate elements that will later make up the physical database tables. An entity is characterized by its attributes. Attributes are used to define the data elements of an entity. After the initial entities have been defined, the process of describing each entity through its characteristic properties begins.

Attribute Definition

Identifying attributes is the next step in ensuring a successful data modeling process. In defining attributes you are setting out to define entity composition. Each entity will have descriptive elements that pertain solely to that element. An attribute is a descriptive element or property of an entity. Fields will represent the attributes when the logical design progresses to the physical design stage.

Attributes are characteristics or properties defined within a single entity, and they correspond to real-world properties of a place, thing, or concept.

Attributes such as names and addresses are almost always present for people and organizations. Other attributes provide further information for the entity as required for the business process being defined.

Deciphering attributes from written descriptions and reports is more of a real-world scenario. The exam will provide the attributes; you will be expected to pick appropriate entities.

Try to find out the attributes that fit each of the entities. More attributes may have to be added later as the model becomes more complete. If you missed an attribute or added extra attributes at this time, they will likely be pointed out when the model is normalized. The normalization of a data model will be discussed later in this chapter, in the section "Data Normalization with Normal Forms." Attribute decisions will vary from person to person, depending on your business scenario perspective for which the data is being modeled.

The identification and creation of attributes is a developed skill; there is no true method for defining all attributes of an entity. Each business problem will require a variation of entity content, so the business process itself will lead to a lot of attribute choices.

A few guidelines to use in the identification, creation, and naming of attributes will help ease this process. The first is how you name your entities. A good name makes an attribute look professional and helps in its readability. Appropriate naming conventions are often developed as a corporate or development standard within an organization. Often mechanisms for shortening names or using common prefixing or suffixing is part of a programming team's standard. Here are some good guidelines that help in naming entities. Consistently following these guidelines will help to keep all of your designs up to the same standard:

➤ An entity or an attribute should be named in its singular form, thereby implying that it is only a single instance. An *instance* is a single occurrence of an entity.

➤ The use of underscores (_), spaces, and other special characters is not a good habit because special characters have particular meanings in some software packages, and the mixture of text and other characters is difficult to type. Try to distinguish a word from another by using mixed case, as in LastName instead of Last_Name.

➤ Entity (and all other object name) identification should be kept small while still providing a description of the object. Names should be kept as small as possible but should still provide a meaningful object title.

➤ Entity names should be unique.

➤ Reserved words, though permitted in the context of SQL names, should be minimized to ease development. Later this will also add to the performance of procedures.

Keep in mind that many of these guidelines refer to all object naming, and when developing the names for attributes, you should still be providing a descriptive name that is concise and unique within the entity. Attribute names should be consistent across entities. For example, if you name an attribute LastName within one entity, you should not name a similar attribute Surname in other entities.

Decomposing an Attribute

Many attributes can be handled as a single attribute. It is also common for some attributes to be broken down into other, smaller attributes. This process is commonly known as *decomposing* attributes. Decomposing an attribute takes an attribute from its original form and divides it into its components. A good example of this is the breaking down of the Address attribute. An Address attribute can easily be broken down into attributes that store data as shown here:

Street	Stores the street address of the user
City	Stores where the user lives
Region	Stores the state or province the user lives in
Postal Code	Stores the user's zip code or other postal code
Country	Stores the user's nation

The process of decomposing an attribute helps to develop a normalized structure, as defined later in this chapter. Decomposing is a function of usage as well. If, for example, a person's name is needed only in its full form, then a decision may be made to not break it up into the separate attributes of first name and last name. This is common for a ContactPerson attribute in an entity that relates to a corporation.

Decomposing an attribute provides many benefits, in contrast to generic compound attributes that are not decomposed. Data integrity is improved. *Data integrity* is a measurement of how well data is kept consistent and flawless throughout the whole ER Model. When attributes are decomposed, different methods of ensuring data integrity can be applied to the broken-down segments rather than the attribute as a whole. It can be difficult to check the validity of an entire address, but when decomposed, the elements can be more easily checked.

Decomposing also aids in the sorting of data for use in specific business processes, such as mass mailing. You will, in most cases, also be improving data retrieval performance when decomposed attributes are used. A generic attribute, Address, contains the street, city, region, postal code, and country. To get just the region of a customer in Washington, you have to select the whole Address attribute and parse it to find Washington, thereby degrading performance because of the redundant data retrieved. If you have four separate attributes, you can select the Region column and get your results more quickly. This same rule applies to updating data. It's easier to update a single part of an Address than to parse and then update the whole Address attribute.

As shown by the example provided in Figure 2.3, the Address has been fully decomposed for all entities, but the name has been decomposed only for the Employee entity.

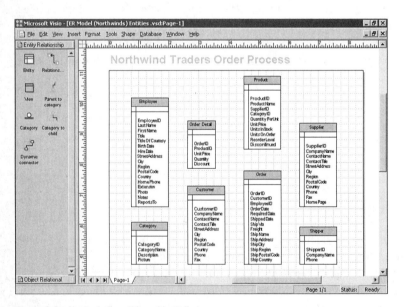

Figure 2.3   Northwind's entities with attributes.

Key Attributes

The use of an attribute can vary from system to system, but some attributes will be present in most systems to help sort data and perform relationship ties between one entity and another. A *key attribute* is almost always present within an entity to act as an identifier, much as a person's name identifies that person as being a unique individual. Entities are usually interdependent: Each holds information that relates to other entities. These relationships can be defined by their correlated dependencies. Key attributes are also therefore used for the purpose of relating one entity to another.

Recognizing Key Attributes

After all attributes have been defined and keys have begun to be recognized, the modeling process will be completed with the application of relationships and the normalization of data. These two processes are closely related, as you will see later, but before they can begin, key attributes must be recognized. These are specialized attributes referred to as *identifiers*. An identifier is an attribute or a set of attributes that defines one unique element of an entity. The use of identifiers allows for the individual selection of records from an entity. As the design progresses to the physical stage, identifiers will become the *primary* and *foreign keys*, allowing entities to be tied together through association or relationships. For Example, a product's identifying attribute is usually a unique product ID.

Identification of Primary and Foreign Keys

A *primary key* is a specialized attribute that is generally defined for each entity. The primary key is almost always defined, though is not necessarily required for all entities in a data model. However, the provision of a primary key does allow for a considerable number of benefits and should be considered in every instance. When defining a primary key, you should keep various factors in mind. The primary key normally defines uniqueness in an entity in that every record of a table has its own unique primary key. Also, when defined, a primary key should not be permitted to be empty. If a primary key is empty, you have a situation in which data integrity is difficult (if not impossible) to maintain.

A primary key should be defined as a single attribute that doesn't allow for duplicates or empty content. The primary key should be as small as possible. It is possible to create a compound primary key that uses multiple attributes or a key that contains a large number of bytes, but in the physical design this will increase the overhead and response time associated with data retrieval. A compound primary key consisting of multiple attributes is used in instances in which a singular attribute by itself does not enforce uniqueness within an entity. As we move through the modeling process, we will discover the need to use such a compound structure in some instances.

In most cases, an attribute is identified for each entity that will act as a key. This attribute could be a customer number, a product number, or simply an attribute to serve no other purpose than to act as a key identifier. When an attribute is added solely for the sake of being an identifier, it is known as a *surrogate key*. Whether you use a natural or surrogate key, that key will represent an important part in establishing relationships. In most circles surrogate keys are preferred because there is never a need to have this surrogate key change. The process of altering a key value can have repercussions on the business process and can also effect many elements of the database system.

 A longtime favorite answer on Microsoft database exams is to use surrogate keys in all entities. As mentioned previously, there are several benefits to doing this.

A *foreign key* is used to tie one entity to the primary key or unique data value of another entity. The relationship is created for the purpose of creating a dependency between the entities. A single attribute or combination of attributes can act as a foreign key depending on the makeup of the referenced primary key. A foreign key doesn't have to be unique. In fact, foreign keys are often in a many-to-one relationship with a primary key in another entity. Foreign key values* should be copies of the primary key values. No value in the foreign key, except a null value, should ever exist unless the same value exists in the primary key of the referenced entity.

A foreign key works in conjunction with a primary key or some other unique attribute to enforce referential integrity among entities. A relationship is created to enforce referential integrity between these two related entities. Foreign key connections may not be fully recognized for the model until you begin to look at the interrelationships of the entities. After a relationship is defined, the connection developed for the relationship will contain the foreign key pointing to the correlated primary key attribute.

For a foreign key to be created, a primary key must first be properly defined. Once defined, this primary key can be referenced by the foreign key. To quickly summarize the use of primary keys, keep the following in mind:

➤ Primary keys consist of sets of attributes whose values uniquely identify the rows in an entity.

➤ Primary keys give an ID to a row. They make the row unique throughout the entity. This means that rows can easily be located by this identifier.

➤ Primary keys can be used only for columns or attributes that don't allow empty entries. Allowing empty values would mean that a row would not be uniquely identified.

➤ The attribute chosen to hold a primary key must have values unique throughout the entity.

Foreign keys help in the relational process between two entities. When a primary key is created on a parent entity, it is connected to another entity by linking to the other entity's foreign key. For example, in an invoice situation, there are usually two entities: one for invoice general information and the other for invoice details. The invoice details would contain a hook on to the invoice general entity through the use of a foreign key, potentially the invoice number or a surrogate key.

NOTE Keys are usually created as part of the table creation process, but they can be added to the table after the initial generation. The syntax for the creation of keys and their association to tables are discussed in Chapter 3.

Before we are ready to draw all relationships into the model, the data model should begin a process of *normalization*. Some of the relationships can no doubt already be seen; however, when normalization standards are applied to the model, more relationships may be found. Only after the model has been fully normalized will you have a complete view of the entity relationships.

Data Normalization

The process of *normalization* is the division of entities in an attempt to provide the most efficient use of data storage. At times, denormalization is planned redundancy that is subsequently performed to improve response time and better use of resources. The process of designing the logical structure of a database is an attempt to provide a degree of normalization combined with aspects of denormalization to produce optimum storage efficiency while still providing acceptable levels of performance and resource utilization. In most instances, data is fully normalized before any aspects of denormalization are considered. In fact, denormalization usually is not approached until the physical model is in development.

Normalization is usually applied in practice from the outset of data modeling. After you're comfortable with all the modeling concepts, you will find yourself implementing normalized structures as a form of good practice. As with all other good development habits, you must first work through the concepts at a granular level before they begin to become second nature.

Normalization in general refers to how you implement and store data. Normalization is a design process intended to eliminate duplicate data. In a normalized entity, the redundant data is removed and the entity is simplified to its most basic form. This usually leads to a more involved entity structure with more entities. In the same way, the process of database normalization and planned denormalization is the process of simplifying data and data design to achieve maximum performance and simplicity. This denormalization process involves the planned addition of redundant data.

Although both normalization and denormalization are valid, necessary processes, the two achieve opposite goals. They don't by themselves achieve maximum performance and simplicity, though they do strive for a perfect balance between performance (denormalization) and simplicity (normalization). Normalization means no duplicate data.

Data Normalization with Normal Forms

In 1970, Dr. E. F. Codd designed three regulations a relational database adheres to, known as *normal forms*. Today they are known as the first, second, and third normal forms. (Normal forms do exceed three, but the first three are the only ones widely used.) The goal of the initial database design is to simplify the database into the third normal form.

Using normal forms provides these basic advantages:

➤ No data redundancy contributing to data integrity

➤ Index columns for faster sorting and searching

➤ Smaller entities that reduce table locking and data contention

➤ Query optimization

 Although in most cases a data model is taken only to the third normal form, it is worth noting that there are actually five forms. Because development to the fourth and fifth normal forms is not a requirement for the exam, we mentioned those forms here only for completeness.

The rules provided by these normal forms are discussed in the following sections.

First Normal Form

The *first normal form*, or *1NF*, defines the foundation for the relational database system. An attribute that is represented only once, and thus is not repeating, is known as an *atomic value*. Attributes should be atomic, which means that they cannot (or should not) be further broken down, based on the business needs for the use of the attribute. The first normal form defines that all attributes be atomic, which is to say they cannot be decomposed and must be nonrepeating.

In relational database terms, an attribute of an entity shouldn't have more than one definable piece of data or repeating groups. 1NF states that all attributes must be defined in their most singular form, which means that attributes must be decomposed and not further divisible.

A full name should never be used. For example, a field called `customer name` could be divided into `first name` and `last name` and would therefore break the first normal form rule. The first name is a piece of data that is independent from the last name and therefore it should be a separate attribute.

Second Normal Form

The purpose behind the second normal form is to ensure that each attribute belongs in the entity. Any non-key attribute of an entity must depend on the entire primary key, not just a portion of the key. For example, if the primary key of an `orders` entity contained two fields, `customer id` and `product id`, the attribute field `product description` wouldn't belong, because it has no connection to the `customer id`, only the `product id`. This would break the second normal form rule.

Third Normal Form

The third normal form states that a non-key field must not depend on another non-key field. The most obvious example of this rule is in the case of address information. The zip code is dependent on the address area; the city is dependent on the address itself. A large corporation or government agency may choose to have zip code information stored in a separate table and not within the base data to a perfect normalized form. Although in most table designs this situation is denormalized, in a pure normal form a separate entity would be used to provide additional address information such as city and zip code based on the address.

Two other normal forms do exist but aren't commonly implemented. It's entirely possible that by adhering to a third normal form, you may actually accomplish the fourth and fifth forms.

Fourth and Fifth Normal Forms

The fourth normal form dictates that a third normal form has no multivalued dependencies. In other words, every value of an attribute must appear in at least one row with every other value of the other attribute.

The fifth normal form is intended to eliminate joint dependency constraints. This is a theoretical consideration that is thought to have no practical value. If you disregard these forms, the design of the database might be less than perfect, but it should have no loss of functionality.

Normalizing a database is seemingly good but it can hamper performance. In many cases a designer has to consider denormalizing a database. Planned redundancy or denormalization is often brought into the design to provide for better performance or to clarify data.

Denormalization

Purposely adding redundant data and other fields that disobey normal forms is *denormalization*. Denormalizing as a process is more part of the physical design and will also be revisited during the implementation to improve performance. The concept is covered here for continuity and also to show the contrast with data normalization. After you have a logical design completely normalized, rarely will you keep it in that state as you proceed to the physical design of the actual database.

NOTE

Although normalization gives you a great deal of storage efficiency and might result in increased performance in some situations, there are some drawbacks to a completely normalized database. You should consider the trade-offs in storage efficiency, performance, and maintainability in your final design.

If you go too far with the normalization process, you might actually reverse the effect you're trying to achieve. Although normalization will reduce data redundancy, result in smaller tables with fewer rows, and provide a logical and consistent form, it will also require table joins for the implementation and will not allow for summary, duplicate, or other data that a user might expect to find in a single table. Normalizing a database design too far can decrease performance and make it difficult to alter the underlying table structure, and might make it harder to work with the data.

Denormalization may occur at any number of levels. At the absolute extreme, a database schema can be completely duplicated to a number of servers across the network by implementing replication. This could be warranted if you need to distribute the access to the data across slow network links or to multiple remote locations. Many advantages are gained through database replication, because the data is more easily available at the locations where it will be used. The drawback of this is increased maintenance of a number of servers. Also, if database replication isn't configured properly, it could monopolize a WAN. In addition, if there are network problems or there is a poor setup, the data might not be synchronized to a level that keeps it up-to-date. Data can be maintained as an exact duplication against a number of servers, but this would require a high-speed network and the configuration of a two-phase commit.

Other, simpler examples of planned denormalization would be to maintain complete address information for customers, suppliers, employees, and so on in the tables with the rest of their general information. This is what most users expect, and it is difficult to maintain a separate address table. There are no defined rules for denormalization, but some definite guidelines will help you understand what level might be appropriate in a given situation.

Data warehousing schemas often use a denormalized approach referred to as a *star* or *snowflake* schema. This schema structure takes advantage of typical decision support queries by using one central "fact" table for the subject area and many dimension tables containing denormalized descriptions of the facts.

There are also several other situations to consider. If a join requires the implementation of more than three tables, denormalization should be considered. In some situations in which the number of columns in a table can grow very large, a denormalized structure would split the table into more easily handled portions and use a one-to-one relationship to connect the information.

The completed structure will have to be modified over time as the live use of the database warrants. Never consider a database design to be perfect or complete. It often takes several years of actual use to determine the best levels of normalization and denormalization to use.

 Some forms of replication and data transfer accommodate redundancy by allowing the data to be on two servers simultaneously. If so, one server is usually treated as a read-only server and is used for offloading query processing from the updatable server. This is discussed in depth later in the book and is definitely an exam topic to be prepared for.

Relationships Between Entities

Relationships are the final component in an ER Model, allowing for a logical linkage between one entity and another. A relationship in an ER Model connects the data elements of two entities that contain information about the same element. The primary entity in a relationship provides some of the data, and other entities provide further related data. A relationship definition states how two entities are connected.

In the modeling process, we attempt to discover which things are related to one another, and how they are related, within the business problem we are modeling. They are usually defined as a link connecting the entities together based on the number of data elements in one entity that are related to one or more elements in the other entity. This is known as the *cardinality of a relationship*.

The cardinality of a relationship is used to define how many elements in one entity match up with elements of another entity. Relationships are usually defined as a numeric link connecting the entities together based on the number of data elements in one entity that are related to one or more full elements in another entity. It can be described as how many of one thing can relate to how many of something else.

Relationships cause a situation known in data modeling as a *dependency*. A dependency is a circumstance in which one entity either can't exist or has little meaning without at least one other entity in the database. When a dependency exists, it becomes a table relationship in the physical database design. There are three basic types of entity dependencies, and these dependencies are based on element cardinality. They are discussed in the points that follow:

➤ *One-to-one dependency*—A one-to-one dependency is the rarest form, because each record in one entity correlates to exactly one record in the other.

➤ *One-to-many dependency*—A one-to-many dependency is the most common form of relationship. One record in a primary entity has ties to many records in a secondary entity.

➤ *Many-to-many dependency*—A many-to-many dependency exists when many records in one entity can relate to many records in another entity.

Relationships are implemented as parent and child entities. In all cases in the ER Model, a key attribute from a child entity is attached to a related key value in a parent. All cardinality of relationships is implemented in this way, meaning that whether you have a one-to-one, one-to-many, or many-to-many relationship, you always maintain integrity by having the key of the child related to a parent.

Identification of Relationships

Setting up the relationships will finalize a draft of the ER Model. This draft will undergo modifications as the database approaches a physical design. Because at this stage of design all the basic elements of data model have been completed using the Entity Relationship approach, we now have a working model allowing us to proceed further into development. A general listing of attributes for each entity and the relationships between these entities is an important springboard to use to progress through the database design to the eventual completed system.

Implementing the relationships and applying normalization principles are often performed as parallel processes because decisions made in one process effect the other process and vice versa. Normalization helps in determining cardinality and the cardinality is a requirement of each relation. The three basic cardinality types, one-to-one, one-to-many, and many-to-many, are partially a result of knowing the business scenario being modeled and partially derived from applying normal forms.

One-To-One Relationship

The one-to-one type of relationship occurs when one row or data element of an entity is associated with only one row or element in the second entity. This type is used mostly when an entity has an extraordinarily large number of attributes so the entity is split in two to make it easier to manage. Also, an extra entity might be desired when developing the physical storage locations of the data. By separating seldom-used data from more frequently used information, you can accommodate faster data retrieval and updates. It is for this reason that these types of relationships are pulled into the model until the physical design of the database has begun.

In modeling a one-to-one relationship, a common key must be present in each of the entities being related. This common key allows for the collective attributes of both entities to be retrieved using a single value. Consider, for example, a product that has many descriptive attributes. Two product entities could be used to separate the different properties. Each entity would use a product number or similar value as a key. This is illustrated in the model segment shown in Figure 2.4.

In the preceding example the ProductCommon entity is used to store the attributes that are most readily used, and the ProductAtypical entity contains other attributes that, though still needed, are less frequently used. It is much more common to find relationships existing in a one-to-many cardinality.

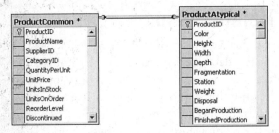

Figure 2.4 Two product entities in a one-to-one relationship.

One-To-Many Relationship

One-to-many relationships exist when a single instance of an entity (the parent entity) relates to many instances of another entity (the child entity). One-to-many dependencies are a natural occurrence in the real world—for example, a customer will have many orders, and a manufactured product could have many components.

One-to-many relationships can be expressed as many-to-one as well, though one-to-many is a common standard. It depends on how the relationship is being viewed.

This relationship is a classic *parent-child dependency*. A foreign key in a child entity will point to the associated primary key of the parent. When this relationship is related, removal of a parent could cause orphaning of the child because of its dependency. There are many examples of this type of relationship in the Northwind order process. The following list represents those seen in the diagram to this point:

➤ One supplier to many products

➤ One order to many order details

➤ One product exists within many order details

➤ One employee has many orders

➤ One customer has many orders

➤ One shipper is used in many orders

➤ One category will contain many products

Although one-to-many usually establishes "many" as the normal numerical component, you *can* have zero or only one child row. Customers *can* have zero or one order as well. In fact, cardinality notation allows for this with `0..*`. As we complete more of the information in the business scenario for Northwind, we will see more of these dependencies occur. One-to-many relationships are also a facet of implementing many-to-many relationships, as discussed in the next section.

Many-to-Many Relationship

A modeling differentiation is made in preparing the many-to-many type of relationship. *Many-to-many relationships* exist when many elements of one entity are related to many elements of another. For this reason, many-to-many relationships are implemented a bit differently in a database environment. In itself, this relationship is not solely one entity to another. In the ER model and database design, a third, joining entity is used to complete two one-to-many relations.

This type of relationship is not uncommon in the real world. As stated, a many-to-many relationship is implemented using three entities. The two main entities are connected together using a third entity. The third entity contains keys connected to the other two entities. In our basic data model the Order Detail entity is just such an entity. In the Northwind example this entity, however, also exists in its own right and contains additional attributes of its own.

In many models the third entity is created for the purpose of joining two other entities and has no other attributes except for those needed as key values to connect to the original entities. Consider, if you will, an educational scenario in which a teacher instructs several different bodies of students and a student has several different teachers. A third entity, TeacherStudent, could be created to connect the main entities.

This new entity that is created is known as an *associate entity* or a *join entity*. Resolving many-to-many relationships involves creating two one-to-many relationships from each of the original entities onto the associative entity. Take the many-to-many relationship between student and teacher. A student can have many teachers while a teacher has many students. A many-to-many relationship will need to be resolved by creating an associative entity and then linking a one-to-many relationship from the Teacher and Student entities to the TeacherStudent entity, as shown in Figure 2.5.

Along with these very standard relationships, you will find in some occurrences that a relationship is made within a single entity. In the case of a relationship in which an entity is related to itself, you have a unique situation, which in modeling terms is called a *unary* or a *self-referencing entity*. In a physical implementation this relationship is implemented through a self-join.

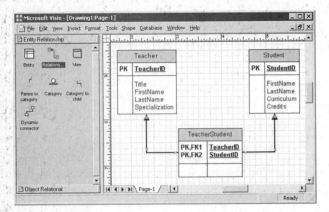

Figure 2.5 A teacher/student many-to-many relationship.

An example of this type of relationship is present within the Northwind system. Within the Employee entity, the ReportsTo attribute will hold the value of an Employee Identifier. This identifier refers to another employee element that is the boss or some other responsible person. The ReportsTo element will be a foreign key that refers to the primary key of the Employee entity. The modeling of this type of relationship is shown in Figure 2.6.

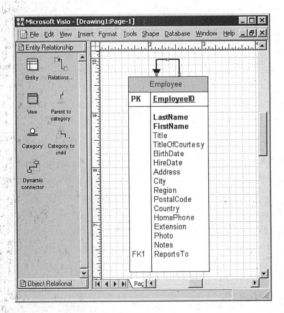

Figure 2.6 A unary relationship.

A unary relationship will constitute a very small percentage of the relationships defined in any given model. These relationships can be defined using a one-to-one or one-to-many cardinality. In an employee scenario a manager can have a single assistant (one-to-one) or any number of employees can report to the same manager (one-to-many).

Relationships will continue to be added to the model as elements in the system evolve. A potential model for the Northwind Trader order process can now be assembled and is provided in Figure 2.7.

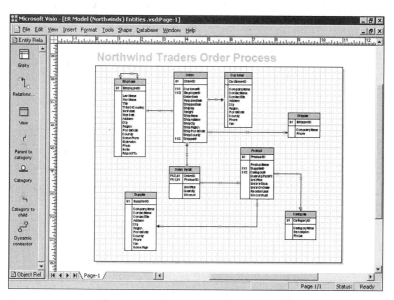

Figure 2.7   The completed Northwind model.

Exam Prep Questions

1. You are a database developer for Northwind Traders. A system that you are developing for your company's SQL Server 2000 will store an online transaction-processing database. Many of the entities are expected to have a very large number of data elements, and these elements will contain a large number of attributes. You want to develop a model for optimal performance. What should you do? (Choose one.)

   ❏ A. Develop a fully normalized structure to minimize the number of joins used to process data.

   ❏ B. Develop a fully normalized structure and then split entities in half, placing the same number of attributes into each entity. Create one-to-one relationships between the two entities.

   ❏ C. Develop a fully normalized structure and then split entities in half based on frequently and infrequently used attributes. Use appropriate relationships to connect the entities.

   ❏ D. Develop a fully normalized structure and then split entities in logical divisions based on commonalities within data element sets to minimize the number of records in each entity.

   ❏ E. Develop a denormalized structure that limits the number of attributes and records in any entity. Create many entities that will have smaller content and apply appropriate relationships.

   Answer: C. Answer A is incorrect because a fully normalized structure will not usually provide for optimum performance. B is not the best approach to provide for performance because there is no measure for usage of attributes or other reasoning for the entity divisions. D, although minimizing the number of rows, does nothing to limit the number of attributes. E is taking the approach too far and will end up with more entities than desired, which will also detract from performance. C is the best approach because it addresses the entity size and performance issues and does so based on sound reasoning.

2. You are a database developer for Northwind Traders. The company is planning to put in place a training facility for employee enrichment purposes. The single room will be scheduled based on the three shifts currently worked by the employees. A senior employee on that shift will teach each course. The entity design, which will also utilize the Employee entity, has been roughly sketched and will contain the following:

   ```
   Schedule Entity
   . ScheduleID
   . CourseID
   . EmployeeID
   . CourseTime
   Course Entity
   . CourseID
   . CourseTitle
   . Description
   ```

. InstructorLastName
. InstructorFirstName
. InstructorTitle

You want to promote quick response times for queries and minimize redundant data. What should you do? (Choose one.)

❏ A. Create a new table named **Instructors**. Include **InstructorID**, **InstructorFirstName**, **InstructorLastName**, and **InstructorTitle** attributes. Remove these elements from the **Course** entity and replace them with an **InstructorID** attribute.

❏ B. Move all the columns from the **Course** entity and place them in the **Schedule** entity, creating just a single entity.

❏ C. Remove the **InstructorFirstName**, **InstructorLastName**, and **InstructorTitle** attributes from the **Course** entity. Replace them with an **EmployeeID** attribute.

❏ D. Remove the **CourseTime** attribute from the **Schedule** entity and place it into the **Course** entity.

Answer: C. Answer A would be an appropriate answer if the instructors for the courses were external to the company. Because these instructors are internal, the personal information can be drawn from the Employee entity, making C a better choice. Making a singular entity as suggested in B would provide far too much redundant storage of data. D is incorrect because the CourseTime attribute is a function of the Schedule not of the Course.

3. You are designing a database model for Northwind Traders that will be used in a customer order process. Customers will be able to order multiple products each time they place an order. You review the model to date, shown here:

```
Customer
.CustomerID
.OrderID
.CompanyName
.ContactName
.Address
.City
.Region
.PostalCode
Order
.OrderID
.ProductID
.OrderDate
.Quantity
.Discount
Product
.ProductID
.Description
.UnitPrice
```

You want good performance while removing redundant data. What should you do? (Each correct answer presents part of a correct solution; choose three.)

❏ A. Create a new entity named **OrderDetail**. Add **OrderID**, **ProductID**, **Quantity**, and **Discount** attributes to this entity.

❏ B. Ensure that a composite primary key on the **OrderID** and **ProductID** attributes is defined on the **Orders** entity.

❏ C. Remove the **ProductID** and **Quantity** attributes from the **Order** entity.

❏ D. Decompose the **ContactName** attribute of the **Customer** entity to provide for **FirstName** and **LastName** attributes.

❏ E. Move the **UnitPrice** attribute from the **Product** entity to the **Order** entity.

❏ F. Remove the **OrderID** attribute from the **Customer** entity and place a **CustomerID** attribute into the **Order** entity.

Answer: A, C, and F. Both A and C are part of the same principle in data modeling and remove the redundant storage of Discount information. Because a customer can make many orders, the relationship needs to be made such that an Order refers to a Customer and not the other way around. The UnitPrice attribute is a property of a Product and for that reason should stay in that entity. Though the ContactName could conceivably be decomposed, there is nothing in the problem statement that would indicate this as a requirement.

4. You are a database consultant for Northwind Traders and you have been hired to develop a database design. This design will be used to develop a database system to be used by a brick-and-mortar store. The information to be maintained in the database will track product categories and suppliers. You create an entity named Product that contains the following:

```
Product
.ProductID
.CategoryID
.SupplierID
.QuantityPerUnit
.UnitPrice
.UnitsInStock
.UnitsOnOrder
.ReorderLevel
.Discontinued
```

You must ensure that each product has a valid value for the Category and Supplier attributes. What should you do? (Choose one.)

❏ A. Define the **Product** entity to have a compound primary key that uses the **ProductID**, **CategoryID**, and **SupplierID** attributes.

❏ B. Create two relationships in which the **SupplierID** and **CategoryID** attributes each refer to other kernel entities.

☐ C. Create a **CategorySupplier** entity and relate the **Product** table to this entity using both the **CategoryID** and the **SupplierID**.

☐ D. Remove the **CategoryID** and **SupplierID** attributes from this entity and move them to a more valid kernel entity.

Answer: B. The CategoryID and SupplierID attributes represent foreign keys that will refer to primary keys within a kernel entity. They are in the correct entity for this purpose and should be referencing the Category and Supplier entities, respectively.

5. You are designing a portion of the database model that will be used by Northwind Traders for its order process. A quick sketch of the model has been made and is shown here:

```
Product
.ProductID
.Description
.QuantityPerUnit
.UnitsInStock
.Unitprice
.SupplierName
OrderDetail
.OrderID
.ProductID
.CustomerID
.Quantity
.Discount
Order
.OrderID
.OrderDate
.Freight
Customer
.CustomerID
.CompanyName
.ContactName
.Address
.City
.Region
.Phone
.Fax
```

You want to obtain speed and efficiency within the model. What changes should be made? (Choose one.)

☐ A. Decompose the **ContactName** attribute so that there are **FirstName** and **LastName** attributes.

☐ B. Remove the **SupplierName** attribute from the Product entity and place it into the Order entity.

☐ C. Remove the **ProductID** from the **OrderDetail** entity and place it into the **Order** entity.

☐ D. Remove the **CustomerID** attribute from the **OrderDetail** entity and place it into the **Order** entity.

☐ E. Remove the **Quantity** attribute from the **OrderDetail** entity. Add a **Quantity** column to the **Order** entity.

Answer: D. The CustomerID present within the OrderDetail entity would be repeated several times per Order when it is needed only once. It is therefore more appropriate for the CustomerID to be in the Order entity.

6. You are a database developer for Northwind Traders. The company is planning a major expansion and desires to begin tracking sales information on a regional basis. Employees of the company will be assigned to a region and are permitted to perform sales only within their designated area. To accommodate this facet of the Order process, a rough sketch has been created of two entities that are to be used. These two entities are illustrated here:

```
RegionSale
.RegionSaleID
.OrderID
.RegionID
Region
.RegionID
.RegionTitle
.EmployeeID
```

You would like the new entities to exist within the system as already defined. You would also like to have the system operate quickly with as little redundant information as possible. You would also like key usage to remain consistent with the rest of the system. What should you do? (Select two answers; each answer represents a part of the correct solution.)

- ❏ A. Create only a single entity for the process, combining the attributes from the two sketched entities.
- ❏ B. Create a third new entity, **RegionEmployee**, to connect the **Region** entity to the **Employee** entity.
- ❏ C. Remove the **EmployeeID** attribute and add a **RegionID** attribute to the **Employee** entity.
- ❏ D. Remove the **RegionSaleID** attribute from the **RegionSale** entity.
- ❏ E. Move the **EmployeeID** from the **Region** entity to the **RegionSale** entity.
- ❏ F. Remove the **OrderID** attribute from the **RegionSale** entity.

Answer: C and D. To remain consistent with the other many-to-many relationships in the system, the RegionSaleID should be removed and a compound primary key should be based on the OrderID and the RegionID. The employee should have an attribute for region and not vice versa.

7. You are a database developer for Northwind Traders. You are creating a database model that includes an entity named Order. The Order entity contains attributes as indicated in the following sketch:

```
Order
.OrderDate
.RequiredDate
.ShipDate
.Freight
```

Employees take orders from the customers and receive a commission on each fulfilled order. Orders can be taken only from the listing of existing customers. Shippers can be selected only from a set of existing shippers. Which additional attributes should be included to complete the entity design? (Choose one.)

- ❑ A. **OrderID, CustomerID, ShipperID**
- ❑ B. **OrderID, CustomerID, ShipperID, EmployeeID**
- ❑ C. **OrderID, ShipperID, EmployeeID**
- ❑ D. **OrderID, CustomerID, EmployeeID**

Answer: B. The order entity as defined by the order process relates to the Customer, Shipper, and Employee entities and should for that reason have foreign keys for each of those kernel entities.

8. You are a database developer for Northwind Traders. The company heads would like to track customer demographics so that they can target advertising budgets and promotions. It is desired to have all budgets based on the past purchases of existing customers. The idea is to target buying patterns by one or more demographics. The demographics to be tracked are the following:

```
gender
age
postal code
region
```

To implement this, area management has sketched the following entities:

```
CustomerDemo
.DemographicID
.DemographicDescription
CustCustomerDemo
.CustomerID
.DemographicID
```

What should you do? (Choose one.)

- ❑ A. Leave the entities as they are to represent an appropriate many-to-many relationship.
- ❑ B. Combine the entities to form one singular entity.
- ❑ C. Add additional attributes to the **CustCustomerDemo** entity.
- ❑ D. Add additional attributes to the **CustomerDemo** entity.

Answer: A. This is a proper many-to-many relationship in which each customer can fit into many demographic categories and any demographic can apply to a number of customers.

9. You are a database developer for Northwind Traders. You are designing a entity to record information about potential new products. A rough sketch of the entity is shown here:

```
TestProduct
.TestProductID
.CategoryID
.SupplierName
.SupplierPhone
.Rating
```

You would like the new entity to be consistent with the remaining system while still storing data in an efficient manner. What should you do? (Choose one.)

- ❏ A. Relate the **TestProduct** entity to the **Product** entity.
- ❏ B. Define a compound primary key that uses both the **TestProductID** attribute and the **CategoryID** attribute.
- ❏ C. Ensure that the **TestProductID** is unique from an existing **ProductID**.
- ❏ D. Replace the **SupplierName** and **SupplierPhone** attributes with a **SupplierID**.

Answer: D. There is already a Supplier entity in the system that could easily be used in a relationship with the newly defined TestProduct entity. Placement of the SupplierName and SupplierPhone attributes into this new entity is therefore redundant.

10. As part of the preparation for the database model for Northwind Traders, you have sketched out a set of entities. The sketch as it stands is shown here:

```
Order
.OrderID
.CustomerID
.EmployeeID
.OrderDate
.RequiredDate
.ShippingDate
.Shipvia
.Freight
.Shipname
.ShipAddress
.ShipCity
.ShipRegion
.ShipPostalCode
.ShipCountry
.ShipperID
OrderDetail
.OrderID
.ProductID
.UnitPrice
.Quantity
Product
.ProductID
.ProductName
.SupplierID
.CategoryID
```

```
.QuantityPerUnit
.UnitPrice
.UnitsInStock
.UnitsOnOrder
.ReorderLevel
.Discontinued
Supplier
.SupplierID
.CompanyName
.ContactName
.ContactTitle
.Address
.City
.Region
.PostalCode
.Country
.Phone
.Fax
.HomePage
```

You are now setting up the relationships for the entities. How should these be applied? (Each correct answer represents part of the solution; choose three.)

❑ A. Create a one-to-many relationship on the **Product** entity that references the **OrderDetail** entity.

❑ B. Create a many-to-one relationship on the **Product** entity that references the **OrderDetail** entity.

❑ C. Create a one-to-many relationship on the **Product** entity that references the **Supplier** entity.

❑ D. Create a many-to-one relationship on the **Product** entity that references the **Supplier** entity.

❑ E. Create a one-to-many relationship on the **Order** entity that references the **OrderDetail** entity.

❑ F. Create a many-to-one relationship on the **Order** entity that references the **OrderDetail** entity.

Answer: A, D, and E. There will be many OrderDetail elements for each Order, many products to a supplier, and many OrderDetail elements that refer to any product.

Implementing the Physical Database

Terms you'll need to understand:

- ✓ RAID
- ✓ Gigabit
- ✓ Database
- ✓ Table
- ✓ Record
- ✓ Row
- ✓ Column
- ✓ Field
- ✓ Filegroups
- ✓ Clustered index
- ✓ Nonclustered index
- ✓ Trigger
- ✓ Primary key
- ✓ Foreign key
- ✓ Constraint
- ✓ Stored procedure
- ✓ Log file
- ✓ Model database

Techniques you'll need to master:

- ✓ Hardware setup/file placement
- ✓ Database creation
- ✓ Object creation
- ✓ Setting/altering properties
- ✓ Setting constraints

Introduction

This chapter deals with the physical components of a SQL Server database system. Beginning with the server hardware, organizing the data storage and creating the physical files is where a lot of future performance will be determined. There are many options to consider for a production environment, and one thing is certain: The minimum installation requirements will not be sufficient. The computer hardware components are only the beginning of the physical elements.

Although we tend to think of the physical realm as things that we can touch and feel, within a DBMS environment it also defines the components of the database itself. The database layout, the key structures, constraints, and other software elements are all considered physical elements. It's time for the entities discussed in the logical design to become tables.

In any physical design, the goal is to provide an efficient and responsive database system that also lends itself to appropriate maintenance tasks without becoming a database administrator's burden. At this stage of a database implementation, care is taken to provide a system structure that is usable, provides for optimum user response time, can be readily maintained, and above all meets the needs of the business for which it was designed.

In moving from an idea to a logical structure to the actual physical elements, you must remember to consider elements that contribute to performance, reliability, and data integrity. Having a model of the system is one thing, but it must be able to meet the demands of an environment in which inevitably the system must meet the intended goals of the company and add to the bottom line.

In a book of this nature, trying to fit all topics into the fray in a logical manner can sometimes be awkward. In this chapter we will discuss some of the hardware implementations that probably should wait for a database design and other criteria. We will approach the hardware next from a standpoint of what the baseline rules are for establishing the server.

A Hardware Dialogue

In a production environment, budget is going to limit some of the hardware decisions being made. Often, new hardware isn't even considered, though in many cases it is needed. Let us approach the topic first from a minimum hardware perspective and then progress to a usual or best-practice scenario. Finally, we will look at the optimum hardware—the hardware we would choose if there were a very large budget available to cover equipment costs.

Let's start with something that may be found on the Administration exam, though less likely seen within the design topics. These are the minimum requirements as specified by Microsoft:

➤ Pentium 166MHz or higher

➤ 64MB minimum, 128MB or more recommended

➤ SQL Server database components: 95MB–270MB, 250MB typical

➤ VGA or higher resolution

➤ CD-ROM drive

Now if I were to walk into an office and see this system as my production machine, I would likely immediately turn and run away. Even as a test system, this would be a frightening configuration. Let's be a little more realistic with all components.

Depending on the load, you want to see a multiple processor system for your database server. One processor is fine with a low-end server, if it is 1GHz or above, but two processors are better and four or more processors are preferred. SQL Server is designed to work best in a symmetric multiprocessor environment.

Given the price of RAM in today's business environment, it doesn't make any sense to skimp in order to lower costs. Put as much RAM into the machine as the hardware and budget can handle. Increasing the memory of a server is the most cost-effective change you can make to achieve better performance on an existing machine. I hate to even put a low end on RAM, but let's suggest 1GB for starters, and don't be afraid to move up a considerable distance from there.

The disk system is also very important. For a strong server you should use a minimum of 5 drives. A 3-drive RAID array would be used to store data, and the other 2 drives would mirror each other and store the operating system and application programs. The more drives you can add into the array, the better the performance and the larger the capacity available to store data. This peaks out at about 10 drives, which is a little overboard anyway, but a 5-drive array performs very well for most implementations.

RAID (redundant array of independent/inexpensive disks) is a technology in which two or more disk drives can be configured in such a manner as to provide the following:

➤ Larger volumes, because space on multiple disks is combined to form a single volume

➤ Improved performance, by interacting with more than one physical disk at a time (disk striping)

➤ Safeguarding of data, by providing mechanisms (mirror or parity) for redundant data storage

Even though software implementations of RAID must be known to pass certification exams, and will be found in production systems, they are not nearly regarded as reliable as hardware RAID. For any high-volume, mission-critical application, it is therefore preferred to set up data redundancy mechanisms at the hardware level.

A gigabit backbone should be configured for the network around the server. It is even worth considering multiple network cards connected to the server to increase the bandwidth available to the machine.

If you are looking on the very high end, then two sets of small RAID arrays of three drives, each on two separate controllers, can provide some additional performance gain and flexibility with data and index placement. It is also often recommended that the log files be kept separated from the data so as to improve performance and reduce disk contention.

 Keeping the log files separate from the data can help improve performance and reduce disk contention.

Defining a SQL Server Database

A database is similar to a work file folder, which contains information pertaining to related topics. In the same way, a database is a group of files used to store data pertaining to a single business process. Databases are organized with fields, records, and tables. A field is a single characteristic, attribute, or property that provides information about an object. A record is a complete set of all the fields combined together for a particular object. A table is a group of all related records.

SQL Server is a relational database management system. A relational database contained within SQL Server is a collection of objects in which data and other information are stored in multiple tables. The numerous tables are related in some way, either directly or indirectly via other tables. A relational database contains all database objects, structures, and raw data pertaining to that database.

Because we have just looked at the hardware, let's start with a focus on where to put the files for the database server. Of consideration here are the operating-system files, the application program files, and the database files consisting of two types of files: *data files* and *log files*.

It is also worth considering the separation of indexes because some performance gains can be realized if the indexes are stored on a drive other than the one on which the data is stored. This is done through the use of filegroups. When the index is created on a different filegroup, each group can make use of different physical drives and their own controllers. Data and index information can then be read in parallel by multiple disk heads.

In an ideal configuration (somewhat tongue in cheek), you might want to separate the operating system from its page file. You would then place the log onto its one drive, separate from the data, with the data configured over a RAID volume as described in the following section. You'd then take the seldom-used data (column or table data) and separate it from data that will be accessed more frequently. After placing the indexes off on their own volume as well, for about $150,000–$200,000 you would have the optimum performance in a database server.

Remember that the DBMS will rely heavily on the file system. The file format in SQL Server 2000 has not significantly changed from the previous version (SQL Server 7). SQL Server uses a set of files to store the data, indexes, and log information for a database. A primary file also has some header information in it, providing SQL Server with necessary information about a database. Each database has a minimum of two files associated with it, one for the data and a second for the log. It is also possible to create multiple files for each of these purposes as described in the following paragraphs. File placement, and object placement within these files, plays an important role in the responsiveness of SQL Server. A database consists of two or more files with each file used for only a single database. A single file cannot be shared by multiple databases.

The File System

Each database has one or more files used to store indexes and data. In a lot of database scenarios, you will not implement more than one data file and one log file. In some instances, however, you might want to implement a filegroup. You might also have a performance gain through the appropriate placement of objects within these groups.

The first file created for this purpose is referred to as the *primary file*. The primary file contains the information needed to start up a database and is also used to store some or all of the data. If desired, secondary files can be created to hold some of the data and other objects. Some databases might be large enough or complex enough in their design to have multiple secondary files used for storage. Normally, the log is maintained in a single file. The log file is used to store changes to the database before these changes are recorded in the data files themselves. The storage of information into log files in this manner enables SQL Server to use these files as an important part of its recovery process. Every time the SQL Server is started, it uses the log files for each of the databases to determine what units of work were still being handled at the time the server was stopped.

The filenames given to all data and log files can be any desired name, although it is recommended that you select a name that indicates the content of the file. The file extensions for the primary data file, secondary data file(s), and log files can also be any chosen set of characters. It is recommended for consistency and standardization that the extensions be .mdf, .ndf, and .ldf for the primary, secondary, and log files, respectively.

Creating Files and Filegroups

Filegroups enable a group of files to be handled as a single unit, and thus make implementations that require multiple files easier to accommodate. With filegroups, SQL Server provides an administrative mechanism of grouping files within a database. You might want to implement filegroups to spread data across more than one logical disk partition or physical disk drive. In some cases, this provides for increased performance as long as the hardware is sufficient to optimize reading and writing to multiple drives concurrently.

You can create a filegroup when a database is created, or you might add them later when more files are needed or desired. After a filegroup has been assigned to a database, you cannot move its files to a different filegroup. Therefore, a file cannot be a member of more than one filegroup. SQL

Server provides for a lot of flexibility in the implementation of filegroups. Tables, indexes, text, ntext, and image data can be associated with a specific filegroup, allocating all pages to one specific group. Filegroups can contain only data files; log files cannot be part of a filegroup.

If you place indexes into their own filegroup, the index and data pages can be handled as separate physical read elements. If the associated filegroups are placed onto separate physical devices, each can be read without interfering with the reading of the other. This is to say that while an index is read through in a sequential manner, the data can be accessed randomly without the need for manipulating the physical arm of a hard drive back and forth from the index and the data. This can improve performance and at the same time save on hardware wear and tear.

Placing an entire table onto its own filegroup offers many benefits. If you do so, you can back up a table without having to perform a much larger backup operation. Archived or seldom-used data can be separated from the data that is more readily needed. Of course, the reverse is true: A table that needs to be more readily available within a database can be placed into its own filegroup to enable quicker access. In many instances, planned denormalization (the purposeful creation of redundant data) can be combined with this feature to obtain the best response.

Placing text, ntext, and image data in their own filegroup can improve application performance. Consider an application design that allows the data for these column types to be fetched only upon user request. Frequently, it is not necessary for a user to view pictures and extensive notes within a standard query. Not only does this accommodate better-performing hardware, but it also can provide faster query responses and less bandwidth saturation, because data that is not required is not sent across the network.

Filegroups can provide for a more effective backup strategy for larger database environments. If a large database is placed across multiple filegroups, the database can be backed up in smaller pieces. This is an important aspect if the time to perform a full backup of the entire database is too lengthy.

After a determination has been made to use a filegroup strategy for storing data, always ensure that when a backup is performed against a filegroup the indexes are also backed up at the same time. This is easily accomplished if the data and indexes are stored in the same filegroup. If they are located on separate filegroups, ensure that both the data and the index filegroups are included in a single backup operation. Be aware that SQL Server does not enforce backup of data and index filegroups in a single operation. You must ensure that the files associated with the indexes tied to a particular dataset are backed up with the data during a filegroup backup.

Objects can easily be moved from one filegroup to another. Using the appropriate property page, you just select the new filegroup into which you want to move the object. Logs are not stored in filegroups. You can, however, use multiple log files and place them in different locations to obtain better and more varied maintenance and allow more storage space for log content.

File Placement for Performance and Reliability

The placement of the files related to a SQL Server 2000 database environment helps to ensure optimum performance while minimizing administration. Recoverability can also be improved in the event of data corruption or hardware failures if appropriate measures are taken. On the exam, you must be prepared to respond to these requirements and properly configure the interactions with the file system.

It is absolutely mandatory to understand the basics of the file system and its use by SQL Server. Know when to split off a portion of the database structure and storage to a separate physical disk drive. Many processes performed within SQL Server can be classified as sequential or random. In a sequential process, the data or file can be read in a forward progression without having to locate the next data to be read. In a random process, the data is typically more spread out, and getting at the actual physical data requires multiple accesses.

Where possible, it is desirable to keep sequential processes running without physical interruption caused by other processes contending for the device. Using file placement strategies to keep random processes separate from sequential ones enables the configuration to minimize the competition over the placement of the read/write heads.

As a minimum requirement for almost any implementation, you should separate the normal sequential processing of the log files from the random processing of the data. You also improve recoverability by separating the data from the log and placing them on separate physical volumes. If the volume where the data is stored is damaged and must be restored from backup, you will still have access to the last log entries. The final log can be backed up and restored against the database, which gives something very close to 100% recoverability right to the point of failure.

An interesting and flexible strategy is to provide a separate drive solely for the log. This single volume does not have to participate in RAID architecture, but RAID might be desired for full recoverability. If you give the log the space of an entire volume, you give the log more room to grow and accumulate over time without the need for periodic emptying. Less frequent log backups are needed and the best possible log performance is achieved.

Two primary concerns in most data environments are data recoverability in the event of the inevitable failures and considerations for minimal downtime. In the industry, one of the optimum ratings to strive for is the elusive "five nines" (99.999). This rating means that over any given period (a generally accepted standard of 365 days minimum), the server remained online and servicing the end user 99.999% of the time. In other words, the total downtime for an entire year would be a little more than five minutes.

Database Creation

An absolute necessity of building databases that interact with SQL Server 2000 is using the appropriate database objects to obtain a usable database system while improving response times and maintaining data integrity. There are considerations and trade-offs for choosing one technique over the other. The selection of the most appropriate method to obtain the desired result requires that you know where each technique is best implemented. The exam will test on the appropriate application of each of these objects.

Creating and altering databases involves selecting the physical volume type for each database file, setting the appropriate file properties, placing the objects into the files/filegroups, and ensuring that appropriate adjustments are made as the database matures. The type of business needs that the database is being designed to meet helps to indicate the measures needed to ensure adequate performance.

Try to place onto separate volumes any files that might tend to compete with each other for read cycles during a single operation. Place log files away from the data to ensure adequate recovery, and make sure that database properties have been set in such a way as to ensure that maintenance tasks can be performed.

When you create a database for the first time, that database initially takes most of its attributes from the Model database. The Model database is a system database that SQL Server uses as a kind of template for database creations. It is a good and common practice to set the properties and contents of the Model database based on the majority of new databases that are to be created.

In practice, many objects are stored in the Model database to minimize the need to re-create these objects every time a database is created. Common elements placed in the Model often include specialized user-defined functions and data types that are present and frequently used by the development staff in their coding. In theory, objects are created for use in a single database, but all developers realize that object and code reuse is an important facet of easing the development process.

Often an object, such as a user-defined function, standard security role, or corporate information table, can be found in most if not all databases within a company. A property value, such as recovery level, might also have a standard implementation across all servers in the enterprise. If an object or a property value will be present in most of the user databases, placing the object into the Model database or setting a property accordingly can save you the work of performing the activity as a post-creation task.

All files needed for a database can be created through a single activity using SQL Server's Enterprise Manager (as shown in Figure 3.1) or with a single CREATE DATABASE Transact SQL statement. Either of these methods can be used to initialize all files and create the database and logs in a single step.

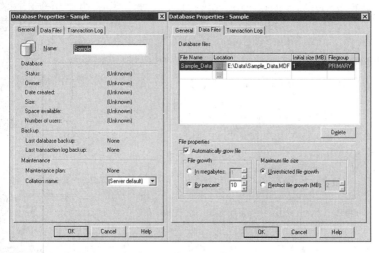

Figure 3.1 Database creation from the Enterprise Manager.

SQL Server 2000 enables you to set database files so that they expand and shrink automatically, eliminating the need for additional administration. By default, SQL Server enables data files to increase in size as needed for data storage. Therefore, a file can grow to the point where all disk space is exhausted. You can specify that a file is not to grow beyond its creation size or implement a maximum size for file growth. Ensure that disk space is not exhausted by using the MAXSIZE option of the CREATE DATABASE or ALTER DATABASE statements to indicate the largest size to which a file can grow.

The default names for the primary database and transaction log files are created using the database name you specified as the prefix—for example, `NewDatabase_Data.mdf` and `NewDatabase_Log.ldf`. These names and locations can be changed, if desired, from the default values provided for the new database file. The T-SQL syntax for creating a simple database is as follows:

```
CREATE DATABASE MyDatabase
ON
(NAME = 'DataStore',
    FILENAME = 'd:\data directory\DataStore_MyDatabase.mdf',
    SIZE = 1MB, MAXSIZE = 5MB, FILEGROWTH = 1MB)
LOG ON
(NAME ='LogStore',
    FILENAME = 'e:\log directory\LogStore_MyDatabase.ldf',
    SIZE = 1MB, MAXSIZE = 5MB, FILEGROWTH = 1MB)
```

Following are some important issues with regard to appropriate use of the `CREATE DATABASE` statement:

➤ The default growth increment measure is MB, but it can also be specified with a KB or a % suffix. When % is specified, the growth increment size is the specified percentage of the size of the file at the time the increment occurs.

➤ A maximum of 32,767 databases can be defined on a server.

➤ The minimum size for a log file is 512KB.

➤ Each database has an owner. The owner is the user who creates the database. The database owner can be changed through `sp_changedbowner`.

➤ The Master database should be backed up after a user database is created.

➤ The default unit of measure for the `size` and `maxsize` settings is MB if you supply a number, but no measure is provided. If no options are supplied, `maxsize` defaults to `unlimited` and the `filegrowth` is `10%`.

In a volatile environment, the database and its related files might frequently increase and decrease in size, and this activity might be the desired operation of the server. In most instances, an implementation providing for more stability in the file system is the desired result. A determination has to be made as to whether the database stays at about the same size or grows or shrinks over time. In most scenarios, a database grows over time and needs to be reduced only when data is archived.

When creating the files, you should set the `SIZE`, `MAXSIZE`, and `FILEGROWTH` parameters so that the database can increase in volume over time. The

FILEGROWTH configuration should be implemented in larger increments so that growth within the file system isn't occupying too much of the server's resources. Growth of files occurs in the background and can be minimized by using a larger growth increment. Always provide a MAXSIZE entry even if the entry itself is close to the capacity of the volume.

You can use the CREATE DATABASE statement to create a database from script. Saving the script enables you to re-create a similar database on another server in the future. Any SQL Server object can have its creation script saved. Using the CREATE DATABASE statement to create a database using multiple files and log files would look similar to this:

```
CREATE DATABASE Example
ON
PRIMARY ( NAME = ExampleData,
FILENAME = 'c:\mssql\data\sampdat.mdf',
          SIZE = 10MB,
          MAXSIZE = 20MB,
          FILEGROWTH = 2MB),
        ( NAME = ExampleIndexes,
FILENAME = 'c:\mssql\data\sampind2.ndf',
          SIZE = 10MB,
          MAXSIZE = 20MB,
          FILEGROWTH = 2MB),
        ( NAME = ExampleArchive,
FILENAME = 'c:\mssql\data\samparch.ndf',
          SIZE = 10MB,
          MAXSIZE = 20MB,
          FILEGROWTH = 2MB)
LOG ON  ( NAME = ExampleLog1,
FILENAME = 'd:\mssql\log\samplog1.ldf',
          SIZE = 10MB,
          MAXSIZE = 20MB,
          FILEGROWTH = 2MB),
        ( NAME = ExampleLog2,
FILENAME = 'd:\mssql\log\samplog2.ldf',
          SIZE = 10MB,
          MAXSIZE = 20MB,
          FILEGROWTH = 2MB)
```

When you create the database and its associated files, you provide values to determine the initial file sizes, indicate whether and how the files will grow, and specify some other basic database and file properties. The initial settings are used as a basis for future file-system activities. If the initial settings are in need of alteration later, you can perform this activity through the Enterprise Manager or by using the ALTER DATBASE T-SQL statement. Alterations can impact the front-end applications, so extra caution must be taken when changing a database from its original form. In particular, the alteration of the collating sequence can have serious repercussions.

Using a Collation Sequence

A *collation sequence* is a set of rules governing the characters that are used within a database and the means by which characters are sorted and compared. In SQL Server 2000 this sequence can be set on a database-by-database basis. In previous versions of SQL Server, the collation sequence was a server-wide setting. You therefore had to either perform a whole series of rebuilding actions to create a database that did not use the server collation, or install the database on a separate server altogether.

In SQL Server 2000 you can specify a nondefault collation for any database on the server. This means that one database does not have to have the same characters or sorting rules as the rest of the databases on the server. If all but one or two of your databases have the same set of characters, a single server can now implement the functionality that previously would have taken two separate machines.

To create a database with a nondefault collating sequence, provide the COLLATE clause on the CREATE DATABASE command. You might also select the collation name from the drop-down box in the Enterprise Manager when you create the database from the GUI.

Collation for an individual column can be different. A collation can be selected for an individual column but is not recommended because it causes great difficulty in the development of front-end applications. Be careful in the use of multiple collating sequences because it makes the transfer and entry of data more complex. It might also limit the application development environment and techniques normally used for data entry and editing.

Be certain of the collation sequence used upon creation of a database. After the collation sequence is set, it can be changed only through rebuilding of the database. If possible, collation decisions should be made during the logical design of the system so that you don't have to rebuild. Although collations can be different, if you want to change the sequence post-creation, you will have to rebuild the database.

Altering Database Properties

Several database properties affect the way in which some SQL Server commands operate. You can use the Enterprise Manager to make appropriate adjustments to some of the database properties. Alternatively, you can use the ALTER DATABASE T-SQL statement to script these changes. You may prefer setting options using T-SQL. The system-stored procedure sp_dboption can still be used to set database options, but Microsoft has stated that in future versions of SQL Server this functionality might not be supported.

In altering a database, you can add or remove files and filegroups and/or modify attributes of the files and filegroups. ALTER DATABASE also enables you to set database properties, whereas in previous versions these properties could be changed only using the sp_dboption stored procedure.

After you've set up the options, the next thing to consider is the creation of objects within the database. Database objects include constraints, indexes, stored procedures, tables, triggers, user-defined functions, views, and more. Each object is discussed in detail, paying particular attention to the impact on the system as a whole. In many implementations, there are various approaches to meeting a particular need. Selecting the appropriate technique for a task requires trade-offs among functionality, performance, and resource utilization.

Inside the Database

A database has quite a variety of objects. Tables are arguably the most important, because they hold the data necessary for the business system to function, but they are just the beginning of the objects you will find present. In every database, user and system alike, you will find several groups of objects, as shown in Figure 3.2.

Figure 3.2   SQL Server database object groupings.

Each database is composed of all of these object groupings, though it is not mandatory for a database to have some of the objects. Even if a particular object is not present within a database, the grouping will still be found.

You need to know a little about all of these objects stored in the database, though some are used more often than others. Knowing an object's purpose could save you from selecting an inaccurate answer on the exam. In particular, the table objects, their content, and their relationships must be expertly known.

Tables

Each database contains a number of tables other than those used to store data. These tables store information that enables SQL Server to keep track of objects and procedures within the database. The sysobjects and syscomments system tables maintain entries containing the object definitions and other tracking information for each object. Various other tables also exist to maintain information about specific objects. For more information regarding system tables, refer to SQL Server Books Online. These tables are used whenever SQL Server needs object information. You should never alter system tables directly, but instead allow SQL Server to manipulate the entries as needed.

When you're defining tables, it is a good idea to have some form of data dictionary prepared to help you make appropriate choices for individual properties. A data dictionary defines data usage and is an extension of the logical data modeling. In SQL Server, the term "database diagram" is usually used rather than "dictionary," although a database diagram is not a complete data dictionary in the sense of documentation.

Diagrams

Diagrams are of particular interest to developers because they can provide a visual appearance of the tables within the database. A data dictionary is a form of documentation generally considered a complete reference for the data it describes. The dictionary is usually a lot more than just a collection of data element definitions. A complete dictionary should include schema with reference keys and an entity-relationship model of the data elements or objects. A pseudo data dictionary can be represented using the database diagram tool provided with SQL Server, as shown in Figure 3.3.

There are a lot of nice features of the diagram tool that allow you to design and enact changes against the database using an attractive, intuitive interface.

It is a handy tool for post-implementation documentation, as well as a training assistant. Documenting the tables in the system is an important aspect of business application development.

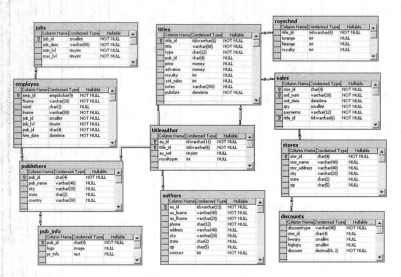

Figure 3.3 A database diagram of the pubs database.

Views

A *view* is a stored query that is executed against the data stored in the tables. The tables of the database hold the data in rows and columns. Views represent the data stored; although they store no data, they can still be used to represent the data in columns and rows.

Stored Procedures

Another execution element stored within the context of a database is stored procedures. A *stored procedure* is a set of T-SQL statements that can be saved as a database object for future and repeated executions. With stored procedures, you can enable a lot of the development and processing to be performed on the server, producing much more efficient and lightweight front-end applications. Any commands that can be entered via SQL Query tools can be included in a stored procedure.

Many system-stored procedures have already been created and are available upon installation of SQL Server. Extended stored procedures, which enable DLL files to be accessed from the operating system, are preestablished and present in the Master database.

Extended stored procedures, like many of the system-stored procedures, are loaded automatically when you install SQL Server. Extended stored procedures access DLL files stored on the machine to enable the calling of the functions contained in the DLLs from within a SQL Server application. You might add to this set of procedures stored in the Master database using the sp_addextendedproc procedure as shown here:

```
sp_addextendedproc 'MyFunction', 'MyFunctionSet.DLL'
```

Stored procedures and views alike can be used as part of a broader security plan.

Users and Roles

Users of the database either must be explicitly defined within the Users container or must gain access by belonging to a group that can gain access to the database. Role-based security can also be implemented at the server, database, or application level. All of these aspects make use of objects stored in the database to help secure the system. Securing the database is discussed later in the book in Chapter 9, "Designing a Database Security Plan."

Rules

Rules are a backward-compatibility feature that performs some of the same functions as CHECK constraints. Rules are discussed briefly here to ensure thorough coverage of table objects. Rules, however, are not likely to be found on the exam except as an incorrect answer. CHECK constraints, which are discussed later in the chapter, are the preferred, standard way to restrict the values in a column. CHECK constraints are also more concise than rules; there can be only one rule applied to a column, but multiple CHECK constraints can be applied. Rules are similar but are created as separate objects and then bound to the column.

Defaults

A DEFAULT is an object that can be defined for a database and is used by columns of tables within the database. A DEFAULT is used to provide a value when no explicit value is given upon input of data. A DEFAULT object must be bound to each column to which it will apply. If a DEFAULT object is bound to a column, it is still possible to specify a different default value for that column in a any given table. This implements a default constraint and unbinds the existing DEFAULT object from the column before the new default value is set.

In this respect the default becomes a property of the column as opposed to a separate object.

User-Defined Data Types and Functions

User-defined data types, as explained in Chapter 1, "Database Development on SQL Server 2000," are really just an extension of the SQL Server system data types. User-defined functions are defined by the developer to be used as a coding object to perform a task within the business system. User-defined functions are dealt with at length in Chapter 6, "Programming Business Logic."

Full-Text Catalogs

The remaining object group is used to hold Full-Text catalogs. These catalogs contain Full-Text indexes that store information about significant words and their location within a given column of data within the database. Full-Text indexing, catalogs, and queries together allow you to search for English words within text fields. There are also fuzzy search capabilities that allow for searching using word forms and similar-sounding words.

In the past, Full-Text indexing has been a considerable exam topic, but it seems to have fallen out of favor with Microsoft and will not likely be seen on the exam.

As you can see, the makeup of a database includes a lot of different objects, much more than just tables full of data. The makeup of a table in SQL Server is more than just simply data definition. A complete table definition includes column descriptions, storage location, constraints, relationships with other tables, indexes, and keys, as well as table-level permissions and text indexing columns.

What's on the Table

After the file structure and content of each file has been determined, the tables themselves can be created and assigned to the files. If the purpose of the table is to hold data that is frequently accessed, the file placement of the table should take that into consideration. Tables that hold archive data and other less frequently accessed data require less maintenance and don't have to be as responsive to user queries.

Keep in mind when assigning objects to files that some objects can be placed away from the mainstream data through the use of filegroups. You can select the object placement from Table Design Properties in the Enterprise Manager or through the use of an ON clause in a CREATE/ALTER statement. SQL Server enables you to place the following table objects:

➤ Tables

➤ Indexes

➤ Text, ntext, or image data

You won't necessarily always be moving objects around. In most instances, the application won't be large enough to justify these measures. You need to address this situation only in very large database systems.

Data Element Definition

The initial definition of each column within a table consists of a name for the column, the type and length of data for the column, and an indicator as to whether the column must have data or allow NULL content. A number of additional column descriptors can be included to define characteristics of how the column obtains its value and how the column is treated within the table. A complete list of potential column descriptors is given here:

➤ Column Name—Should be meaningful so as to describe the column content.

➤ Data Type—Any one of 25 possible definitions provides the basis for the data a column will contain. Choices include several possibilities for each data type. (Data types are discussed more fully later in this book.)

➤ Length—For many of the data types, the length is predetermined. You must, however, specify a length for character, Unicode (nCHAR), and binary data. A length must also be specified for variable-length data columns. If a char or an nCHAR data type is only a single character, no length has to be defined.

➤ Allow Nulls—You can provide an indicator for allowing NULL content for any variable except those assigned as primary keys.

➤ Primary Key—Enforces unique content for a column and can be used to relate other tables. Must contain a unique non-NULL value.

➤ Description—Provides an explanation of the column for documentation purposes. (This is an extended table property.)

➤ Default Value—Provides a value for a column when one is not explicitly given during data entry. A default object must be created and then bound to a column, but the preferred technique is to provide the default definition, directly attached to the column in the CREATE/ALTER table definition. It is defined at the database level and can be utilized by any number of columns in a database.

➤ Precision—The number of digits in a numeric column.

➤ Scale—The number of digits to the right of a decimal point in a numeric column.

➤ Identity—Inserts a value automatically into a column, based on seed and increment definitions.

➤ Identity Seed—Provides the starting value for an Identity column.

➤ Identity Increment—Defines how an Identity will increase or decrease with each new row added to a table.

➤ Is RowGuid—Identifies a column that has been defined with the Unique Identifier data type as being the column to be used in conjunction with the ROWGUIDCOL function in a SELECT list.

➤ Formula—Provides a means of obtaining the column content through the use of a function or calculation.

➤ Collation—Can provide for a different character set or sort order than other data. (Use with extreme caution, if at all, because dealing with different character sets impairs front-end development and hampers data input and alteration processes.)

Many characteristics of column definitions will have an impact on the definition of other columns, tables, and databases. For a more complete definition of any of these properties, consult SQL Server Books Online.

Keys to Success

A table key is an attribute used to identify a particular row of the table. Both primary and foreign keys are defined in the form of a constráint. These keys work together to accommodate table relationships. A foreign key refers to the primary key in the parent table, forming a one-to-one or one-to-many relationship. Remember from the discussion of the logical design that a many-to-many relationship is really two one-to-many relationships using a joining table.

When multiple tables maintained in a database are related to each other, some measures should be taken to ensure that the reliability of these relationships stays intact. To enforce referential integrity, you create a relationship between two tables. This can be done through the database diagram feature of the Enterprise Manager or through the CREATE and ALTER TABLE T-SQL statements. Normally, you relate the referencing or foreign key of one table to the primary key or other unique value of a second table.

PRIMARY KEY Constraint

A PRIMARY KEY constraint enforces entity integrity in that it does not permit any two rows in a table to have the same key value. This enables each row to be uniquely defined in its own right. Although a primary key should be created when a table is initially created, it can be added or changed at any time after creation. The primary key can be added upon creation of the table as given here:

```
CREATE TABLE OtherAuthors
( au_id id NOT NULL
    CONSTRAINT [UPKCL_othauind] PRIMARY KEY  CLUSTERED,
  au_lname varchar (40) NOT NULL ,
  au_fname varchar (20) NOT NULL ,
  phone char (12) NOT NULL ,
  address varchar (40) NULL ,
  city varchar (20) NULL ,
  state char (2) NULL ,
  zip char (5) NULL ,
  contract bit NOT NULL ) ON [PRIMARY]
```

A primary key cannot have NULL content, nor can there be any duplicate values. SQL Server automatically creates a unique index to enforce the exclusiveness of each value. If a primary key is referenced by a foreign key in another table, the primary key cannot be removed unless the foreign key relationship is removed first.

The definition of a primary key for each table, though not a requirement of the SQL Server database environment, is recommended. A primary key helps records maintain their identities as unique rows of a table and also provides a means of relating tables to other tables in the database to maintain normal forms. (For further information on normalization and normal forms, see Chapter 2, "Creating a Logical Data Model.") A foreign key is defined in a subsidiary table as a pointer to the primary key or other unique value in the primary table to create a relationship.

The most common relationships are one-to-many, in which the unique value in one table has many subsidiary records in the second table. Another form of relationship, which is normally used to split a table with an extraordinary number of columns, is a one-to-one relationship. The use of one-to-one splits a table and associates a single unique value in one table with the same unique value in a second table. A many-to-many relationship can also be defined, but this form of referencing requires three tables and is really two separate one-to-many relationships.

 If, on the exam, you run into the topic of setting relationships based on unique values, the correct answer is likely to be one chosen based on the documentation and not on actual functionality. The capability to set a relationship to any unique column is not noted in documentation. The correct technique to use when answering an exam question would be one that involves a foreign key set to a **PRIMARY KEY** or **UNIQUE** constraint.

Utilizing referential integrity guidelines helps maintain the accuracy of data entered into the system. A database system uses referential integrity rules to prohibit subsidiary elements from being entered into the system unless a matching unique element is in the referenced table. The system also protects the data from changes and deletions, assuming that cascading actions (defined later in this chapter) have been carefully and properly implemented.

FOREIGN KEY Constraint

A FOREIGN KEY constraint is defined so that a primary and subsidiary table can be linked together by a common value. A foreign key can be linked to any unique column in the main table; it does not necessarily have to be linked to the primary key. It can be linked to any column that is associated with a unique index.

You can define a foreign key and its relationship when creating or altering a table definition. The following example defines a relationship using T-SQL:

```
CREATE TABLE OrderDetails
    ( DetailsID           smallint,
      OrderID             smallint
          FOREIGN KEY (OrderID) REFERENCES Orders(OrderID),
      QtyOrdered bigint,
      WarehouseLocation   smallint
      )
```

With a foreign key defined, you cannot add a value to the foreign key column if a matching value is not present in the primary table. If a child entry with an ID is not found in the parent table, then that is known as an orphan child and is a breach of referential integrity rules.

Using Cascade Action

New to SQL Server with the 2000 release is a cascading action feature that many other database environments have been enjoying for quite some time.

Cascading actions affect update and delete activity when an existing foreign key value is changed or removed. Cascade action is controlled through the CREATE and ALTER TABLE statements, with clauses for ON DELETE and ON UPDATE. You can also select these features using the Enterprise Manager.

 The cascading actions feature is a new feature, and you can expect that something about it will be asked on the exam. Also be prepared for the exam by knowing all the results and implications of cascading actions. For example, you might be asked what occurs when a record contained in the parent table is deleted or has its key value changed.

In a cascading update, when you change the value of a key in a situation in which a foreign key in another table references the key value, those changed values are reflected back to the other tables. A similar thing happens with a delete operation: If a record is deleted, all subsidiary records in other tables are also deleted. For example, if an invoice record is deleted from an invoice table that has invoice details stored in another table and referenced by a foreign key, then the details would also be removed.

A series of cascading actions could easily result from the update or deletion of important keys. For example, the deletion of a customer could cause the deletion of all that customer's orders, which could cause the deletion of all the customer's invoices, which in turn could cause the deletion of all the customer's invoice details. For this reason, careful system design is important, and the potential archiving of data through the use of triggers should be considered.

In the case of multiple cascading actions, all the triggers to be fired by the effects of the original deletion fire first. AFTER triggers then fire on the original table, and then the AFTER triggers in the table chain subsequently fire.

Maintaining Order with Indexes

Putting the data into sequence to accommodate quick retrieval, and at the same time provide meaningful and usable output to an application, usually requires that a variety of indexes be defined. A clustered index provides the physical order of the data being stored, whereas a nonclustered index provides an ordered list with pointers to the physical location of the data.

Indexing is most easily defined and understood if you compare the data and index storage of a database to that of a book. In a book the data itself is placed onto the pages in a sequence that is meaningful if you read the book sequentially from cover to cover. An index at the back of the book enables you to read the data randomly. You can locate a topic by looking through a list of topics that is accompanied by a physical page reference to the place where the topic can be found. To read a single topic, you need not skim through the entire book.

In a similar manner, data in a database can be handled randomly or in sequence. A single record can be located in the database by looking it up in the index, rather than reading through all the rest of the data. Conversely, if a report is to be generated from all the data in a database, the data itself can be read sequentially in its entirety.

Index storage in SQL Server has a B-tree structured storage. The indexes are maintained in 8KB pages qualified as root, intermediate, and leaf-level pages. In a clustered index the leaf level is the data itself, and all other levels represent index pages. In a nonclustered index all pages contain indexes (see Figure 3.4).

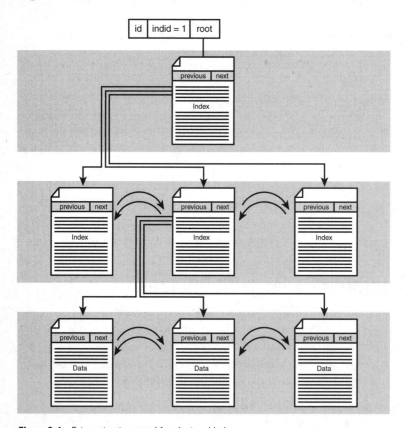

Figure 3.4 B-tree structure used for clustered indexes.

If a clustered index has not been defined for a given table, the data is stored in a "heap." A data heap does not maintain data in any particular order; it simply stores the data in the order in which it is entered. In some applications, in which data is never retrieved in any particular order on a regular basis, this might actually be advantageous.

Indexes can be created using the T-SQL CREATE INDEX command. When you're creating indexes, it is good practice to leave space for later insertions of data. The following example creates a compound, nonclustered index that is 75% full:

```
CREATE INDEX IXProductItem
ON ProductOrderLine (OrderMateKey, ProductLineKey)
WITH FILLFACTOR = 75
```

The two different organizations of indexes, *clustered* and *nonclustered*, provide for the ordering of data either through physically rearranging the data as in a clustered index or through the use of data pointers as in a nonclustered index. If the organization is not specified, as in the previous example, nonclustered will be defaulted to.

Indexing Through Reordering—Clustered

The selection of the appropriate column(s) on which to base a clustered index is important for several reasons. As previously mentioned, a clustered index represents the order in which the data is physically stored on the disk. For this reason, you can define only a single clustered index for any table. If you choose not to use a clustered index in a table, the data on the disk will be stored in a heap. A clustered index, if present, has clustering keys that are used by all nonclustered indexes to determine the physical location of the data.

The basis for the index usually is determined by the order in which the majority of applications and queries want their output. The clustered index values are also present in other indexes, and the size of the defined index should be kept as small as possible. When you select a clustering key, try to utilize a numeric data type because character types cause index storage to occupy much more space.

Always define a clustered index first before you define any of the nonclustered indexes. If you do these tasks in reverse order, all nonclustered indexes rebuild themselves upon creation of the clustered index.

Indexing Through Data Pointers—Nonclustered

Nonclustered indexes provide a means of retrieving the data from the database in an order other than that in which the data is physically stored. The only alternative to the use of these indexes would be provisions for a sort operation that would place undue overhead on the client system and might not produce the desired response times. A data sort implementation is usually performed only for one-time operations or for applications that will have very limited usage.

Although the creation of indexes saves time and resources in a lot of cases, avoid the creation of indexes that will rarely be utilized. Each time a record is added to a table, all indexes in the table must be updated, and this might also cause undue system overhead. For that reason, careful planning of index usage is necessary.

One of a Kind—Unique Indexing

When indexes are created, it is important to guarantee that each value is distinctive. This is particularly important for a primary key. SQL Server automatically applies a unique index to a primary key to ensure that each key value uniquely defines a row in the table. You might want to create additional unique indexes for columns that are not going to be defined as the primary key.

Room for Additions

Fill factor is the percent at which SQL Server fills leaf-level pages upon creation of indexes. Provision for empty pages enables the server to insert additional rows without performing a page-split operation. A page split occurs when a new row is inserted into a table that has no empty space for its placement. As the storage pages fill, page splits occur, which can hamper performance and increase fragmentation.

You will normally find that queries (the reading of existing data) outweigh data updates by a substantial margin. Providing the extra room slows down the query process. Therefore, you might not want to adjust the fill factor value at all in static systems in which there are smaller numbers of additions.

Equally, setting the fill factor too low hampers read performance because the server must negotiate a series of empty pages to actually fetch the desired data. It is beneficial to specify a fill factor when you create an index on a table that already has data and will have a high volume of inserts. If you do not specify this setting when creating an index, the server default fill factor setting is chosen. The fill factor for the server is a configuration option set through the Enterprise Manager or the sp_configure stored procedure.

The percentage value for the fill factor is not maintained over time; it applies only at the time of creation. Therefore, if inserts into a table occur frequently, it's important to take maintenance measures for rebuilding the indexes to ensure that the empty space is put back in place. A specific index can be rebuilt using the CREATE INDEX T-SQL command with the

DROP EXISTING option. Indexes can also be defragmented using the DBCC INDEXDEFRAG command, which also reapplies the fill factor.

The Pad Index setting is closely related to the setting for fill factor to allow space to be left in non-leaf levels. Pad Index cannot be specified by itself and can be used only if you supply a fill factor. You do not provide a value for this setting; it matches the setting given for the fill factor.

Data Entry Using Defaults

A default is used to provide a value for a column to minimize data entry efforts or to provide an entry when the data is not known. A default provides a value for the column as a basis for initial input. Any data that is entered for the column overrides the default entry. You can apply a default definition to a column directly using the CREATE or ALTER TABLE statement or through the Design Table option from within the Enterprise Manager. You can also create a default as its own object and then bind it to one or more columns.

A default definition that is provided as part of a table definition is a standard and preferred method of implementing default entries. The advantages of this technique are that the default is dropped when the table is dropped and that the definition is stored within the table itself. A default object must be created and bound to the column in a two-step operation. To create and bind a default object, use the following code:

```
CREATE DEFAULT StateDefault AS 'IN'
    sp_bindefault StateDefault, 'customers.state'
```

To create a default within a table definition, use the following:

```
CREATE TABLE SampleDefault
    ( SampleID          smallint NOT NULL
        CONSTRAINT UPKCL_SampleID PRIMARY KEY CLUSTERED,
      City              varchar(50)
        DEFAULT         ('Woodstock'),
      State             char(2)
        DEFAULT         ('NY')
    )
```

When an INSERT operation is performed on a table, you must supply values for all columns that do not have a default entry defined or that do not allow NULL content.

Checks and Balances

A CHECK constraint is one of several mechanisms that can be used to prevent incorrect data from entering the system. Restrictions on data entry can be applied at the table or column level through the use of a CHECK constraint. You might also apply more than a single check to any one column, in which case the checks are evaluated in the order in which they were created.

A CHECK constraint represents any Boolean expression that is applied to the data to determine whether the data meets the criteria of the check. The advantage of using a check is that it is applied to the data before it enters the system. However, CHECK constraints do have less functionality than mechanisms, such as stored procedures or triggers.

One use for a CHECK constraint is to ensure that a value entered meets given criteria based on another value entered. A table-level CHECK constraint is defined at the bottom of the ALTER/CREATE TABLE statement, unlike a COLUMN CHECK constraint, which is defined as part of the column definition. For example, when a due date entered must be at least 30 days beyond an invoice date, a table-level constraint would be defined this way:

```
(DueDate - InvoiceDate) >= 30
```

A column-level check might be used to ensure that data is within acceptable ranges, such as in the following:

```
InvoiceAmount >= 1 AND InvoiceAmount <= 25000
```

A check can also define the pattern or format in which data values are entered. You might, for example, want an invoice number to have an alphabetic character in the first position, followed by five numeric values, in which case the check might look similar to the following:

```
InvoiceNumber LIKE '[A-Z][0-9][0-9][0-9][0-9][0-9]'
```

Finally, you might want to apply a check when an entry must be from a range of number choices within a list. An inventory item that must be one of a series of category choices might look similar to this:

```
ProductCategory IN ('HARDWARE', 'SOFTWARE', 'SERVICE')
```

A COLUMN CHECK (or other constraint) is stated as a portion of the column definition itself and applies only to the column where it is defined. A TABLE CHECK (or other constraint), on the other hand, is defined independently of any column, can be applied to more than one column, and must be used if more than one column is included in the constraint.

A table definition that is to define restrictions to a single column (minimum quantity ordered is 50), as well as a table constraint (date on which part is required must be later than when ordered), would be as shown here:

```
CREATE TABLE ProductOrderLine
     (ProductLineKey  BigInt,
      OrderMatchKey   BigInt,
```

```
ProductOrdered  Char(6),
QtyOrdered      BigInt
  CONSTRAINT Over50 CHECK (QtyOrdered > 50),
OrderDate       DateTime,
RequiredDate    DateTime,
  CONSTRAINT CK_Date CHECK (RequiredDate > OrderDate))
```

Usually a single table definition would provide clauses for key definition, indexing, and other elements that have been left out of the previous definition to focus in more closely on the use of CHECK constraints.

As you can see, constraints come in all shapes and sizes, controlling table content, inter-table relationships, and validity of data. Although we have discussed many objects, there are a few loose ends to tie up in order to get a full perspective on objects.

Other Bits and Pieces

There are many different objects within a database and surrounding the table content. A few objects left to discuss are rather specialized in their use and in where they are applied. Permissions (which we will leave until Chapter 9) are a wide array of rights and privileges that are present at several levels, from the server to the database to the table, all the way down to an individual column. There are also packages that contain definitions of procedures used by DTS to get data from one place to another (DTS packages are discussed in Chapter 5, "Retrieving and Modifying Data").

Alerts, *operators*, and *jobs* work together to aid in administration over the server by allowing for the modification of tasks and informing individuals of important events on the server. These, along with articles, publications, and subscriptions, are defined in the next chapter, "Advanced Physical Database Implementation." The only object left undefined from a data perspective is triggers.

Trigger Utilization

Triggers are like stored procedures in that they contain a set of T-SQL statements saved for future execution. The big difference is that, unlike stored procedures, triggers are executed automatically based on data activity in a table. A trigger may fire based on UPDATE, INSERT, or DELETE operations.

In SQL Server 2000, triggers can be fired *after* an operation completes (SQL Server default) or *instead of* the triggering operation. An AFTER trigger can be used to archive data when it is deleted, to send a notification that the new data has been added or changed, or to initiate any other process you might want to automate based on data activity. An INSTEAD OF trigger can be used to perform more advanced activities (such as advanced data checking), to enable updates in a view to occur across multiple tables, and to perform many other functions that might be necessary in place of a triggering activity.

Triggers represent a mechanism in which code can be executed based on activity in the data. Triggers are expanded on and fully illustrated in Chapter 6.

Troubleshooting Failed Object Creation

Troubleshooting is certainly a broad topic in the real development world, and certainly on all Microsoft exams. In this chapter the focus for troubleshooting is on the interactions with objects and the server, as well as application settings that are required for an object to be created and used. On the exam troubleshooting will be approached from a wide variety of angles. In the "real world" it is good practice to always view a procedure from a problem-solving perspective. Always be ready to ask yourself, "What could go wrong?" and "What can be done to resolve the problem?"

Most problems associated with creating and/or accessing objects can be resolved through setting appropriate object access permissions. However, other elements that can hamper the creation or use of objects include (but are not limited to) the following:

➤ Backup and restore operations

➤ Other users' operations locking parts of the system

➤ Hardware or resource problems

➤ Network connectivity

➤ Configuration settings

➤ Operating system

➤ Metadata corruption

A good starting point from which to resolve most problems is the wealth of feedback SQL Server gives in the form of the OS Application Event Log, SQL Server Logs, and the Current Activity Window, as well as the permission properties of the users, roles, and objects.

To create a database, you need to be a member of System Administrators or Database Creators server roles or have the Create Database permission. To create objects within a database, you must be a member of db_owner or db_ddladmin database roles or have the specific permission to create the object as given by statement-level permissions. Statement-level permissions can be found on the Permissions tab of the database Properties dialog box.

As databases and their objects are created, the system uses the default file-group for the physical storage of the element. It is a good practice to create a storage group for user objects and make that the default filegroup. This way, as the user creates objects, those objects don't compete for storage with other data.

If a user lacks the permission to create or alter an object, an alternative is available that grants the user creation permission without giving the user too much control over the environment. An Application role that has permission to work with objects in this manner can be assigned to a stored procedure that creates the objects for the user. When the user executes the procedure, objects can be created or altered in a controlled manner.

Exam Prep Questions

1. As a developer for a large healthcare provider, you are assigned the task of developing a process for updating a patient database. When a patient is transferred from one floor to another, an internal identifier, CurrentRoomID, which is used as the primary key, needs to be altered while the original key, AdmittanceRoomID, is maintained. If a patient is moved more than once, only the original key and the current key need to be maintained. Several underlying tables have been configured for referential integrity against the patient table. These underlying tables must change in an appropriate manner to match with one or the other of the room keys in the patient table. These relationships will be altered based on different situations in other tables. Figure 3.5 illustrates the PatientTracker table design exhibit. What method would you use to accommodate the update?

PatientTracker					
Column Name	Condensed Type	Nullable	Data Type	Length	▲
🔑 CurrentRoomID	char(3)	NOT NULL	char	3	
AdmittanceRoomID	char(3)	NOT NULL	char	3	
PatientID	int	NOT NULL	int	4	
▶ BedID	tinyint	NOT NULL	tinyint	1	▼

Figure 3.5   The **PatientTracker** table design exhibit.

- ❏ A. Use the Cascade Update Related Fields option to have changes in the primary key automatically update the keys in all referenced tables.
- ❏ B. Use an indexed view to enable the user to make changes to multiple tables concurrently.
- ❏ C. Disable the Enforce Relationship for Inserts and Deletes option to enable an AFTER TRIGGER to handle the necessary changes.
- ❏ D. Define an INSTEAD OF UPDATE TRIGGER to perform the necessary updates to all related tables.

Answer: D. The INSTEAD OF trigger was designed specifically for this type of situation and also to handle complicated updates in which columns are defined as Timestamp, Calculated, or Identity. Cascade operations are inappropriate because the updated key is not always stored. Indexed views by themselves do not allow for the type of alteration desired and would have to be complemented with the actions of a trigger. Disabling referential integrity is a poor solution to any problem, especially considering the medical nature of this application and the possible ramifications. For more information, see the earlier section "Trigger Utilization."

2. A large organization needs to maintain image data on a database server. The data is scanned in from documents received from the federal government. Updates to the images are infrequent. When a change occurs, usually the old row of data is archived out of the system and the new document takes its place. Other column information that contains key identifiers about the nature of the document is frequently queried by an OLAP system. Statistical information on how the data was queried is also stored in additional columns. The actual document itself is rarely needed except in processes that print the image. Which of the following represents an appropriate storage configuration?

❏   A. Place the image data into a filegroup of its own, but on the same volume as the remainder of the data. Place the log onto a volume of its own.

❏   B. Place all the data onto one volume in a single file. Configure the volume as a RAID parity set and place the log into a volume of its own.

❏   C. Place the image onto one volume in a file of its own and place the data and log files together on a second volume.

❏   D. Place the image into a separate filegroup with the log on one volume and the remainder of the data on a second volume.

Answer: D. Because the image data will seldom be accessed, it makes sense to get the remainder of the data away from the images while moving the log away from the data. This will help to improve performance while providing optimum recoverability in the event of a failure. For more information, see "The File System."

3. An Internet company sells outdoor hardware online to more than 100,000 clients in various areas of the globe. Servicing the website is a SQL Server whose performance is barely adequate to meet the needs of the site. You would like to apply a business rule to the existing system that will limit the outstanding balance of each customer. The outstanding balance is maintained as a denormalized column within the customer table. Orders are collected in a second table containing a trigger that updates the customer balance based on INSERT, UPDATE, and DELETE activity. Up to this point, care has been taken to remove any data from the table if the client balance is too high, so all data should meet the requirements of your new process. How would you apply the new data check?

❏   A. Modify the existing trigger so that an order that allows the balance to exceed the limit is not permitted.

❏   B. Create a check constraint with the No Check option enabled on the customer table, so that any inappropriate order is refused.

❏   C. Create a rule that doesn't permit an order that exceeds the limit and bind the rule to the Orders table.

❏   D. Create a new trigger on the Orders table that refuses an order that causes the balance to exceed the maximum. Apply the new trigger to only INSERT and UPDATE operations.

Answer: A. Because a trigger is already in place, it can easily be altered to perform the additional data check. A rule cannot provide the required functionality because you cannot compare the data. The CHECK constraint may be a viable solution but you would have to alter the trigger to check for an error and provide for nested operations. The number of triggers firing should be kept to a minimum. To accommodate additional triggers, you would have to check the order in which they are being fired and again set properties of the server and database accordingly. For more information, see "Trigger Utilization."

4. An existing sales catalog database structure exists on a system within your company. The company sells inventory from a single warehouse location that is across town from where the computer systems are located. The product table has been created with a non-clustered index based on the product ID, which is also the Primary Key. Non-clustered indexes exist on the product category column and also the storage location column. Most of the reporting done is ordered by product category. How would you change the existing index structure?

- ❑ A. Change the definition of the Primary Key so that it is a clustered index.
- ❑ B. Create a new clustered index based on the combination of storage location and product category.
- ❑ C. Change the definition of the product category so that it is a clustered index.
- ❑ D. Change the definition of the storage location so that it is a clustered index.

Answer: D. Because the majority of the reporting is going to be performed using the storage location, it would be the likely candidate. The clustered index represents the physical order of the data and would minimize sorting operations when deriving the output. For more information, see "Maintaining Order with Indexes."

5. You are designing an application that will provide data entry clerks the capability of updating the data in several tables. You would like to ease entry and provide common input so the clerks need not enter data into all fields or enter redundant values. What types of technologies could you use to minimize the amount of input needed? Select all that apply.

- ❑ A. Foreign key
- ❑ B. Cascading update
- ❑ C. Identity column
- ❑ D. Default
- ❑ E. NULL
- ❑ F. Primary key
- ❑ G. Unique index

Answer: B, C, D, E. All these options have activities that provide or alter data so that it does not have to be performed as an entry operation. In the case of NULL, data need not be provided, possibly because the column contains non-critical information. For more information, see "Keys to Success."

6. A database that you are working on is experiencing reduced performance. The database is used almost exclusively for reporting, with a large number of inserts occurring on a regular basis. Data is cycled out of the system four times a year as part of quarter-ending procedures. It is always important to be able to attain a point-in-time restoration process. You would like to minimize the maintenance needed to accommodate increases and decreases in file storage space. Which option would assist the most in accomplishing the task?

- ❑ A. SIMPLE RECOVERY
- ❑ B. AUTOSHRINK
- ❑ C. MAXSIZE
- ❑ D. AUTOGROW
- ❑ E. COLLATE

Answer: D. Use AUTOGROW to set the system so that the files will grow as needed for the addition of new data. You may want to perform a planned shrinkage of the database as part of the quarter-ending process and save on overhead by leaving the AUTOSHRINK option turned off. For more information, see "Creating Files and Filegroups."

7. You are the administrator of a SQL Server 2000 computer. The server contains a database named Inventory. Users report that several storage locations in the `UnitsStored` field contain negative numbers. You examine the database's table structure. You correct all the negative numbers in the table. You must prevent the database from storing negative numbers. You also want to minimize use of server resources and physical I/O. Which statement should you execute?

❑ A.
```
ALTER TABLE dbo.StorageLocations
      ADD CONSTRAINTCK_StorageLocations_
➥UnitsStoredCHECK (UnitsStored >= 0)
```

❑ B.
```
CREATE TRIGGER CK_UnitsStored On _
➥StorageLocations FOR INSERT, UPDATE AS
      IF INSERTED.UnitsStored < 0 ROLLBACK TRAN
```

❑ C.
```
CREATE RULE CK_UnitsStored As
      @Units >= 0
      GO
      sp_bindrule 'CK_UnitsStored''_
➥StorageLocations.UnitsStored'
      GO
```

❑ D.
```
CREATE PROC UpdateUnitsStored(@StorageLocationID_
➥ int, @UnitsStored bigint) AS
      IF @UnitsStored < 0
            RAISERROR (50099, 17)
      ELSE
            UPDATE StorageLocations
              SET UnitsStored = @UnitsStored
              WHERE StorageLocationID = @StorageLocationID
```

Answer: A. You need to add a constraint to prevent negative data entry. The best method of implementing this functionality is a constraint. A trigger has too much overhead and the RULE is not accurately implemented. A procedure could handle the process but is normally used only for processes requiring more complex logic. For more information, see "What's on the Table."

8. You are the administrator of a SQL Server 2000 computer. The server contains a database named Inventory. In this database, the Parts table has a primary key that is used to identify each part stored in the company's warehouse. Each part has a unique UPC code that your company's accounting department uses to identify it. You want to maintain the referential integrity between the Parts table and the OrderDetails table. You want to minimize the amount of physical I/O used within the database. Which two T-SQL statements should you execute? (Each correct answer represents part of the solution; choose two.)

❑ A. CREATE UNIQUE INDEX IX_UPC On Parts(UPC)

❑ B. CREATE UNIQUE INDEX IX_UPC On OrderDetails(UPC)

❑ C. CREATE TRIGGER UPCRI On OrderDetails _
  ➥FOR INSERT, UPDATE As
      If Not Exists (Select UPC From Parts
  ➥ Where Parts.UPC = inserted.UPC)
          BEGIN
              ROLLBACK TRAN
          END

❑ D. CREATE TRIGGER UPCRI On Parts FOR INSERT, UPDATE As
      If Not Exists (Select UPC From Parts
  ➥ Where OrderDetails.UPC = inserted.UPC)
          BEGIN
              ROLLBACK TRAN
          END

❑ E. ALTER TABLE dbo.OrderDetails
      ADD CONSTRAINTFK_OrderDetails_Parts _
  ➥FOREIGN KEY(UPC)REFERENCES dbo.Parts(UPC)

❑ F. ALTER TABLE dbo.Parts
      ADD CONSTRAINTFK_Parts_OrderDetails
  ➥ FOREIGN KEY (UPC)REFERENCES dbo.Parts(UPC)

Answer: A, E. The UNIQUE constraint on the Parts table UPC column is required first so that the FOREIGN KEY constraint can be applied from the OrderDetails.UPC column referencing Parts.UPC. This achieves the referential integrity requirement. It also reduces I/O required during joins between Parts and OrderDetails, which make use of the FOREIGN KEY constraint defined. For more information, see "FOREIGN KEY Constraint."

9. You are the database developer for a leasing company. Your database includes a table that is defined as shown here:

```
CREATE TABLE Lease
(Id Int IDENTITY NOT NULL
    CONSTRAINT pk_lesse_id PRIMARY KEY NONCLUSTERED,
Lastname varchar(50) NOT NULL,
FirstName varchar(50) NOT NULL,
SSNo char(9) NOT NULL,
Rating char(10) NULL,
Limit money NULL)
```

Each SSNo must be unique. You want the data to be physically stored in SSNo sequence. Which constraint should you add to the SSNo column on the Lease table?

❑ A. UNIQUE CLUSTERED constraint

❑ B. UNIQUE UNCLUSTERED constraint

❑ C. PRIMARY KEY CLUSTERED constraint

❑ D. PRIMARY KEY UNCLUSTERED constraint

Answer: A. To obtain the physical storage sequence of the data, you must use a clustered constraint or index. Although a primary key would also provide for the level of uniqueness, it is not the desired key for this table.

10. You are building a database and you want to eliminate duplicate entry and minimize data storage wherever possible. You want to track the following information for employees and managers: first name, middle name, last name, employee identification number, address, date of hire, department, salary, and name of manager. Which table design should you use?

❑ A. Table1: EmpID, MgrID, Firstname, Middlename, Lastname,
        Address, Hiredate, Dept, Salary.
     Table2: MgrID, Firstname, Middlename, Lastname

❑ B. Table1: EmpID, Firstname, Middlename, Lastname,
        Address, Hiredate, Dept, Salary.
     Table2: MgrID, Firstname, Middlename, Lastname. _
     ➥ Table3: EmpID, MgrID

❑ C. Table1: EmpID, MgrID, Firstname, Middlename, _
     ➥ Lastname,
        Address, Hiredate, Dept, Salary

❑ D. Table1: EmpID, Firstname, Middlename, Lastname,
        Address, Hiredate, Dept, Salary.
     Table2: EmpID, MgrID Table3: MgrID

Answer: C. A single table could provide all the necessary information with no redundancy. The table could easily be represented using a self-join operation to provide the desired reporting. Join operations are discussed in detail in the Chapter 5.

11. You are developing an application and need to create an inventory table on each of the databases located in New York, Detroit, Paris, London, Los Angeles, and Hong Kong. To accommodate a distributed environment, you must ensure that each row entered into the inventory table is unique across all locations. How can you create the inventory table?

- ❑ A. Supply Identity columns using a different sequential starting value for each location and use an increment of 6.
- ❑ B. Use the IDENTITY function. At the first location use IDENTITY(1,1), at the second location use IDENTITY(100000,1), and so on.
- ❑ C. Use a UNIQUEIDENTIFIER as the key at each location.
- ❑ D. Use the Timestamp column as the key at each location.

Answer: A. Using identities in this fashion enables records to be entered that have no overlap. One location would use entry values 1, 7, 13, 19; the next would have 2, 8, 14, 20; the third, 3, 9, 15, 21; and so on. For more information, see "Data Element Definition."

12. You are building a new database for a company with 10 departments. Each department contains multiple employees. In addition, each employee might work for several departments. How should you logically model the relationship between the department entity and the employee entity?

- ❑ A. Create a mandatory one-to-many relationship between department and employee.
- ❑ B. Create an optional one-to-many relationship between department and employee.
- ❑ C. Create a new entry, create a one-to-many relationship from the employee to the new entry, and create a one-to-many relationship from the department entry to the new entry.
- ❑ D. Create a new entry, create a one-to-many relationship from the new entry to the employee entry, and then create a one-to-many relationship from the entry to the department entry.

Answer: C. This is a many-to-many relationship scenario, which in SQL Server is implemented using three tables. The center table, often referred to as the connecting or joining table, is on the many side of both of the relationships to the other base table. For more information, see "FOREIGN KEY Constraint."

Advanced Physical Database Implementation

Terms you'll need to understand:

✓ View
✓ Indexed view
✓ Partitioned view
✓ Schema
✓ Schema binding
✓ Log shipping
✓ Replication
✓ Publisher
✓ Subscriber
✓ Article
✓ Merge
✓ Snapshot
✓ Transactional
✓ Distributor

Techniques you'll need to master:

✓ Configuring server options
✓ Database configuration
✓ Defining indexed and partitioned views
✓ Defining replication

Introduction

This chapter covers some of the more advanced aspects of the physical database design. Of particular interest to anyone preparing for the exam will be the discussion of schema binding and data partitioning because these two topics represent functionality that has been provided over and above the previous version of SQL Server. You can certainly expect questions on schema binding and data partitioning when you take the exam. Also, traditional topics like views, with this version's idiosyncrasies, will be explored.

We will also explore various technologies that exist in handling multiple server environments. Knowing what each technology offers—as well its restrictions—helps you adapt a database system applied across multiple machines. Considerations for controlling data alterations, having the data available when needed, and responding to queries in a timely manner will be the aim of questions within this area of the exam.

In preparing properly for some of these more advanced topics, you must ensure that you have a thorough understanding of the variety of objects and technologies available within the realm of physical design. Know what each technique accomplishes (advantages) and also watch out for associated pitfalls (disadvantages).

In many aspects of the database server, the interaction between SQL Server and the OS (operating system) is crucial. Some of the physical design concepts that are discussed point out the role that the OS performs and the reason for its participation.

The Need for a More Complex Design

Sometimes you need something more than the data alone can provide. A different perspective on the data may be needed to simplify matters or supply a security layer between the user and the data store. This functionality is provided by views.

In an attempt to achieve as little downtime as possible, it is essential to consider a strategy that involves multiple servers and redundant other hardware. Data redundancy, adequate backups, and some form of disaster recovery plan must all be a part of a complete solution.

Although most of the topics surrounding server clustering fall out of the scope of this book, the partitioned views are discussed at length in the section "Other Multiple Machine Database Implementations," later in this chapter. This functionality includes such topics as data replication, partitioned views, and log shipping.

User Interaction Through Views

A view is a predefined SELECT statement that creates a dynamic virtual table. Although not a real table, a view can be used for many tasks for which an actual table can be used and is often referenced in the same way as a table. A VIEW can be used in SELECT, INSERT, UPDATE, and DELETE statements as if it were a table. No data is stored within views (except indexed views).

Often you would like to design an application that gives the user a list of specific columns out of a table but does not grant the user access to all data. A view can be used to limit what the user sees and the actions the user can perform over a portion of the data in a table.

An alternative to creating a view would be to handle column-level permissions over a table, which can be a true nightmare to administer. A new interface feature in SQL 2000 does enable you to use the GUI to set column-level permissions. However, this feature should be used as little as possible, if ever, because handling permissions at a granular level will lead to administrative headaches.

The problem with column-level permissions is that the initial creation process of the permission is time-consuming, and the granularity of maintenance of the permissions requires extremely careful documentation. Imagine a table with 100 columns and 1,000 or more users, groups, and roles. Trying to document and keep track of all the permissions is an immense task that will overwhelm even the best administrator.

Use a view to simplify administration and provide a more meaningful perspective on the data for the user. The following example shows the creation of a view:

```
CREATE VIEW InStock AS
SELECT ProductID, Description, QTYOnHand FROM Products
WHERE QTYOnHand > 0
```

In the preceding example the view limits the data to items that are in stock. If it were used in place of the entire table, when displayed onto a sales terminal, it would reduce errors in attempting to order items that were not in stock. View access permission can also be granted to specific users throughout your database, which produces a flexible security management plan. Views can be used to define numerous combinations of rows and columns from one or more tables. When views use only a few of the columns in a table, the table data is referred to as being vertically filtered; and when views use only a portion of the rows in a table, the table data is referred to as being horizontally filtered. The capability to filter data is a great advantage of using views. If only a subset of data is desired, a view prevents users from seeing too much data.

The concept of filtering data can be taken further because views can be used with horizontally or vertically partitioned data through a partitioned view. This is where data that could have been put into one table is split into several tables to improve performance. A view can then be used to join all this data together. If the data is on different servers, you are working with a distributed partitioned view. Server Federations utilize horizontal and/or vertical partitioning of data across several servers.

On the largest of databases you will need multiple servers to achieve the capacity and performance needed in a business scenario. In this type of system, a multiple server system will be needed to balance the processing load for the database. SQL Server 2000 shares the database processing load across a group of servers by horizontally partitioning the SQL Server data. These servers are managed independently, but they cooperate to process the database requests from the applications; such a cooperative group of servers is called a federation.

A view can contain 1,024 columns that are extracted from a single table or multiple tables, and they have other restrictions, explored later in this chapter. A view can return an unlimited number of rows, so the number of rows is dependent on the number of rows in the table or tables referenced and the combination of filters applied.

Views provide many benefits and, because of this, are very common throughout an enterprise database environment. The number-one reason a view is created is to protect data from inquisitive eyes. This means that the developer has to worry only about allowing access to the view and further restricting the rows that are returned. Views provide many other benefits, including the following:

➤ *Make querying easier.* Views enable users to execute specific SELECT statements without requiring users to provide the entire SELECT statement each time it executes.

➤ *Hide irrelevant data.* Views enable you to use SELECT to select only the data that is needed or of interest.

➤ *Enforce security.* Users can view only what you let them see. This may be a set of rows or columns or both. This feature is especially important when sensitive information is involved, such as salary and credit card information. Views provide a more efficient data retrieval process and easier security management because permissions are checked and maintained at only one level.

➤ *Export data easily.* Views can gather data from different views and tables, thus making it easy to export data. This data can be exported using the Bulk Copy Program (BCP) or Data Transformation Services (DTS). Regardless of the tool you are using, it is easier to create an export statement if you can tell it to take all the data in a specific table. The view can be used to consolidate this data for this purpose.

Views offer some great advantages but have several restrictions that do not exist in normal SELECT statements. Before examining the view creation process, you should review some facts and restrictions that deal with views. SQL Server will not let you forget these facts when you are creating your views; it throws up an error, usually detailing what you are missing or doing wrong. The most important of these facts, other than those already mentioned, are the following:

➤ The view's definition can comprise rows and columns from one or more tables in the current or other databases.

➤ Defaults, triggers, and rules are not allowed to be associated with a view. The only exception to this rule is the new INSTEAD OF trigger.

➤ View names must follow the rules for identifiers.

➤ Views cannot be created using the ORDER BY clause unless they use the TOP clause (as in TOP 100 PERCENT).

➤ Views cannot be created using the COMPUTE BY or SELECT_INTO clauses.

➤ View names must adhere to uniqueness rules.

➤ Views cannot be created on temporary tables.

➤ Temporary views cannot be created.

➤ Views can be nested up to 32 levels.

Views can be created using the Enterprise Manager, the Create View Wizard, or the T-SQL CREATE VIEW statement. You will usually want to filter only a portion of a table selected with the view. A good example of this might be when you want to hide a salary column of a table, and therefore create a view that references all columns except the salary column.

For designing views of all types, you may find it advantageous to use the View Designer, accessible from the Enterprise Manager when you select

Create View of New View from within a database. The designer is presented in Figure 4.1, showing a view that could be used to access orders that have no discounts applied.

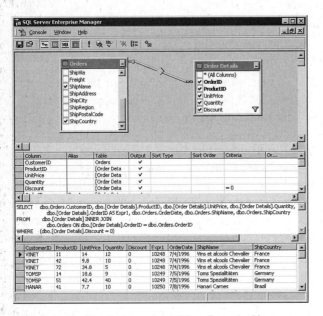

Figure 4.1 The View Designer accessed from Enterprise Manager.

Notice from Figure 4.1 that the syntax of the view is created as you work with the designer. Also notice that the criteria element on the Discount line shows =0, which would represent horizontal filtering with the use of a WHERE clause.

You can create view definitions beyond a standard SELECT statement. Utilizing views, you can join multiple tables, use aggregate functions, or combine the use of user-defined functions to make capable things normally restricted within views. These are really just features of more advanced query techniques, which will be discussed at length in Chapter 5, "Retrieving and Modifying Data."

Getting a Better View

A resultset can use joins to gather data from a number of tables. You can reference up to 256 tables in a single SELECT statement or view. You can make use of the power and versatility of data selection to essentially provide any information from the data.

Similar to the way in which a table serves as the base for a view, a view can gather its information from another view. Creating a view using an existing view as the underlying information source helps when you want to further refine criteria on an existing view. To create a view referencing a base view, examine the following code listing. If we were interested only in obtaining a list of employees from the United States, our previously created EmployeeListing view could be used as the basis for another view, as shown here:

```
CREATE VIEW AmericanEmployees
AS
SELECT LastName, FirstName, Address, City,
               PostalCode, Country, Region, HomePhone
FROM EmployeeListing
WHERE Country = 'USA'
```

You may need to change a view definition. You accommodate this by dropping and re-creating the view, but doing so would reset any previously granted permissions. Using the ALTER VIEW statement, you can easily reshape the definition of a view without affecting the permissions granted. Altering the AmericanEmployees view to include an employee ID could be performed as shown here:

```
ALTER VIEW AmericanEmployees
AS
SELECT EmployeeID, LastName, FirstName, Address, City,
               PostalCode, Country, Region, HomePhone
FROM EmployeeListing
WHERE Country = 'USA'
```

Don't be careless with the changes to views. Altering views or tables that are used by views may cause the dependent views to stop working. SQL Server does not back-check all table or view alterations to ensure that they do not create errors. This is where the SCHEMABINDING option helps out. If you have SCHEMA-bound objects, you cannot ALTER the source objects at all. It may be preferable to drop and re-create a series of objects, rather than having objects that do not function. This process is defined later in the chapter, in the section "Indexed Views."

You may find that SQL Server does not allow you to perform tasks because of one dependency or another. For instance, all objects are dependent on their owner, so you are not able to drop a user from the database if that user owns objects. The number of database objects that the server checks for dependencies is very large, but it is easy to find out what objects they are. A quick query of sysobjects can reveal any object ownership dependencies. To remove a view from a database, use the DROP VIEW statement. Dropping a view removes the definition of the view from the database and an entry in the sysobjects, while not affecting the underlying tables and views. If object deletions are performed from the Enterprise Manager, the dependencies can be viewed before removal, as shown in Figure 4.2.

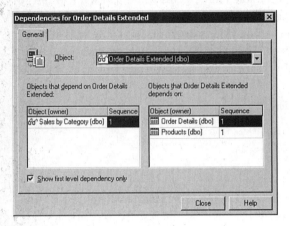

Figure 4.2 Enterprise Manager dependency listing.

Scripts, stored procedures, and views can exist anywhere, and refer to tables or views in your database. There is no easy location that can be checked that tells SQL Server who is referencing your table or view. Another user can reference your view from an entirely different server, without your knowledge, if that user has been granted the SELECT permission to it. Therefore, there is no back-checking of integrity when you change the structure of tables or views.

Utilizing Views

Views serve many useful purposes in a database system. As previously mentioned, a view can be substituted for a table in most instances, but this is only the beginning of where you can apply a view to solve a business problem. Data can be viewed, modified, inserted, and deleted through the use of views. Views are extremely useful in extracting desired data to be ported to other systems. There are a few items to keep in mind when you are developing a system around views. When modifying data in a view, you cannot alter any calculated result; there is no capability to make the changes to the data that provided the derived information. In a view that contains more than one table, the data changed can affect only one table at a time. Altering data in both tables of a two-table view would require two updates.

Any inserts performed against the underlying table must provide values for all NOT NULL columns, unless DEFAULT values are declared for those columns. Any inserted data must also conform to any constraints that are in place and may affect the newly added data. It is possible that a definition could let you INSERT data that is not actually visible through the view. Views can partition data through conditional operation or otherwise limit output using table joins. If you want to prevent the INSERT of data that does not conform to the view, you can use the WITH CHECK OPTION when creating your view.

There are many view options on the exam. You could easily see an exam question that asks you to ensure that the data seen, deleted, inserted, and updated through a view conforms to the view definition. Remember that one of the purposes of a view is to hide and/or protect the underlying data.

You can easily see the power of using views in many instances. As long as a few simple conventions are followed, views are a flexible and commanding tool in the developer's arsenal. But we have only scratched the surface, and we still have a few major areas of views to examine. With these additional topics, come many more idiosyncrasies that can easily be exam material.

Indexed Views

In a standard view there is a great deal of overhead associated with the view object operating over the data that is stored in a table. The view must dynamically build the information from the table(s) each time the view is accessed. The overhead can be considerable in views that involve complex processing of a large amount of data. In cases in which these views are frequently needed in a business solution, you can improve performance by using a clustered index. When a unique clustered index is created on a view, the view is executed and the resultset is stored in the database in the same way a table with a clustered index is stored. Indexed views are available only through the use of the Enterprise version of SQL Server—other versions of the software do not allow the option. If you want to use indexed views, a number of session-level options must be set to ON when you create the index. You need to set NUMERIC_ROUNDABORT to OFF. The options that need to be set to ON are listed here:

➤ ANSI_NULLS

➤ ANSI_PADDING

➤ ANSI_WARNINGS

➤ ARITHABORT

➤ CONCAT_NULL_YIELDS_NULL

➤ QUOTED_IDENTIFIER

Become comfortable with these configuration options. You are likely to find exam questions about the options needed to set up indexed views. Ensure that you are comfortable with the configuration required.

Schema Binding

Note that SCHEMABINDING has to be specified when you create indexed views. Also, when SCHEMABINDING is specified, you have to adhere to the owner.object syntax when referencing tables or views in the creation of your view. A lot of specific options need to be in place to allow for indexed views to be defined.

Schema binding involves attaching an underlying table definition to a view or user-defined function. Normally, if this process is not used, a function or view definition does not hold any data or other defining characteristics of a table. The definition is stored as a set of T-SQL statements and handled as a query or procedure. With binding, a view or function is connected to the underlying objects. Any attempt to change or remove the objects fails unless the binding has first been removed. Normally, you can create a view, but the underlying table might be changed so that the view no longer works. To prevent the underlying table from being changed, the view can be "schemabound" to the table. Any table changes, which would break the view, are not allowed.

 The word *schema* has several different uses and definitions within SQL Server; the exam will leverage this fact and attempt to confuse the separate definitions. Make sure that you are aware of how the term is used in relation to XML, indexed views, and maintaining metadata. For more information about these particulars, you can consult Chapter 5 in the "Extensible Markup Language" section; this chapter, in the "Indexed Views" section; and Chapter 7, "Tuning and Optimizing Analysis," in the "Information Gathering" section.

Indexed views, defined previously in the chapter, require that a view be defined with the binding option and also that any user-defined functions referenced in the view also be bound. In previous versions of SQL Server, it was not possible to define an index on a view. With the advent of binding, however, meaningful indexes can now be defined over a view that has been bound to the underlying objects. The following example uses T-SQL for the creation of a schema-bound view:

```
CREATE VIEW SampleBoundView WITH SCHEMABINDING AS
        SELECT ProductID, Description, PurchPrice,
  PurchPrice * Markup AS SalesPrice
        FROM dbo.ProductTable
```

Other than setting the specific set of options, nothing more needs to be done for the optimizer to utilize an index with a query on a view. Essentially, the SQL Server Optimizer handles the view query in the same manner in which it would handle a standard query against a table. The view cannot reference another view; only underlying tables are permitted, and you must create the view with the SCHEMABINDING option. Only the Enterprise and Developer editions support the creation of an indexed view.

There are some limitations to the content of the SELECT statement for the view definition:

➤ There may be no use of *.

➤ A column name used as a simple expression cannot be specified in more than one view column.

➤ There may be no derived tables.

➤ Rowset functions are not permitted.

➤ UNION, outer joins, subqueries, or self-joins cannot be used—only simple joins can be used.

➤ There may be no TOP, ORDER BY, COMPUTE, or COMPUTE BY clause.

➤ DISTINCT is not permitted.

➤ COUNT(*) cannot be used, but COUNT_BIG(*) is allowed.

➤ The aggregate functions AVG, MAX, MIN, STDEV, STDEVP, VAR, and VARP are not permitted.

➤ A SUM function cannot reference a nullable expression.

➤ The full-text predicates CONTAINS or FREETEXT may not be used.

We have introduced a lot of new terms in this list. These terms are new in our discussion but will be revisited later in the book.

Note that although indexed views are advantageous for performance reasons, in some cases they can not be utilized if greater functionality is desired within the information presented by the application. Another performance consideration that usually comes into play with extremely large datasets is the use of partitioned views.

Partitioned Views

A partitioned view enables the creation of a view that spans a number of physical machines. These views can fall into one of two categories: local or distributed. A distinction is also made between views that are updatable and those that are read-only. The use of partitioned views can aid in the implementation of federated database servers, which are multiple machines set up to share the processing load.

Multiple server operations balance the load so that updates are potentially separated from queries and query load can be spread across multiple machines. For more information on federated server implementations, see SQL Server Books Online, "Designing Federated Database Servers." Federated Servers are beyond the scope of the exam and therefore this book as well.

Partitioned views drastically restrict the underlying table designs and require several options to be set when indexes are used. Constraints need to be defined on each participating server so that only the data pertaining to the table(s) stored on that server is handled. Although CHECK constraints are not needed to return the correct results, they enable the query optimizer to more appropriately select the correct server to find the requested data.

To use partitioned views, you horizontally split a single table into several smaller tables, each having the same column definitions. Set up the smaller tables to accept data in ranges and enforce the ranges using CHECK constraints. Then you can define the distributed view on each of the participating servers. Add linked server definitions on each of the member servers. An example of a distributed view definition is as follows:

```
CREATE VIEW AllProducts AS
        Select * FROM Server1.dbo.Products9999
UNION ALL
        Select * FROM Server2.dbo.Products19999
UNION ALL
        Select * FROM Server3.dbo.Products29999
```

Partitioning attempts to achieve a balance among the machines being used. Data partitioning as defined previously involves the horizontal division of a singular table into a number of smaller tables, each dealing with a range of data from the original and split off onto separate servers. Some configuration options can help gain performance when operating against partitions. Setting the Lazy Schema Validation option using sp_serveroption can optimize performance. When used, it is set for each linked server definition. This optimizes performance by ensuring that the query processor does not request metadata for any of the linked tables until actually needed. Attempting to ensure that the correct query goes to the appropriate server also helps to improve performance while minimizing bandwidth use.

A partitioned view is considered to be updatable if a set of SELECT statements is combined into one resultset using UNION ALL operations, as shown previously in this section. Indexes based on calculated columns are not permitted within any table definitions, and all tables must have a primary key and an ANSI_PADDING set.

When you use a partitioned view to insert data, all columns must be included in the INSERT statement, even if the table definitions provide DEFAULTs or allow for NULL content. Also, IDENTITY columns cannot be referenced; therefore, no underlying tables can have IDENTITY columns, nor are they permitted to have timestamp columns.

Remote partitioned views require that you keep a few additional considerations in mind. A distributed transaction is automatically initiated to ensure that integrity is maintained throughout all operations, and the XACT_ABORT option must be set to ON. Smallmoney and smalldatetime data types in the remote tables are mapped to money and datetime types locally.

Partitioning Strategies

Partitions can be designed in a symmetric or asymmetric fashion, and although it is most useful to design symmetrically, the access requirements of a lot of systems necessitate an asymmetric design.

A symmetrical design is one in which all related data is placed on the same server so that most queries do not have to cross network boundaries to access the data. It is also easier to manage the data if the division of tables can be performed in such a manner that each server has the same amount of data. In most real-world applications, data is accessed in a random fashion that can make the designer lean toward an asymmetric implementation. The design can be configured so that one server has a larger role and/or contains more data than the others. Performance can be improved if you weigh each server's use and make one server work harder on the partitioned applications, because the other servers perform larger tasks that deal with other unrelated processes.

Designing for distributed partitioned views requires appropriate planning of front-end applications to ensure that, whenever possible, data queries are sent to the appropriate server. Middleware, such as Microsoft Message Queue or an application server or other third-party equivalents, should attempt to match queries against data storage. When preparing for data communication with the front-end application, the operating-system settings of the server will affect the server's interaction with the application.

Operating-System Service Properties

There are four services acting within the operating system that provide the functionality to the database system. The SQL Server Service is responsible for data retrieval and any other interactions with the data. The SQL Server Agent Service is responsible for the execution of scheduled tasks and the performing of maintenance activities. The Microsoft Search Service is a full-text indexing and search engine that is an optional portion of a server installation. Text-searching capabilities can be used to find data matches when searching using English text and phrases. Finally, the Distributed Transaction Coordinator Service is optionally used to control interactions between multiple servers. For any of the features provided by these services to be utilized, they must be installed and running on the server.

In SQL Server 2000, two aspects of the server's operating system allow for a successful service restart in the event of failure. The operating system's services can be configured to automatically start on computer startup and can also be set up to respond to service interruptions. To set service properties, you must locate the MSSQLServer Service. This service can be found in your administrative tools, Services on a Windows 2000 or 2003 operating system, or Control Panel Services for an NT-based system.

For the configuration options as displayed when using the Windows 2000 services properties, see Figures 4.3. Besides configuration through the operating-system services interface, there are also settings that are accessible from the Enterprise Manager that will affect the server's operations. These settings can also be controlled through the use of T-SQL.

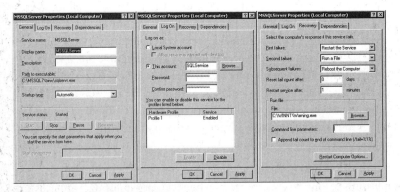

Figure 4.3   Configuring Windows 2000 Services.

The database recovery interval can be set for the number of minutes each database takes to start up after an outage or controlled server startup. You can find the Recovery Interval option in the Enterprise Manager by right-clicking the server, selecting Properties from the pop-up menu, and navigating to the Database Settings tab.

User accounts should be assigned for the SQL Server and SQL Server Agent services. Separate user accounts can be identified for each of the services. Conversely, the same account can be used for all services and several servers. As a standard implementation, it is usually best to use the same account. You might want to use separate accounts for each server, particularly if you want each server to send and receive email as a separate identity.

Server Configuration Settings

Standard configuration settings are available through the Server Properties dialog box in the Enterprise Manager, or they can be accessed using the sp_configure stored procedure. Descriptions of these configuration settings are presented in the subsections that follow. Some of the more advanced options require that you enable Show Advanced Options. You can set advanced options on by using the following:

```
sp_configure 'show advanced options', 1
reconfigure
```

You won't need to know all the server and database configuration options on the exam. On the two SQL Server MCDBA exams, though, you will be confronted with a number of them, so having a good idea as to what most of them are used for is strongly recommended.

Affinity Mask (Advanced)

Use the Affinity Mask option in systems that have four or more processors. It increases performance when the system is under a heavy workload. You can specify which processors Microsoft SQL Server is to use. You can exclude SQL Server activity from processors that have been given specific workload assignments by the Windows NT 4.0 or Windows 2000 operating systems.

Allow Updates

The Allow Updates option is used to allow the direct alteration of system tables. When Allow Updates is set to 1, any user with appropriate permissions can either update system tables directly with ad-hoc updates or create stored procedures that update system tables.

AWE Enabled (Advanced)

Address Windowing Extension (AWE) is an advanced option used to support up to a maximum of 64GB of physical memory.

C2 Audit Mode

Use C2 Audit Mode to review both successful and unsuccessful attempts to access statements and objects. Allowing for the documentation of system activity and observance of security policy violations, C2 auditing tracks C2 audit events and records them to a file in the \mssql\data directory or the \mssql$instancename\data directory for named instances of SQL Server. If the file reaches a size limit of 200MB, C2 auditing starts a new file.

Cost Threshold for Parallelism (Advanced)

Use the Cost Threshold for Parallelism option to specify the threshold at which SQL Server creates and executes parallel query plans. Parallel query plans are executed only when the estimated cost to execute a serial plan for the same query is higher than the value set. The cost refers to an estimated elapsed time in seconds that is required to execute a standard plan. Set Cost Threshold for Parallelism only on symmetric multiprocessors.

Cursor Threshold (Advanced)

Use the Cursor Threshold option to indicate the number of rows in the cursor set at which cursor keysets are generated asynchronously. If you set Cursor Threshold to -1, all keysets are generated synchronously, which benefits small cursor sets. If you set Cursor Threshold to 0, all cursor keysets are generated asynchronously. With other values, the query optimizer compares the number of expected rows in the cursor set and builds the keyset asynchronously if it exceeds the number set in Cursor Threshold. Do not set Cursor Threshold too low because small resultsets are better built synchronously.

Default Language

Use the Default Language option to specify the default language for all newly created logins.

Fill Factor (Advanced)

Use the Fill Factor option to specify how full the server should make each page when it creates a new index using existing data. The Fill Factor percentage affects performance because SQL Server must take time to split pages when they fill up. The default for Fill Factor of 0 (zero) does not mean that pages are 0% full. It is treated similarly to a fill factor value of 100 in that indexes are created with full data pages and nonclustered indexes with full leaf pages. The default setting is different from 100 in that SQL Server leaves some space within the upper level of the index tree.

Index Create Memory (Advanced)

Use the Index Create Memory option to control the amount of memory used by index creation sorts. This option is self-configuring and should operate without requiring adjustment. If difficulties are experienced creating indexes, consider increasing the value. Query sorts are controlled through the Min Memory Per Query option. The default value for this option is 0 (self-configuring).

Default Full-Text Language (Advanced)

Use the Default Full-Text Language option to specify a default language value for full-text indexed columns. The default value of this option is the language of the server.

Lightweight Pooling (Advanced)

The Lightweight Pooling option provides a means of reducing the overhead associated with the excessive context switching sometimes seen in multi-processor environments. When excessive context switching is present, Lightweight Pooling might provide better throughput.

Locks (Advanced)

The Locks option sets the maximum number of available locks, limiting the amount of memory the server uses. The default setting is 0, which enables SQL Server to allocate and deallocate locks dynamically based on changing system requirements.

Max Degree of Parallelism (Advanced)

The Max Degree of Parallelism option limits the number of processors to use in parallel plan execution. The default value is 0 (the actual number of CPUs) and the maximum is 32.

Max Server Memory/Min Server Memory

These two settings, Max Server Memory and Min Server Memory, establish upper and lower limits to the amount of memory the database engine uses. The database engine starts with only the memory required to initialize. As the workload increases, it acquires additional memory. The database engine frees any of the acquired memory until it reaches the amount specified in Min Server Memory.

Max Text Repl Size

The Max Text Repl Size option specifies the maximum size (in bytes) of text and image data that can be added to a replicated column in a single INSERT, UPDATE, WRITETEXT, or UPDATETEXT statement.

Max Worker Threads (Advanced)

The Max Worker Threads option configures the number of worker threads available to the server and its processes. SQL Server uses the threads so that one or more threads simultaneously support each network that SQL Server supports; another thread handles database checkpoints; and a pool of threads handles user connections.

Media Retention (Advanced)

Use the Media Retention option to provide a default for the length of time each backup should be retained. Overridden by the RETAINDAYS clause of the BACKUP statement, Media Retention helps protect backups from being overwritten until the specified number of days has elapsed.

Min Memory Per Query (Advanced)

Use the Min Memory Per Query option to specify the minimum amount of memory that will be allocated for the execution of a query.

Nested Triggers

The Nested Triggers option enables actions that initiate performance of another trigger. When the Nested Triggers option is set to 0, triggers cannot cascade. When the Nested Triggers option is set to the default setting of 1, triggers can cascade to as many as 32 levels.

Network Packet Size (Advanced)

Use the Network Packet Size option to set the packet size used across the entire network. The default packet size is 4096 bytes. If an application does bulk-copy operations, or sends or receives large amounts of text or image data, a packet size larger than the default can improve efficiency because it results in fewer network reads and writes. If an application sends and receives small amounts of information, you can set the packet size to 512 bytes, which is sufficient for most data transfers.

Open Objects (Advanced)

Use the Open Objects option to set the maximum number of database objects that can be open at one time. Database objects are those objects defined in the `sysobjects` table: tables, views, rules, stored procedures, defaults, and triggers.

Priority Boost (Advanced)

The Priority Boost option specifies the processor scheduling priority. If you set this option to 1, SQL Server runs at a priority base of 13 in the Windows NT 4.0 or Windows 2000 Scheduler. The default is 0, which is a priority base of 7.

Query Governor Cost Limit (Advanced)

The Query Governor Cost Limit option specifies an upper limit for the time in which a query can run. Query cost refers to the estimated elapsed time, in seconds, required to execute a query.

Query Wait (Advanced)

Memory-intensive queries, such as those involving sorting and hashing, are queued when not enough memory is available to run the query. The query times out after a set amount of time that SQL Server calculates (25 times the estimated cost of the query) or the time amount specified by the non-negative value of the Query Wait.

Recovery Interval (Advanced)

Use the Recovery Interval option to set the maximum number of minutes per database that the server needs in order to recover the database activity. The recovery process is initiated each time SQL Server starts or as the basis for completing a restore operation. The recovery process rolls back transactions that did not commit and rolls forward transactions that did commit. This configuration option sets an upper limit on the time it should take to recover each database. The default is 0, indicating automatic configuration by SQL Server. In practice, this means a recovery time of less than one minute, and a checkpoint marker is placed into the transaction log approximately every one minute for active databases.

Remote Access

Use the Remote Access option to control logins from remote servers running SQL Server. Set Remote Access to 1 (the default) to enable logins from remote servers. Set the option to 0 to secure a local server and prevent access from a remote server.

Remote Login Timeout

Use the Remote Login Timeout option to specify the number of seconds to wait before returning from a failed remote login attempt.

Remote Proc Trans

The Remote Proc Trans option protects the activities of a server-to-server process through the use of the Distributed Transaction Coordinator. Set Remote Proc Trans to 1 to provide an MS DTC-coordinated distributed transaction that protects the ACID properties of transactions. Sessions begun after setting this option to 1 inherit the configuration setting as their default.

Remote Query Timeout

The Remote Query Timeout option is used to indicate the number of seconds that must elapse when processing a remote operation before the operation times out. The default of 600 sets a 10-minute wait.

Scan for Startup Process (Advanced)

Use the Scan for Startup Process option to scan for automatic execution of stored procedures at startup time. If it is set to 1, SQL Server scans for and executes all automatically executed stored procedures defined on the server. The default value is 0 (do not scan).

Set Working Set Size (Advanced)

The Set Working Set Size option reserves physical memory space for SQL Server that is equal to the server memory setting. SQL Server, based on workload and available resources, configures the server memory setting automatically. It varies dynamically between the Min Server Memory and Max Server Memory settings.

Two Digit Year Cutoff

Use the Two Digit Year Cutoff option to specify an integer from 1753 to 9999 that represents the last year for interpreting two-digit years as four-digit years.

User Connections (Advanced)

Use the User Connections option to specify the maximum number of simultaneous user connections. The actual number of user connections allowed also depends on the version of SQL Server you are using and the limits of your application(s) and hardware. SQL Server enables a maximum of 32,767 user connections.

User Options

The User Options option is used to specify global defaults for all users. A list of default query processing options is established for the duration of a user's work session. A user can override these defaults by using the SET statement. You can configure user options dynamically for new logins. After you change the setting of user options, new logins use the new setting; current logins are not affected.

Reconfigure

The Reconfigure option updates the server configuration. It is used after the application of sp_configure to change server settings and make the new settings take effect. Because some configuration options require that a server stop and restart before the currently running value can be updated, Reconfigure does not always update the currently running value. Use the With Override option of this command to force a value that might or might not meet ranges of allowed values or recommended settings.

The SQL Server configuration options are used to fine-tune the database environment. Many options provide a mechanism for an administrator or a developer to obtain optimum performance and achieve a more secure and stable server. A total approach to an optimum environment also involves the proper use of database configuration options. Server property adjustments affect all the databases stored on the server where database configuration options are used to control a database and not affect other databases.

Database Configuration Options

Database options are set to allow for application or procedural requirements and to provide for administrative configuration. You will interact with these settings to set up backups, allow for specific procedures, and provide appropriate access levels, depending on what is needed for a given process. Learn the settings that are required for each process and know the resulting effect on the system under different operating configurations.

Standard database configuration settings are available through the Database Properties in the Enterprise Manager, or they can be accessed using the sp_dboption stored procedure. Some of the more advanced settings cannot be set singly; they must be set in combination with other settings.

There are five categories of database options:

➤ *Auto options*—AUTO_CLOSE, AUTO_CREATE_STATISTICS, AUTO_UPDATE_STATISTICS, and AUTO_SHRINK.

➤ *Cursor options*—CURSOR_CLOSE_ON_COMMIT and CURSOR_DEFAULT LOCAL or GLOBAL.

➤ *Recovery options*—RECOVERY FULL or BULK_LOGGED or SIMPLE and TORN_PAGE_DETECTION.

➤ *SQL options*—ANSI_NULL_DEFAULT, ANSI_NULLS, ANSI_PADDING, ANSI_WARNINGS, ARITHABORT, NUMERIC_ROUNDABORT, CONCAT_NULL_YIELDS_NULL, QUOTED_IDENTIFIER, and RECURSIVE_TRIGGERS.

➤ *State options*—OFFLINE or ONLINE, READ_ONLY or READ_WRITE, SINGLE_USER or RESTRICTED_USER or MULTI_USER, and WITH ROLLBACK AFTER or WITH ROLLBACK IMMEDIATE or NO_WAIT.

These options are described in the following sections.

Settings for Automatic Actions

One group of settings tell a database to take actions in an automated fashion. Actions that the server would normally wait for specific instruction to perform can be set to automatically occur based on properties of the environment. These options in most cases allow for better resource usage, but some may also have associated overhead. These options are summarized in the following subsections. The sp_dboption procedure is always executed within the context of the master, as in the following:

```
Use Master
sp_dboption 'pubs', 'read only', 'TRUE'
```

AUTO_CREATE_STATISTICS

When the AUTO_CREATE_STATISTICS option is set to ON, statistics are automatically created on columns used in a predicate. A predicate is an expression that evaluates to TRUE, FALSE, or UNKNOWN. Predicates are used in the search condition of WHERE clauses and HAVING clauses, and the join conditions of FROM clauses. Adding statistics improves query performance because the optimizer can better determine how to evaluate queries. If the statistics are not used, SQL Server automatically deletes them. When this option is set to OFF, SQL Server does not automatically create statistics; instead, statistics can be manually created.

AUTO_SHRINK

When the AUTO_SHRINK option is set to ON, the database files are set up for periodic shrinking. Any database-associated file, data, or log can be shrunk automatically. When the option is set to OFF, the database files are not automatically shrunk during periodic checks for unused space. By default, this option is set to ON for all databases in SQL Server Desktop Edition, and OFF for all other editions, regardless of the operating system.

AUTO_UPDATE_STATISTICS

When the AUTO_UPDATE_STATISTICS option is set to ON, existing statistics are automatically updated when the statistics become out-of-date because the data in the tables has changed. When this option is set to OFF, existing statistics are not automatically updated; instead, statistics can be manually updated.

AUTO_CLOSE

When the AUTO_CLOSE option is set to ON, server resources are freed up as soon as the database is closed and shut down cleanly when the last user of the database exits. By default, this option is set to ON for all databases in the Desktop Engine, and OFF for all other editions. The database reopens automatically when a user tries to use the database again. When this option is set to OFF, the database remains open even if no users are currently using it.

Arguably the AUTO_CLOSE options is also a cursor option because it will also affect the resources tied up through the use of cursors.

Moving the Cursor

Cursor activities are usually set in motion by an application, but they can utilize resources on the server. Operating as a record selector, cursors locate the current data being acted on and keep track of data manipulations. There are a couple of options that can be set to help control how these resources react, as detailed next.

CURSOR_CLOSE_ON_COMMIT

When CURSOR_CLOSE_ON_COMMIT is set to ON, any open cursors are closed automatically when a transaction using the cursor is committed. By default, this setting is OFF and cursors remain open across transaction boundaries, closing only when the connection is closed or when they are explicitly closed, which is usually when a procedure finishes.

CURSOR_DEFAULT LOCAL or GLOBAL

When CURSOR_DEFAULT LOCAL is set and a cursor is not defined as GLOBAL when it is created, the scope of the cursor is local to the batch, stored procedure, or trigger. The cursor name is valid only within this scope. When CURSOR_DEFAULT GLOBAL is set and a cursor is not defined as LOCAL when it is created, the scope of the cursor is global to the connection. The cursor name can be referenced in any stored procedure or batch the connection executes.

Settings for Recovery

Aiding in system recovery is important for the next set of options. A little proactive maintenance through the use of these options can save time when you're attempting a full or partial data recovery.

TORN_PAGE_DETECTION

The TORN_PAGE_DETECTION recovery option enables SQL Server to detect incomplete I/O operations caused by power failures or other system outages. When set to ON, this option causes a bit to be reversed for each 512-byte sector in an 8KB database page as the page is written to disk. If a bit is in the wrong state when the page is later read by SQL Server, the page was written incorrectly; a torn page is therefore detected.

RECOVERY FULL or BULK_LOGGED or SIMPLE

When FULL is specified, database backups and transaction log backups are used to provide full recoverability from media failure. All operations, including bulk operations, such as SELECT INTO, CREATE INDEX, and bulk loading data, are fully logged. When BULK_LOGGED is specified, logging for all SELECT INTO, CREATE INDEX, and bulk loading data operations is minimal and therefore requires less log space. In exchange for better performance and less log space usage, the risk of exposure to loss is greater than with full recovery. When SIMPLE is specified, the database can be recovered only to the last full database backup or last differential backup.

Some of the database properties that were available in previous releases of SQL Server have been combined to form what is referred to in SQL Server 2000 as recovery models. Setting the appropriate model can enable most, if not all, data activity to be recovered in the event of system failures. Three models are supported: Simple, Bulk-Logged, and Full.

The Simple recovery model ensures higher performance during bulk-copy operations and maintains a smaller database log. However, the model does not support transaction log backups and, therefore, there will be data loss in the event of a failure because the database can be restored only to the point of the last full or differential database backup.

Bulk-Logged recovery also allows for high-performance bulk procedures that use minimal log space. Some data might be lost, but because you can perform log backups, usually the only loss will be bulk operations since the last backup.

If recoverability to a specific point in time with as little data loss as possible is the goal, the Full recovery model should be set. The Full recovery model makes the heaviest use of the database logs.

Set Coding Reaction with SQL Options

How the server reacts to a front-end application or any other connection can be configured through the use of several SQL options within the database, is discussed next.

ANSI_NULL_DEFAULT

The ANSI_NULL_DEFAULT option enables the user to control the default nullability. When NULL or NOT NULL is not specified, a user-defined data type or a column definition uses the default setting for nullability. When this option is set to ON, all user-defined data types or columns that are not explicitly defined as NOT NULL during a CREATE TABLE or ALTER TABLE statement default to allowing null values. Columns that are defined with constraints follow constraint rules regardless of this setting.

ANSI_NULLS

When ANSI_NULLS is set to ON, all comparisons to a null value evaluate to NULL (unknown). When set to OFF, comparisons of non-Unicode values to a null value evaluate to TRUE if both values are NULL. By default, the ANSI_NULLS database option is OFF.

ANSI_PADDING

When ANSI_PADDING is set to ON, trailing blanks in character values inserted into varchar columns and trailing zeros in binary values inserted into varbinary columns are not trimmed. Values are not padded to the length of the column. When this option is set to OFF, the trailing blanks and zeros are trimmed. This setting affects only the definition of new columns. It is recommended that ANSI_PADDING always be set to ON. SET ANSI_PADDING must be ON when creating or manipulating indexes on computed columns or indexed views.

ANSI_WARNINGS

When ANSI_WARNINGS is set to ON, errors or warnings are issued when conditions such as divide-by-zero occur or null values appear in aggregate functions. When it's set to OFF, no warnings are raised when null values appear in aggregate functions, and null values are returned when conditions such as divide-by-zero occur. By default, ANSI_WARNINGS is OFF.

ARITHABORT

When ARITHABORT is set to ON, an overflow or divide-by-zero error causes the query or batch to terminate. If the error occurs in a transaction, the transaction is rolled back. When this option is set to OFF, a warning message is displayed if one of these errors occurs, but the query, batch, or transaction continues to process as if no error occurred.

NUMERIC_ROUNDABORT

If NUMERIC_ROUNDABORT is set to ON, an error is generated when the loss of precision occurs in an expression. When it's set to OFF, losses of precision do not generate error messages, and the result is rounded to the precision of the column or variable storing the result.

CONCAT_NULL_YIELDS_NULL

When CONCAT_NULL_YIELDS_NULL is set to ON, if one of the operands in a concatenation operation is NULL, the result of the operation is NULL. When this option is set to OFF, concatenating a null value with a character string yields the character string as the result.

QUOTED_IDENTIFIER

When QUOTED_IDENTIFIER is set to ON, identifiers can be delimited by double quotation marks, and literals must be delimited by single quotation marks. All strings delimited by double quotation marks are interpreted as object identifiers. Quoted identifiers do not have to follow the T-SQL rules for identifiers. They can be keywords and can include characters not generally allowed in T-SQL identifiers. When this option is set to OFF (the default), identifiers cannot be in quotation marks and must follow all T-SQL rules for identifiers. Literals can be delimited by either single or double quotation marks. Identifiers must be enclosed in square brackets ([ ]) if they contain spaces or other characters or keywords.

RECURSIVE_TRIGGERS

When RECURSIVE_TRIGGERS is set to ON, triggers are enabled to fire recursively. When it's set to OFF (the default), triggers cannot be fired recursively. Just as this set of SQL options controls the interaction with the front end, so does the next set of options. State options, however, control the status of the database or accessibility of the data to connections.

The State of the Server

State options determine whether data is accessible to one or more connections. The database state can be temporarily changed to allow for administration or other specialty tasks.

OFFLINE or ONLINE

When OFFLINE is specified, the database is closed and shut down cleanly and marked offline. The database cannot be modified while it is offline. When ONLINE is specified, the database is open and available for use.

READ_ONLY or READ_WRITE

When READ_ONLY is specified, users can retrieve data from the database but cannot modify the data. Automatic recovery is skipped at system startup and shrinking the database is not possible. No locking takes place in read-only databases, which can result in faster query performance. When READ_WRITE is specified, users can retrieve and modify data.

SINGLE_USER or RESTRICTED_USER or MULTI_USER

SINGLE_USER enables only one user at a time to connect to the database. All other user connections are broken. The timeframe for breaking the connection is controlled by the termination clause of the ALTER DATABASE statement. New connection attempts are refused. RESTRICTED_USER enables only members of the db_owner fixed database role and dbcreator and sysadmin fixed server roles to connect to the database, but it does not limit their number. MULTI_USER enables all users with the appropriate permissions to connect to the database.

WITH termination

The termination clause of the ALTER DATABASE statement specifies how to terminate incomplete transactions. Breaking their connections to the database terminates transactions. If the termination clause is omitted, the ALTER DATABASE statement waits indefinitely, until the transactions commit or roll back on their own. ROLLBACK AFTER 'integer' SECONDS waits for the specified number of seconds. ROLLBACK IMMEDIATE breaks unqualified connections immediately. NO_WAIT checks for connections before attempting to change the database state and causes the ALTER DATABASE statement to fail if certain connections exist. When the transition is to SINGLE_USER mode, the ALTER DATABASE statement fails if any other connections exist. When the transition is to RESTRICTED_USER mode, the ALTER DATABASE statement fails if any unqualified connections exist.

Each of the database options plays a role in the server's interaction with the database and as a result will effect performance and resource utilization. This may also affect the design of the front-end application. As seen before, many of these settings must be in effect to utilize indexed views through binding.

Working from a single server, you have settings for the operating system, each of its services, the SQL Server itself, and each of its databases. That leaves us with only one major topic to discuss within the realm of advanced physical design: the implementation of system models that involve more than one machine. The topic of database systems spanning multiple machines was covered to a small extent earlier in the chapter with a look at partitioned views. As far as the capabilities of SQL Server within a multiple machine environment go, partitioned views represent only one aspect.

Other Multiple Machine Database Implementations

Many high-demand implementations require the use of multiple servers to handle the workload. Various options exist for using SQL Server on multiple servers. Partitioning, log shipping, replication, federated servers, and clustering are all potential implementations for using multiple servers and obtaining load balancing.

Partitioning and federated servers provide load balancing for a single application and work together to provide users with better response. This type of implementation is in place of a multiple server cluster where all machines load balance to share the workload. In a federation, each server is completely independent; it is the application and database design that implements the load balancing.

Microsoft failover clustering provides for availability by enabling a secondary server to take over activities if a primary server fails. For further information on failover clustering, see SQL Server Books Online, "Creating a Failover Cluster."

Replication places potentially updatable copies of the same data on multiple servers so that applications that allow for site independence can, at the same time, keep all copies of the data synchronized. Most models have a degree of latency or delay between the initial updates and the moment when all data is in agreement.

Standby Servers and Log Shipping

To achieve availability and performance, redundancy is the starting point. Data redundancy can be obtained at the table and database level through denormalization, and at the server level through the use of log shipping, replication, and/or partitioning. We investigated the denormalization of a database design in the preceding chapter. In the physical environment the variety of implementation choices occurs at a machine level. Each technique has a set of requirements that must be closely adhered to.

A warm backup server or standby server is a lower-cost implementation that is often selected as an alternative to replication or clustering. The premise is to back up the production server on a regular basis, restoring it to a second machine that can be put into production in the event of failure in the first computer. A standby server can also assist in taking some of the workload from the production machine if it is used as a read-only query server.

In SQL Server 2000 you can use the Maintenance Plan Wizard to implement a standby server configuration. The wizard prompts you through the configuration of backups and regularly scheduled log shipments to the standby machine.

Using log shipping is a way to have two separate servers that contain the same database and split the query load away from the updating of data. The log information is periodically copied to a read-only, standby server that can then be used for query purposes, thereby offloading some of the work from the main production machine. For further information on log shipping implementations, see SQL Server Books Online, "Maintenance Planning Wizard."

Standby server implementations utilizing log shipping is one form of multiple machine implementations that create redundant data in multiple databases. It is a relatively simple implementation. Other multiple machine implementations involve much more concise configuration. SQL Server offers up a technology referred to as data replication to get data in an orderly fashion from one database to another on the same server or on separate servers. Replication allows for various topologies that control the flow of data between machines.

 The exam requires you to choose the appropriate technology and also asks about particular aspects of replication. It is imperative, therefore, that you have a complete understanding of what replication offers in contrast to other aspects of SQL Server.

Replicating Data

Replication is the process by which data and database objects are distributed from SQL Server to other database engines that reside across your enterprise; this data can be distributed to other SQL Server databases or even non-SQL Server databases such as Oracle and others. This replication is performed using a Publisher/Distributor/Subscriber metaphor, which is a metaphor consisting of a Publisher, Subscriber, and Distributor that forms the basis of replication.

To understand replication, you must understand and become familiar with the basic concept of the Publisher/Distributor/Subscriber metaphor. This metaphor defines the different roles SQL Server can play throughout the replication process. SQL server can also play a third role: the Distributor. Each role provides functionality that aids in the replication process. The Publisher is the server that makes the data available so that it can be sent to the Subscriber. The Distributor is the intermediary that collects the data from the Publisher and transports it to the Subscriber. The Subscriber is the server that ends up receiving the data.

Publisher

In replication terminology, the Publisher is the server that produces the original data for the use of the replication process. The Publisher can produce many publications or sets of data to be distributed to other subscribing machines. One Publisher can produce data to be replicated to many Subscribers. Also, many Publishers may produce data to be distributed to just a single, central Subscriber. The former is implemented as a standard Central Publisher/Distributor/Subscriber replication model, and the latter is referred to as a Central Subscriber replication.

Distributor

In SQL Server terminology, the Distributor is the server that contains the distribution database, data history, and transactions; as its name implies, it sends data to Subscribers. The Distributor can be implemented on the same physical server as the Publisher or Subscriber, though it doesn't need to be. It can reside on a separate server across the world connected via a network. The placement of the Distributor and its characteristics depends on the type of replication used.

Subscriber

A Subscriber in SQL Server terms is the server that receives replicated data through the Distributor. A Subscriber receives publications by subscribing to them—not, however, by subscribing to individual articles that represent only a portion of a publication. It is also possible to use stored procedures to set up subscriptions, in which case it is possible to subscribe to a single article. Subscribers can choose from the publications available at the Publisher and don't necessarily need to subscribe to all of them. Other replication terminologies are also important to the process and fall into line with the subscription metaphor. When a subscription is set up, a Publication made up of one or more articles is configured.

Articles and Publications

Simply put, articles are data structures made up of selected columns and/or rows from a table. An article could also be the entire table, although it is recommended that the content of an article be kept to just the minimum amount of data needed for the specifics of an implementation. One or more articles are bundled into a publication to be used for replication. Articles must be grouped into a publication before they are ready to be replicated. In short, then, a publication is a collection of one or more articles and is capable of being replicated.

Replication Strategies

Replication, with its many benefits, serves as a backbone for many businesses. Placing the same data on multiple servers, with each server closer to the user's location, can reduce the use of bandwidth and provide the user with faster update operations and retrieval of data. Without replication, businesses would be incapable of carrying out robust branch operations across the globe. DBAs favor replication for the following reasons:

➤ In using replication, businesses are capable of having data copied from server to server in a multisite enterprise, providing flexibility and more efficient use of networking resources.

➤ Replication allows for a greater concurrent use of data, allowing more people to work with the data at the same time.

➤ Copies of the database can be distributed, bringing data closer to the end user and providing a form of load balancing.

➤ Replication is perfect for the traveling salesman or roaming disconnected user. It enables mobile users who work on laptops to be updated with current database information when they do connect and to upload data to a central server.

Replication techniques can be applied to three replication models, as well as several different physical models. The physical aspects and models have no direct correlation. The replication model supplies the functionality, whereas the physical aspects lay out the placement and roles of individual servers.

Merge, snapshot, and transactional replication all involve essentially the same basic elements to begin with. However, each model has idiosyncrasies of its own that require some thought during the design of the actual implementation.

The application of the initial snapshot that begins the entire replication process can be compressed and/or saved to a CD so that some of the necessary communications can be offloaded. Doing so makes more efficient use of network bandwidth in slow-link or dial-up environments in particular.

Subscriptions can be set up as either a push subscription or a pull subscription. A push subscription is one in which the Publisher initiates a subscription and provides the basis for scheduling the replication process. The pull subscription is one in which the Subscriber initiates the subscription and provides the basis and timing on which data is to be obtained. In either case, whoever initiates a subscription selects the appropriate articles to be transmitted.

Replication can be set up in various ways. The different scenarios in which replication is set up each provide specific benefits and qualities. SQL Server can serve as Publisher, Subscriber, or Distributor. The individual roles can all be set up on a single machine, although in most implementations there is at least a separation between a Publisher/Distributor and the subscribing machine(s). In some other scenarios, the Subscriber of the data from one machine may republish the data to still other Subscribers. The possibilities are endless. You can choose to implement any of the following common scenarios, which cover the basics of a physical replication model. In real-world scenarios, however, the actual physical model used could have any combination of these elements, based on a business's individual needs:

➤ Central Publisher, multiple Subscribers

➤ Multiple Publishers, multiple Subscribers

➤ Multiple Publishers, single Subscriber

➤ Single Publisher, remote Distributor

Central Publisher, Multiple Subscribers

In this form of replication, the data originates at the publishing server, and that original data is sent to multiple Subscribers via the Distributor. Depending on the form of replication used, changes to the data at the destination servers can enable updates to be propagated back to the Publisher and other Subscribers, or it can be treated as read-only data, in which updates occur only at the Publisher. This type of scenario is typically used when a company has a master catalog at the headquarters and has many different Subscribers located elsewhere.

An advantage of this configuration is that multiple copies of the data from a central server are available for user processing on multiple machines. Data can be distributed to the locations where it is needed. With this form of replication, data can be brought closer to the user, and the load on a single server can be reduced. Expensive bandwidth can also be utilized in an improved manner.

Multiple Publishers, Multiple Subscribers

In this replication, every server publishes a particular set of rows that relate to it and subscribes to the publications that all the other servers are publishing so that each of them can receive data and send data. This form is typically used in a distributed warehouse environment with inventory spread out among different locations, or any other situation in which the data being held at each location-specific server needs to be delivered to the other servers so that each location has a complete set of data.

For this form of replication, the correct database design is crucial to having each server publish and subscribe to the correct information. The table structure for the data involved in the publication is usually implemented with a compound primary key or unique index, although it is possible to use an identity or another algorithm that enables each location to be uniquely identified within the entire table. One portion of the key is an identifier for the location, whereas the second element is the data identifier.

Multiple Publishers, Single Subscriber

In the "multiple Publishers, single Subscriber" scenario, a server subscribes to publications on some or all of a number of other publishing servers. This is needed when overall data is required at only one site, possibly the headquarters. Data can be collected from widely dispersed areas, and the central location, the Subscriber, would end up with a master database from all the Publishers combined.

Single Publisher, Remote Distributor

Replication does not need to include a Distributor residing on the same server or even within close proximity to the Publisher. Instead, the machine handling the distribution can be implemented as a totally separate segment. This is practical when you need to free the publishing server from having to perform the distribution task and minimize costs that can be incurred over long-distance or overseas network connections. Data can also be replicated faster and delivered to many Subscribers at a much lower cost while minimizing the load on the Publisher. In situations in which the connection between the Publisher and the Subscriber is over a slow link or over high-cost connections, a remote Distributor should be used to lower the cost and increase data transfer rates.

The individual roles of each server are implemented in all types of replication; the physical configuration does not dictate the type of replication used. The next section examines the types of replication and their implementation.

Types of Replication

Each model provides different capabilities for distributing data and database objects. There are many considerations for selecting a replication type or determining whether replication is a suitable technique for data distribution. The many considerations to determine the suitability of each of the models include transactional consistency, the Subscriber's capability or lack of capability to update data, latency, administration, site autonomy, performance, security, update schedule, and available data sources. Each of these is defined as replication, and they are discussed through the next several sections.

Other data distribution techniques that don't involve replication can offer a different set of features but may not provide for the flexibility offered by replication. To determine which replication type is best suited to your needs, consider the three primary factors: site autonomy, transactional consistency, and latency. These three considerations are illustrated in Figure 4.4, which also compares and contrasts data distribution techniques.

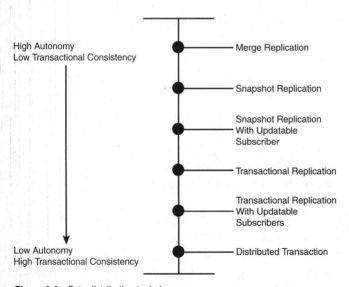

High Autonomy
Low Transactional Consistency
— Merge Replication

— Snapshot Replication

— Snapshot Replication With Updatable Subscriber

— Transactional Replication

— Transactional Replication With Updatable Subscribers

Low Autonomy
High Transactional Consistency
— Distributed Transaction

Figure 4.4 Data distribution techniques.

When you are in the position of selecting between the data distribution techniques, there are essentially three questions to be asked: How soon is data needed to agree at all replication locations (latency)? How much site independence is required in processing changes to the data (autonomy)? How consistent does data need to remain after changes are made? The answer to each of these questions will determine the approach used.

Site Autonomy in Replication

Site autonomy measures the effect of your site's operation on another site. A site having full autonomy is completely independent of all other sites, meaning that it can function without even being connected to any other site. High site autonomy can be achieved in SQL Server replication where it would not be possible using other data distribution techniques. Not all replication configurations achieve autonomy; such high site autonomy can be seen best with merge replication.

Site autonomy directly affects transactional consistency. To achieve an environment that both is autonomous and has a high degree of transactional consistency, the data definition must provide a mechanism to differentiate one site from the other. A compound primary key, for example, in a "central Subscriber" or "multiple Publisher, multiple Subscriber" scenario, allows autonomy while achieving transactional consistency. If an implementation enables each site to update the same data, it will always have some degree of transaction inconsistency or at least a delay before consistency is achieved.

Transactional Consistency in Replication

Transactional consistency is a measure of changes made to data, specifically those changes that remain in place without being rolled back. Changes can get rolled back due to conflicts, and this will affect user changes and other user activities. In replication you have multiple distinct copies of your data, and if you allow updates to each copy, it is possible for different copies of a piece of data to be changed differently. If this situation is allowed, as is the case in some forms of replication, you have imperfect (low) transactional consistency. If you prevent two copies from changing independently, as is the case with a distributed transaction, you have the highest level of transactional consistency.

In a distributed transaction, the application and the controlling server work together to control updates to multiple sites. Two-phase commits implemented in some forms of replication also help. The two phases used are preparation and committal. Each server is prepared for the update to take place, and when all sites are ready, the change is committed at the same time on all servers. After all sites have implemented the change, transactional consistency is restored.

Latency in Replication

Latency can be thought of as how long data in the Subscriber has to wait before being updated from the copy of the data on the Publisher. Several factors contribute to latency, but it is essentially the length of time it takes changes to travel from the Publisher to the Distributor and then from the Distributor to the Publisher. If there is no need for the data to be the same, at the same time, in all Publishers and Subscribers, then the latency resident within a replication strategy will not negatively affect an application. A two-phase commit, as SQL Server implements through the use of immediate updating, can minimize latency on updates coming from the Subscriber, but it has no effect on updates sent from the Publisher. Latency can be affected by the workload on the Publisher and Distributor, the speed and congestion of the network, and the size of the updates being transported.

Each type of replication offers advantages and disadvantages. You must select the type based on the requirements of the business application. The three types of replication—snapshot, transactional, and merge—move data using different principles.

Use of Snapshot Replication

Snapshot replication distributes data and database objects by copying the entire contents of the published items via the Distributor and passing them on to the Subscriber exactly as they appear at a specific moment in time, without monitoring updates. A snapshot is stored on the Distributor, which encapsulates data of published tables and database objects; this snapshot is then taken to the Subscriber database via the Distribution agent.

Snapshot replication is advantageous when replicated data is infrequently updated and modified. A snapshot strategy is preferable over others when data is to be updated in a batch. This does not mean that only a small amount of data is updated, but rather that data is updated in large quantities at distant intervals. Because data is replicated at a specific point in time and not replicated frequently, this type of replication is good for online catalogs, price lists, and the like, in which the decision to implement replication is independent of how recent data is.

Snapshot replication offers high levels of site autonomy. It also offers a great degree of transactional consistency because transactions are enforced at the Publisher. Transactional consistency also depends on whether you are allowing Updating Subscribers, and what type (immediate or queued).

Transactional Replication

Transactional replication is defined as the moving of transactions captured from the transaction log of the publishing server database and applied to the Subscriber's database. The transactional replication process monitors data changes made on the Publisher.

Transactional replication captures incremental modifications that were made to data in the published table. The committed transactions do not directly change the data on the Subscriber but are instead stored on the Distributor. These transactions held in distribution tables on the Distributor are sent to the Subscriber. Because the transactions on the Distributor are stored in an orderly fashion, each Subscriber acquires data in the same order as is in the Publisher.

When replicating a publication using transactional replication, you can choose to replicate an entire table or just part of a table using a method referred to as filtering. You can also select all stored procedures on the database or just certain ones that are to be replicated as articles within the publication. Replication of stored procedures ensures that the definitions they provide are in each setting where the data is to be found. Processes that are defined by the stored procedures can then be run at the Subscriber. Because the procedures are being replicated, any changes to these procedures are also replicated. Replication of a stored procedure makes the procedure available for execution on the local server.

Merge Replication

Merge replication is the process of transferring data from the Publisher to the Subscriber, enabling the Publisher and Subscriber to update data while they are connected or disconnected, and then merge the updates after they both are connected, providing virtual independence. Merge replication therefore allows the most flexibility and adds the most autonomy to the replication process. Merge replication is also the most complex replication because it enables the Publisher and Subscriber to work virtually independently. The Publisher and Subscriber can combine their results at any certain time and combine or merge their updated results.

The Snapshot agent and the Merge agent help in carrying out the process of merge replication. The Snapshot agent is used for the initial synchronization of the databases. The Merge agent then applies the snapshot; after that, the job of the Merge agent is to increment the data changes and resolve any conflicts according to the rules configured.

Conflicts are likely to occur with merge replication. Conflicts occur when more than one site updates the same record. This happens when two users concurrently update or modify the same record with different values. When a conflict occurs, SQL Server has to choose a single value to use. It resolves the conflict based on either the site priority on the database site or a custom conflict resolver. You could give more priority to, for instance, a user in the HR department than one from the sales department. When a conflict is detected, it is resolved immediately after the conflict resolver is executed. A conflict occurs when the Publisher and Subscriber have both changed the record since they last shared a common version. Conflicts can be record based or column based. The default is column based.

What has been presented in this chapter outlines the basics of replication, and although we have discussed many of the principles and strategies, the actual configurations can be quite involved. As you have seen, there are many design considerations to be considered, and the administration over the replication sites can be considerable.

If you are to successfully implement replication, you must get much further into the depths of the agents and implementations. These techniques fall under the scope of the administration processed and are thus out of the scope of this book. For additional assistance or information, you can find a considerable amount of data within SQL Server Books Online, as well as the Microsoft Web Resources.

The only remaining physical design to discuss would be the implementation of distributed transactions. Transactions in general and their implementation over distributed servers are discussed in Chapter 6, "Programming Business Logic."

Exam Prep Questions

1. You are working for a large international organization that supplies packaging materials for companies that require custom commercial designs. The number of products is becoming too large for the current computer system to handle, and you need to provide a solution that will spread the load over the current server and a new machine coming into the system. Queries need to be performed over a wide variety of products, and there is no predictable pattern to the queries. What is an appropriate technique to implement the changes?

   ❑ A. Configure replication using the new machine as a Subscriber and the original machine as the Publisher/Distributor to balance the workload.

   ❑ B. Separate the table into two smaller tables and place one table on each server. Configure a partitioned view and appropriate constraints on each of the machines.

   ❑ C. Implement multiserver clustering so that each of the two servers can respond to data activities, thus achieving a balanced workload.

   ❑ D. Configure log shipping on both servers to have a copy of the data on each of the servers and propagate all changes to the alternate machine.

   Answer: B. This is a perfect example of where partitioning a table into two smaller objects enables you to use two machines to help reduce the load on the overall application. Remember that failover clustering is the only form of clustering supported by SQL. It therefore does not actually reduce the load; it only assists in obtaining an around-the-clock operation. Log shipping assists in offloading query load, but it does little to reduce update load because it leaves the second server in a read-only state. Merge replication may enable updates to span many servers, but the associated overhead and data latency make it a less than desirable alternative. For more information, see the "Partitioned Views" section of this chapter.

2. You are the administrator of a SQL Server 2000 computer. The server contains your company's Accounts database. Hundreds of users access the database each day. You have been experiencing power interruptions, and you want to protect the physical integrity of the Accounts database. You do not want to slow down server operations. What should you do?

   ❑ A. Enable the torn page detection database option for each database.

   ❑ B. Disable write caching on all disk controllers.

   ❑ C. Create a database maintenance plan to check database integrity and make repairs each night.

   ❑ D. Ensure that the write caching disk controllers have battery backups.

Answer: D. Good controllers suitable for database use will have a battery backup. The battery should be regularly tested under controlled circumstances. Disabling caching if currently in place is likely to affect performance, as will enabling torn page detection. Torn page detection might help point out whether data is being corrupted because of failures. A maintenance plan is recommended, although it is not an entire solution in its own right.

3. You are the sole IT person working in a small branch office for a non-profit organization that deals with natural resource conservation issues. A noncritical database is maintained on the database server. You have been given the task of configuring appropriate database properties that would allow for a minimum use of execution time and storage resources. Which of the following set of properties is most appropriate?

- ❏ A. Full recovery, auto shrink, torn page detection
- ❏ B. Bulk recovery, auto shrink, single user
- ❏ C. Simple recovery, auto close, auto shrink
- ❏ D. Simple recovery, auto shrink, single user
- ❏ E. Bulk recovery, auto close, auto shrink

Answer: C. Simple recovery uses the least amount of log space for recording changes to the database. Full recovery uses the most space because it fully logs any bulk operations. Bulk recovery represents a midpoint between the two. Auto close frees up resources at the earliest possible point during process execution, and auto shrink minimizes the space used in the file system by periodically reducing the files when there is too much unused space. For more information, see the section "Recovery Interval (Advanced)."

4. Tom needs to achieve optimum performance within his application. He is examining different view technologies as a way to improve data access performance. He is currently managing a database that is replicated between five servers (for load balancing) and contains customer information for six sales divisions. The Customer table currently contains a consolidated list of 100,000,000 customer records. What could Tom try to implement to improve server performance?

- ❏ A. Indexed views
- ❏ B. Partitioned views
- ❏ C. Complex views
- ❏ D. Full outer views

Answer: B. Partitioned views, and specifically distributed partitioned views, may improve the data access for Tom's database. Because a large number of rows could be separated by sales division per server (with one server maintaining information for two divisions), his database tables may be ideal candidates for distributed partitioned views. For more information about partitioned views, see the section "Partitioned Views."

5. You are the administrator of a SQL Server 2000 computer at your company's warehouse. All product orders are shipped out from this warehouse. Orders are received at 30 sales offices throughout the country. Each sales office offers a range of products specific to its own region. Each sales office contains one SQL Server 2000 computer. These servers connect to the warehouse through dial-up connections once a day. Each sales office needs data pertaining to only its own region. You need to replicate inventory data from the server at the warehouse to the servers at the sales offices. You have decided to use transactional replication. You want to minimize the amount of time needed to replicate the data. Which actions should you take? (Choose three.)

- ❑ A. Create one publication for each Subscriber.
- ❑ B. Create one publication for all Subscribers.
- ❑ C. Enable horizontal partitioning.
- ❑ D. Enable vertical partitioning.
- ❑ E. Use pull subscriptions.
- ❑ F. Use push subscriptions.

Answer: A, C, E. It is necessary to design the structure of the database so that the publications can include an article specific to each location. This will mean having a compound primary key containing regional information and an article for each Subscriber that is horizontally partitioned based on the region. Because the connection is initiated by the Subscriber dial-up, you must also set up pull subscriptions. For more information, see the section "Types of Replication."

6. You configure transactional replication on the Headquarters server and make numerous publications available. Later, a member of the Sales department subscribes to one of the publications. However, the only article from the publication that he needs is MonthlyRevenues. He needs data quickly and needs to avoid receiving the redundant data that would come from subscribing to the whole publication. What can be done to solve this dilemma?

- ❑ A. Change the style of replication being used to snapshot replication.
- ❑ B. Filter the publication so that only MonthlyRevenues can be replicated; push this subscription to the Sales department.
- ❑ C. Create a new publication that contains only a single article, MonthlyRevenues.
- ❑ D. There is no way to solve this problem. He needs to subscribe to the whole publication.

Answer: C. Of the options offered, creating a new publication is the best choice because it is the only option that will work. Creating filters can be done only vertically (columns) or horizontally (rows). A more experienced individual could use stored procedures to subscribe to a single article, but this option is not present in the answer choices. For more information, consult the "Partitioned Views" section.

7. Transactional replication offers low site autonomy, and merge replication offers high site autonomy. What is meant by "site autonomy"?
   - ❑ A. The measuring of the consistency of transactions
   - ❑ B. How long data in the Subscriber can stay without being renewed
   - ❑ C. The independence of one site in relation to others
   - ❑ D. How many Subscribers and Publishers are involved in a replication process

Answer: C. Site autonomy refers to one site's independence from all other sites for processing modifications. Autonomy measures the effect of your site's operation on another. A site that has full autonomy is completely independent of all other sites, meaning that it can function without even being connected to another site. See "Types of Replication" for more information on autonomy and other considerations.

8. You work in a finance company where changes to the values in the Finance table are made quickly, and thus you want these incremental changes to be propagated to Subscribers as they occur. These Subscribers are always connected to the Publisher with a reliable connection. Which type of replication is used when you want updated changes at the server in almost real-time?
   - ❑ A. Snapshot replication
   - ❑ B. Snapshot replication with Updating Subscribers
   - ❑ C. Transactional replication
   - ❑ D. Merge replication

Answer: C. Transactional replication is a good solution when you want updated changes at the server in almost real-time. Because of the frequency of the changes, snapshot replication is not a good solution. Merge replication can be set up in a single direction but is generally used only when the Publisher and Subscribers make updates while connected or disconnected. See the section "Transactional Replication" for more details.

9. You and Josh are replicating data to multiple Subscribers who need to update data at various times and propagate those changes to the Publisher and to other Subscribers. These Subscribers need to be able to make changes offline and later synchronize data; this means that they need a replication strategy that offers high autonomy. Which type of replication offers almost complete site autonomy?

   ❑   A.   Snapshot replication

   ❑   B.   Snapshot replication and transactional replication

   ❑   C.   Merge replication

   ❑   D.   Transactional replication

   ❑   E.   Transactional replication with Updating Subscribers

   Answer: C. Merge replication allows the most flexibility and adds the most autonomy to the replication process, enabling the Publisher and Subscriber to work virtually independently. The Publisher and Subscriber can combine their results and updates at any time. See the section "Merge Replication" for more details.

10. Your company has just purchased an accounting application from a vendor. The application stores its data in a database named Accounting. The tables in this database contain columns that function as primary keys, but PRIMARY KEY and FOREIGN KEY constraints are not used.

   You need to replicate data from this database to another SQL Server computer. This server will use the replicated data to generate reports. Most reports will run each month, but the accounting department needs to have the ability to run reports at any time. Reports should be accurate through the last full working day.

   You cannot make any changes to the database, but you need to implement replication. Which two actions should you take? (Each correct answer represents part of the solution.)

   ❑   A.   Implement merge replication.

   ❑   B.   Implement snapshot replication.

   ❑   C.   Implement transactional replication.

   ❑   D.   Schedule replication to run continuously.

   ❑   E.   Schedule replication to run during off-peak hours.

   Answer: B, E. Because there is no primary key and no other changes to the database can be performed, the only alternative that can be used is snapshot replication. Because the data does not need to be up-to-the-minute, a scheduled data refresh occurring overnight or during other nonpeak times is most appropriate. See the section "Use of Snapshot Replication" for more details.

11. Your company has just purchased an accounting application from a vendor. The application stores its data in a database named Accounting. The tables in this database contain columns that function as primary keys, but PRIMARY KEY and FOREIGN KEY constraints are not used.

   You need to replicate data from this database to another SQL Server computer. This server will use the replicated data to generate reports infrequently. Most reports will run each month, but the accounting department needs to have the ability to run reports at any time. Reports should be accurate through the last full working day.

   Disk space is at a premium and you want to conserve space as much as possible. Which action should you take?

   ❑ A. Use transactional replication.
   ❑ B. Use snapshot replication.
   ❑ C. Use a linked server for reporting.
   ❑ D. Use DTS to the reporting server.
   ❑ E. Use XML to the reporting server.

   Answer: C. Use of a linked server will allow for heterogeneous data access without taking up any additional disk space. The other solutions use some disk space; without this restriction, all the other solutions are possible.

Retrieving and Modifying Data

Terms you'll need to understand:

- ✓ BCP
- ✓ DTS
- ✓ **OPENXML**
- ✓ **SELECT**
- ✓ **WHERE**
- ✓ **GROUP BY**
- ✓ **HAVING**
- ✓ **ORDER BY**
- ✓ **COMPUTE**

- ✓ XML
- ✓ Schema
- ✓ Cursor
- ✓ Lock
- ✓ **INTO**
- ✓ **INSERT**
- ✓ **DELETE**
- ✓ **UPDATE**

Techniques you'll need to master:

- ✓ Importing and exporting data
- ✓ Manipulation of data from various sources

- ✓ Data retrieval, filtering, grouping
- ✓ Summarizing data
- ✓ Data modifications
- ✓ Utilizing XML options

Introduction

We now turn our attention to the concept of data retrieval and modification. This is a very diverse topic. We will begin with the fundamentals of SQL coding, the SELECT statement, and progress through to one of the most recently added features, extracting data through the use of XML. Also, because the same coding mechanisms are used for updating data as are used in retrieval, we will conclude our discussion and the chapter itself with the coding mechanisms of the UPDATE, INSERT, and DELETE statements.

Moving a Mountain of Data

There are several ways of moving large amounts of data, either within a single server or between servers. Importing and exporting tasks vary in SQL Server, and each task has an appropriate implementation. The first technique we will discuss is a more traditional mechanism for moving data, BCP. A closely related technique involves the use of BULK INSERT, a relatively new feature that's really just an extension of the BCP functionality.

Backup/restore is also a common method used for moving data. In this approach, data can be backed up, placed onto CD, and easily transported to another location for restore. This technique is also common when a test or training copy of the data is desired within the same server where the "live" data resides.

Another technique, which actually represents several different techniques, involves the use of replication. Replication of data is a feature of SQL Server specifically used to create copies of data. Completed copies, partial copies, and warm backups all use data replication as the primary method of implementation.

Data Transformation Services (DTS) is probably the most full-featured and flexible technique for moving data. It is usually implemented in instances in which data is to be massaged during the movement of the information. Whether it be minor processing of the information or something more lucrative, the DTS tools are quite diverse and very capable of handling any such task.

The previously mentioned techniques are the most common, but there are also some custom techniques involving a little coding and scheduling of jobs that can be used. Such is the case when loading data cubes into data warehouses in preparation for data analysis. With so many different techniques available, it is important to know the advantages and disadvantages of each method. So in the next several sections we will look into each means to see where each is most appropriately put into service.

Mass Movements of Data via BCP

The Bulk Copy Program (BCP) is most often used when the database can be taken out of production temporarily to import large amounts of data. Of course, BCP also allows for the export of data, in which case the database can remain online. Using BCP for importing data is extremely fast. As the name indicates, BCP is a process used to copy large amounts of data.

BCP is not a specific implementation of SQL Server. The BCP command-line tool is often used from batch files. The command-prompt window is often forgotten as an execution environment. In the current world of graphics, colors, pictures, and automation, it is easy to become intimidated with a black empty window that contains only a blinking cursor. In fact, many end users never see this perspective on the operating system as shown in Figure 5.1. In fact, however, this window is pretty easy to use if you need quick access to the operating system to execute applications.

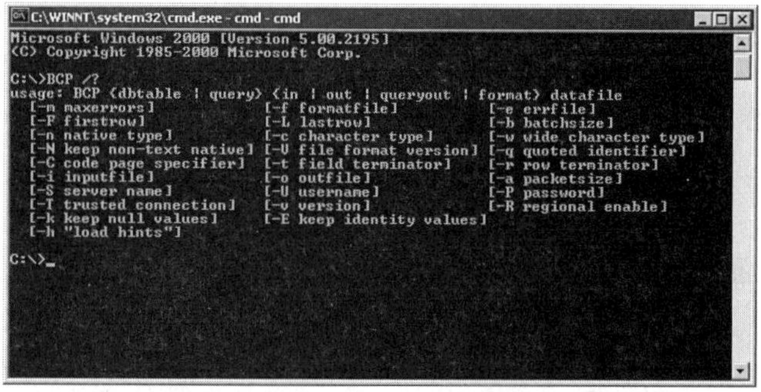

Figure 5.1   Command-line entry window with BCP assistance.

BCP's biggest asset is its speed. It moves information into and out of a database using data files. BCP is normally used to do one of the following:

➤ Bulk copy from a table, view, or the resultset into a native-mode data file in the same format as the table or view.

➤ Bulk copy from a table, view, or the resultset into a data file in a format other than the one that the table or view is in. In this instance, a format file is created that defines the characteristics of each column. If all columns are converted to character format, the resulting file is called a character-mode data file.

▶ Bulk copy from a data file into a table or view. A format file can be used to determine the layout of the data file.

▶ Load data into program variables and then import the data into a table or view a row at a time.

As with most command-line operations, a listing of options can be provided easily using the /? command switch. Knowing the listing of options, or switches as they are more appropriately known, doesn't always make it easier to use the command. BCP has several unique standard implementations, each using a separate set of switches.

As stated, BCP is best suited to loading data into a database quickly. BCP does not create tables. You must have a table set up and waiting for BCP before you run BCP. This is the basic syntax of the BCP operation:

```
bcp <table> <in or out> <file> <security information> <format information>
```

To avoid unnecessary confusion, we will avoid a lot of the specifics of each implementation and variation of the coding. Mastering all the options of the BCP command will require a lot of practice and additional research beyond the scope of this book. The following represents a simple export of data:

```
bcp "Northwind.dbo.Products" out "Products.txt" -c -q -U"sa" -P"password"
```

Assuming a very simple password for the sa account of password, the command will create a text file from the Products table of the Northwind database.

Although BCP is a long-standing tool available to use with SQL Server, you are not likely to see it on the exam other than by definition of how it is used. You are not likely to be asked for the specifics of its command coding structure. Focus on knowing where to implement BCP and knowing the available BULK INSERT options.

For large files with more than a couple thousand rows, perhaps, you should turn on the SELECT INTO/BULKCOPY option for the database, or set the database recovery mode to SIMPLE. This option disables all transaction log backups while they are turned on, and you must do a full backup to get transaction log backups to work afterward. The option affects certain operations, namely those involving SELECT INTO and BULK COPY, by changing how transaction logging works. If you do set the recovery mode to SIMPLE, it is recommended that you turn it back to FULL when you have completed your process.

BCP is a pretty powerful tool, but it's kind of difficult to use when you need to just read a file from within SQL Server as part of a script or scheduled job. It sure would be nice if there were a T-SQL equivalent.

The BULK INSERT statement implements part of BCP inside SQL Server, so it has all the speed of BCP with an easier-to-use interface. BULK INSERT will allow for the copying of a data file into a database table or view with a user-specified format. However, the BULK INSERT statement cannot copy data from a SQL Server out to a data file. The BULK INSERT statement allows you to copy data one way only. BULK INSERT copies data into SQL Server using the functionality of BCP from within SQL Server via a T-SQL statement. Although it uses most of the same options, it doesn't need to know which server to use or what security to use because you use it from within T-SQL, so it runs on that server with the security context with which you logged in. Both of the BCP variations require a lot of command knowledge. BCP can be rather complex and it is worth taking a look at how to import and export data using the graphical tools.

Using Backup/Restore for More Than Recovery

Although the most common use of the BACKUP and RESTORE operations (DUMP and LOAD were the previous versions) is for safeguarding data, the two commands are also useful in moving large amounts of data. In particular, when a set of data is needed for testing or training purposes, the backing up of one database can be restored into another. This is a quick and thorough technique for gaining a copy of the original data for testing.

 Use Backup/Restore to move copies of data over long distances, particularly when there is a large amount of data to be moved. A CD/DVD can be couriered faster than electronic transmission over a slow WAN link.

A complete backup can be restored into the same database for recovery, but it can also be restored to a different database or server to create a duplicate set of data. In this event the data will need to be refreshed on a periodic basis. The data refresh of a test or training database can be scheduled. The restore operation of data into the test database needs to be scheduled to occur after the backup operation of the live database.

A restore operation can be scheduled through the use of the T-SQL Restore command, the basics of which are easily implemented. If you are using the restore operation to overwrite a different database, you will need to use a few more options as given in the following code:

```
Restore FileListOnly From Backups
Restore Database Back From Backups
 With Move 'LiveData.mdf' To 'Back.mdf',
 Move 'LiveData.ldf' To 'Back.ldf',
 Replace
```

The initial restore operation obtains the list of files on a backup device. This is needed if you're restoring from a device not originally associated with the database being restored into. The second restore will perform the actual operation, moving the files that were originally backed up, and will replace the database, overwriting the previous contents.

Data Movement with Manipulation

Basic imports and exports of data can be performed using the Data Transformation Services Import/Export Wizard. This tool uses SQL Server DTS to copy data into and out of SQL Server using nice, easy-to-understand graphical tools. In addition to working with SQL Server, DTS can copy from any data source that is ODBC compliant to any other data source. This functionality means that data can be combined from all sources regardless of the program used to process and store the data originally.

The only really tricky part of the entire wizard is the transformations. DTS enables you to write transformations in VBScript that can make simple changes to data, such as formatting or localizing. By clicking on the Transform window, you can go into the transformation and change the VBScript so that it changes the data format.

After you have completed the definition via the wizard, you can save the package for future use—and this is only the beginning. The DTS editing environment allows you to turn a simple input/output operation into a complex business process that can be repeated and scheduled to occur on a regular basis.

There is little purpose behind the storage of data if you can't get the data out of the system in a meaningful manner. The SELECT statement is the basis for most of the activity performed in data retrieval. It is the first statement for a SQL developer to master, because its use is varied and can involve many options.

Selecting Information from the Data

After data is in the database, it is inevitable that the data will need to be accessed, changed, and reported on. To perform these basic operations, you need to be able to apply the programming constructs of Structured Query Language (SQL)—specifically, Microsoft's implementation referred to as Transact-SQL (T-SQL). The most common of these statements performs the basis for getting data out of the system: the SELECT statement.

SELECT statements can be made very complex with the use of options that can join many tables together and with functions that can calculate and summarize data at the same time. SELECT statements also can often be as simple as one line of code that retrieves the requested data. The complete SELECT syntax is very involved with many optional portions. The complete syntax reference can be found in SQL Server Books Online (BOL) under "SELECT, SELECT (described)." Many of the options are used only under special circumstances.

To start out simple, you will often be retrieving all the data from a particular table. Even if the final query is not intended to get all the data, you can often begin the data analysis by examining all the rows and columns of data in a particular table. The following example retrieves the employee data from the Northwind database:

```
SELECT * FROM MYSERVER.Northwind.dbo.Employees
```

Note the asterisk used to obtain all columns from the Employees table. It is also worth noting the use of the four-part name (Server.Owner. Database.Object). This name includes the server name, MYSERVER, database name, Northwind, the owner name, dbo, and the name of the table itself, Employees.

Four-part names are used to perform queries when a one-part name of the table itself does not sufficiently qualify the table being queried. If the query is being executed within the scope of the server itself with the Northwind database in use and you are the owner or the owner is dbo, then the four-part name is not necessary. There are therefore several valid variations on queries for the Employees table. Each of the following will produce the same results:

```
SELECT * FROM Employees

SELECT * FROM dbo.Employees

SELECT * FROM Northwind.dbo.Employees

SELECT * FROM Northwind..Employees
```

Although often a query will go after all the data in a table, there are a considerable number of options available for the query statement. You can choose some of the columns of the table, provide record-level conditions to limit the number of rows returned, put the output into groups, provide group-level conditions to selectively choose the groups, put the output into a sorted order, and produce calculated results. You can also get into some very complex queries through the use of JOIN, UNION, and subquery operations.

 The clauses of a **SELECT** query must be provided in the correct order to have valid syntax. As a mechanism for remembering the order, you can use the following acronym and phrase: SIFWGHOC—Some Infinitely Funny Winos Get High On Champagne. **SELECT**, **INTO**, **FROM**, **WHERE**, **GROUP BY**, **HAVING**, **ORDER BY**, **COMPUTE (BY)**.

The exam objectives require you to know how to access data in different ways, providing for different looks into the data with user-friendly views and other reporting methods from the data source. Most cases don't want the extraction of all the data from the tables. Usually queries want to limit the number of columns and rows displayed from the database. This will provide the functionality to meet most scenarios while providing for improved performance and response times to the user. You need to limit and specifically apply conditions over the data that is transmitted to the user interface.

Narrowing the Scope of Data Retrieval

The first portion of the SELECT statement identifies which columns will come from a table. When specifying column names, be sure to use a comma-delimited list and don't place a comma after the final column name. When specifying column names, you can use an asterisk (*), designating that all columns are to be returned from the specified table or tables. The asterisk can be provided by itself as seen previously or supplied in addition to columns selected. The following query selects a few of the columns from the Employees table:

```
SELECT EmployeeID, FirstName, LastName, Title FROM Employees
```

You can optionally supply column headers to give a user-friendly listing of the data. By default, the column headers that are displayed in the resultset are the same as the columns specified in the column select list, such as FirstName and LastName. But why not change this column header to something more readable? You can change the name of a resultset column by specifying the keyword AS, this being the traditional SQL-92 ANSI standard. Changing the column name with an equals sign (=) or implied assignment is also an alternative syntax choice. The following example illustrates the use of column aliasing (of course, you would normally use only one of the three techniques and the industry standard is SQL-92 ANSI):

```
SELECT EmployeeID AS 'Employee ID',
    'First Name' = FirstName,
    LastName 'Last Name',     Title
    FROM Employees
```

```
SELECT EmployeeID AS 'Employee ID',
     'First Name' AS FirstName,
     LastName AS 'Last Name',
     Title
     FROM Employees
```

Notice that the previous column aliases have been enclosed within single quotation marks. This enclosure needs to be made when the column alias includes spaces. The alias name needs to be enclosed within brackets when the alias is a reserved SQL Server keyword.

Sometimes you need to show two columns as one by combining two columns together. When you do this, you are using a method called string concatenation. Concatenation can be thought of as joining strings together just as you can combine words into phrases. The operator used to perform the concatenation is the plus (+) sign. You can create a singular name column by combining the last name and first name values:

```
SELECT TitleOfCourtesy + ' ' + FirstName + ' ' + LastName
     AS 'Employee Name',
                 Title
     FROM Employees
```

As you can see, multiple strings can be concatenated together, creating more meaningful content. When SELECT features are used in this manner, information is beginning to be pulled out of the raw data. In fact, the SELECT statement with the addition of the INTO clause can create a table drawn from the original table. In this manner the newly created table can contain a subset of columns and/or rows.

The SELECT INTO statement can perform a data insertion and create the table for the data in a single operation. The new table is populated with the data provided by a FROM clause. The SELECT INTO statement creates a new table with a structure identical to that of the columns provided in the query. It then copies all data that meets the WHERE condition into this newly created table. It is possible to combine data from several tables or views into one table, and again a variety of sources can be used. The following example creates a new table within the database that would contain only two columns:

```
SELECT TitleOfCourtesy + ' ' + FirstName + ' ' + LastName
     AS 'Employee Name',
                 Title
     INTO HRTable
     FROM Employees
```

The INTO clause creates a table, so it is important that the table does not exist when you're using the command. If the desire is to add data to an existing table, an INSERT INTO operation must be performed. We will look at the INSERT statement later in the chapter. An INTO operation is often used to denormalize data. By definition, data will be duplicated into another location. The second table is often used in circumstances in which it is easier and/or more efficient to work with a subset of the data. This duplication is purposely performed but some queries can result in unwanted duplicates.

Use of the DISTINCT clause eliminates duplicate rows from any resultset. A SELECT query may return records with equal values, but using DISTINCT eliminates duplicates and leaves only singular values in the resultset. You might use the DISTINCT keyword when you need to know only whether a value exists, rather than how many records of a value exist. This DISTINCT option, when specified, selects only the values that are unique throughout a row. See Figure 5.2 for a contrast between listing all data values and listing only DISTINCT data values.

Figure 5.2 Listing **DISTINCT** cities.

The DISTINCT keyword is optional when calculations are performed using SUM, AVG, and COUNT. When DISTINCT is used, duplicate values are eliminated before the calculation is performed. Limiting the number of rows returned from queries is common and serves a number of purposes. This narrowing of data is referred to as horizontal filtering.

The WHERE clause is used to limit the number of rows in the resultset based on defined restrictions. These restrictions are specified as conditional arguments, such as Salary>10000, LastName LIKE 'G%', or State = 'FL'. SQL Server will always execute the WHERE action first to discover which rows should be looked at before other operations needed by a given SELECT clause. This acts as a layer of filtration in a basic SELECT query.

Similar to the WHERE clause is the HAVING clause. In a SELECT statement these clauses control the rows from the source tables that are used to build the resultset. WHERE and HAVING are filters. They specify a series of search conditions, and only those rows that meet the terms of the search conditions are used to build the resultset. To address how these clauses are used, we must understand the conditions that can be applied within these clauses.

Conditional Filtering of Data

Filtering data is used for determining the data to be selected based on conditional requirements. Essentially, all conditions come down to one of three possible outcomes. If two values are compared, the result is positive, negative, or equal (greater than, less than, or equal to).

Operators play an important part in determining the content of any conditional operations. An operator is a symbol specifying an action performed on one or more expressions. In SQL Server these operators are divided into a few elementary categories, as presented in the next few paragraphs. Each operator category represents a piece of functionality that provides many operators. In some instances there are several dozen operator choices.

Comparison Operators

Comparison operators can be used with character, numeric, or date data expressions. Their purpose is to determine a Boolean result based on the comparison of the expressions. Table 5.1 lists all comparison operators that are valid in SQL Server.

Table 5.1	Comparison Operators
Operator	Meaning
<	Less than
>	Greater than
=	Equal to
<=	Less than or equal to
>=	Greater than or equal to
!=	Not equal to
<>	Not equal to
!<	Not less than
!>	Not greater than

Whereas comparison operators evaluate the differences between two or more values, arithmetic operators aid in processing mathematical functions against values.

Arithmetic Operators

Arithmetic operators perform mathematical operations on two expressions. A complete listing of the available arithmetic operators and their uses is shown in Table 5.2.

Table 5.2	Arithmetic Operators
Operator	**Meaning**
+ (Add)	Addition
- (Subtract)	Subtraction
* (Multiply)	Multiplication
/ (Divide)	Division
% (Modulo)	Returns the integer remainder of a division

Although these operators usually perform actions against numeric data, the plus (+) and minus (-) operators can also be used to perform arithmetic operations on date values.

Logical Operators

Logical operators are also known as Boolean operators. The three logical operators are AND, OR, and NOT. Their meanings are pretty straightforward: AND adds an additional filter condition to the one specified and returns TRUE only when both or all conditions specified are met. The OR logical operator adds another filter condition to the existing condition as well, but it returns TRUE when either condition is met. NOT tells SQL to get everything in the query except for what it has specified. An example of the three operators in use is provided in Figure 5.3.

Brackets can significantly alter the results of operations that use logical operators. Test all conditions and alter the precedence by using brackets. According to the order of operations, bracketed comparisons are performed first. The logical operators are evaluated in the order: () first, then NOT, then AND, and finally OR.

Bitwise and Unary Operators

Bitwise operators are used on int, smallint, or tinyint data. The - (bitwise NOT) operator can also use bit data. All bitwise operators perform an operation on one or more specified integer values as translated to binary expressions within T-SQL statements. The bitwise NOT operator changes binary 1s to 0s and 0s to 1s. Bitwise operators perform bit manipulations between two expressions of any of the data types of the integer data type category. The set of operators is shown in Table 5.3.

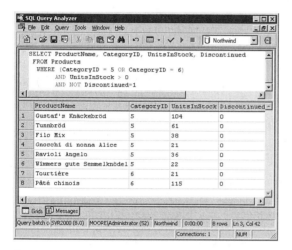

Figure 5.3 Compound conditions using the logical operators **AND**, **OR**, **NOT**.

Table 5.3	Bitwise Operators
Operator	**Meaning**
&	Bitwise **AND**
I	Bitwise **OR**
^	Bitwise exclusive **OR**
~	Bitwise **NOT**

The operands for bitwise operators can be any of the data types of the integer or binary string data type categories, with the exception that both operands cannot be any of the data types of the binary string data type category.

Unary operators (see Table 5.4) perform an operation on only one expression of any of the data types of the numeric data type category. The + (positive) and - (negative) operators can be used on any expression of any of the data types of the numeric data type category. The ~ (bitwise NOT) operator can be used only on expressions of any of the data types of the integer data type category.

Table 5.4	Unary Operators
Operator	**Meaning**
+	Value is positive
-	Value is negative
~	Returns the ones complement of the number

BETWEEN, IN, and EXISTS

Ranges can also be specified when using the WHERE clause with the help of the BETWEEN keyword. Simply put, BETWEEN provides a range of values within which the data should lie; otherwise, the data does not meet the condition. BETWEEN is inclusive, meaning that the range includes the lower value specified and the upper value specified. The following query therefore would also have the value 20 as a possibility in the results:

```
SELECT * FROM Products WHERE UnitPrice BETWEEN 10 AND 20
```

If the intent was to exclude the value 20, the query would be written like this:

```
SELECT * FROM Products WHERE UnitPrice BETWEEN 10.00 AND 19.99
```

You can also incorporate something known as a list when using the WHERE clause. Essentially, a list specifies the exact values a column may or may not take. If the record does not contain the value for the column specified in the IN list, it is not selected. IN determines whether a given value matches a set of values listed. For example:

```
SELECT * FROM Customers WHERE Country IN ('UK', 'USA')
```

This example limits the values of Country to only UK and USA. Customers who live in the countries mentioned in the IN list will be the only ones listed.

The use of IN is similar to that of EXISTS. When a subquery is introduced with the keyword EXISTS, it functions as an existence test. The WHERE clause of the outer query tests for the existence of rows returned by the subquery. The subquery does not actually produce any data; it returns a value of TRUE or FALSE. The following is an example of the use of EXISTS to find only those customers in the United States:

```
SELECT DISTINCT Pub_Name FROM Publishers
    WHERE EXISTS (SELECT * FROM titles
                            WHERE Pub_id = Publishers.Pub_id
                            AND Country = 'USA')
```

Existence tests can be useful in solving some problems, but because of the use of subqueries, the query itself is very inefficient and can usually be accomplished more efficiently by using a JOIN operation.

Similar Conditioning Using **LIKE**

You can retrieve rows that are based on portions of character strings by using the LIKE predicate. The LIKE predicate determines whether a given character string matches a specified pattern. The types of data a LIKE statement can work with are char, varchar, nvarchar, nchar, datetime, smalldatetime, and text. A pattern specified in the LIKE predicate can include regular characters and wildcard characters. During pattern matching, regular characters must exactly match the characters specified in the column value. Wildcard characters can be matched with any character or set of characters according to the wildcard character used, as shown in Table 5.5.

Table 5.5 The Wildcard Characters Allowed in T-SQL	
Character	Meaning
[ ]	Any single character within the specified range (**[f-j]**) or set (**[fghij]**)
_ (underscore)	Any single character
%	Any number of zero or more characters
[^]	Any single character not in the specified range or set

If your application repeatedly calls the LIKE predicate and performs numerous wildcard searches, you should consider using the MS Search Service if it is installed and in use on the server. Consider the value of the response time over the storage resources that the MS Search Service and full-text search capabilities require. MS Search Service is required to use full-text search. Full-text search enables a variety of powerful wildcard searches. You should avoid LIKE searches that have a % wildcard at both the beginning and the end. The following example of how to use the LIKE clause uses the % wildcard to select all customers whose CustomerID begins with the letter A:

```
SELECT CustomerID, ContactName FROM Customers
 WHERE CustomerID LIKE 'A%'
```

You can also use the NOT keyword with the LIKE predicate, which simply retrieves a query that does not contain records matching the specified elements in the LIKE clause. With character matching it is sometimes more efficient to exclude characters with the use of NOT. It is common to use a negative test in particular when looking for values that represent true data, as in NOT NULL.

Selecting Rows Based on **NULL** Values

A NULL value is a value given to a field that that has no value. Many people confuse NULL values with zero-length strings or the value zero, but such is not the case. NULL is just a fancy word for a value that is unknown. In SQL Server, you can select the desired NULL values or reject them using IS NULL or IS NOT NULL.

Many queries involving NULL tests depend on the ANSI connection settings for the session. When you SET ANSI NULLS ON, a comparison in which one or more of the expressions is NULL returns UNKNOWN as the result of the comparison. A value that is not known cannot be compared against another value. Use the IS NULL or IS NOT NULL instead to test for NULL values. T-SQL does support an extension of the traditional behavior that allows for comparison operators to return TRUE or FALSE as a comparison result. If you SET ANSI NULLS OFF, comparisons to NULL return TRUE when the value being compared against is also a NULL. The comparison returns FALSE for any other value. Regardless of the ANSI NULLS setting, NULL values are always considered equal for the purposes of the ORDER BY, GROUP BY, and DISTINCT keywords.

Putting It All in **ORDER**

Putting data in order provides for a more meaningful display of data and enables the data to be presented in a manner that meets additional reporting requirements set by most front-end applications. Data can be ordered in either ascending or descending sequence (ASC/DESC). ASC is the default and can be optionally provided with the command. DESC must be provided if a descending sequence is desired. When you are ordering rows that contain NULL values, the NULL-valued records are displayed first, provided that the default sort order is used (ASC).

ORDER BY determines the sequence of data based on column(s) selected and sequencing requested: ascending (ASC) or descending (DESC). Descending orders rows from highest to lowest; ascending orders rows from lowest to highest. Ordering can even be performed based on columns not included in the SELECT list. There is no limit to the number of items in the ORDER BY clause; however, there is a limit of 8,060 bytes.

After data selection has been determined, the actual data sent is ready for an ordering process if one has been defined. The ordering of data is optional, and if it is not present in a request, the data is sent in an order determined at the data source. Ordering data is a necessity when using the TOP condition.

Returning **TOP** rows

The TOP clause limits the number of rows returned in the resultset to a specified number or percentage at the top of a sorted range.

Select top 50: Returns the top 50 rows

Select top 50 percent: Returns the top 50% of the rows

There is an alternative to TOP. You can also limit the number of rows to return using SET ROWCOUNT N. The difference between these two is that the TOP keyword applies to the single SELECT statement in which it is specified. SET ROWCOUNT stays in effect until another SET ROWCOUNT statement is executed, such as SET ROWCOUNT 0 to turn the option off.

You can optionally specify that the TOP keyword is to use the WITH TIES option, in which case any number of records can possibly be displayed. WITH TIES displays all records that are equivalent to the last matching element. If you are looking for the top 10 employees and there is a tie for 10th between two employees, 11 or more records are displayed. If the tie is for 9th or a higher position, only 10 records are listed.

Of course, after you begin placing data into the desired order, the next thing would be to group the output and perform calculations based on the group. Grouping allows the production of subtotals and also provides more usable output in applications that require grouped output.

Displaying Groups in Output

The GROUP BY clause of the SELECT statement creates groups within the data. These groups can be used to display data in a more orderly fashion or produce more meaningful results through the use of aggregate functions.

The GROUP BY clause specifies the groups into which output is to be shown and, if aggregate functions are included, calculations of summary values are performed for each group. When GROUP BY is specified, either each column in any non-aggregate expression in the select list should be included in the GROUP BY list, or the GROUP BY expression must match exactly the select list expression.

It is important to note that if the ORDER BY clause is not specified, groups returned using the GROUP BY clause are not in any particular order. It is recommended that you always use the ORDER BY clause to specify a particular ordering of the data. Data will still be collected into groups. Examine the following example:

```
SELECT Country, Count(DISTINCT City) AS 'Number of Cities'
  FROM Customers GROUP BY Country
```

Countries are collected together and are placed in the order chosen by SQL Server (usually ascending). The number of unique cities will be counted and displayed beside the related country. By supplying the ORDER BY clause as in the following example, you sort data into descending sequence, placing the country with the greatest number of unique cities at the top:

```
SELECT Country, Count(DISTINCT City) AS 'Number of Cities'
 FROM Customers GROUP BY Country
 ORDER BY Count(DISTINCT City) DESC
```

You may not want all groups to be included in the output. To exclude groups from the recordset, you can utilize the HAVING clause, which operates against the groups of data in the same way that the WHERE clause acts against the individual rows. In the next example, as shown in Figure 5.4, the listing has been narrowed down by the elimination of countries with fewer than three unique cities.

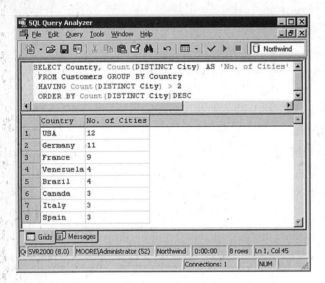

Figure 5.4 **GROUP BY**, **HAVING**, and **ORDER BY** used together.

COMPUTE and COMPUTE BY options of the SELECT statement also fall into the topic of grouping data. These two clauses can serve a purpose similar to that of the GROUP BY clause. GROUP BY will produce a single output in which there is a single row for each group. The output will contain only the grouping columns and aggregate functions, and the select list can contain only the grouping columns and aggregate functions. COMPUTE produces multiple results, the detail rows for each group containing the expressions from the select list and aggregate for the group, or the total aggregate for the statement. A COMPUTE list can contain expressions other than the grouping columns or aggregate functions, and aggregate functions are specified in the COMPUTE clause, not in the select list, as shown in the following example:

```
SELECT DISTINCT Country, City
 FROM Customers
 ORDER BY Country, City
 COMPUTE Count(City) BY Country
```

More Advanced Query Groups

CUBE and ROLLUP, along with GROUPING, can be used to effectively summarize data. The CUBE operator is primarily used in data warehousing applications. It is used to generate a resultset that is a multidimensional cube. Without getting too deep into a data warehousing discussion, a data cube is based on columns that are needed for data analysis. These columns within data cubes are more appropriately referred to as dimensions. The cube is a resultset containing a cross-tabulation of all the possible combinations of the dimensions.

The CUBE operator is specified in the GROUP BY clause of a SELECT statement. The select list contains the dimensions and aggregate expressions. The resultset contains all possible combinations of the values in the dimensions, along with the aggregate values from the underlying rows. Figure 5.5 represents the output from using CUBE.

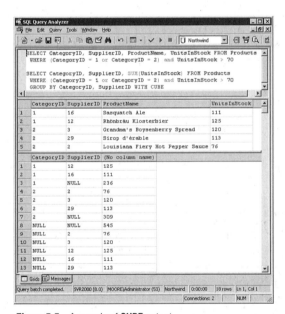

Figure 5.5   A sample of **CUBE** output.

The query in Figure 5.5 returns a resultset that contains the units-on-hand subtotal for all possible combinations of category and supplier. Note the rows that contain the NULL values. These rows report subtotals for each category (where the supplier is NULL) and supplier (where the category is NULL). The row containing the two NULL values represents the grand total.

NULL values can present a problem in distinguishing a NULL generated by the CUBE from a NULL in the actual data. You can solve this quandary using the GROUPING function. GROUPING returns 0 if the value came from the data, and 1 if the value is a NULL generated by the CUBE. GROUPING is represented in Figure 5.6.

Figure showing SQL Query Analyzer window:

```
SELECT CategoryID, SupplierID, SUM(UnitsInStock),
   GROUPING(CategoryID) As 'Cat', GROUPING(SupplierID) As 'Sup' FROM Products
   WHERE (CategoryID = 1 or CategoryID = 2) and UnitsInStock > 70
   GROUP BY CategoryID, SupplierID WITH CUBE
```

	CategoryID	SupplierID	(No column name)	Cat	Sup
1	1	12	125	0	0
2	1	16	111	0	0
3	1	NULL	236	0	1
4	2	2	76	0	0
5	2	3	120	0	0
6	2	29	113	0	0
7	2	NULL	309	0	1
8	NULL	NULL	545	1	1
9	NULL	2	76	1	0
10	NULL	3	120	1	0
11	NULL	12	125	1	0
12	NULL	16	111	1	0
13	NULL	29	113	1	0

Query batch completed. SVR2000 (8.0) MOORE\Administrator (53) Northwind 0:00:03 13 rows Ln 4, Col 3 Connections: 2 NUM

Figure 5.6 GROUPING with **CUBE.**

Roll Up the Cube

The ROLLUP operator is similar to CUBE but somewhat more useful in standard applications that do not necessarily pertain to data warehousing. The ROLLUP operator is used in generating reports that contain subtotals and totals. Whereas the CUBE operator generates its results for all combinations of values, the ROLLUP operator generates only a set of values for a hierarchy. The ROLLUP operation does not report on values from the lower elements of the hierarchy. A similar query as previously used in Figure 5.5 produces a much smaller resultset, as shown in Figure 5.7.

> You must know the basics of **CUBE**, **ROLLUP**, and **GROUPING** for this exam, but don't get too hung up on the granular details. Data warehousing is a complete topic in its own right. Is has its own certification exam covering the material in depth.

We have peered into a little of what data warehousing is about, but let's bring the focus back to the heart of the design exam. SQL Server is a relational database management system. This section focuses on the "relational" part. It covers how tables relate to one another. In Chapter 2, "Creating a Logical

Data Model," you covered how primary keys and foreign keys are used in a database model, and how they impact storing of data. This chapter shows you how to retrieve data from a relational database. This involves using the various join types: INNER, RIGHT, LEFT, and CROSS. You're also going to learn about using a technique called derived tables to simplify query writing.

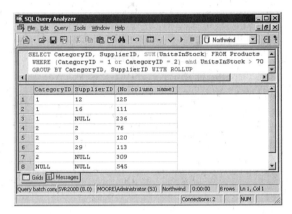

Figure 5.7   A sample of **ROLLUP** output.

Joining Multiple Sets of Data

Joins and derived tables will figure prominently in your exam. Joins are the backbone of relational databases; they actually put the "relation" in relational databases. They're used in all the main SQL statements (SELECT, INSERT, UPDATE, and DELETE). They're very important. Also, derived tables tend to be overlooked, and they're perceived as complicated even though they're not; so they're also likely to show up.

Joining tables is pretty much a natural occurrence within a relational database system. Many of the queries performed on a regular basis will involve multiple tables. Whenever you query data from two tables, you need to find some way to relate the two tables. Connecting one table to another mandates a common element of the tables. You would use this whenever you want to see a resultset that includes columns from several tables.

There are three basic join types, as well as a union operation that can be used to connect tables. An inner join shows results only where there are matches between the elements. An inner join leaves out all the records that don't have a match. An outer join can show all the records from one side of the relationship, records that match where they are available, and NULL values for records that do not have a match. An outer join shows all the same records as an inner join, plus all the records that don't match. The final join, a cross join, returns all possible combinations of rows between the two sides of the join. The number of records in the resultset is equal to the number of records on one side of the join multiplied by the number of records on the other side of the join. No correlation is attempted between the two records; all the records from both sides are returned.

Cross joins are less frequently used than inner and outer joins. With an outer join you are guaranteed to have all records returned from one side or the other. With inner joins the only rows returned will be those that match in the joined tables. It is easier to contemplate the overall processes if you consider join operations first. What you put in the WHERE clause and other clauses is applied after the joins are processed. So bear in mind that when a join returns a specified set of records, the SQL statement may or may not return all those records, depending on what you've specified in the WHERE clause.

With all of that out of the way, let's look at each of the different join operators, starting with INNER JOIN.

Return Output Only When It Matches—Inner

The INNER JOIN statement is the easiest and most often used. For this reason, when an INNER JOIN operation is performed, the INNER portion of the syntax is optional. A rowset is returned from the operation for the records that match up based on the criteria provided through the ON clause. A one-to-many relationship is handled inside of an application with the INNER JOIN. To show all orders for a particular customer, the join operation would be this:

```
SELECT Orders.* FROM Orders
 JOIN Customers
 ON Orders.CustomerID = Customers.CustomerID
```

The results from the preceding query may appear a little on the unusual side because no sorting is performed. Typically an order is specified or information is grouped to make the output more usable. In performing this type of query, each column that occurs in more than one of the tables must be prefixed with the table name or an alias. Figure 5.8 shows a couple of examples of how the join operation might be used.

Inner joins can involve the use of more than two tables and in many cases are more useful to an application. To look into this further, an order process can be considered in much more detail. A customer has many orders, an employee makes many sales, a single order can have multiple line items/order details, and a product can occur within multiple orders. To relate all of this within a single SELECT operation, you would have something like this:

```
SELECT * FROM Orders AS O
 JOIN Customers AS C ON O.CustomerID = O.CustomerID
 JOIN Employees AS E ON O.EmployeeID = E.EmployeeID
 JOIN [Order Details] AS OD ON O.OrderID = OD.OrderID
 JOIN Products AS P ON OD.ProductID = P.ProductID
```

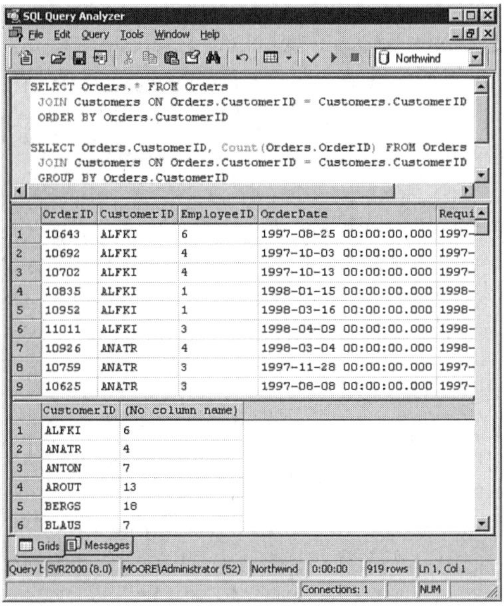

Figure 5.8 Customer/Orders **INNER JOIN**.

Of course, you probably would not want to return all the rows from all the tables, but the preceding example was intended to show the syntax with multiple tables. You will note that each table has been aliased to make it easier to write the query. Of course, in the preceding query data is returned only where there is a match in the ID. If you wanted to see data for all customers regardless of whether they have placed an order or something similar, an outer join is necessary.

Return Output Even When It Doesn't Match—Outer

You can use an outer join when you want to return all of one entire list of rows from one side of the join. There are three types of outer joins: left, right, and full. The terms "left" and "right" are used based on the positioning of the tables within the query. The first table is the right; the second, the left. You may find it easier drawing a picture to represent the table when you are first learning outer joins.

A right outer join, often abbreviated to right join, returns all the rows belonging to the table on the right side and only the matching rows on the table on the left side. Conversely, a left outer join returns all the rows from the table on the left side. A full outer join returns all the rows from both sides with correlations where they exist.

Left and right outer joins, for all intents and purposes, are the same operations; it is simply a matter of the position of the tables within the queries. For this reason the following examples use only the left outer join syntax, which is the one typically used. The following query will produce a listing of all customers and their orders. If a customer has never placed an order, he would still be in the listing accompanied by a NULL for the OrderID.

```
SELECT * FROM Customers AS C
 LEFT JOIN Orders AS O
  ON C.CustomerID = O.CustomerID
```

Be careful in using conditions within these operations. A join operation is solved by the query analyzer before a WHERE condition. If you are looking for a listing of all customers and their orders and want to limit the listing to a single month, you must not place the condition with the ON clause in a WHERE. Placement of the condition in the WHERE would reduce the output after the join has occurred, and you would end up with a list that did not contain all customers. The correct query would be as follows:

```
SELECT C.CustomerID, O.OrderID FROM Customers AS C
 LEFT OUTER JOIN Orders AS O
 ON C.CustomerID = O.CustomerID AND MONTH(OrderDate) = 6
```

Contrast the difference in the output, as shown in Figure 5.9.

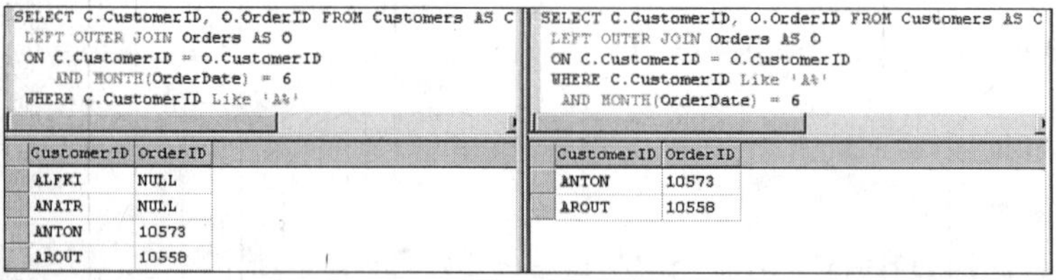

Figure 5.9 **ON** versus **WHERE** conditions in joins.

Notice that when the WHERE condition included the month restriction, not all customers were included in the results. The full outer join would include all elements from both the left and the right tables. This is helpful when you want to see all the records from both tables regardless of whether there was a correlation. Therefore, the following query would show all customers and all orders. If there was an order for which there was no customer on file, the

CustomerID would be NULL. If there was a customer who had not placed an order, the OrderID would be NULL.

```
SELECT C.CustomerID, O.OrderID FROM Customers AS C
 FULL OUTER JOIN Orders AS O
 ON C.CustomerID = O.CustomerID
```

It should be identified that in the Northwind database it is not possible for an order to occur unless there is a matching customer. This is because of the restrictions that are in place through maintaining referential integrity. Although the full join allows you to see all the rows from either table, there is one more query, the cross join, that joins every row in both tables.

Joining Everything to Everything—Crossing

Performing a cross join on two large tables is probably not a good idea. The number of rows in the return set, or in intermediate sets used by SQL Server, can get out of hand quickly, causing server-wide performance degradation. If you have 100 records in the Person table, and 100 records in the Sales table, and then perform a cross join between the two tables, you'll end up with 10,000 records in your resultset (100*100 = 10,000).

Scale a cross join up to one table with 50,000 records and a second table with 100 records, and the resulting join produces five million records. This is not desired in most applications. If you figure that each of those returned records contains about 300 bytes, you can end up with a resultset that weighs in at 1.5 gigabytes, which would probably overwhelm any client computer you aimed it at.

Cross joins are rarely used except in some forms of statistical analysis. This is because most of the connections made really have nothing to do with something in common between the tables. It is simply a matter of connecting every row on one side to every row on the other regardless of content.

Multiple Datasets—Unions

Unions are similar to joins in that the resulting output contains combined information. A union, however, is the operator used to join two separate queries together end to end. A union operator takes the output of two or more SELECT statements and creates one recordset.

Each SELECT statement in the list must return the same number of columns, and the columns must be of compatible types. So if the first SELECT statement returns an int, a float, a varchar(15), and a char(6), the second SELECT has to contain two pieces of data that can be converted to numbers followed by two pieces of data that can be converted to characters.

If the columns are different types but are compatible, the output set will contain as close to the types of the first SELECT as possible. If any of the SELECT statements returns a mix of variable-length and fixed-length fields, the output will be variable length. If the SELECT statements contain columns of different lengths, the longest length is used for the output. If the two values are numerics, the value with the most precision is used.

If you have an integer and a float, the output is a float, because a float has the most precision. If you have an integer and a string that is a number (such as 42), you will have an integer; but if the string was 42.00, you'll have a numeric type that can contain two decimal places and a full integer.

Many SELECT queries can be combined using a UNION to create a single result-set. The following example creates a large set of addresses by combining the output from three separate tables:

```
SELECT ContactName, Address, City, Country, Phone
    FROM Customers
 UNION
SELECT FirstName + ' ' + LastName, Address, City, Country, HomePhone
    FROM Employees
 UNION
SELECT ContactName, Address, City, Country, Phone
    FROM Suppliers
```

Notice that the FirstName and LastName columns of the Employees table have been combined and are treated as a single column. The resulting UNION uses the same number of columns in each of the three queries. When ordering the data from a UNION, the ORDER BY clause is attached to the final SELECT statement. If you want to create a new table that combines the output, you supply the INTO clause on the first SELECT. Therefore, to create a sorted address table using the preceding example, the syntax would be this:

```
SELECT ContactName, Address As 'StreetAddress', City, Country, Phone
    INTO Addresses FROM Customers
 UNION
SELECT FirstName + ' ' + LastName, Address, City, Country, HomePhone
    FROM Employees
 UNION
SELECT ContactName, Address, City, Country, Phone
    FROM Suppliers
 ORDER BY Country, City
```

The column names for the resulting table are taken from the first query in the set of UNION operators. If you want to change the column names, you would simply need to add aliases to the columns of the first SELECT similar to what has been done in the preceding example with the StreetAddress alias.

One unique feature of the UNION is that it automatically removes duplicates from the final resultset. To achieve a complete UNION operation that would include the duplicates, you would use the UNION ALL command instead of simply using UNION.

Adding and Modifying Data

Any business application includes many more processes than the retrieval of data. As time passes, new data will no doubt need to be inserted, redundant data will need to be deleted, and existing data will need to be updated. This is representative of a basic ACD (add, change, delete) implementation that is performed in virtually every database environment.

Data modifications are performed using UPDATE, and removal of data is achieved through the use of a DELETE command. Although there are many ways to insert data into an existing table, the primary coding method is by using the INSERT statement. The statement causes the data values to be inserted as one or more rows into an existing table.

Data inserted must meet the parameters defined by the table structure. This means that NOT NULL columns must have data provided either through input or through the use of column definitions that provide for their own values. A column can obtain its input value through a DEFAULT, IDENTITY, formula, or default object. Data must also meet all rules and constraints that have been defined in the table schema.

Data can be inserted into a table directly or through the resulting dataset from another command such as a SELECT query or an EXECUTE operation. When a query is performed, it enables a large amount of data to be extracted from a table or view and stored into another table.

A SELECT statement can be used within the INSERT statement to add values into a table from one or more other tables or views. Using a SELECT subquery is also a mechanism that enables more than one row to be inserted at one time. This type of INSERT statement is often used to insert data into a separate table from some other table or data source. In this manner the data can be copied or just separated off for handling of exceptions or specialty tasks.

For example, imagine that you would like to copy all your current employees into a customer table. This will enable your employees to make purchases and, of course, allow for an employee discount (not implemented in the Northwind example). The query to perform this operation might look similar to the following:

```
INSERT INTO Customers
     SELECT EmployeeID, 'Northwind',
```

```
            FirstName + ' ' + LastName,
            'Employee', Address, City, Region,
            PostalCode, Country, HomePhone, NULL
      FROM Employees
```

The SELECT list of the subquery must match the column list of the INSERT statement. If no column list is specified, the SELECT list must match the columns in the table or view being inserted into, as in the example. Note that NULL has been provided for a fax number at the end of the column list, because none is included in the Employees table. The INSERT SELECT statement can be used to insert data from any viable source. This includes SQL Server tables and views, and sources outside SQL Server.

An EXECUTE statement (typically abbreviated to EXEC) that returns data with SELECT or READTEXT statements can be used to return the insert values to an INSERT operation. Each resultset must be compatible with the columns in the table or in the column list being used by the INSERT. In this manner a stored procedure can be executed and the data returned as input to a table. If an operation returns data with the READTEXT statement, each individual READTEXT statement can return a maximum of 1MB. The EXEC operation can also be used with extended procedures (not available in previous versions of SQL Server).

Using an operation in this manner enables complex logic to be saved into a stored procedure, and the resulting output can be used for the insertion. Using this facility, you can get virtually any data from anywhere and feed it to any destination. Some of these alternatives to query feeds are explored in Chapter 6, "Programming Business Logic."

Alternatively, you can specify just the VALUES keyword, which is a more convenient method. VALUES is required unless you are doing INSERT, SELECT OR INSERT, or EXECUTE. The same results are produced with the following query:

```
INSERT INTO PetTable Values(30, 'May', 2002, 'male', 'black', 'cat')
```

Of course, adding data is only the first aspect of ACD operations. After data is initially inputted into the system, over time it will need to be altered. Alterations to data are performed through the use of an UPDATE.

Just as with the input of data, any alterations made to the data are subject to the rules and constraints as defined in the table schema. Any data modifications made that do not meet these defined standards result in errors being generated that the front-end application may have to trap and control.

Most data modifications will be based on a conditional operation or alternatively will be an in-place UPDATE of the current record. The following represents a basic UPDATE statement that will adjust the data based on the criteria given:

```
UPDATE Customers
  SET Region = 'South America'
  WHERE Country IN ('Argentina', 'Brazil', 'Venezuela')
```

Along with data modifications, data over time will become obsolete and will need to be removed. Data removal is accomplished through the use of the DELETE statement. It is extremely important to provide a condition when performing data deletions because it is too easy to remove all data if you do not exercise caution. The following command removes all records from the specified table:

```
DELETE FROM Customers
```

If you would like to delete all rows, a fast, nonlogged method is already supplied: TRUNCATE TABLE. It immediately frees all space used by indexes and data by that table, as opposed to DELETE, which should be used when partial data removal is desired. Although both TRUNCATE TABLE and a DELETE statement with no WHERE clause remove all rows in a table, TRUNCATE TABLE is faster and uses fewer system and log resources. The DELETE statement removes rows one at a time, recording an entry in the transaction log for each row. TRUNCATE TABLE removes the data by deallocating the data pages used to store the table's data, and only the page deallocations are recorded in the log. TRUNCATE TABLE removes all rows from a table, but the table structure and its columns, constraints, and indexes remain intact. The counter used by any identity columns is reset to the seed value for the column. If you want to retain the identity counter, use DELETE instead.

Removal of data may impact other tables if cascading deletions have been specified for a relationship. This could mean the removal of other records based on a single DELETE operation. Also, a relationship definition may prevent the deletion of data and return an error condition to the operation. The DELETE statement removes one or more records from a table based on a condition in the WHERE clause. A simplified sample DELETE statement is shown here:

```
DELETE FROM Products
   WHERE Discontinued = 1
```

Traditional applications could be completely centered around the four basic SQL commands: SELECT, INSERT, UPDATE, and DELETE. Essentially, these statements handled about every operation that needed to be performed against the data.

Extensible Markup Language (XML)

XML (Extensible Markup Language) is really quite like a database itself, in that it stores the data along with the basic data definition and with an XML schema defines the complete data structure and business rules. XML is much more portable than a database and is quickly becoming the standard for data exchange among websites, applications, and other implementations that require exchange of data. The language itself is derived from HTML, which in turn was designed to provide an application-independent, character-set-independent method of transferring data, especially transaction-oriented data, across systems.

XML has gained acceptance as a means to communicate data across platforms, especially over the Internet. This exam objective requires you to know how to retrieve data from SQL Server to exchange with other systems. In particular, you will be required to know how to import and manipulate data using OPENXML.

In general, XML is a document format that can be used to transfer data between systems. Within the SQL Server environment, XML documents can be created with the FOR XML clause of the SELECT statement. This clause provides several options for formatting XML output.

Now here is a new feature that is drilled to death on the exam. Expect several questions because it is a new feature and a strong technology. The implementation of XML is a little rough in this release of SQL Server and there is hope for improvement; but just the fact that the capability is present is worth noting. With an industry push on this standard interprogram communication technique, it is worth spending some time to master SQL Server's implementation of XML.

Okay, this is a technical book so here it is in the proverbial technical nutshell. XML is a subset of SGML, which is a huge standard that is so complex nobody has ever completely implemented it. HTML is also a subset of SGML but is quite limited; XML is less limited (and more complex) than HTML but is still far less complex than SGML. Got it? Okay, then let's move on and take a little more of a basic approach.

An XML document consists of one or more elements, which are bound between angle brackets (< >). The first word that appears inside the angle brackets is the name of the element. The rest of the element consists of element attributes. For example, here's an element:

```
<row xmlns="x-schema:#Schema1" ID="9" First="Danny" Last="Thomas"/>
```

The name of the element, or the element type, is row. The xmlns property specifies the name of the schema, which is the format that the element will take. The element then has other attributes, such as ID, First, and Last, which all have values. The element ends with a forward slash and an angle bracket, indicating the end of the element.

An element can also contain other elements as shown here:

```
<SalesPerson ID="1" First="Danny" Last="Thomas">
<Sales Qty="4"/>
<Sales Qty="3"/>
</SalesPerson>
```

In this case, the SalesPerson element contains two Sales elements. Notice that on the first line there isn't a slash before the ending bracket; the matching slash for this element is on the last line. This is how objects are nested in XML.

Simplifying XML Use

To output data in XML format, the SELECT statement includes an operator called FOR XML. This specifies to SQL Server that instead of returning a rowset, it should return an XML document. There are three different options for generating the XML: RAW, AUTO, and EXPLICIT.

Where is the schema? To produce XML output that also contains the schema information for the XML, you must tack the **XMLDATA** qualifier to the end of the **FOR XML** clause.

In AUTO mode, SQL Server returns the rowset in an automatically generated nested XML format. If the query has no joins, it doesn't have a nesting at all. If the query has joins, it returns the first row from the first table, then all the correlated rows from each joined table as a nested level. For example, the following query shows order details nested inside of orders:

```
SELECT O.OrderID, O.CustomerID, OD.ProductID, OD.UnitPrice, OD.Quantity
    From Orders AS O
 JOIN [Order Details] AS OD ON O.OrderID = OD.OrderID
 WHERE O.OrderID < 10251
  FOR XML AUTO
<O OrderID="10248" CustomerID="VINET">
<OD ProductID="11" UnitPrice="14.0000" Quantity="12"/>
<OD ProductID="42" UnitPrice="9.8000" Quantity="10"/>
<OD ProductID="72" UnitPrice="34.8000" Quantity="5"/></O>
<O OrderID="10249" CustomerID="TOMSP">
<OD ProductID="14" UnitPrice="18.6000" Quantity="9"/>
<OD ProductID="51" UnitPrice="42.4000" Quantity="40"/></O>
<O OrderID="10250" CustomerID="HANAR">
<OD ProductID="41" UnitPrice="7.7000" Quantity="10"/>
<OD ProductID="51" UnitPrice="42.4000" Quantity="35"/>
<OD ProductID="65" UnitPrice="15.8000" Quantity="15"/></O>
```

Note that the aliases for each table become the row identifiers within the XML output. Unfortunately, Query Analyzer by default shows only the first 256 characters of a string that's returned. For most XML queries that will not be adequate, and a setting of the maximum 8192 is recommended. To set the option within the query analyzer, select Tools, Options, Results from the menu. It is for this reason that we have tried to limit the data output size in most of the examples throughout this section by including a WHERE clause to filter the number of rows.

To produce a listing that also supplies the schema elements of the XML (now *that* is really hard to read), you tack the XMLDATA onto the end of the FOR XML clause:

```
SELECT * FROM Products WHERE ProductID = 1 FOR XML AUTO, XMLDATA
<Schema name="Schema3" xmlns="urn:schemas-microsoft-com:xml-data" xmlns:
dt="urn:schemas-microsoft-com:datatypes"><ElementType name="Products"
content="empty" model="closed"><AttributeType name="ProductID" dt:type=
"i4"/><AttributeType name="ProductName" dt:type="string"/><AttributeType
name="SupplierID" dt:type="i4"/><AttributeType name="CategoryID" dt:type
="i4"/><AttributeType name="QuantityPerUnit" dt:type="string"/>
<AttributeType name="UnitPrice" dt:type="fixed.14.4"/><AttributeType
name="UnitsInStock" dt:type="i2"/><AttributeType name="UnitsOnOrder" dt:
type="i2"/><AttributeType name="ReorderLevel" dt:type="i2"/><Attribute
Type name="Discontinued" dt:type="boolean"/><attribute type="ProductID"/
><attribute type="ProductName"/><attribute type="SupplierID"/><attribute
 type="CategoryID"/><attribute type="QuantityPerUnit"/><attribute type=
"UnitPrice"/><attribute type="UnitsInStock"/><attribute type="UnitsOn
Order"/><attribute type="ReorderLevel"/><attribute type="Discontinued"/>
</ElementType></Schema><Products xmlns="x-schema:#Schema3" ProductID="1"
 ProductName="Chai" SupplierID="1" CategoryID="1" QuantityPerUnit="10
 boxes x 20 bags" UnitPrice="18.0000" UnitsInStock="39" UnitsOnOrder="0"
 ReorderLevel="10" Discontinued="0"/>
```

When you run the query, the actual XML comes out all on one line as a stream of data. XML output does not use linefeeds or make things readable in any fashion. The easiest way to write queries for XML, then, is to write them with the FOR XML clause left off, make sure that they are returning the data you want, and then add the FOR XML back onto the end of the query. That eliminates the need for a lot of extra formatting.

The use of the RAW mode of XML output is best suited in situations in which minimum formatting is desired. In RAW mode each row is returned as an element with the identifier row. Here's an example of the same query as you just saw, returned in RAW mode:

```
<row OrderID="10248" CustomerID="VINET"
ProductID="11" UnitPrice="14.0000" Quantity="12"/>
<row OrderID="10248" CustomerID="VINET"
ProductID="42" UnitPrice="9.8000" Quantity="10"/>
<row OrderID="10248" CustomerID="VINET"
ProductID="72" UnitPrice="34.8000" Quantity="5"/>
<row OrderID="10249" CustomerID="TOMSP"
ProductID="14" UnitPrice="18.6000" Quantity="9"/>
```

```
<row OrderID="10249" CustomerID="TOMSP"
ProductID="51" UnitPrice="42.4000" Quantity="40"/>
<row OrderID="10250" CustomerID="HANAR"
ProductID="41" UnitPrice="7.7000" Quantity="10"/>
<row OrderID="10250" CustomerID="HANAR"
ProductID="51" UnitPrice="42.4000" Quantity="35"/>
<row OrderID="10250" CustomerID="HANAR"
ProductID="65" UnitPrice="15.8000" Quantity="15"/>
```

If you have binary data stored in text or image data types, SQL Server ignores the data when generating XML. If you want the data to be included, you use the BINARY BASE64 option:

```
SELECT * FROM Employees
 FOR XML RAW, BINARY BASE64
```

Another option available for extracting data in an XML format is EXPLICIT. The EXPLICIT option enables you to specify the format of the XML that will be created. To define the format, you have to alias the first column of output to the name Tag, name the second column Parent, and then alias each consecutive column to relate it to a specific Tag. The column names after Parent are named this way:

```
[ElementName!TagNumber!AttributeName!Directive]
```

So the example

```
SELECT 1 AS TAG, NULL AS Parent,
       [Order Details].Quantity AS [Order!1!QtyPurchased],
       Products.ProductID AS [Order!1!ProdID],
       Products.ProductName AS [Order!1!Product],
       Products.UnitsInStock AS [Order!1!OnHand]
FROM Products INNER JOIN [Order Details]
   ON Products.ProductID = [Order Details].ProductID
WHERE OrderID = 10248 FOR XML EXPLICIT
```

returns this data:

```
<Order QtyPurchased="12" PersonID="11"
Product="Queso Cabrales" OnHand="22"/>
<Order QtyPurchased="10" PersonID="42"
Product="Singaporean Hokkien Fried Mee" OnHand="26"/>
<Order QtyPurchased="5" PersonID="72"
Product="Mozzarella di Giovanni" OnHand="14"/>
```

These types of queries are quite arduous and "clunky," to say the least, but they do produce useful results.

You are not going to become an XML expert overnight, and the material presented in this book is light, to say the least. Essentially, all we have done is shown how to draw data out of SQL Server in an XML format. We have not tried to explain XML or produce an XML reference text, but knowing the material presented in this section and the one to follow should get you through the XML portion of the exam.

You use the FOR XML clause to retrieve XML data, and it is really pretty easy to use after you get the hang of it. Getting XML data into a database is a little more tricky and not too user friendly.

Moving Data Using XML

Use the Transact-SQL OPENXML function to insert data represented as an XML document. OPENXML is used to allow access to XML data as if it were like any other table or rowset. You must first have an XML document in memory to work with. OPENXML can be used in SELECT, as well as in SELECT INTO statements where a source table or view can be specified. Here is a breakdown of the process:

1. Store into a variable or otherwise attain XML data that is loaded into memory.

2. Use the sp_xml_preparedocument system stored procedure to read and parse the XML data and create a document handle.

3. Access the XML data using the OPENXML statement to define the format of the XML document and return the rowset.

4. Use the sp_xml_removedocument system stored procedure to destroy the document handle created for XML access.

One of the trickiest parts of the whole procedure is simply having the data available in an XML format so that the rest of the process can continue. The XML data can simply be created through the use of another query if you are moving data from one database to another. You may also want to access the data through a stream or another source. To keep the material presented in this unit focused on what you need to accomplish to prepare for the exam, we will not burden you with the steps needed to access stream or file data. Instead, we will look at data loaded through other queries and directly loaded into variables for use.

To prepare an XML document, you somehow need to get the document into a T-SQL variable. After you have determined your XML source, you need to use the stored procedure for handling XML documents. There are two related procedures that will open a handle to the document and subsequently close the handle when it is no longer needed:

sp_xml_preparedocument

sp_xml_removedocument

The prepare document function will read XML text that can be provided as input directly or via a character variable. The procedure then parses the text using the XML parser. This is a dynamic link library (Msxml2.dll) used to understand the XML information being presented by the internal document. Next the data is provided as a parsed document in a state ready for consumption. This parsed document is a tree representation of the XML data. The following simple example demonstrates the use of the procedure with a direct XML text feed:

```
DECLARE @hdoc INT
EXEC sp_xml_preparedocument @hdoc OUTPUT,
    '<SalesPerson ID="9" First="Danny" Last="Thomas">
    <Sales Qty="5"/><Sales Qty="10"/></SalesPerson>'
EXEC sp_xml_removedocument @hdoc
```

The first thing you'll notice is the variable declaration. The @hdoc is a variable that holds a temporary value for use later, in the sp_xml_removedocument as well as in the OPENXML. The next thing to note is that an sp_xml_preparedocument and sp_xml_removedocument are paired up. This is critical to ensure appropriate use of resources. Without the removal of the document handle, the only way to recover the memory is to restart SQL Server.

The sp_xml_preparedocument stored procedure has one optional argument: the xpath_namespace argument, which is used to specify an alternative namespace for the document. By default, the system uses the default namespace `<root xmlns:mp="urn:schemas-microsoft-com:xml-metaprop">`. If you specify an alternative namespace string, it replaces the `"urn:schemas-microsoft-com:xml-metaprop"` with whatever you specify.

The OPENXML function has three parameters and an optional WITH clause. It takes the document handle, which is returned by the sp_xml_preparedocument procedure, the rowpattern, which specifies which rows to return, and a single-byte value that can specify flags. In most cases you will want to use a rowset filter to achieve more useful output:

```
SELECT * FROM openxml(@hdoc, '/SalesPerson', 1)
```

Using this filter will return only the attributes that pertain to the SalesPerson. Now, if you could just put the rows where they need to be, you'd have it made:

```
SELECT * FROM openxml(@hdoc, '/SalesPerson', 1)
          WITH (FirstName varchar(30), LastName varchar(30))
```

That WITH clause does the trick, and you finally get decent output:

```
FirstName      LastName
-------------  -------------
Danny          Thomas
```

So now you have the data you want, extracted from an XML rowset. Using the WITH clause is basically the same syntax as laying out the columns in a table: the column name, some space, the data type, a comma, and then the next column name.

OPENXML is extremely cumbersome. You can't read XML from a file easily; you have to spend time fighting with arcane bit-field flags, and you get to completely reformat your data—and you do all that just to get a few rows. You can't declare a variable of type TEXT, so you can hold only about 8KB of XML in SQL Server at a time.

Exam Prep Questions

1. You have two tables that were created like this:

```
create table birds ( BirdID int IDENTITY(1,1),
    BirdName varchar(30) )
create table BirdFeathers ( BirdID int, FeatherID int )
```

You need to find all the FeatherIDs for each BirdName. Which of the following queries will do the job?

❑   A.
```
select BirdName, FeatherID from birds b inner
    join birdfeathers bf on b.BirdID = bf.birdid
```

❑   B.
```
select BirdName, FeatherID from birds b left
    join birdfeathers bf on b.BirdID = bf.birdid
```

❑   C.
```
select BirdName, FeatherID from birds b right
    join birdfeathers bf on b.BirdID = bf.birdid
```

❑   D.
```
select BirdName, FeatherID from birds b cross
    join birdfeathers bf on b.BirdID = bf.birdid
```

Answer: A. They're all valid syntax except for the ON clause in the CROSS JOIN, making option D completely invalid, but only option A returns the correct rowset. This is all about structuring joins, which is covered in the section "Joining Multiple Sets of Data."

2. You need to send an XML rowset to a parts supplier for your business that produces radio kits. The rowset should contain a parts list for your order for next week. The supplier has provided you with a schema you must use. Which of the following FOR XML options will enable you to conform to his schema?

❑   A. FOR XML RAW, XMLDATA
❑   B. FOR XML AUTO, BINARY BASE64
❑   C. FOR XML EXPLICIT
❑   D. FOR XML AUTO

Answer: C. To successfully exchange data in a provided schema, you're going to have to dig through the documentation and figure out how to do explicit XML. If you need help creating XML files from rowsets, check out the section on "Extensible Markup Language (XML)."

3. There's a performance problem on one of your SQL Servers that you use to process XML. After a period of time processing XML data, the server's memory utilization is very high and the server won't allow any more XML statements to be prepared. Which of the following is the most likely cause of the problem?

   ❑ A. Cursors in the Transact-SQL batches aren't deallocating properly.

   ❑ B. The XML that is being parsed is not well formed.

   ❑ C. The server has a hardware problem.

   ❑ D. The XML strings are not properly removed after preparation and use.

   Answer: D. The sp_xml_removedocument stored procedure must be called to free memory by deallocating the memory for the XML strings, and if you lose the handles, the resulting memory leak will eventually cause SQL Server to be unable to process more XML. The section "Moving Data Using XML" goes into great detail about how all this works.

4. Leeks Unlimited has just acquired another company, the Garlic Crock. The company is trying to import the several million rows of data from the Garlic Crock's databases by exporting the data from Garlic Crock's mainframe into text files and then using BCP to bulk copy the data into the Leeks Unlimited database server. The problem is that the transaction log of the database keeps filling up. Which of the following options would not help alleviate the problem?

   ❑ A. Rather than using BCP, use the same options with BULK INSERT.

   ❑ B. Use the batch size limiter on the BCP command line.

   ❑ C. Use the batch size limitation as a bulk copy hint.

   ❑ D. Make sure that the SELECT INTO/BULKCOPY option is turned on.

   Answer: A. The BULK INSERT statement with the same parameters will fill up the logs just as fast as BCP. Any of the other options will help, though. There is a great section in this chapter to check out: "Mass Movements of Data via BCP."

5. After importing all the Garlic Crock data from its mainframe, Leeks Unlimited needs to read a bunch of Garlic Crock's data from its Web server database back ends, which are currently using Microsoft Access. Which of the following tools would be the best for the job?

   ❑ A. The Bulk Copy Program

   ❑ B. OPENXML

   ❑ C. The BULK INSERT command

   ❑ D. The DTS Import/Export Wizard

   Answer: D. The only tool that can directly read Microsoft Access databases and import them is the DTS Import/Export Wizard. The other tools listed require either exporting the data to text files or exporting it to XML. The DTS Import/Export Wizard is covered in the section "Data Movement with Manipulation."

6. Eric has a couple of fairly large tables that handle the food inventory for his snack-smuggling operation. He wants to cause a problem for his system administrator, preferably by just using up resources unnecessarily. What's the best way to do this?

❑ A. Cross-join the two tables.

❑ B. Left-join the two tables and union them together.

❑ C. Inner-join the tables and union them together.

❑ D. Right-join the tables and union them together.

Answer: A. Cross-joins consume the most resources because they have the largest rowset, which is the size of table 1 times table 2. None of the other queries can come even close. A quick jump back to the section "Joining Multiple Sets of Data" would be in order if that one tripped you up.

7. Things have been pretty boring lately, so Barney the security guard wants to put some random top-secret data on a laptop and then throw it over the wall at the local embassy. He wants to make sure that the data is nice, complete, and easy-to-read XML. Which of the following should he use?

❑ A. FOR XML AUTO, XMLDATA

❑ B. FOR XML RAW

❑ C. FOR XML BASE BINARY64

❑ D. FOR XML BASE PORTABLE

Answer: A. The XMLDATA flag puts the schema, including all the data types, into the XML document for easy viewing. Putting data into XML files is covered by the section "Moving Data Using XML," earlier in this chapter.

8. A small manufacturing company has a considerable number of data sources because no standardization has occurred across any platform. One of the database servers has SQL Server installed; the others come from various vendors. For a project you are working on, you need to gather data from the SQL Server and merge it together with data from two other sources. You then need to bring the data into Excel to do some charting. How would you accomplish this task?

❑ A. Export the data from the other sources into a comma-delimited file. Then export from SQL Server the data that is to be imported into Excel.

❑ B. Export the data from all three sources so that it can be imported into Excel.

❑ C. Use DTS to transfer all the data from all sources directly into Excel.

❑ D. Use Excel to transfer data from all three sources into a spreadsheet.

Answer: C. SQL Server is ideal for this situation. Depending on the actual details of the process, this can be performed directly using replication or Data Transformation Services (DTS). Given the complexity of the scenario, it is likelier that DTS would be used because of its limitless flexibility. For more information, consult SQL Server Books Online.

9. You have been given the assignment of preparing a set of user-friendly queries to produce a series of reports for a building construction supply company. You would like a query that places customers in order by country, state, and then city. Which of the following queries would solve the problem?

❑ A.
```
SELECT * FROM Customers
    ORDER BY Country, State, City
```

❑ B.
```
SELECT CustomerName, City, State, Country
    ORDER BY Country, State, City, CustomerName
```

❑ C.
```
SELECT * FROM Customers
    ORDER BY City, State, Country
```

❑ D.
```
SELECT CustomerName, City, State, Country
    ORDER BY City, State, Country, CustomerName
```

❑ E.
```
SELECT CustomerName, City, State, Country
    ORDER BY CustomerName, City, State, Country
```

Answer: A. Assuming that all data from the table is needed, A is correct. It is not necessary to include all columns from a select list when using ORDER. For appropriate use of ORDER BY, see the section "Putting It All in ORDER."

10. You are working on a database view that will be used by a group of salespeople to query a database for sales statistics. The report that you are debugging is printing duplicates for some states, and in some instances there are three or more duplicates. How would you try to resolve the problem?

❑ A. Correct the FROM clause.
❑ B. Correct the WHERE clause.
❑ C. Correct the TOP clause.
❑ D. Correct the ORDER BY clause.
❑ E. Correct the DISTINCT clause.

Answer: E. Appropriate use of the DISTINCT clause could eliminate the recurring data being noted. To diagnose this problem, the correct syntax must be implemented. The following code represents a plausible solution:

```
SELECT DISTINCT Country FROM Customers ORDER BY Country
```

For further details on the use of DISTINCT, see the section "Selecting Information from the Data."

11. A local branch of a large hotel chain maintains guest information on a single SQL Server 2000 computer. You are creating an application that will change the contents of a database programmatically through a Visual Basic interface on a local area network. Which technology would you utilize?

❑ A. ADO

❑ B. RDO

❑ C. DAO

❑ D. SQL-DMO

❑ E. XML

Answer: A. An XML implementation may be more suited to an active server page Internet application than a LAN application. RDO and DAO represent older technologies that aren't as efficient and versatile as ADO. SQL-DMO is for development of system applications that interact with SQL Server on a non-data level. For more details about any of the technologies, see SQL Server Books Online.

Programming Business Logic

Terms you'll need to understand:

✓ Deterministic
✓ Nondeterministic
✓ Stored procedure
✓ User-defined function
✓ Parameter

Techniques you'll need to master:

✓ Coding SQL Server objects
✓ Handling transactions
✓ Using parameters within procedures
✓ Implementing error handling
✓ Utilization of various trigger types

Introduction

Programming business logic under the SQL Server framework involves several different mechanisms. There are seven areas in which you can perform coding using T-SQL:

➤ Stored procedures

➤ User-defined functions

➤ Triggers

➤ Jobs

➤ Ad-hoc querying

➤ Views

➤ DTS

Stored procedures enable you to modularize frequently used queries and complex logic into an easy-to-manage object. User-defined functions provide similar functionality, but with the additional capability to return single values or tables to the caller, which provides a great deal of flexibility.

With SQL Server you can perform coding from various environments. The command prompt can be used with BCP and OSQL. Third-party products can code SQL and "pass through" to the server in a language understood by SQL Server. The Query Analyzer is a powerful T-SQL editing environment that is quite comfortable to use.

When using the Query Analyzer to write code, you will often find it useful to open a couple of instances, in particular when testing multiple user interaction. Within each instance any number of windows can be open to provide access to multiple portions of a project in one easy-to-handle coding application. Multiple instances and multiple windows allow you to work with different data simultaneously.

Start with Data Analysis
Prior to Coding

When any data retrieval query is being run, it is compulsory to specify where the data is coming from. Specifying which tables are going to be accessed can be done with the FROM clause of the SELECT statement. FROM table lists do not necessarily have to be just standard tables. It is also valid to specify derived tables, joined tables, views, user-defined functions that return tables, and system functions that return tables.

A derived table is a subquery that retrieves rows from the database. A SELECT clause within a FROM clause of another SELECT, referred to by an alias, produces a derived table. The resulting rows take on a construct similar to that of a standard table. Derived tables produce a performance hit in most situations, and where possible, a join should be coded to replace the derived table.

The name of a view is often substituted for a table name. A view, stored as a query on the server, often provides necessary column restrictions and application considerations that makes it a beneficial data source.

User-defined functions can generate recordset output and in that form be used in place of a table name. A function can declare an internal table variable, insert rows into the variable, and then return the variable as its return value. A class of user-defined functions known as in-line functions return the resultset of a SELECT statement as a variable of type table.

System functions often generate a set of records that can be envisioned as a table. These rowset functions return an object that can be used in place of a table reference in a T-SQL statement.

Data sources can be located throughout the organization. They can be located at many sites, be on different computers and are created using many data management tools. SQL Server has the functionality available to connect to and use data anywhere it resides. Of course the data in its raw format won't be presentable and will require formatting. After a data source has been determined, the coding can begin.

Making Data Presentable

Often data returned from the database is not presented in a manner that the end user can identify with and access in a reasonable manner. Many SQL Server functions allow for the alteration of the data type or more appropriate presentation to the user. If data is not in a type presentable to the user, the CONVERT() and CAST() functions will be the first ones used.

Data needs to be converted from one form to another when you are using diverse functions or data types that don't match up with the type needed by a particular function. Data can be converted from one data type to another with the CONVERT() and CAST() functions. CAST() is based on the SQL-92 standard and is favored over CONVERT(), although both CONVERT() and CAST() have their particular strengths in handling individual types of data.

You will need to supply both the expression that needs to be converted and the data type to convert the given expression to perform conversion operation. SQL Server automatically converts certain data from one data type to another. For example, if a smallint is compared to an int, the smallint is automatically converted to an int before the comparison proceeds. These are called implicit conversions because you don't have to use the CAST() or CONVERT() functions. When data is converted to a new data type and the data is too large for the new data type to handle, SQL Server displays an asterisk or identifies the problem with an error message, depending on the data types involved.

The CONVERT() function transforms data from one data type to another. CONVERT() is also used extensively with date operations to format a date. The following example converts the Price column into a CHAR data type so that you can concatenate it with another string expression. Remember, concatenation can be done only using strings, so it must be converted:

```
SELECT 'The book costs ' + CONVERT(CHAR(5), Price) FROM Titles
```

The CAST() function is similar to the CONVERT() function in that it converts data. It is preferred over the CONVERT() function because it's based on the SQL-92 standard.

CAST() is usually preferred over **CONVERT()** for operations with more advanced processing requirements.

The following example illustrates the use of CAST() to convert numeric data to a string to allow for its use in a concatenation:

```
SELECT 'The book costs ' + CAST(Price AS CHAR(5)) FROM Titles
```

When working in character strings, whether converting, concatenating, or applying string data to another application, you may need to trim off space at the beginning or end. Often data is space filled. Within T-SQL there are two functions for trimming spaces: RTRIM() and LTRIM(). If you want to trim all spaces, these can be combined, and though it looks awkward, it does accomplish the task.

```
LTRIM(String)
RTRIM(String)
LTRIM(RTRIM(String))
```

By formatting data you're presenting the information so that more value is produced in the finished product. Formatting information can be as simple as placing output in the correct sequence; however, formatting can also mean the use of these procedures for the analysis and display of data.

Functions Make Data Work

There are functions for making strings more usable. There are functions for performing mathematics. There are functions that work the calendar and functions that tell time, functions that move data around and functions that rhyme. Functions perform tasks against the data, they perform activities, and they produce results.

All functions are either deterministic or nondeterministic. The specification of whether a function is deterministic or nondeterministic is called the determinism of the function. Deterministic functions always return the same result anytime they are called with a specific set of input values. Nondeterministic functions may return different results each time they are called with a specific set of input values.

An example of a deterministic function would be DATEADD(), a built-in function that always returns the same result for any given set of argument values. GETDATE() is not deterministic because it is always invoked with the same argument, yet the value it returns changes each time it is executed.

Be careful with the use of appropriate functions because nondeterministic functions cannot be used in a lot of processes. An index cannot be created on a computed column if the expression references any nondeterministic functions, and a clustered index cannot be created on a view if the view references any nondeterministic functions.

The most commonly used nondeterministic functions are the aggregate functions that provide answers based on the entire set of data being assimilated.

Aggregate Collective Functions

Aggregate functions are functions that provide summary data about sets. Questions like "How many rows are in that table?" "How many widgets did we sell last week?" and "What is the average price we charged for a widget?" are all answered with aggregate functions. Some are more commonly used than others, and anyone familiar with working in a spreadsheet environment has seen these before.

Aggregate functions take one of three types of arguments. Some take a simple wildcard (*). This means either that the operation doesn't apply to rows or that it should apply to all rows. In COUNT(*) the wildcard returns the number of rows in the table. The number of rows that are in the table is independent of any individual column. The function is applied across the entire group, regardless of the content of each row.

All the functions take a column name as an argument, and then the aggregate applies only to that column. COUNT(PersonID) returns the number of non-null PersonIDs in the table. Some functions enable you to apply the function to distinct values. COUNT (DISTINCT PersonID) provides a count of the number of distinct IDs in the column, ignoring duplications.

The AVG() Function

The AVG() function returns the average value for a given column. It requires a column name, and optionally you can use DISTINCT() to get an average for just the distinct values in the table. Here's an example that determines the average size of an order from the sample Sales table:

```
SELECT AVG(QtyPurchased) FROM Sales
```

The COUNT() and COUNT_BIG() Functions

The COUNT() function returns an integer representing the number of rows in the table. The COUNT_BIG() function does the same thing, but it returns a number of type bigint, instead used for analyzing large datasets.

The MAX() and MIN() Functions

MAX() and MIN() are simple. They return the maximum or the minimum value in the set. The highest and lowest values within the set being evaluated will be returned in the data type of the column being used for the analysis.

The SUM() Function

The SUM() function is nearly as simple—it just returns the sum of all the values in the group. SELECT SUM(Quantity) FROM [Order Details] will provide a total for the number of products sold.

Functions Used for Deviation and Variance

Without delving too deep into statistical operations, we'll say that these sets of functions are useful in analyzing populations. The VAR() and VARP() functions calculate the variance of the group. The STDDEV() and STDDEVP() functions calculate the standard deviation of the group. Variance and standard deviation are used in statistics to determine the spread of a sample set. A sample set has a high variance and a high standard deviation if there is a wide range of values in the sample set. If there is a small range of values, the variance and standard deviation is smaller. The STDEVP() and STDEV() functions differ in that the STDEV() determines the sample standard deviation, whereas STDEVP() returns the population standard deviation. VAR() and VARP() are similar.

Checksum Operations

A checksum is a number generated from a data value that essentially summarizes the data value. If you store that value and then change the data, you can test the checksum to quickly notice this change. Checksums are used frequently in data storage to denote data corruption.

 If you're working with large datasets, though, the capability to compare checksums saves an immense amount of time over comparing strings together.

There is an approximately two in four billion chance of a checksum being the same for two pieces of data being tested. The checksums return some number that's an integer, and the chances that two pseudorandom integers will be the same are very small. This is a useful function for detecting changes in rows as an alternative to timestamps.

The CHECKSUM() and CHECKSUM_BINARY() functions aren't true aggregate functions. They return a checksum for whatever you ask them to, typically for a row. The difference between CHECKSUM() and CHECKSUM_BINARY() is that a CHECKSUM() checks data that has been localized for the server, whereas CHECKSUM_BINARY() checks raw data. In this case, "localized" means that the string is translated to how it would compare before computing the checksum. So if you're on a server that's set up as not case sensitive, which is the default, the CHECKSUM() for "Widget" and "widget" would be the same, whereas the BINARY_CHECKSUM() would be different.

The CHECKSUM_AGG() function is the aggregate function used to compute checksums over sets. This function enables you to get the aggregated checksum for an entire table. Look at some examples. First, here's an example of using just the CHECKSUM() function on a table:

```
SELECT CHECKSUM(*) FROM
```

This returns a checksum for each row based on the entire content of the row. Now, if you want to use a checksum for the entire table, you can do this:

```
SELECT CHECKSUM_AGG(CHECKSUM(*)) FROM [Order Details]
```

This gives you a checksum for the entire table. Now, look at a way to use this information. The key thing to remember about using a checksum is that it's a snapshot. To find differences, you've got to have a checksum before and a checksum after the changes occur.

Of Calendars and Clocks

In T-SQL, as with many other programming languages, date and time manipulation have been given special importance by the many functions available. Dates and times are implemented as datetime and smalldatetime data types and need to be treated with special functions. To first examine dates, you must realize that dates cannot be added or subtracted using the regular operators. The date functions available in SQL Server enable you to change and manipulate dates easily.

The DATEADD() Function

The DATEADD() function adds a number to the part of the date you specify, such as month or day, and then returns the new datetime value. The function adds an interval to a date specified. The following example adds three days to the ShipDate column of a BackOrders table:

```
SELECT DATEADD(day, 3, ShipDate) FROM BackOrders
```

The portion of the date that you work with allows for several different entries, as presented in Table 6.1.

Table 6.1	Possible Values for Date Portion Entries
Date-Part	**Abbreviations**
Year	yy, yyyy
Quarter	qq, q
Month	mm, m
Dayofyear	dy, y
Day	dd, d
Week	wk, ww
Hour	hh
Minute	mi, n
Second	ss, s
Millisecond	ms

The DATEDIFF() Function

The DATEDIFF() function is used in a similar manner. This function, however, calculates the amount of time in date-parts between the second and first of two dates you specify. DATEDIFF() subtracts the start date from the end date to produce the result. Look at the following example:

```
SELECT PubDate,
  DATEDIFF(year, PubDate, getdate()) AS 'Difference'
    FROM Titles
```

The method of counting across boundaries, such as minutes, seconds, and milliseconds, makes the result given by DATEDIFF() consistent across all data types. The result is a signed integer value equal to the number of date-part boundaries crossed between the first and second date. For example, the number of weeks between Monday, March 5, and Monday, March 12, is 1.

The GETDATE() Function

To get the current date, use the GETDATE() function. This function can be useful when you are producing reports that need to be dated. The GETDATE() function returns the current system date and can be used in a SELECT statement. You can use GETDATE() in designing a report to have the current date and time printed every time the report is produced. GETDATE() is also useful for functions such as logging the time a transaction occurred on an account. You can use GETDATE() anywhere to return the current system date.

The DATENAME() Function

The DATENAME() function can be used in determining part of a date in the form of a string. You may, for instance, need to know specifically the day or month of a publication. The DATENAME() function returns a character string representing the specified date-part from the date. Here's an example of using DATENAME() to find the name of the current month:

```
Select datename(mm,getdate()) as 'month'
```

The DATEPART() and DATENAME() functions produce the specified part of a datetime value (the year, quarter, day, hour, and so on) as either an integer or a string. Because smalldatetime is accurate only to the minute, when a smalldatetime value is used with either of these functions, the seconds and milliseconds returned are zero.

Using DATEPART()

DATEPART() is similar to DATENAME() except that it returns an integer value indicating the date rather than a character string. The following is an example of using DATEPART() to find the current month and display it numerically:

```
SELECT datepart(mm,getdate()) AS 'month'
```

Many useful date functions give the developer flexibility in dealing with what is traditionally one of the more pesky data types: dates. With history reflecting unfavorably on the storage of date information, it is important to consider this data type to be infinite in that dates need to remain unique as time progresses.

Using Mathematical Functions in T-SQL

In most programming languages numeric data types have always had useful functionality supplied with the coding environment. SQL Server is no exception with its adoption of a standard set of mathematical functions.

A mathematical function performs a math operation on numeric expressions and returns the result of the operation. Math functions operate on any of the SQL Server numeric data types (decimal, integer, float, real, money, smallmoney, smallint, and tinyint). The initial precision of built-in operations on the float data type data is six decimal places.

By default, a number passed to a mathematical function is interpreted as a decimal data type. The CAST() or CONVERT() functions can be used to change the data type to something else, such as a float.

You can use the diverse set of math functions provided by T-SQL to fulfill many database needs. SQL Server provides numerous mathematical functions so that you can perform the most complex calculations possible. These numerous functions are provided in most programming language environments. Some of the more commonly used math functions are listed in Table 6.2.

Table 6.2	Mathematical Functions in T-SQL	
Function	Parameters	Result
ABS	(Numeric expression)	The absolute value of a number
CEILING	(Numeric expression)	Smallest integer greater than or equal to the expression
EXP	(Float expression)	Exponential value
FLOOR	(Numeric expression)	Largest integer less than or equal to the expression
PI	( )	Returns 3.1415926535897931
POWER	(Numeric expression, **y**)	Value of expression to the power of **y**
RAND	(Seed)	Random value between zero and one
ROUND	(Numeric expression, length)	Numeric expression rounded off to the precision (length) of a number
SQRT	(Float expression)	Square root of the expression
SQUARE	(Float expression)	Square of the expression

The following example shows you a query that uses some of the many mathematical functions in SQL Server. Notice that when a query is non-data retrieval, as this one is, a FROM clause does not have to be specified.

```
SELECT pi() AS 'PI' , abs(-44) AS 'Absolute',  power(2,3) AS 'Power'
```

Discussion of mathematical functions would be an involved endeavor for this medium. This book does not set out to make mathematical geniuses out of every SQL developer. To become fully versed in all mathematical functions would require a significant education in the science of mathematics.

Character functions interact against alphanumeric data in a similar fashion as numeric data interacts with mathematical functions. Some of these were discussed within the realm of formatting data, but there are a few more worth looking into.

String It Up

SQL Server also provides a full array of character (string) functions. Character functions enable you to easily manipulate attributes that are character specific. Most of the functions provided in Table 6.3 are normally used, and therefore you should regularly practice using them.

Table 6.3	Character Functions in T-SQL	
Function	**Parameters**	**Result**
+	**expr1 + expr2**	Concatenates strings, joining them together.
ASCII	**String expression**	Gets the ASCII code value of the string.
CHAR	**Integer expression**	Changes the ASCII integer into a character.
LEN	**String expression**	Identifies the length of an expression.
PATINDEX	**Pattern expression**	Returns the position of the beginning of a pattern. If the pattern is not found, it returns zero.
REPLICATE	**String expression, integer expression**	Repeats a character expression the number of times specified.
REVERSE	**String expression**	Returns the reverse of a string expression.
SPACE	**Integer expression**	Returns a string of repeated spaces.
STUFF	**String expr1, expr2 start, length, String**	Deletes a specified length of characters and inserts another set of characters at a specified starting point.
SUBSTRING	*String expr, start, length*	Returns part of a string expression.

Concatenation of string expressions is a quite common process. Joining strings together can assist in presenting data in a more readable form. You must be somewhat cautious in using concatenation with expressions that can result in a NULL value. Concatenation of a string value to a NULL string results in NULL. A check should be performed for string content in situations in which concatenated information could be partially or completely NULL.

String functions are quite useful in specific situations. You may want to delve into each of the functions with pertinent examples in SQL Server Books Online. Most of these functions are quite straightforward and easily used. The one function that may warrant a short illustration is the SUBSTRING() function.

The **SUBSTRING()** Function

It may be that you want to return a part of a string rather than the whole string. The SUBSTRING() function, which returns a part of a character or binary string, can be used for this task. The SUBSTRING() function, in a WHERE clause, may perform a table scan where an index was supposed to function (if an index was implemented). When the SUBSTRING() function does not include the first letter of the column being searched, a table scan is performed. This is not efficient processing. The following example illustrates the use of SUBSTRING() in a concatenation process:

```
SELECT AU_FName + ' ' + AU_LName AS 'Full Name',
  SUBSTRING (AU_FName, 1,1) + SUBSTRING (au_lname, 1,1) AS 'Initials'
    FROM Authors
```

All the string functions have their own place where they can be applied to assist with string manipulations. For the most part, you should find them very straightforward to use and not the focus of exam elements because of their ease of use. The final area of SQL Server functionality left to discuss is a series of functions that allow for various system-level interactions.

Working with System-Level Functions

As you have seen in the preceding two compilations, many functions are supplied to perform mathematical and character-manipulation operations. You can also use a third category of functions with the SELECT list known as system-specific functions. You can use system functions to retrieve special system or database information through T-SQL and the SELECT statement. Table 6.4 shows a compilation of the numerous system functions available in T-SQL.

Table 6.4	Database/System Functions	
System Function	Parameters	Description
COL_LENGTH()	(*table name, column name*)	Length of a column
COL_NAME()	(*table_id, Column_id*)	Name of a column
DATALENGTH()	(*Expression*)	Byte length of an expression
DB_ID()	(*database_name*)	Database number
DB_NAME()	(*database_ID*)	Database name
GETANSINULL()	(*database_name*)	Nullability setting
HOST_ID()	( )	Number for workstation
HOST_NAME()	( )	Name of workstation
IDENT_INCR()	(*table or view*)	Increment value for identity
IDENT_SEED()	(*table or view*)	Starting number for identity
INDEX_COL()	(*table name, index_id, key_id*)	Indexed column's name
ISNULL()	(*expression, value*)	Changes null values
NULLIF()	(*expression1, expression2*)	Null if equivalent
OBJECT_ID()	(*object_name*)	Object identification number
OBJECT_NAME()	(*Object_ID*)	Database object name
STATS_DATE()	(*Table_ID, Index_ID*)	Date statistics were updated
SUSER_SID()	(*login name*)	User's login identification
SUSER_SNAME()	(*server_user_id*)	User's login name
USER_ID()	(*user_name*)	User's database identification
USER_NAME()	(*user_ID*)	User's database username

ISNULL() can be useful when you want to convert all null values to a particular value. For example, look at the following query. This query converts all null values into zeros:

```
SELECT ISNULL (price, 0.0000), price FROM titles
```

System functions, information schema views, or the system stored procedures can be used to gain access to system information without querying the system tables directly. System tables can change significantly between versions of SQL Server.

SQL Server provides system stored procedures or information schema views for obtaining information about the properties of data, such as the type of data in a column (numeric, text, and so on) or the length of a column. This type of information is called metadata and is maintained by SQL Server for all server and database objects. Metadata can be used to find out information about the structure of data, the contents of a server, or information that specifies the design of objects.

Although it is possible to obtain data by querying any of the system tables directly, the system tables may not provide the information required in the future. It is recommended that system stored procedures, system functions, and information schema views be used because the contents of the system tables may change in future releases.

Information Schema Views

Information schema views provide a method independent of the system tables to view metadata. These views enable applications to work properly even though significant changes may have been made to the system tables and more changes may be made in the future. An application that uses the views rather than a direct query against the system tables should function in the same manner in the future as it does in the current SQL Server release.

The information schema views included in SQL Server conform to the SQL-92 Standard definition for the INFORMATION_SCHEMA. Names used in the SQL-92 standard for these views are different from those used by SQL Server, though the names from SQL Server can equivalently be mapped to those of the standard. The following list shows the SQL-92 names and the SQL Server equivalents:

➤ A SQL-92 "Catalog" is a SQL Server "Database."

➤ "Schema" in SQL-92 is an "Owner" in SQL Server.

➤ "Object" is the same in both SQL-92 and SQL Server.

➤ A "Domain" in SQL-92 is a user-defined data type in SQL Server.

When retrieving metadata from the information schema views, you must use a qualified name that includes the INFORMATION_SCHEMA in the position where you usually specify the username. For example:

```
SELECT * FROM Northwind.INFORMATION_SCHEMA.TABLES
```

For more information on the variety of metadata that can be obtained through the use of information schema views, use the Index tab of SQL Server Books Online. When you type information schema, the index shows links to all the appropriate views. Many system stored procedures can also be used to find information about server and database objects. With many of the procedures, however, you can also perform actions against the server, whereas information schema views are used solely to obtain metadata.

System Stored Procedures

Many administrative and informational activities in SQL Server can be accomplished through the use of SQL Server's many system stored procedures. System stored procedures are available to perform various activities, from obtaining information about server settings and objects to managing processes on the server to performing maintenance activities and much more.

It is not possible to cover all the procedures in this book, and SQL Server Books Online has full definitions and examples for these procedures. At various points throughout the book, references will be made to those procedures you are likely to find on the exam and others that will serve useful purposes in the future.

The following are typical situations that are tested on the exam:

- Date conversion using appropriate date functions
- String concatenation, including building and parsing functions
- System application design, in which system functions are used to programmatically control or manipulate the software functionality

Beyond the hundreds of functions available to SQL Server, there are other entire worlds we have yet to explore that we need to consider when developing and coding applications using T-SQL. We have already visited a few of the basic commands used to perform simple queries.

Providing the Orders to Be Followed

One of the powerful features of SQL Server is the capability to write scripts and batches to manipulate data. T-SQL includes features such as conditional execution constructs (IF...ELSE), looping constructs (WHILE), and cursor functionality. These features combine to make T-SQL a limited yet fairly powerful tool.

T-SQL programs are technically called *scripts*. A script is usually contained within a text file on disk, which is then loaded into some tool (the Query Analyzer, or the command-line equivalent called OSQL) and can be executed. A script is made of one or more *batches*. Each batch is made up of zero, one, or more transactions.

To separate one batch from another, put the word GO on a line by itself between the batches, like this:

```
SELECT * FROM sysobjects WHERE type = 'u'
go
SELECT COUNT(*) FROM sysobjects
```

This script contains two batches, one from the beginning of the file to the word GO, and another from the word GO to the end of the file. Knowing how batches work is important for several reasons. Batches determine variable scope. This subject is covered again later, but you should always remember that a variable can be used only within the batch where it is declared.

SQL Server compiles and runs scripts batch by batch. If you have a script with several batches in it, and one of the batches contains a syntax error, the rest of the batches do execute; but the statement in the batch that had an error does not execute. If one of the statements would cause a constraint violation, that statement doesn't execute, but all the other statements in the batch do execute.

Other runtime errors, such as arithmetic overflow errors, cause the batch to stop executing at that point, with all the preceding commands executed and none of the following commands executed.

When you use tools such as Query Analyzer or the command-line equivalent, OSQL, the tools themselves send the statements to SQL Server in batches, one batch at a time. SQL Server then compiles the single batch, processes it, and returns for the next batch as necessary. The keyword GO, then, isn't used by SQL Server; it is actually used by the various tools to determine when batches start and stop. The following illustrates a few rules you should know about batches:

➤ You can't add columns to a table and then reference them with an UPDATE or INSERT in the same batch.

➤ EXECUTE (EXEC) isn't required if it's on the first executable line of the batch.

➤ You can't combine CREATE VIEW, CREATE PROCEDURE, CREATE RULE, CREATE TRIGGER, or CREATE DEFAULT statements in a batch.

➤ You will have difficulties creating objects and then using them in the same batch. This is a bad practice and it usually doesn't work or produces unpredictable results.

Variables can cause other issues within scripts. Local variables declared within the script fall out of scope after a batch is ended with GO. You can use global variables, but then you open up issues around consuming resources and visibility to outsiders.

Coding with Variables

A variable is a temporary place to put pieces of data that you're working with. This can include dates, values, strings—essentially, anything you need to store during the execution of the script. A variable is very similar to a column. Differentiating a variable from a column is accommodated through the use of a @ or @@ prefix on the name. All variables must be declared before they can be utilized:

```
DECLARE @id int, @total int, @fee varchar(30)
```

You can create variables of most SQL data types, the exceptions to this being TEXT, NTEXT, and IMAGE. Instead of the large data types, you must accept the limitations of a standard string variable that holds up to 8,000 bytes, so you can build a varchar(8000) or an nvarchar(4000) in a variable. (Remember that the nchar and nvarchar types are double-wide characters, so they take up twice as much room as a varchar.) There is also a special variable type called TABLE that can be used to store a recordset. For example, you can declare a table variable and then load it with data something like this:

```
DECLARE @tmp TABLE (Id int, TableName varchar(50))
INSERT INTO @tmp SELECT Id, Name FROM sysobjects WHERE Type = 'u'
```

That creates a table similar to a temporary table that is available only within the current batch. This is faster and requires fewer resources than a temp table, but with a more limited scope. Be aware, however, that this consumes SQL Server memory, so don't put exceptionally large tables into these structures. You cannot use a variable of type table as the target of a SELECT..INTO statement, either. You can populate the table using only INSERT..SELECT, INSERT..VALUES, and UPDATE.

All variables cease to exist at the end of their scope. To keep things simple, SQL Server has only one scope for a variable, which is the local scope. Yes, there are "global variables" but they are reserved as functions for the server itself. The developer can not create global variables. That means that when your script has a GO in it, all variables are deallocated. If you intend to use the values contained within them again later in the script you will need to stow them away into a table. Variables need to be redeclared and reinitialized after the GO.

Setting and Using Variables

There are four ways to put a value into a variable. If you need to put data into a variable that comes out of a SELECT statement, you can do something like this:

```
SELECT @id = id FROM sysobjects WHERE name = 'syscolumns'
```

After executing this, and assuming that the variables are all declared proper-ly, you'll end up with some number in the @id variable. That's one way to put a value into a variable. You can also set a variable using SET:

```
SET @id = 42
   or
SET @today=getdate()
```

Another way to put a value into a variable is with the EXEC statement, utiliz-ing the return value from a stored procedure execution:

```
DECLARE @ReturnCode int
EXEC @ReturnCode = sp_who
```

Return codes used in this manner do not return data. Return codes provide status information such as success or failure of the procedure execution. Return codes are limited to data type int, so you can also use return codes to return integer data. The final way to set a variable is also to use an EXEC, but with an output parameter:

```
EXEC @ReturnCode = SampleProcedure @ID = 9, @Qty = @QtyVar OUTPUT
```

Output parameters (and input parameters, for that matter) are used in many circumstances when you must pass information from one procedure to another. This topic is expanded on later in the chapter, in the section "Results from Procedure Execution." Local variables are equally useful with-in a procedure. Global variables are set up by the server and, post–SQL Server Version 7, are more appropriately called functions.

Server Provided Global Values

Global variables are not variables. They are actually system functions that return various pieces of information about the current user environment for SQL Server. A global variable looks like a variable with a double @@ prefix. You cannot declare global variables. You can put as many @ signs as you want in front of a variable declaration and you will still have a local variable. Each of the following in essence declares the same type of local variable:

```
DECLARE @id int
DECLARE @@id int
DECLARE @@@id int
```

Global variables are functions; however, you cannot directly change them with a SET or SELECT statement. So if you use one of these special functions somewhere, realize that although it looks like a variable and can act like one, you can't assign any data to it; you can only read data from it. Table 6.5 lists some of the most common global variables in SQL Server 2000. There are many other functions available, but because they are less frequently used and you are unlikely to see them on the exam, they have been omitted from the list. To see the complete list, refer to Global Variables in SQL Server Books Online.

Table 6.5 Common Global Variables in SQL Server 2000	
Global Variable	Function
@@CURSOR_ROWS	The number of rows in the previously opened cursor
@@ERROR	The error number for the last SQL statement executed
@@FETCH_STATUS	The status of the last cursor fetch operation
@@IDENTITY	The value used for the last **INSERT INTO** for an identity
@@ROWCOUNT	The number of rows returned by the last statement
@@SERVERNAME	The name of the current server
@@SPID	The current process identifier used by SQL Server
@@TRANCOUNT	The number of nested transactions for the current statement
@@VERSION	The version string (date, version, and processor type)

To access the content of global variables, you can use a SELECT command or you can assign the values through use of a SET. You can also display the value using a PRINT statement. As we are now well into T-SQL coding, before we get much further, you should be documenting your work. The use of comments is essential in producing readable code that is usable by members of a development team.

Document As You Go

Comments have two entirely different purposes within a T-SQL batch or stored procedure. First, they can be used to document code, to make it easier for folks who have to maintain software in the future. Second, they can be used to temporarily disable lines of code within your batch when you're trying to get it working. Using comments is the most reliable way of ensuring that you or anyone else can figure out what your code does.

SQL Server has two methods for putting comments in your code. The first commenting method is to start the comment with a double dash (--). The double dash can appear anywhere on the line, and anything between the double dash and the end of the line is a comment and is not executed. For example:

```
--this is a comment on the whole line
SET @i = 42    --this is a comment, but the preceding code will execute
--Nothing on this line executes    SET @i = 21
```

The other style of comment, which is not seen as often anymore, is the slash-star comment:

```
/*              **************
Note that this is a multiple-line comment. This type
of comment can begin and end anywhere. It can start
or end in the middle of a line, though for readability
the markers on either end are usually segregated from
the comments.
****************          */
```

One thing to watch for is that the string GO within a comment on a line by itself causes an error. The more common convention by far is to use the double-dash style of comment. The new Query Analyzer for SQL Server 2000 provides you with a tool to create multiline comments quickly and easily. Just highlight the lines you want to comment and press Ctrl+Shift+C. This adds a double dash to the beginning of each highlighted line. To uncomment the text, just use Ctrl+Shift+R. This is a quick, easy, and painless way to comment out large chunks of code for testing and put them back later. There aren't any restrictions on any special words in the double-dash comment.

Statement Blocks with **BEGIN...END**

The BEGIN and END keywords work jointly to group statements together. They are used in later constructs for loops and conditional statements. BEGIN and END are used to create a statement block, which is a group of statements that can be used anywhere one statement can be used. For example, you could write this:

```
BEGIN
        UPDATE mytable SET emptype = 'manager' WHERE name ='fred'
        UPDATE mytable SET name = 'george' WHERE id = 42
END
```

Note that traditionally the indentation is the preferred style, although it is not required. BEGIN and END must occur as a pair. That's why they are indented as they are: The indentation makes it easy to spot if one of them is missing, and it makes it easy to tell where the statement block ends. The keyword RETURN exits out of a statement block without executing any further commands:

```
BEGIN
      UPDATE mytable SET emptype = 'manager' WHERE name =_ 'fred'
      RETURN
      UPDATE mytable SET name = 'george' WHERE id = 42
END
```

In the preceding example the second UPDATE never runs. It's not very useful now, but when used in combination with a conditional operation, such as IF...ELSE, it becomes a very useful command.

Conditional Statements with **IF...ELSE**

In many instances you want things to be performed only if certain conditions are met. Although there are several conditional constructs, by far the most common and easiest to use is the IF...ELSE construct. In T-SQL, an IF statement looks like this:

```
IF expression
      statement
ELSE
      statement
```

When multiple statements are to be executed based on the condition, you must use a statement block similar to the following:

```
IF expression
  BEGIN
      statement
      statement
      statement
  END
ELSE
  BEGIN
      statement
      statement
      statement
  END
```

The expression has to be an expression that evaluates to a true or false condition, unlike in some languages that use zero and nonzero. To evaluate something to true or false, you need to use the comparison operators.

Multiple Conditions with **CASE**

A CASE expression works like an IF statement, but it can be used in locations where an IF statement cannot. Specifically, a CASE expression returns one of a specific set of values based on the outcome of one or more expressions. Here's an example:

```
Select CASE datepart(weekday, getdate())
      WHEN 1 then 'Sunday'
      WHEN 2 then 'Monday'
      WHEN 3 then 'Tuesday'
      WHEN 4 then 'Wednesday'
      WHEN 5 then 'Thursday'
      WHEN 6 then 'Friday'
      WHEN 7 then 'Saturday'
      ELSE 'Unknown'
END
```

This example gets the day of week for today and turns it into a string that represents the text for the day of week. If, for some reason, the day of the week returned by the datepart() function is invalid, it returns the string Unknown. The result is placed into the variable @Result. This is the proper syntax to use when the comparison you want to use is equality—in this situation, datepart(weekday, getdate()) = 1. Notice that the expression starts with the keyword CASE and ends with the keyword END. This is the only time you can use an END without a BEGIN. This is called a "simple" CASE statement, in contrast with the "searched" CASE statement, discussed later in this section.

CASE statements are a flexible mechanism for adding logic within a query anywhere an expression is permitted. This means that you can also use a CASE expression in the WHERE clause, in an ORDER BY clause, or anywhere else an expression is allowed, similar to the following:

```
SELECT Name FROM sysobjects
  WHERE CASE id % 2 WHEN 1 THEN 1 ELSE 0 END = 1
```

The percent sign in this example is the modulo operator: It returns the remainder of the first number divided by the second number. Basically, what this SELECT statement does is return the names of all the odd-numbered (divisible by 2 with a remainder of 1) objects in the current database. When the ID modulo 2 returns a value of 1, then it's an odd number; the CASE statement returns 1, which the WHERE clause then compares to the number 1, and the row is included in the resultset. Otherwise, the CASE statement returns 0, which does not equal 1, so the row is not included in the resultset. The keen of wit will note that a better way to write this would be the following:

```
SELECT name FROM sysobjects WHERE id % 2 = 1
```

That, however, would not have demonstrated the point of using CASE statements in a WHERE clause, nor would it be nearly as convoluted. It would, however, be readable and efficient. A statement that is a shortcut for a CASE statement is called COALESCE. It takes a series of values and returns the first one that's not null. To condense many conditions into a single statement, use the following:

```
SELECT COALESCE(sid, 0) FROM sysusers
```

It is important to recognize that in many situations the first syntax you think of may not be the best way to write code based on ease of execution and efficiency. Always be willing to reexamine what you have written to see whether it can be done better. This is particularly important when examining complex queries and looping structures.

Loops in T-SQL

Whereas most languages provide many different looping constructs, T-SQL offers essentially only one: WHILE. A WHILE loop is similar to an IF statement, but after executing any conditional statements it retests the condition and returns to the top to start over again. A WHILE loop continues to execute until the conditional expression controlling the loop becomes false. If the expression never becomes false, you have a problem known as an infinite loop.

A classic looping structure has three steps. The initialization step sets up the variables and populates them to initial values. The test step evaluates the expression and determines whether the loop should be repeated. The augmentation step performs useful work, usually changes the expression somehow, and returns to the test step. Remember that the WHILE loop is the only construct provided for executing a counting loop, so a simple loop that counts to 100 would look like this:

```
DECLARE @i int
SET @i = 1  --initialization
WHILE @i <= 100 --test
BEGIN
     PRINT @i
     SET @i = @i + 1  --augmentation
END
```

Two special keywords can be used to control the execution of a WHILE loop. The CONTINUE keyword short-circuits the statement being executed and immediately goes back up to the loop test, ignoring the rest of the statement block. The BREAK keyword exits the WHILE loop and starts executing the statement after the end of the statement block. Here's an example of the BREAK keyword:

```
DECLARE @i int
SET @i = 1 --initialization
WHILE @i <= 100 --test
BEGIN
     PRINT @i
     SET @i = @i + 1   --incrementation
     IF @i = 42 BREAK
END
```

This causes the loop to stop counting when it reaches the number 42, but after it has printed 41. The number 42 will not be printed. Here's an example of using a CONTINUE keyword:

```
DECLARE @i int
SET @i = 1  --initialization
WHILE @i <= 100 --test
BEGIN
     PRINT @i
```

```
        SET @i = @i + 1    --augmentation
        IF @i = 42
        BEGIN
                SET @i = @i + 1
                continue
        END
END
```

This skips printing the number 42 and goes straight on to printing 43 and up to 100. Why does it increment the variable before using CONTINUE? If it didn't, the statement would actually print the number 42 and continue along, just as the first WHILE loop did.

Although loops are great, how often do you need to count things in T-SQL? It would be great if you could use this structure to work on one row from a table and then loop to perform the same operation with data from the next row. It is in working with cursors that looping operations become of primary importance. Cursors allow you to exercise a looping structure against a dataset and thus process a recordset from beginning to end.

Traditional Data Processing

Cursors are used to take the results of a SELECT statement and assign the output from the recordset to a set of variables, one row at a time. This enables you to walk through the recordset one record at a time and process the information.

Creating a cursor involves five steps:

1. Declare the cursor with the DECLARE CURSOR statement.

2. Open the cursor with the OPEN statement.

3. Use FETCH to get rows from the cursor.

4. Close the cursor with CLOSE.

5. Use DEALLOCATE to deallocate it.

Here's a short example:

```
DECLARE @Name sysname
DECLARE SysObj cursor for SELECT name FROM sysobjects
OPEN SysObj
FETCH NEXT FROM SysObj INTO @Name
WHILE @@FETCH_STATUS = 0
BEGIN
        PRINT @Name
        FETCH NEXT FROM SysObj INTO @Name
END
CLOSE SysObj
DEALLOCATE sysobj
```

The first line declares a variable called @Name of type sysname. The sysname data type is a special nvarchar data type that is used to hold the names of different system objects. If you're putting system names into a variable, it's the correct type to use because if the length of names changes from this version of SQL Server to the next, your code will still work.

The DECLARE CURSOR line declares what the cursor is going to do. In this case, the cursor is going to return the Name column in sysobjects. It is possible to return multiple fields, and data can be filtered with a WHERE clause. You can do anything in the SELECT statement that you can do in any other SELECT statement, including joins. The OPEN actually makes the cursor usable by allocating resources for it.

The FETCH NEXT fetches the next row from the cursor. Because you haven't fetched any rows from the cursor yet, it fetches the first one. It takes the value returned and places it into the @Name variable. Note that the returned data and the variable have to be the same type, or if they are two different types, they have to convert implicitly. FETCH NEXT automatically sets the global variable @@FETCH_STATUS to 0 if the fetch was successful, and to other values (refer to Table 6.6) for other results. The WHILE loop will continue execution as long as there are records within the dataset to process, in other words, @@FETCH_STATUS = 0.

Table 6.6	Return Values from a Fetch Operation
Return Value	Significance
0	The **FETCH** statement was successful.
-1	The **FETCH** statement failed or the row is beyond the resultset.
-2	The row fetched is missing.

After the sample code executes the printing, there's another FETCH. This operation iterates the loop, advancing the cursor to the next record in the dataset and changing the @@FETCH_STATUS when there is no data left to execute. After the FETCH is the end of the loop, which then returns up to the test. Although @@FETCH_STATUS doesn't change every time, it changes when the end of the cursor is reached, so the loop doesn't go on forever.

The CLOSE and DEALLOCATE are what you use to tell SQL Server that you're finished with the cursor. These close the cursor, which releases any locks you have, and deallocate the cursor, freeing the memory resources used by the cursor. Now, this was just a basic example. There are far more useful illustrations of using a cursor to follow within this segment.

A few options are available in the DECLARE CURSOR statement. The cursor used in the previous example was the default cursor type. It is important to recognize the default behavior of a cursor if no other behavior is specified. It puts a shared lock on rows in the cursor for the duration of the cursor, so they cannot be modified while the cursor is reading them. To avoid the locking problem, tell SQL Server to make a copy of the data and run the cursor from the copy by using the INSENSITIVE keyword. The cursor takes longer to open because SQL Server actually copies all the data to run the cursor into a temporary table.

Another thing you can do with cursors is scroll back and forth through them. This is done with the SCROLL keyword. Those are the options for scrolling and fetching. Now see what things look like for inserts and updates through a cursor. By default, a cursor is updatable. To prevent updates to a cursor, use the FOR READ ONLY clause, which is placed after the SELECT statement in the DECLARE cursor:

```
DECLARE Flintstone SCROLL CURSOR
        FOR SELECT Id, Value FROM Bedrock ORDER BY 1
        FOR READ ONLY
```

To update through a cursor, you need to tell SQL Server that you're going to update the cursor using the FOR UPDATE clause, which goes in the same place as the FOR READ ONLY in the preceding code example. To actually update the data, you perform a positioned update by using a special form of the UPDATE statement, UPDATE WHERE CURRENT OF:

```
DECLARE @ID int, @Value varchar(30)
DECLARE Flintstone cursor
        FOR SELECT Id, Value FROM Bedrock
        FOR UPDATE
OPEN Flintstone
FETCH NEXT FROM Flintstone INTO @ID, @Value
UPDATE Bedrock SET Value = 'Fredrick'
        WHERE CURRENT OF Flintstone
CLOSE Flintstone
DEALLOCATE Flintstone
```

Several rules have to be followed to update through a cursor. First, the cursor cannot be read-only. That's fairly obvious, but it implies that the cursor does not have the INSENSITIVE or SCROLL options turned on, in addition to not having the READ ONLY option turned on. Many other options (which are discussed later) cause a cursor to be read-only. The FOR UPDATE in the cursor declaration is optional, but suggested. A cursor defaults to an updatable state, but if you explicitly state that the cursor is going to be updated, your code will be easier to read. It would be even better if the update specified FOR UPDATE OF *columnname*, because that's the only column that is updated.

Everything that has been discussed so far about cursors is part of the ANSI SQL-92 standard, so the code is fairly generic and should be portable to any other database management system that is SQL-92 compliant. There are many T-SQL–specific extensions to the cursor syntax that enable you to make performance enhancements for your cursor operations. Some of these extensions are described in the following list:

➤ LOCAL—This is the optional state for a cursor. It means that the cursor is available for only the current batch and the current connection. To change the default behavior, set the Default to Local Cursor database option.

➤ GLOBAL—"Global" in this case means "global to the current connection." Declaring a cursor as global makes it available to subsequent batches or stored procedures that are run by the connection. The cursor is not available to other connections, even if the connection is from the same user.

➤ FORWARD_ONLY—This tells SQL Server that the cursor is going to run only from the beginning of the recordset to the end of the recordset. The cursor is not allowed to go backward or skip around. The only fetch that works is FETCH NEXT. This is an optimization; it allows SQL Server to consume less overhead for the cursor.

➤ STATIC—This does the same thing as the INSENSITIVE keyword in the SQL-92 syntax.

➤ KEYSET—If you use this, your cursor will not be able to access data inserted by other users after the cursor is opened. Also, if a row is deleted by another user, an @@FETCH_STATUS of -2 (row is missing) will be returned if you attempt to fetch a deleted row. This type of cursor has less overhead than a DYNAMIC cursor, but (unless FORWARD_ONLY is also specified) all the different FETCH options are available.

➤ DYNAMIC—A DYNAMIC cursor is the opposite of a KEYSET cursor. All inserts and deletes done by users are immediately available to the cursor. However, FETCH ABSOLUTE does not work with a dynamic cursor because the underlying data may change the position of the records.

➤ FAST_FORWARD—This is a cursor that has all the properties of a FORWARD_ONLY and READ_ONLY cursor, and it's designed to go forward quickly with little overhead.

➤ READ_ONLY—This does not allow updates to the cursor.

➤ SCROLL_LOCKS—This causes SQL Server to exclusively lock each row that is touched by the cursor as the rows are read in, to prevent other users from updating the record.

➤ OPTIMISTIC—This causes SQL Server to not lock any rows during the scrolling of the cursor, and you have to just hope that none of the rows being changed by the cursor is simultaneously being changed by somebody else. Attempting to change a row through the cursor results in an error.

➤ TYPE_WARNING—If somehow your cursor changes type implicitly, a warning is issued.

A few notes about the preceding list. First, the default LOCAL or GLOBAL status of a cursor can be changed by changing the server-wide Default to Local Cursor configuration setting. Next, if you specify FORWARD_ONLY and don't specify STATIC or KEYSET, the cursor behaves as a DYNAMIC cursor. In other words, the cursor sees any records inserted by other connections while the cursor is open. In addition, if you don't use the SCROLL, STATIC, KEYSET, or DYNAMIC options to specify that a cursor should scroll, the cursor will be FORWARD_ONLY. Also, you cannot use FORWARD_ONLY and FAST_FORWARD together.

Cursors are flexible mechanisms that can be used to solve problems when no other solution exists. Keep in mind, however, that there are many approaches to solving most database issues that don't require cursors. Don't get caught in a cursor trap; they carry significant overhead and are required only for specialty tasks. Most day-to-day database transactions won't require their use. They are, however, a useful coding mechanism to add to the scripting toolbox.

The two most similar of the coding implementations are stored procedures and user-defined functions. Stored procedures and user-defined functions can be used to manipulate and store data by encapsulating SELECT, INSERT, UPDATE, and DELETE functionality.

Converting Constructs to Code

Both stored procedures and user-defined functions allow you to pass and return parameters. To control what stored procedures and functions do, different values can be passed that control how they work. In addition, parameters provide a way to retrieve the data found by the execution.

Using Stored Procedures

Stored procedures are the mainstay of application programming with SQL Server. Typically, applications that perform well and that are easily managed employ stored procedures exclusively for their data retrieval and update needs. This helps facilitate centralized management of queries, the capability to change data models and tune queries without rewriting code, and the capability to manage transactions without user intervention.

Playing the role of the middle tiers in n-tier architecture, stored procedures, and user-defined functions provides facilities for validating and modifying data to conform to business rules.

Using stored procedures is a powerful and flexible technique for performing tasks within an application. A stored procedure, when it is first used, is compiled into an execution plan that remains in the procedure cache. This provides for some of the performance over ad-hoc operations. The performance improvements in SQL 7 and 2000 are not as drastic as in previous versions because changes in the way that other operations now execute provide them with some of the same benefits as stored procedures. A stored procedure can accept parameters, process operations against any number of databases, and return results to the calling process.

A stored procedure, like other operations, can be encrypted to protect the details of the operation. An application might need to send several operations across a network and respond conditionally to the results. This can be handled with a single call if the logic is contained in a single stored procedure. The use of local and global cursors can expose information to the application or other applications as needed, giving provisions for complex development processes with conversations between separate processes.

A stored procedure is any set of T-SQL statements compiled into a single execution plan and stored within the database for future execution. When a stored procedure is compiled into an execution plan, it is compiled once and stored into RAM, where the execution plan may be reused by the server. This presents a slight improvement in performance over noncached coding implementations.

Temporary stored procedures used frequently in earlier versions are still supported by SQL Server, although improvements in other areas should eliminate or reduce the need for their use. The most significant improvement is the capability to compile and maintain most SQL operations in cache for prolonged periods.

A stored procedure can have input and output parameters. A stored procedure also has an integer return value that can be used to indicate success or failure or can be used as an alternative output. This means that a stored pro-cedure can return results in several ways: with an integer return code, with one or more resultsets, and with output parameters.

The T-SQL CREATE PROCEDURE statement is used to create a stored procedure. You can execute this statement from the Query Analyzer, or you can access it through the Enterprise Manager by right-clicking on Stored Procedures under the database and choosing the New Stored Procedure option. The procedure is then saved within the current database as an object.

Creating Stored Procedures

Stored procedures are created using the CREATE PROCEDURE statement. The CREATE PROCEDURE statement has to be the first executable line in a batch, and the stored procedure continues until the end of the batch, which is until the end of the file or until the word GO. You can abbreviate the word PROCEDURE to just PROC.

Stored procedures are used as a way to perform complex activities, and they can be used to hide the details of a process for security reasons. In this respect, stored procedures share similar qualities as views, providing the nec-essary results without the need for the knowledge of the underlying objects. If a user has permission to execute a procedure, he can perform activities not normally covered by his own permissions. A user who is not permitted to delete or insert data could do so through the execution of a procedure that performs these activities on behalf of the user. This may seem like a breach of security, but remember that the procedure only does exactly as it's told and removes data only as instructed in a controlled manner.

A simple procedure could be nothing more than a saved query. In the fol-lowing example a procedure is created that will list all tables in the current database.

```
CREATE PROCEDURE TableList AS
SELECT name FROM sysobjects WHERE xtype = 'u'
GO
```

The procedure returns the same thing all the time: the list of tables that include the objects of type 'u' in the database in which the stored procedure was created. An improvement in the procedure to allow for more flexibility could possibly allow a parameter to be passed in so that any object types could be listed. A better name should also then be chosen, as in the following:

```
CREATE PROCEDURE ObjectList
   @ObjectType varchar(2)
 AS
```

```
SELECT name FROM sysobjects WHERE xtype = @ObjectType
GO
```

This procedure makes use of a parameter, supplied to allow for input to the procedure. A parameter is a variable that is passed in to a stored procedure to give the stored procedure a little guidance on how to get things done. When you use parameters in this manner, the finished product is a far more usable and flexible stored procedure. One problem exists, however: If a parameter is not provided, you end up with an error. For this reason, in many circumstances you will want to provide parameter defaults within the procedure so that the parameter itself becomes optional. Many programming languages have implementations for optional parameters, and in T-SQL it is simply a parameter with a default value supplied, as in the following completed version of the process:

```
CREATE PROCEDURE ObjectList
   @ObjectType varchar(2) = 'u'
 AS
SELECT name FROM sysobjects WHERE xtype = @ObjectType
GO
```

Look at how this procedure can now be used. Using this single procedure, we can list primary keys using a type 'PK' or system tables using a type 'S'. When no parameter is passed into the procedure, the default, a type 'u', will be utilized by the process.

Parameters are commonplace within stored procedures. Input parameters within our example allow for flexibility in the use of a procedure, but you may also desire a procedure that provides feedback in the form of parameter information passed out of the procedure. Output parameters are one of three mechanisms for obtaining output from a procedure.

Results from Procedure Execution

There are essentially two types of procedures needed by most systems. A common type of procedure is one that performs a necessary process. In many cases there is no need for much output from the process. The purpose of the process is to perform the task and that is all. The second type of procedure is one that provides output. Anything from a simple query, complex joining of data, or another form of feedback is needed by the process to provide information from the system.

The most common form of output provided by a stored procedure is a recordset, a set of data in the form of columns and rows to provide information as an end result of the procedure. The results of a query or complex logical process that provides the recordset define the makeup of the procedure but represent only one form of data that can be returned. When a stored procedure is executed, a separate recordset is provided as the output for each SELECT.

Another common form of output is a return value indicating the success, failure, or other status of the procedure. A return value is always an integer value and is passed from the procedure upon completion using a RETURN statement. A common use of a return value is to indicate the result of a procedure execution. A zero returned from the procedure would indicate successful execution; a negative value could indicate an error; a positive value could indicate a choice made. Return values have somewhat limited usage because they can be only of an integer data type.

Other possible outputs from a procedure include messages from the system such as how many records were processed, printed output resulting from the execution of a PRINT statement, and error messages provided when problems exist in the code or in the data.

True Customization with User-Defined Functions

User-defined functions, a new feature for SQL Server 2000, provide further encapsulation of logic into highly reusable and efficient components. In some applications, the functions available from the SQL Server installation do not suit all needs. It is for these instances that user-defined functions were intended. The functions can contain any combination of T-SQL statements. These functions act similarly to stored procedures with the exception that any errors occurring inside the function cause the entire function to fail.

SQL Server supports three varieties of user-defined functions:

➤ Scalar functions

➤ Inline table-valued function

➤ Multi-statement table-valued functions

The functions defined can accept parameters if needed and return either a scalar value or a table. A function cannot change any information outside the scope of the function and therefore maintains no information when processing has been completed. Other activities that are not permitted include returning information to the user and sending email. The CREATE FUNCTION statement is used to define a user-defined function similar to the following:

```
CREATE FUNCTION MyFunction (@Num1 smallint, @Num2 smallint)
      RETURNS real AS
```

```
BEGIN
Declare @ReturnValue real
            If (@Num1 > @Num2)
             Set @ReturnValue = @Num1 * 2 + 30
            If (@Num1 = @Num2)
             Set @ReturnValue = @Num1 * 1.5 + 30
            If (@Num1 < @Num2)
             Set @ReturnValue = @Num1 * 1.25 + 30
            If (@Num1 < 0)
             Set @ReturnValue = @Num2 * 1.15 + 30
            Return(@ReturnValue)
END
```

 You will definitely see user-defined functions on the exam. The coding is similar to that of stored procedures. The short description given here does not indicate the lack of exam coverage for this topic. It simply shows that it would be redundant to go through all the information presented in the preceding section again.

User-defined functions (UDFs) represent powerful functionality that has a wide variety of uses within the SQL Server environment.

Alternative Coding Mechanisms

Triggers are sections of SQL Server programming code that execute when data modification is performed on a table in the database. Triggers offer a method of constraining data input and performing other tasks when data is added, deleted, or updated in the database. Other methods of constraining data include using constraints and rules.

Trigger and constraints handle data control differently. Constraints such as FOREIGN KEY and CHECK constraints are fast and efficient, but triggers offer more functionality. If you are looking for quick and easy, use constraints. If you need flexibility and functionality, use a trigger.

Because our current topic focuses more on coding and the implementation of T-SQL, the focus for our constraint discussions will center around triggers. We will revisit the discussion of choices based on security and performance in Chapter 8, "Designing for Optimized Data Access," and Chapter 9, "Designing a Database Security Plan."

Code Responses to Actions

Triggers perform an important role in SQL Server 2000: They enable you to control what happens when a user inserts, deletes, or updates data in the tables or views in your database. This control can be used to restrict the values that are inserted, prevent deletion of records, update related tables, store denormalized data, or log actions. Triggers might be used for these reasons and others, but many triggers are used to restrict or constrain data input when traditional constraints are not capable enough. A trigger contains code that is similar to a stored procedure, but it is automatically executed when an INSERT, DELETE, or UPDATE statement is invoked. Triggers are often used to help enforce and follow business logic for your organization.

There is no way to force a trigger to execute without performing the associated data modification on the table. Triggers can be used to enforce the business rules in a database when constraints are not sufficient. Typically, triggers are a more CPU-intensive way to implement tasks, and you are usually better off to implement restrictions through constraints, such as FOREIGN KEY or CHECK constraints, because they do not cause performance to suffer as much. Most of the performance impact that triggers suffer from occurs when they reference tables that are not in memory.

Triggers can enforce complex restrictions by raising a user-defined error using the RAISERROR() command. Triggers can be used to track or log changes to a table. More than one AFTER trigger can be created on a table. With INSTEAD OF triggers, only one trigger of each type (INSERT, UPDATE, or DELETE) can be created on a table. Triggers consume relatively more performance than FOREIGN KEY constraints. If the trigger references only tables that are in memory, performance is similar. Stored procedures, both local and remote, might be executed from triggers.

When you're working with triggers, it is important to remember the order in which they execute. INSTEAD OF triggers execute instead of the attempted data modification (INSERT, UPDATE, or DELETE). The INSTEAD OF trigger could actually proceed to perform the modification to the table itself. Constraints are applied after the INSTEAD OF trigger, and AFTER triggers are executed after the constraints and data modification take place.

When comparing stored procedures to triggers, and assuming that the code used is of similar complexity, both offer some advantages. Stored procedures might be less CPU intensive on data failures than AFTER triggers, because an AFTER trigger reverses the data modifications, whereas a stored procedure just doesn't make the data modification. Stored procedures follow the same ownership chain rules as views do. For example, if you own a table, and you own the stored procedure that performs an action on the table (such as a DELETE), then you only need to grant the EXECUTE permission to the stored procedure and do not need to grant the DELETE permission to the table. In this way, the stored procedures can offer greater data security; but when you implement a trigger, the code will be executed when the data is modified in the table, regardless of whether the stored procedure is used. This function of triggers is useful because some people are granted access directly to the table and the code will still be executed.

Many AFTER triggers can be specified for each INSERT, UPDATE, or DELETE action. If multiple triggers exist, you can specify the first and last trigger to fire. The others are fired in no particular order, and you cannot control that order. An AFTER trigger can be defined only on a table. Only one INSTEAD OF trigger can be defined for each of the triggering actions; however, an INSTEAD OF trigger can be defined on a view as well as a table.

 In previous releases, you could use triggers to help enforce referential integrity constraints. This was difficult and required that you eliminate other elements, such as **FOREIGN KEY** constraints. In SQL Server 2000, it is far more efficient to use cascading actions.

To define a trigger, you can select the Manage Triggers option from the Table Design window. You can also go to the table to which you want to attach a trigger, and you can find the option as an extension of the pop-up menu off the All Tasks option.

You can use the T-SQL CREATE TRIGGER statement to create triggers for all applicable operations. You can access this command from the Enterprise Manager by using the Managing Triggers option. Managing Triggers in the Enterprise Manager (and in other objects as well) provides you with the shell of a CREATE statement even if you are changing an existing trigger. The Enterprise Manager enables you to change an existing trigger, first dropping the trigger before re-creation. The ALTER TRIGGER statement is used to change the definition of a trigger without dropping it first, and it is used only through T-SQL. An example of the creation of a trigger using T-SQL is as follows:

```
CREATE TRIGGER UpdatedCustomer ON CustomerTable
FOR INSERT, UPDATE AS
            declare @phone nvarchar(20)
            declare @Contact nvarchar(100)
            select @phone = phoneno,
                @contact = contactname from inserted
            RAISERROR(50100, 1, 1, @Contact, @Phone)
```

This procedure is one of my favorite implementations for use in customer applications. In the case of customer information, an automated alert that sends an email message to the salesperson could be defined around the error being raised. On an INSERT, a clerk or salesperson may make an initial client contact call based on an email that the alert may send. In the event of an UPDATE, the clerk could call the client to ensure that the new information is accurate. The benefit is that the trigger automatically fires when new rows are added to the table or changes are made to the customer information.

Triggers are powerful tools for development of a database system. Consider the following points when you are creating and using trigger functionality in a DBMS environment:

➤ Triggers can process all three actions: UPDATE, DELETE, and INSERT.

➤ AFTER triggers apply to a single table and can be made column-level.

➤ AFTER triggers cannot be created on views or temporary tables.

➤ INSTEAD OF triggers are the only triggers that can be created on views.

➤ Triggers can be created with the SQL Server Enterprise Manager, the Query Analyzer, and programmatically through SQL-DMO.

➤ Triggers are database objects and follow object-naming conventions.

➤ Triggers can be created and altered by the sysadmin, db_owner, and db_ddladmin roles, as well as the table owner.

➤ Triggers cannot use any of the following statements:

ALTER DATABASE	ALTER TABLE	CREATE
DISK	DROP	GRANT
LOAD DATABASE	LOAD TRANSACTION	RECONFIGURE
RESTORE DATABASE	REVOKE	SELECT INTO
UPDATE STATISTICS		

If possible, you should avoid creating triggers for simple tasks; constraints perform the task faster and with less CPU overhead. Triggers should be used only when constraints do not offer the power or flexibility required.

After a trigger is created, you might need to make slight changes to the way it processes because policies or procedures change in your organization. This is not a problem. You can easily change the way a trigger processes, either by deleting and then re-creating the trigger, or by altering the trigger via a one-step process using ALTER TRIGGER. It is worth noting that when you change a trigger from within the Enterprise Manager, it shows you a CREATE trigger operation even though it is an ALTER that is actually used behind the scenes.

ALTER is the preferred method over dropping and re-creating because the ID in the syscomments table remains the same. If you have other scripts on your server that have been coded to look for the trigger by its object_ID, these scripts will fail if the object_ID is changed; coding your scripts with these types of dependencies is generally a bad practice. The syntax for

ALTER TRIGGER is comparable to that of the CREATE TRIGGER statement and has all the same arguments.

Triggers might also be renamed by any user who has the correct permission and by the database owner. Triggers must follow the rules for naming identifiers. You are not likely to have to rename a trigger very often, but you might end up with a naming conflict with another item you want to add to the database. If policy or procedures prevent you from being able to rename the new item, you might have to rename your trigger.

When a trigger is renamed, any references to the trigger name inside of other objects are not updated, and they have to be updated manually or they will not work. You should run sp_depends 'trigger_name' to find out where the trigger is referenced before you rename the trigger. To rename a trigger, use the sp_rename system stored procedure. In some instances you might want to delete the trigger and re-create it with a new name. The next topic is deleting or dropping triggers.

Dropping Triggers

Deleting triggers is as easy as renaming them. Deleting a trigger does not affect the underlying table or data contained in the table. To remove triggers using the SQL Server Query Analyzer, you have to use the DROP TRIGGER statement. When dropping a trigger, you should first find out whether any tables or objects reference it. To find out which objects reference a trigger, run sp_depends 'trigger_name' before you drop the trigger. If you do not check to see which objects reference the trigger, you risk having those objects fail to function. You cannot perform this check after you have deleted the trigger.

Appropriate Use of **INSTEAD OF** Triggers

INSTEAD OF triggers can change any data-modification statement into a customized action. INSTEAD OF triggers place all the rows of a DELETE statement that would have taken place into the Deleted table, and in the case of an INSERT statement, all the rows that would have been inserted into the Inserted table. You can then script an appropriate set of steps to validate the proposed action, before the application or violation of any constraints that might be implemented. Constraint violations roll back your last statement, whereas the INSTEAD OF trigger can test for violations and then modify the proposed action to avoid the constraint violation. If an INSTEAD OF trigger has already been executed, and the constraints are still violated, then any actions taken in the INSTEAD OF trigger are rolled back. With the INSTEAD OF INSERT trigger, the proposed update (including who attempted it) can be logged, and you can issue a rollback before the constraints are applied.

Before SQL Server 2000, the only type of trigger available was an AFTER trigger—a trigger that contains a set of statements that fire after a modification to a table has been made and after any applicable constraints have been applied. INSTEAD OF triggers are new to SQL Server 2000 and execute instead of the triggering action.

INSTEAD OF triggers are not fired recursively. If the INSTEAD OF INSERT trigger fires, and then proceeds to issue the INSERT on the table, the INSTEAD OF trigger would be skipped, constraints would be checked, and the AFTER trigger would fire. Failure at the constraints would cause the statement to be cancelled, and a rollback could be issued if the AFTER trigger fails. A rollback would reverse all actions performed since the original statement was issued, so any actions performed by the INSTEAD OF trigger would also be rolled back.

One of the great benefits of INSTEAD OF triggers is that they can be added to views. The INSTEAD OF trigger is the only type of trigger that can be placed on a view. Normally, views that reference multiple tables are not updatable because changes can be made to only one table at a time. With the help of an INSTEAD OF trigger, these views can be made to appear to update multiple tables at once. Also, views based on multiple tables using joins cannot normally have data deleted, but with an INSTEAD OF trigger, this too can be accomplished. An INSTEAD OF trigger has access to the deleted table, so it can use this deleted information to find which underlying base table needs to have data deleted.

The following are some guidelines you should observe when creating INSTEAD OF triggers:

➤ There can be only one INSTEAD OF trigger for each action on a table.

➤ INSTEAD OF triggers are new to SQL Server 2000 and execute before the triggering statement. INSTEAD OF triggers are the only triggers that can be implemented on a view.

➤ INSTEAD OF triggers are never recursively fired. That is, if an INSTEAD OF trigger fires a custom INSERT statement to the same triggered table, the INSTEAD OF trigger will not fire again.

➤ INSTEAD OF triggers cannot be used on tables that have cascaded updates.

➤ INSTEAD OF triggers can reference text, ntext, and image columns in their Inserted and Deleted tables.

Trigger Firing Order

Only a few options allow you to change when a trigger is executed. One is when the trigger is created, and the other is with the sp_settriggerorder procedure. Recursion can also play a role in how triggers are fired or executed. The first thing to look at is the different types of triggers.

When you create a trigger, you create an INSTEAD OF, AFTER, or FOR trigger. Depending on the type of trigger, your trigger will execute at a different time. This is an issue that has been previously discussed in this chapter, but it is important, and it's worth covering again.

When creating a trigger, you use one of the following statements:

➤ CREATE TRIGGER *name* ON *table* INSTEAD OF *action*—Trigger fires before constraints are checked and before that data modification is processed.

➤ CREATE TRIGGER *name* ON *table* AFTER *action*—Trigger fires after the data modification and after constraints are checked. Constraints can cancel the statement, causing the trigger to never fire.

➤ CREATE TRIGGER *name* ON *table* FOR *action*—Trigger fires after data modification and after constraints are checked. There is no difference between FOR and AFTER. Microsoft's SQL Server includes both FOR and AFTER for backward compatibility but treats them the same way. Before SQL Server 2000, all triggers were FOR triggers.

In addition to the type of trigger you are working with, you can set a FIRST and LAST trigger when you are working with AFTER triggers. Because there can be only one INSTEAD OF trigger of each type on a table, there is no need or reason to attempt to set the fire order of INSTEAD OF triggers. However, there can be many AFTER triggers of each type set on a single table.

You might have multiple triggers so that you can define multiple actions to take when data in a table is modified. Rather than having multiple triggers, you can alter a trigger, making it larger and larger to accommodate all the logic. In many cases, smaller, more specific triggers can be easier to manage, code, and troubleshoot. Because there are multiple triggers of each type, you might have a reason to want one to fire before the others, and therefore want to set the order of triggers. To change the fire order of triggers, you can use the sp_settriggerorder stored procedure.

Outside of FIRST and LAST, you have no control over how triggers will fire. If you have already specified a FIRST or LAST trigger, you cannot specify another trigger as FIRST or LAST. If you want to remove a FIRST or LAST option, the ALTER TRIGGER statement always removes this setting when it is executed. If you alter a trigger and want to leave it as FIRST or LAST, you will have to reexecute the sp_settriggerorder statement.

Exam Prep Questions

1. You have an accounting SQL Server database application that is accessed by 50 users on your company network. When a user inserts or updates a record, you want to make sure that all the required columns have appropriate values. Which of the following would be best for this situation?

   ❑ A. A stored procedure and a trigger
   ❑ B. A batch and a trigger
   ❑ C. An UPDATE trigger and an INSERT trigger
   ❑ D. One trigger by itself

   Answer: D. A single trigger can be used to perform validation on more than one event, such as an INSERT and an UPDATE. For more information about the differences between trigger types, see the "Alternative Coding Mechanisms" section of this chapter.

2. You are a developer for a database. Currently the structure of data and the usage have been causing high CPU utilization on the server. You have decided that you must add several triggers to your database to validate data and generate alerts based on data modifications. You are worried about the impact of the triggers on your already heavily utilized server. Generally, how will triggers affect the performance of your server?

   ❑ A. They will incur low performance overhead, most of it involved in referencing tables.
   ❑ B. They will severely impact database performance.
   ❑ C. They do not impact performance whatsoever.
   ❑ D. They consume less resources than any other type of resource in SQL Server; execution of programming logic uses most of the performance.

   Answer: A. Triggers usually require very little CPU time. Most of the time involved in executing a trigger comes from referencing tables, which might have to be read from the disk. Execution time is usually low, but actual impact can be hampered depending on what is done in the programming code of the trigger. You might code CPU-intensive tasks into your trigger by calling on certain stored procedures or commands. These commands might not be typical in a trigger. For more information about triggers, see the section "Code Responses to Actions."

3. You have a database that contains several FOREIGN KEY and CHECK constraints. Users are having problems with data entry on the database, because the data that they are adding is constantly in violation of the CHECK constraints. Corporate policy regarding database design prevents you from modifying the current constraints, so you decide to implement your changes via a trigger. Which types of triggers would be best suited for this task?

❑ A. UPDATE, DELETE, and INSERT triggers.

❑ B. Just UPDATE and INSERT triggers.

❑ C. INSTEAD OF triggers.

❑ D. Triggers cannot be used in this circumstance.

Answer: C. INSTEAD OF triggers would be required for this task, because you must check for constraint violations before the update occurs. If there are constraint violations, AFTER triggers will not fire. Most likely you will be implementing INSTEAD OF INSERT or INSTEAD OF INSERT, UPDATE triggers. When trigger actions are listed, such as an INSERT trigger, you cannot know for sure whether it is an INSTEAD OF or AFTER trigger, but you should assume that it is a FOR or AFTER trigger if not specifically mentioned. For more information about the order in which triggers and constraints are applied, see the section "Trigger Firing Order."

4. You are working for a medical agency that tracks statistics for doctors throughout the country; these statistics are later involved in economic decisions. This year, the medical agency plans on creating statistics for the salaries of doctors and storing them in a SalarySurvey table. To get more accurate statistics, the agency does not include values of salaries that are greater than $200,000 or smaller than $10,000. Which of the following is the best way to implement this plan? All these examples are set to support only single-row inserts, which would not be typical on a production database.

❑ A. The following code:

```
CREATE TRIGGER SalaryCheck
  ON SalarySurvey
  FOR INSERT
  AS
    IF (SELECT MonthlySalary FROM inserted)
      > 200,000 or
      (SELECT MonthlySalary FROM inserted)
      < 10,000
      BEGIN
        RAISERROR('Cant Enter Salary: Range Error',
              16, 1) WITH LOG
        ROLLBACK TRANSACTION
      END
```

❑ B. The following code:

```
CREATE TRIGGER SalaryCheck
  ON SalarySurvey
  FOR INSERT
  AS
    IF (SELECT MonthlySalary FROM updated)
      > 200,000 or
      (SELECT MonthlySalary FROM updated)
      < 10,000
      BEGIN
        RAISERROR('Cant Enter Salary: Range Error',
              16, 1) WITH LOG
        REVERSE TRANSACTION
      END
```

❑ C. The following code:

```
CREATE TRIGGER SalaryCheck
  ON SalarySurvey
  AFTER UPDATE
  AS
    IF (SELECT MonthlySalary FROM inserted)
      > 200,000 or
      (SELECT MonthlySalary FROM inserted)
      < 10,000
      BEGIN
        RAISERROR ( 'Cannot Enter Salary - out of range',
              16, 1) WITH LOG
        ROLLBACK TRANSACTION
      END
```

❑ D. The following code:

```
CREATE TRIGGER SalaryCheck
  ON SalarySurvey
  FOR INSERT
  AS
    IF (SELECT MonthlySalary FROM inserted)
      > 200,000 or
      (SELECT MonthlySalary FROM inserted)
      > 10,000
      BEGIN
        RAISERROR ( 'Cannot Enter Salary - out of range',
              16, 1) WITH LOG
        ROLLBACK TRANSACTION
      END
```

Answer: A. This is the only answer choice that is implemented as an INSERT trigger and has correct use of ROLLBACK TRANSACTION. For more information about INSERT, UPDATE, and DELETE triggers, see the section "Code Responses to Actions."

5. Paul has a five-batch script, and he is creating a T-SQL cursor in batch one. He wants to use the cursor in batches two, three, and four. What must Paul do to access the cursor from any batch? Choose the best answer.

❑ A. Use DECLARE CURSOR in every batch and then repopulate them.

❑ B. Creating this type of cursor is not possible in SQL Server 2000.

❑ C. Create the cursor using the GLOBAL keyword.

❑ D. Create the cursor using the PUBLIC keyword.

Answer: C. Global cursors are available to later batches from the same connection. By the way, there is no such thing as a public cursor. This is a good example of an exam question because none of the answers looks quite right and you'll spend way too much time trying to figure it out. Remember, the instructions are to pick the best answer. There's some information on cursor scope in the section "Traditional Data Processing" that may help if you had trouble with this question.

6. Bob has just finished using his cursor and he will not need it for the rest of the time he is connected. What can Bob do to fully release all system resources held up by the cursor?

❑ A. Run DBCC_CURSOR_PERFORMANCE

❑ B. Run the DEALLOCATE command

❑ C. Run the CLOSE CURSOR command

❑ D. Run the ALL SYSTEMS statement with the CURSOR argument

Answer: B. The DEALLOCATE command releases all the resources used by a cursor. This information is covered in the section "Traditional Data Processing."

7. Paul needs to create a cursor that is sensitive to data updates and deletes. He knows that the number of rows in the query he's using should be around 50. Paul subsequently uses the @@CURSOR_ROWS global variable to check for the number of rows in the cursor, which apparently should be around 50. To his surprise, he notices another value. What is this value?

- ❏ A. 0
- ❏ B. 1
- ❏ C. -1
- ❏ D. NULL

Answer: C. The value of the @@CURSOR_ROWS global variable is -1 only when the cursor is declared as dynamic, and Paul's cursor was declared as dynamic. Information about using global variables is located in the section "Server Provided Global Values," and how cursor status works is in the section "Traditional Data Processing."

8. Stan runs a query and receives an error message with a severity level of 17. How serious is this error?

- ❏ A. The error was not that serious; the user should rerun the query.
- ❏ B. The query contained one or more typographical errors.
- ❏ C. The error was severe, probably caused by a hardware or software fault.
- ❏ D. The severity level has nothing to do with how serious the error was.

Answer: C. The severity levels from 17 to 19 designate hardware and/or software problems. Subsequent processing may be stopped. For more information, check out the section "Traditional Data Processing."

Tuning and Optimizing Analysis

. . . .

Terms you'll need to understand:

✓ Query Analyzer
✓ SQL Profiler
✓ System Monitor
✓ Trace
✓ Filter
✓ Execution plan
✓ Query Optimizer

Techniques you'll need to master:

✓ Viewing current activity
✓ Tracing activity over time
✓ Utilizing the System Monitor
✓ Tracing operations with the SQL Profiler
✓ Diagnosing execution plans
✓ Troubleshooting locking behavior

Introduction

This chapter investigates the tools that are provided with the SQL Server product to allow the database developer or administrator to inspect, optimize, and tune an installation to provide for the best implementation.

The Enterprise Manager Console (EMC) is the primary graphical tool that performs many of the administrative tasks needed in SQL Server. With this tool, databases can be created as well as objects contained in them, such as views and tables. The EMC provides for administration over the SQL Server security environment, server and database configuration, and statistical analysis and management, as well as providing a complete set of administrative tools. Essentially, it is the only tool needed for day-to-day operations of a SQL Server environment.

When you go beyond the day-to-day tasks, however, and require more in-depth analysis of the database environment, you must reach beyond the EMC and walk into the realm of the other tools supplied for the purpose of investigation and problem determination. Over time, the size of the database will need to be adjusted to accommodate new data or data removal. The configuration of the server in any given installation may vary greatly. The applications that a server is intended to handle will direct the configuration. In troubleshooting and tweaking the performance of any installation, you will need to know how the server is being used.

Troubleshooting, performance tuning, and resource optimization require in-depth knowledge of how SQL Server operates, as well as knowledge of the applications to which the database server is being applied. You have seen numerous tools and options that can be used to assist in this process.

The first problem you will face on the exam will be which tool to use, given a set of circumstances. Second, you will need to present a course of action for monitoring and troubleshooting. Third, you will need to read and diagnose the output and then select an appropriate solution. A person who implements databases needs to be comfortable in all these areas, and you will find a few of each type of question on the exam.

Troubleshooting at the server level will require the use of the operating systems' tools. At the database server and database level you should be using the SQL Profiler. Digging deeper and into more granular inspection will require the use of the Query Analyzer and some knowledge of commands and options to provide a look at individual tables and processes.

Various tools, utilities, and information sources are built into SQL Server to help you optimize SQL Server operations. These mechanisms can be used to diagnose, maintain, and optimize all operations. To obtain immediate information about the server, you can observe the current activity using the Enterprise Manager or stored procedures. To observe information from a historical perspective, you can view the SQL Server logs from the Enterprise Manager.

Information Gathering

The SQL Server Enterprise Manager provides a facility where an administrator can go to find out pertinent information about what the server is currently doing. Use the Current Activity window to perform monitoring of SQL Server. This enables you to determine, at a glance, the volume and general types of activity on the system related to current blocked and blocking transactions in the system, connected users, the last statement executed, and locks that are currently in effect.

The Current Activity view provides a display of process information, locks broken down by process identification, and locks broken down by object.

Processes Operating in the Environment

The process information provides information on all activity currently executing against the system. It also lists current connections that may not be active but are still using resources. Here are descriptions of the process information columns:

➤ *Process ID*—SQL Server Process Identifier (SPID).

➤ *Context ID*—Execution Context Identifier, used to uniquely identify the subthreads operating on behalf of the process.

➤ *User*—Identifier of the user who executed the command.

➤ *Database*—Database currently being used by the process.

➤ *Status*—Status of the process.

➤ *Open Transactions*—Number of open transactions.

➤ *Command*—Command currently being executed.

➤ *Application*—Name of the application program being used.

➤ *Wait Time*—Current wait time in milliseconds. When the process is not waiting, the wait time is zero.

➤ *Wait Type*—Name of the last or current wait type.

➤ *Wait Resources*—Textual representation of a lock resource.

➤ *CPU*—Cumulative CPU time for the process.

➤ *Physical IO*—Cumulative disk reads and writes.

➤ *Memory Usage*—Number of pages in the procedure cache that are currently allocated. A negative number indicates that the process is freeing memory allocated by another process.

➤ *Login Time*—Time at which a client process logged in to the server.

➤ *Last Batch*—Last time a client process executed a remote stored procedure call or an EXECUTE statement.

➤ *Host*—Name of the workstation.

➤ *Network Library*—Column in which the client's network library is stored. Every client process comes in on a network connection. Network connections have a network library associated with them that enables them to make the connection.

➤ *Network Address*—Assigned unique identifier for the network interface card on each user's workstation.

➤ *Blocked By*—Process ID (SPID) of a blocking process.

➤ *Blocking*—Process ID (SPID) of processes that are blocked.

The process information presented can be a good starting point to see what is going on within the SQL Server environment. But you are going to have to go into a lot more depth and use many of the other tools available if you are truly going to see what is happening on the server and, perhaps of more interest, how it is happening.

By far the two most diverse and granular tools for analysis of the database system are the Query Analyzer and the Profiler. Gathering information from the operating system tools and the server activity procedures and displays plays an important part in the initial fact-finding that must be performed to alter any of the properties of the server.

It is a good idea to not run the SQL Server 2000 Profiler on the same server you are monitoring. Running the Profiler uses considerable resources and this can noticeably affect the server's performance. Instead, run it on another server or workstation acting as a monitoring machine and have all data collected there.

The processes we are discussing are often used in an implementation as a starting point toward the following:

➤ Developing system documentation

➤ Establishing record-keeping procedures

➤ Troubleshooting system problems

➤ Optimizing the database server

➤ Tracking data trends

As you begin any of these processes, begin with the hardware and operating system and then proceed into the application server. As you get further into data gathering and analysis, you should look into each database and the interactions between the data and the user applications. To view SQL Server tasks in detail, after the initial data-gathering processes, use the SQL Server Profiler to develop a more complete picture. When more granularity is desired and you want to look into the user applications, the functionality provided by the Query Analyzer can be used to obtain the most detailed and granular data.

External Tools Provided by the Operating System

Much of the performance of any database system relies on the application and database designers. The use of the network, processor, memory, and disk storage can all be dictated by the type of database design and the use of the applications operating against the database server. For this reason, the operating system usually acts as only a starting point in any performance analysis testing. If the hardware configuration is not adequate and the operating system is not properly configured, the database engine won't be able to respond optimally.

The first task that the hardware and operating system serve in any database system is to provide a means to store and operate the database software and objects. The operating system is also responsible for reporting hardware and software problems, as well as making it possible for you to monitor everything executing on the machine.

From the Event Viewer you can quickly spot problems and diagnose the series of steps that led up to any given situation. The Event Viewer has options available for you to filter events to specific categories and severity. You can also select other computers to view and find out additional information about any event.

To see only the desired events, you need to configure a view for the log with the appropriate selections. If you view the properties of any of the logs, you can find general and filter information under the appropriate tabs. In the General tab you can see and set pertinent information for the log itself. The Filter tab can be used to view only the desired errors. The application log will show the bulk of the messages you would be interested in under the MSSQLSERVER source. Reporting to the Event Viewer by SQL Server is made to the application event log. Use this log when looking for messages sent by any of the SQL Server–related services. The application log records events that pertain to SQL Server, using any of the following sources:

➤ MSSQLSERVER—This is the primary source for event information and, along with SQLSERVERAGENT, will be responsible for most of your diagnostic focus. The SQL Server service manages all the database files used by an instance of SQL Server. It is the component that processes all statements sent from client applications. The service allocates resources between users and enforces business rules as defined.

➤ SQLSERVERAGENT—The SQL Server agent supports the non–data-specific activity in an installation. It is involved in the scheduling of activities, notification of problems, and definition of important contact personnel. This is done in the form of Jobs, Schedules, Operators, and Alerts.

➤ MSSQLServerOLAPService—The primary service used in OLAP (Online Analytical Processing) to manage statistical operations between data cubes.

➤ MSDTC—The Microsoft Distributed Transaction Coordinator is an operating service accessed by SQL Server for coordinating transaction atomicity across multiple data resources using a two-phase commit. You can enable distributed transaction support in applications by using the appropriate distributed transaction identifiers around the block of T-SQL code to be handled by MSDTC similar to the following:

```
BEGIN DISTRIBUTED TRANSACTION
        /* Commands used in the
           distributed transaction */
END DISTRIBUTED TRANSACTION
```

➤ MSSQLServerADHelper—The MSSQLServerADHelper service performs the two functions necessary for active directory integration. It adds and removes objects used in Active Directory, and it ensures that the Windows account under which a SQL Server service is running has permissions to update the Active Directory objects.

Of course, if you are running multiple versions of SQL Server on the same machines, you will see these also represented as information sources. Some of these sources do not show up on all installations. If a server is not using an aspect of SQL Server, that source does not report any information. Now that the hardware and operating system interactions have been addressed, it's time to move into the server itself to begin a more granular look.

Monitor Activity with the Profiler

The SQL Profiler tool is a graphical mechanism that enables you to monitor SQL Server events. The tool enables you to capture and save data about every event on the server. The data can be stored to a file or SQL Server table. Stored data can then be analyzed and events can be replayed.

The SQL Profiler should be used to monitor only the events of interest. Monitoring all events on the server produces so much data that the data can become overwhelming. Large traces can be filtered so that you are viewing only the information you want to see. You can use filters to view a subset of the event data that was captured. Monitoring too many events also adds excessive amounts of overhead to the server. This overhead can slow the monitoring process and cause the large amounts of output from the trace to create a file or table that is very large. This is particularly important when you are going to be performing the monitoring over long periods.

SQL Profiler is a useful tool for various circumstances. Use SQL Profiler to do the following:

➤ Monitor the performance of SQL Server

➤ Debug T-SQL statements and stored procedures

➤ Identify long-running queries

➤ Step through procedures to ensure that they are working as expected

➤ Capture events on a production system and replay them on a test system

➤ Diagnose problem situations through the capturing of event data

➤ Audit and review events

In troubleshooting the SQL Server environment, you will typically use the SQL Profiler. The tool is best used to find queries that are not performing well or ones that are executing for long periods. It is also useful in identifying the cause of data blocking and deadlock situations. In monitoring a healthy server, the SQL Profiler is generally used to monitor performance and to audit application, user, database, and job activity.

Before you start using the Profiler, you should become familiar with profile templates. A *template* defines the criteria for each event you want to monitor with SQL Profiler. Predefined templates can be used for individual circumstances, and you can create your own template as well, specifying which events, data columns, and filters to use. A template can be saved, and at any time a trace can be loaded and started with the template settings. To help identify long-running queries, use the Profiler's Create Trace Wizard to run the TSQL by Duration template. You can specify the length of the long-running queries you are trying to identify, and then have these recorded in a log.

The SQL Profiler captures data using a trace based on the selected events, data columns, and filters. The trace is the basis for all data collected and can be defined on an ad hoc basis, can be drawn from a template, or can be a combination of the two. Even though you have defined the data collected, you may still apply filters to the data after it is captured to focus on the type of information you want. For this reason you may want to save traces even after you are finished with the current activity. A past trace can possibly be used and applied to various circumstances.

At times, when monitoring with the Profiler, you will find the amount of data provided to be considerable and possibly overwhelming. It can be difficult to find what you are looking for within a trace that covers a broad range of events. A useful technique that can ease this process is to write the trace to a SQL Server table, and then query the table from within the Query Analyzer. Assuming that you know what you are looking for, this method can greatly speed up finding the data in the trace you need.

The Profiler can store captured data in a text file or in a table. If you decide to store the data in a SQL Server table, don't store it in a database you are profiling or, if possible, not even on the same server, because it could affect the performance of the server you are profiling. Instead, store the trace data in a database on another server. After data is captured (which is the easy part of the process), you must sift through the data collected to draw some meaning from the results.

The Profiler can use many existing templates to gather information for various types of circumstances. You may want to select some of these templates to see the actual information that is being gathered. After it has been created, the trace is permanently stored until it is deleted. The trace can be started again by name through the Profiler interface or via stored procedure.

To use the output generated by a trace, you must first determine what type of data you are most interested in from the trace. The next section illustrates how to get the most valuable information from the trace results.

On the exam, you may be expected to select the correct event classes and objects given a specific scenario. Ensure that you are familiar with the classifications of the Profiler trace objects and under what circumstances you would select them. By viewing the objects selected for each of the default templates, you can familiarize yourself with these choices.

Defining a Profiler Trace

When using the SQL Profiler to define a trace, you use event categories to select the events to monitor. Event categories have been grouped into classes of events. The following classes and their descriptions are available to be selected:

➤ *Cursors*—Events produced by use of cursors.

➤ *Database*—Events produced when files grow or shrink automatically.

➤ *Errors and Warnings*—Events produced when an error or warning occurs.

➤ *Locks*—Events produced when a lock is acquired, or other lock activity occurs.

➤ *Objects*—Occur as objects are created, opened, closed, or deleted.

➤ *Performance*—Events produced when SQL data manipulations execute.

➤ *Scans*—Events produced when tables and indexes are scanned.

➤ *Security Audit*—Events used to audit server activity.

➤ *Sessions*—Events produced by clients connecting and disconnecting.

➤ *Stored Procedures*—Events produced by the execution of procedures.

➤ *Transactions*—Events produced by the execution of Microsoft Distributed Transaction Coordinator transactions or by writing to the transaction log.

➤ *TSQL*—Events produced by the execution of T-SQL statements.

➤ *User Configurable*—User-configurable events.

Each event class has various objects that can be monitored. To select any of the objects when defining a trace, use the Events tab of the Trace Properties dialog box. You add and remove objects, not whole classes, although a whole class of objects can be traced, if desired.

Using Profiler Traces to Diagnose Locking

SQL Profiler provides the Locks event classes to monitor locking behavior during trace operations. Several of these classes are useful in monitoring locking, blocking, and deadlocking situations on the server. The following list represents the classes and gives a short narrative description of what each class can be used for:

➤ Lock:Acquired—This event fires to show the acquisition of a resource lock.

➤ Lock:Cancel—An event is fired when a lock on a resource has been cancelled. A lock can be cancelled by SQL Server because of a deadlock or by a programmatic cancellation by a process.

➤ Lock:Deadlock—A deadlock occurs if two concurrent transactions have deadlocked each other by trying to obtain locks on resources that the other owns.

➤ Lock:Deadlock Chain—The chain of events produced for each of the processes leading up to a deadlock situation.

➤ Lock:Escalation—An event fired when the server determines that a lock should be converted to a larger scope.

➤ Lock:Released—The event fires when a resource lock is released.

➤ Lock:Timeout—This event fires when a lock request has timed out because another process is blocking a resource with its own lock.

Lock:Acquired and Lock:Released are used to monitor the timing of lock behavior. These events indicate the type of lock and the length of time the lock was held. Often a redesign of the application that is setting the locks in place can lessen the lock duration considerably.

The Lock:Deadlock, Lock:Deadlock Chain, and Lock:Timeout are used to monitor deadlock and timeout situations. This information is useful to determine whether deadlocks and timeouts are affecting the user and/or application.

Locking is one of the more common aspects queried on the exam. Remember to first check the current activity to get a snapshot perspective on locking. Use the Profiler when you want to analyze locking over time.

The Results window of the SQL Profiler is segmented into two view panes. If you have included TextData as one of the columns in your definition, the bottom pane shows you SQL statement information. The top pane illustrates the current trace data view where event information is displayed based on current filter settings.

After trace event data has been collected, you can save the trace to have it replayed later. The SQL Profiler Playback feature is powerful but carries a little overhead. It is well worth considering having a test machine available to act as a playback and troubleshooting server.

Playback of events is accomplished through the SQL Server multithreaded playback engine. This engine can simulate user connections and SQL Server authentication. The event data can be played back to reproduce the activity captured in the trace. Replay can be very useful in troubleshooting an application or another process problem.

Trace Playback and Diagnosis

After you have identified the problem and implemented corrections, run the trace that was originally collected against the corrected application or process to see whether the proposed solution accomplishes the desired effect. The replay of the original trace can be a useful mechanism in designing solutions. The trace replay feature has advanced debugging support. You can make use of break points and run-to-cursor features.

When the target computer is going to be other than the computer originally traced, you must ensure that the database IDs on the target are the same as those on the source. You can accomplish this by creating (from the source) a backup of the Master database, as well as any user databases referenced in the trace, and restoring them on the target. In this manner a test SQL Server can be used as a debugging server for any multiple-application environment.

The default database for each login contained in the trace must be set on the target. The default database of the trace activity login must be set to the database that matches that login name, even in cases in which the database name might be different. To set the default database of the login, use the `sp_defaultdb` system stored procedure.

You have the option of replaying the events in the order in which they were traced. If selected, this option enables debugging. This enables you to implement debugging techniques such as stepping through the trace. Replaying the events using multiple threads will optimize performance but will disable debugging. The default option is to display the results of the replay. If the trace you want to replay is a large capture, you may want to disable this option to save disk space.

Query Optimization

The SQL Server Query Optimizer is the database engine component of SQL Server 2000. As the database engine, it oversees all data-related interaction. It is responsible for generating the execution plans for any SQL operation. In diagnosing a query, the optimizer must decide on the most efficient means of executing the query and interacting with the database objects.

SQL Server has a cost-based optimizer that can be extremely sensitive to the information provided by statistics. Without accurate and up-to-date statistical information, SQL Server has a great deal of difficulty in determining the best execution plan for a particular query.

SQL Server goes through a considerable process when it chooses one execution plan out of several possible methods of executing a given operation. This optimization is one of the most important components of a SQL Server database system. Although some overhead is incurred by the optimizer's analysis process, this overhead is saved in execution.

The optimizer uses a cost-based analysis procedure. Each possible method of execution has an associated cost. This cost is determined in terms of the approximated amount of computing resources used in execution. The Query Optimizer must analyze the possible plans and choose the one that has the lowest estimated cost.

It is not uncommon for some complex SELECT statements to have thousands of possible plans. Of course, in this case the optimizer does not analyze every possible combination. It uses a complex series of processes to find a plan that has a cost reasonably close to the minimum—a minimum that is only theoretical and unlikely to be achieved.

The Query Optimizer relies on up-to-date statistical information that is maintained within the metadata of a database system. This information is collected and updated based on changes to the index and data structure. Proper maintenance should ensure that the statistical data is maintained and accurately reflects the current database environment.

The primary tool available for the interaction with the Query Optimizer is the SQL Query Analyzer, which is an all-in-one T-SQL editor, debugging environment, and object viewer.

The SQL Query Analyzer

At this juncture in the book, and in your own experience with SQL Server, you should have begun to master using this tool to enter SQL. The object browser and templates, color-coded entry environment, variety of display formats, and powerful toolset all make the tool a mandatory element for use by an administrator or a programmer.

Now that you are familiar with the tool, it is time to turn it into one of the most important elements of the application diagnostic and performance-tuning framework. Capable of reaching into individual commands and objects, this tool provides for the finest level of granularity and deepest interaction with the SQL Server architecture.

When viewing an execution plan, you have the capability of representing the activity that the optimizer needs to perform with a graphic set of icons. Accompanying the graphic is a set of statistics that goes along with that portion of the operation.

Query Execution Plans

The execution plan options graphically display the data retrieval methods chosen by the Query Optimizer. The graphical execution plan uses icons to represent the execution of specific statements and queries in SQL Server, rather than the tabular text representation produced by the SET SHOWPLAN_ALL or SET SHOWPLAN_TEXT statements. Analysis of a query plan is a very important process that helps you understand the performance characteristics of a query.

An execution plan is particularly useful in determining the steps a complex query needs to take. See Figure 7.1 for a sample query and execution plan displays for invoice information. The query combines data from six separate tables. It is possible to see the work involved by looking at the plan SQL Server uses.

```
SELECT O.ShipName, O.ShipAddress, O.ShipCity, O.ShipRegion, O.ShipPostalCode, O.ShipCountry,
       O.CustomerID, C.CompanyName, C.Address, C.City, C.Region, C.PostalCode, C.Country,
       (FirstName + ' ' + LastName) AS Salesperson, O.OrderID, O.OrderDate, O.RequiredDate,
       O.ShippedDate, S.CompanyName 'Shipper', OD.ProductID, P.ProductName, OD.UnitPrice,
       OD.Quantity, OD.Discount,
       (CONVERT(money, (OD.UnitPrice*Quantity*(1-Discount)/100))*100) AS Price, O.Freight
FROM Shippers S
  INNER JOIN (Products P
  INNER JOIN ((Employees E
  INNER JOIN (Customers C
  INNER JOIN Orders O ON C.CustomerID = O.CustomerID)
  ON E.EmployeeID = O.EmployeeID)
  INNER JOIN "Order Details" OD ON O.OrderID = OD.OrderID)
  ON P.ProductID = OD.ProductID)
  ON S.ShipperID = O.ShipVia
```

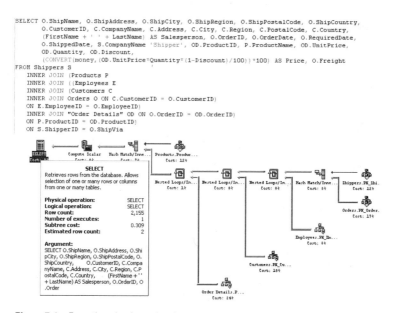

Figure 7.1 Execution plan for an invoice query.

The graphical plan is read from right to left and from top to bottom. By placing your mouse over any of the icons in the plan, you can acquire information about the processes being performed. Each query in the batch that is analyzed is displayed, including the cost of each query as a percentage of the total cost of the batch.

Reading Execution Plans

There are actually two techniques for generating an execution plan. The graphical execution represents an execution plan with icons, whereas the SET SHOWPLAN_ALL or SET SHOWPLAN_TEXT statements use a tabular representation. Each of these mechanisms enables you to look under the hood of the server to see what is actually occurring. The graphical plan is much easier to use and is what you will be expected to master.

 The exam will expect you to be able to look at any of these outputs and decipher what is happening. You will also have to provide recommendations for improvement(s). Being able to see behind the scenes is very useful for understanding the performance characteristics of a query.

The graphical output illustrates all the processes within the engine using pictorial representations. These icons illustrating the many potential processes are shown in Figure 7.2. Some of these processes are discussed in full in this chapter because they pertain to material you are likely to find on the exam. For information on other processes, you should refer to SQL Server Books Online.

Each of the icons specifies a logical and physical operation. An execution plan will have any number of icons depending on the number of operations needed to perform the query. A single query, even a simple one, will have a number of icons, each used to represent a part of the query or statement.

Each node is related to a parent node. All nodes with the same parent are drawn in the same column. Rules with arrowheads connect each node to its parent. Recursive operations are shown with an iteration symbol, and operators are shown as symbols related to a specific parent. When the query contains multiple statements, multiple query execution plans are drawn.

It is easy to see that a simple change to the database design can make a drastic difference in the execution plan. The simple addition of an index can reduce reads and greatly improve performance. The next two graphics illustrate the difference made in the plan when an index is added. Notice in

Figure 7.3 that the rightmost icon is a scan procedure that sequentially reads the data.

Icon	Physical operator				
	Assert		Index Delete		Row Count Spool
	Bookmark Lookup		Index Insert		Sequence
	Clustered Index Delete		Index Scan		Sort
	Clustered Index Insert		Index Seek		Stream Aggregate
	Clustered Index Scan		Index Spool		Table Delete
	Clustered Index Seek		Index Update		Table Insert
	Clustered Index Update		Inserted Scan		Table Scan
	Collapse		Log Row Scan		Table Spool
	Compute Scalar		Merge Join		Table Update
	Concatenation		Nested Loops		Top
	Constant Scan		Parallelism	Icon	Cursor phys.operator
	Deleted Scan		Parameter Table Scan		Dynamic
	Filter (clsColumn)		Remote Delete		Fetch Query
	Hash Match		Remote Insert		Keyset
	Hash Match Root		Remote Query		Population Query
	Hash Match Team		Remote Scan		Refresh Query
			Remote Update		Snapshot

Figure 7.2 The graphical showplan icons.

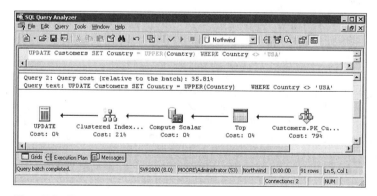

Figure 7.3 The execution plan before index placement.

After a nonclustered index is created against the Country field, the server can more efficiently answer the query through the use of an index seek that reads only the data needed to resolve the conditions of the query, as shown in Figure 7.4.

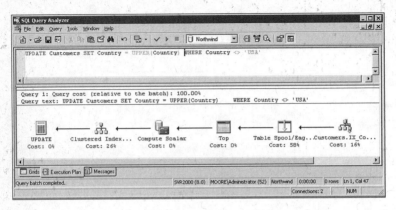

Figure 7.4 The execution plan after an index was placed on the Country column.

Execution Plan Caching and Sharing

The memory used by SQL Server is divided among a number of processes. A pool of this memory is divided between the storage of execution plans and allocation of data buffers. The actual division between the two varies significantly depending on the system use. The portion of this memory pool that is used to store execution plans is referred to as the *procedure cache*. The data buffers are similarly called the *data cache*. In any given execution plan there are two main components: the plan itself and the context on which the query was executed.

Most of the plan is a read-only structure that can be used by any number of applications, connections, and users. No actual user context is stored within the plan itself. The execution context is a data structure stored for each user currently running the query associated with the plan. This area stores any data specific to a single use, such as parameter values.

When a query is executed, the server first looks through the procedure cache to verify that a plan already exists. If present, the plan is reused. This reuse of execution plans saves on the overhead associated with recompiling the query. If no plan exists, the server generates a new one. SQL Server 2000 has integrated logic that enables a plan to be shared between connections without requiring that an application prepare the statement.

In rare instances you may be able to apply index and other optimizer hints to change the way a query is performed. The optimizer in most cases produces the best plan, and attempts at bettering the plan don't usually provide any gains.

Optimizer Hints

A "hint" is a method of providing information in the SQL syntax that tells the Query Optimizer to use a specific plan rather than the one it may normally choose. Index, join, locking, query, table, and views all can be supplied with hint information to be passed to the Query Analyzer. Table 7.1 lists the options available for join, query, and table hints.

Table 7.1	Optimizer Hints in SQL Server	
Type	**Option**	**Description**
Join	**LOOP, HASH, MERGE, REMOTE**	Indicates how to join the rows of two tables.
Query	**HASH, ORDER, GROUP**	Indicates hashing or ordering in **GROUP BY** and **COMPUTE** aggregations.
Query	**MERGE, HASH, CONCAT, UNION**	Indicates how **UNION** operations are performed.
Query	**FAST integer**	Optimizes for retrieval of the specified number of rows.
Query	**FORCE ORDER**	Performs joins in the order in which the tables appear.
Query	**ROBUST PLAN**	Accommodates maximum potential row size.
Table	**FASTFIRSTROW**	Has the same effect as specifying **FAST 1**.
Table	**INDEX =**	Instructs SQL Server to use the specified index(es).
Table	**HOLDLOCK, SERIALIZABLE, REPEATABLEREAD, READCOMMITTED, READUNCOMMITTED, NOLOCK**	Specifies the isolation level.
Table	**ROWLOCK, PAGLOCK, TABLOCK, TABLOCKX, NOLOCK**	Specifies the locking granularity.
Table	**READPAST**	Skips locked rows.
Table	**UPDLOCK**	Takes update locks instead of shared locks. Cannot be used with **NOLOCK** or **XLOCK**.
Table	**XLOCK**	Takes an exclusive lock. Cannot be used with **NOLOCK** or **UPDLOCK**.

Hints can provide additional control over the individual operations performed by the optimizer in the act of retrieving data with a query. Though not necessarily used to improve performance, hints are used for changing the action that would normally be taken. Hints can provide additional functionality that enables system-level applications to be designed that may need access to data beyond the capabilities of a standard data read. In most cases, the use of hints is not recommended because the optimizer usually selects the best mechanism to retrieve the data from a given query.

Join Hints

Join hints are not frequently used. The SQL Server Optimizer rarely makes a poor choice in how to join sets of records together. If you run a few queries and analyze the execution plans, you will see subqueries that are converted to joins and other join selections based on the specifics of the query.

In some rare instances you may be able to improve the performance of a complex query by altering the way the join is made. If you want to get this granular with a particular operation, run tests with different internal approaches to the join and measure their execution. This will seldom improve performance and you should concentrate optimization efforts in other areas.

Query Hints

Query hints are also rarely used and seldom yield any gain in functionality of performance. A Query hint can be used within the OPTION clause of a query, but in most cases will not provide for any performance gain. As with Join hints, if you want to perform some experiments, you may find rare instances in which hints will produce better performance.

Table Hints

Table hints are more frequently used because they can provide necessary functionality needed in some specialized circumstances. Table hints, if used, must be specified following the FROM clause using a WITH clause and must be enclosed in parentheses. Any of the Table hints can be specified using the SELECT, INSERT, UPDATE, and DELETE statements to instruct the server as to the type of locks to use.

Table hints are used when you need to have a greater degree of control over the types of locks acquired on an object. These locking hints, when used, will override the current transaction isolation level for the session. Table 7.2 illustrates these lock hints and provides a short description of the functionality.

Table 7.2   Locking Hints Used Within SQL Server

Locking Hint	Description
HOLDLOCK	Will hold a shared lock until completion of the transaction. **HOLDLOCK** is equivalent to **SERIALIZABLE**.
NOLOCK	Do not issue shared locks and do not honor exclusive locks. Dirty reads of uncommitted transactions are possible.
PAGLOCK	Use page locks where a single table lock would be taken.
READCOMMITTED	(Default) Running at the **READ COMMITTED** isolation level.
READPAST	Causes a transaction to skip rows locked by other transactions that would ordinarily appear rather than block the transaction.
READUNCOMMITTED	Equivalent to **NOLOCK**.
REPEATABLEREAD	Perform a scan with the same locking semantics as a transaction running at **REPEATABLE READ** isolation level.
ROWLOCK	Use row-level locks instead of page- and table-level locks.
SERIALIZABLE	Perform a scan with the same locking semantics as a transaction running at the **SERIALIZABLE** isolation level.
TABLOCK	Use a table lock instead of the row- or page-level locks. SQL Server holds this lock until the end of the statement. However, if you also specify **HOLDLOCK**, the lock is held until the end of the transaction.
TABLOCKX	Use an exclusive lock on a table. This lock prevents others from reading or updating the table.
UPDLOCK	Use update locks instead of shared locks while reading a table, and hold locks. **UPDLOCK** has the advantage of allowing you to read data without blocking other readers and update it later with the assurance that the data has not changed.
XLOCK	Use an exclusive lock that will be held until the end of the transaction.

You need to exercise caution with the use of any of these hints because you will be changing the default behavior and your procedure should document the behavior chosen and reasons for the implementation choice.

Exam Prep Questions

1. As a database implementer you are developing several new stored procedures on an existing SQL Server 2000 database that resides at your company headquarters. You are experimenting with a Query Analyzer session that contains each of the individual queries to be used in these procedures. After running a given SELECT query and using the graphical showplan feature to understand the execution plan, you want to prove that internal statistics are available for a particular column used in the query. How would you best find this information?

   ❑ A. Disable the graphical showplan display.
   ❑ B. Hold the mouse over each individual node relating to the desired column.
   ❑ C. Use a SET SHOWPLAN statement.
   ❑ D. Examine each node of the desired column without mousing over it.

   Answer: B. A feature of the graphical showplan display enables you to see information about each node in the display by holding the mouse over the node. A display shows the node analysis based on the contents of the entire query. Of the choices available, this would be the best mechanism to use to gain the desired information. For more information, see the section "The SQL Query Analyzer."

2. You are a database implementer of a SQL Server 2000 environment that has a single database server. The server contains all your company's databases, including an investment-tracking database. Each day more than 100 operators make approximately 5,000 changes to customer investments. In addition, daily and monthly reports are created from the investment data.

   Another development team at your company needs to optimize a database application. The team members need a sample of database query activity to discover whether they can speed up the transactions. The developers also want to replay the sample on another SQL Server computer.

   You need to capture the sample, but you want to minimize any increase to the workload of the server. What should you do?

   ❑ A. Run Profiler on a client computer. Configure SQL Profiler to monitor database activity, and log data to a .trc file.
   ❑ B. Run Profiler on the server. Configure SQL Profiler to monitor database activity, and log data to a database table.
   ❑ C. Run System Monitor on a client computer. Configure System Monitor to monitor database activity, and log data to a .blg file.
   ❑ D. Start SQL Server from a command prompt. Specify trace flag 1204 to enable verbose logging.

Answer: A. Although it would be most desirable to run the query on another SQL Server, it is always best to select a machine other than the production machine to absorb the overhead of the Profiler itself. For more information, see the section "Monitor Activity with the Profiler."

3. You are the administrator of a SQL Server computer. Users report that the database times out when they attempt to modify data. You use the Current Activity window to examine locks held in the database, as shown in Figure 7.5. You need to discover why users cannot modify data in the database, but you do not want to disrupt normal database activities. What should you do?

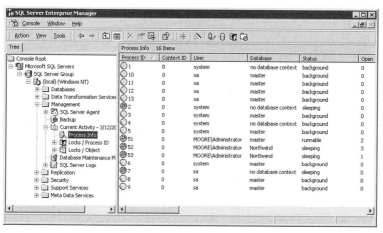

Figure 7.5 The Current Activity window.

❑ A. Use the Current Activity data to discover which resources are locked.
❑ B. Use the sp_who stored procedure to discover who is logged in as spid 52.
❑ C. Use SQL Profiler to capture the activity of the user logged in as spid 52.
❑ D. Use System Monitor to log the locks that are granted in the database.

Answer: A. Although knowing who has the login may be useful later, the first thing to look for is what is executing that is causing the block. For more details, see "Current Activity" in SQL Server Books Online.

4. You are working on a SQL Server 2000 computer that contains a database named Sales. The company's web-based application uses the Sales database to store sales transactions. The company website has grown in popularity, and database utilization has increased. You need to collect data about the utilization of server resources so that you can provide capacity planning. You want to automate the collection process so that information is gathered as quickly as possible. What should you do?

 ❑ A. Configure System Monitor to collect data and store it in a SQL Server table.

 ❑ B. Create a job that executes the sp_statistics stored procedure daily.

 ❑ C. Use SQL Profiler to trace server activity and store the results in tables.

 ❑ D. Configure alerts to store information in the Windows application event log.

Answer: C. To monitor detailed activity of SQL Server, you should use the SQL Server Profiler and configure a trace to take in the necessary data and filter for the desired objects. For more details, see the section "Monitor Activity with the Profiler."

5. You create two transactions. One transaction inserts employee personal information into the database. The other transaction inserts employee demographics. The second query is less important than the first. How could you ensure that when locking problems exits the second query is always the one terminated?

 ❑ A. Set DEADLOCK_PRIORITY to LOW for the transaction that inserts the employee personal information.

 ❑ B. Set DEADLOCK_PRIORITY to LOW for the transaction that inserts the employee demographics.

 ❑ C. Add code that checks for the inserting of personal information. If an error is encountered, restart the transaction.

 ❑ D. Add the ROWLOCK optimizer hint to all UPDATE queries.

 ❑ E. Set the isolation level to SERIALIZABLE when inserting the personal information.

Answer: B. SET DEADLOCK_PRIORITY LOW specifies that the current transaction is the preferred deadlock victim. If this were performed on the transaction that contained the personal information, it would actually be the opposite of what we wanted to accomplish. Adding ROWLOCK hints or altering the isolation levels would not be appropriate in most instances in which there are deadlock possibilities between two known transactions and does nothing to guarantee the server selection for termination.

6. You have a mission-critical application that runs within the context of the company's SQL Server. Database activity is high during the day as sales transactions are entered through network point-of-sale terminals. Sales clerks are reporting that transactions are taking too much time and customers are annoyed with the waiting period for updates to information. What would you do to diagnose the situation?

❑   A.   Increase the amount of memory on the server.

❑   B.   Upgrade the processor on the server or move to a multiple processor machine.

❑   C.   Use `sp_configure` to increase the number of locks available to the server.

❑   D.   Run SQL Profiler in the day, and use the output for the Index Tuning Wizard.

❑   E.   Run SQL Profiler in off-peak times, and use the output for the Tuning Wizard.

Answer: D. You need to perform some diagnosis during the period in which the issues exist. There is no sense in changing the physical configuration of the server until some diagnosis has been performed. Although adding memory and/or upgrading the processor may help the situation, it is impossible to know whether that is even an issue before performing some tests. SQL Profiler tests should be performed during activity; to get an accurate reading of the database usage, a profiler trace should be performed during the day when the system is being used.

7. Your company database contains a table listing the items and quantities available for sale. You have a stored procedure that updates the table. The procedure first checks to see whether there is sufficient quantity for the sale before performing the update. The check is performed with a HOLDLOCK so that the quantity is held for the duration of the transaction. Sometimes this procedure is chosen as a deadlock victim when others are reading data from the same table. You would like to prevent this while maintaining data integrity. What should you do?

❑   A.   Remove the table hint.

❑   B.   Change the table hint to UPDLOCK.

❑   C.   Change the table hint to REPEATABLEREAD.

❑   D.   Set the transaction isolation level to SERIALIZABLE.

❑   E.   Set the transaction isolation level to REPEATABLE READ.

Answer: B. You should alter the lock to an UPDLOCK in this circumstance because you want the data to be in the same state as the read when you actually perform the update. Using this lock will allow other users to still access the data as long as they do not attempt to make an update while the lock is in place. A HOLDLOCK will hold the shared lock until the end of the transaction but not prevent updates. Removing this option without replacing it with something else serves no purpose. SERIALIZABLE does nothing to change the situation because it provides the same functionality as the HOLDLOCK. REPEATABLE READ options do not provide for protection against phantom deletions of the record being updated.

Designing for Optimized Data Access

Terms you'll need to understand:

✓ Concurrency
✓ Lock
✓ Index
✓ Clustered index
✓ Nonclustered index
✓ Index Tuning Wizard (ITW)
✓ Indexed view
✓ **UPDATE STATISTICS**
✓ Serializable
✓ Database consistency checker (DBCC)

Techniques you'll need to master:

✓ Working with transactions
✓ Controlling locking
✓ Creating, altering, and removing indexes
✓ Performing system maintenance

Introduction

From the outset of the first stages of the database design, you will be making decisions that will directly affect performance. To look at the hardware configuration, operating system and other analysis tools are available as part of the NT and Windows 2000 operating system. To monitor hardware and operating system events, you would use the System Monitor tool.

The System Monitor enables you to monitor server performance and activity using predefined objects and counters, or user-defined counters to monitor events. System Monitor is referred to as Performance Monitor in Windows NT. Its role is to collect counts rather than data about the events. You can set thresholds on specific counters to generate alerts and notify the individuals who need to address the problem. Often the best way to start the troubleshooting process is to observe the current activity.

The Current Activity window is found in the SQL Server Enterprise Manager and graphically displays information about processes currently running. It also displays blocked processes, locks, user activity, and other useful information for ad hoc views of current activity. Equally helpful are the logs that SQL Server provides for the reporting of errors. Error logs contain additional information about events in SQL Server beyond what is available elsewhere. You can use the information in the error log to troubleshoot SQL Server–related problems. The Windows application event log provides an overall picture of events occurring on the Windows NT 4.0 and Windows 2000 system as a whole, as well as events in SQL Server, SQL Server Agent, and Full-Text Search. Several stored procedures have been built into SQL Server to provide for specific benefits.

Monitoring and troubleshooting have always played an important part in the activities performed on the job. Microsoft has always made this an exam focus as well. It is important to understand what each of the tools can do to aid in monitoring and troubleshooting. Knowing which tool to select based on symptoms of the problems is the focus of this chapter, and you'll go into further depth in each of these areas.

System functions and system statistical functions enable you to perform operations and return information about values, objects, settings, and statistical information about the system. System functions are also available to find out more information pertaining to the server, databases, objects, and current session.

Many tools are available to assist with the tuning of your database after you begin the implementation, but don't forget about the design from the outset. Many performance gains will come out of the database design itself. The table structures and relationships, indexing, and other physical objects weigh in heavily when contributing to performance gains. You need to consider controlling the environment right from the beginning.

Concurrency and Locking

One of the hallmarks of a true database management system is whether it has the capability to handle more than one user performing simultaneous data modifications. The problem is that when several users in a database make changes, it's likely that they eventually will want to update the same record at the same time. To avoid the problems this would cause, SQL Server and most database management systems provide a locking mechanism.

A locking mechanism provides a way to "check out" a particular row or set of rows from the database, marking them so that they cannot be changed by another user until the connection is finished and the changes are made. For connections that are reading data, locking provides a mechanism to prevent other connections from changing the data for the duration of the read or longer. There are two basic types of locks: shared locks and exclusive locks. A shared lock happens when a user is trying to read a row of data; for some duration, depending on the transaction isolation level (which is covered later in this chapter), the user owns a shared lock on the table. Because the user is just trying to read the record, there can be several shared locks on the row, so many people can read the same record at the same time.

Users obtain exclusive locks when the user needs to change the row. Exclusive locks are not shared; there can be only one user with an exclusive lock on a row at any given time. If a user needs to acquire an exclusive lock to a row that is already locked by another user, the result is lock contention. Some level of contention is normal in a database that is being frequently updated. Typically, an application waits for some arbitrary amount of time for the locks to clear and the transaction to complete. This results in an apparent slowdown of the application and the server, and excessive amounts of contention lead to performance degradation and possibly user complaints.

There are a few things you can do to reduce lock contention. First, make transactions as simple as possible. Keep extraneous logic out of the transaction. The best case is when you do all the gathering of data and validation of that data outside of the transaction, and the transaction is used only to update and insert rows. Second, you should make sure that the application does not have any transactions that wait for user input because users tend to do such things as go to lunch, usually while they have windows open, waiting for them to enter data to complete their transactions.

In general, you should try to collect all the data at once, and then start the transaction, make the changes, and commit. Design applications and databases with concurrency in mind. Keep tables that are frequently updated small by moving columns that don't belong in the table or that aren't changed as often into another table. If a table is going to be updated frequently, make sure that it isn't indexed more than necessary. Data modification statements, such as INSERT, UPDATE, and DELETE, have to change the indexes as they go, so having too many indexes on a table requires them to modify several indexes.

With contention also comes a circumstance known as a deadlock. A deadlock occurs when two processes are locking resources and each one wants the resource that the other has locked away. Sounds like the makings of a street fight to me. Deadlocks occur when two or more transactions cannot complete because of mutual locks. SQL Server detects the deadlock and more or less randomly kills one of the user processes.

Which process is killed in a deadlock isn't exactly random. If one user is the System Administrator and the other one is just a normal user, the normal user's process is terminated. Otherwise, SQL Server picks the user that has the least to lose from having its transaction terminated. If the users stand to lose equally, SQL Server picks one at random. It's also possible to set a connection-level parameter with SET DEADLOCK_PRIORITY LOW to tell SQL Server that the transaction can be terminated if it is involved in a deadlock.

Controlling Lock Behavior

To avoid deadlocks, make sure that all the objects are always accessed in the same order. Make sure that in cases in which a series of updates to different tables are done, they are always done in the same order. Keep transactions as short as possible, prevent user interaction within transactions, and set a low isolation level. Use a transaction setting as in the following example:

```
SET TRANSACTION ISOLATION LEVEL READ UNCOMMITTED
```

SQL Server knows that sometimes it's critical that the data you are reading from the database is absolutely 100% committed data, whereas at other times you want the data to be read quickly, and incomplete or uncommitted transactions just don't matter. To accommodate these situations, SQL Server supports four transaction isolation levels:

➤ *Read Uncommitted*—This isolation level shows you all the data without getting a shared lock first. Another connection may change the data while it is being read. This can be great for applications that are doing system monitoring or reporting, when minimal impact to the rest of the system is desired. This is also called "dirty reads."

➤ *Read Committed*—This isolation level acquires a shared lock during the read of the data but doesn't keep the shared lock for the entire transaction. The resulting data is complete but may change after successive reads, showing new data or indicating missing data with each successive read. This is the default transaction isolation level, and it is generally an acceptable trade-off between reading dirty data and minimizing contention.

➤ *Repeatable Read*—This isolation level acquires a shared lock on the rows for the duration of the transaction but still allows other users to add rows into the resultset. That means that later reads may contain more data, but they won't contain any less.

➤ *Serializable*—This isolation level acquires a shared lock on the entire range of data being queried, preventing inserts or updates from happening for the duration of the transaction. This is a very dangerous thing to do from a concurrency perspective, because it generates a lot of locks and can more easily result in deadlock problems.

There is one more aspect of locking to discuss. SQL Server also has the capability to lock objects at different levels to increase performance. This is called *lock granularity*.

In addition to shared and exclusive locks, SQL Server also locks objects at different levels. SQL Server can lock a single row of a table, a single data page, or an entire table.

Typically, SQL Server operates in the page lock mode, in which it locks the data pages being requested. After a certain amount of blocking is noticed, SQL Server slips into a row locking mode, in which single rows are locked.

On the other end of the scale, when a connection attempts to update a certain percentage of a table, SQL Server automatically escalates to a table lock, in which it automatically locks the entire table either exclusively (in the case of a full table update) or shared (in the case of a full table read). SQL Server also determines lock escalation based on the activity occurring in the table at the time of the lock request. If the activity level is low, it saves itself some time by just escalating the lock sooner because it will have less effect on other users.

That means there are shared page locks, shared row locks, and shared table locks for reads, along with exclusive page locks, exclusive row locks, and exclusive table locks for writes. Locks and the control of locking behavior is important in DBMS systems. To aid in management over the DBMS, you can also implement transactions that will directly affect locking behavior. A transaction implies several things:

➤ *Atomicity*—A transaction cannot be broken up into smaller units; either the entire transaction happens or none of it happens.

➤ *Consistency*—A completed transaction leaves the database in a consistent state.

➤ *Isolation*—A transaction is isolated from other transactions in the database, so transactions can't overwrite each other's data. Transactions, in other words, can't interfere with other transactions that are running concurrently.

➤ *Durability*—A transaction, after it has been applied, sticks in the database.

These qualities are easy to recall by remembering the word "ACID": Atomicity, Consistency, Isolation, and Durability. SQL Server provides the atomicity, isolation, and durability for you, but it's up to you to make sure that a transaction leaves the database in a consistent state. Atomicity and durability are handled by the transaction logging system and, to an extent, by the lazy writer mechanism of waiting for idle time to commit data. Isolation is handled by the lock manager.

Controlling Business Logic Using Transactions

Transactions provide control over the operations that are being performed. In SQL Server this control can be implied or left to the developer to explicitly request. Either way, you can gain a little control over the changes occurring on the data.

It is possible within SQL Server for everything to be controlled within the realm of a transaction. The SET IMPLICIT_TRANSACTIONS command can be used to turn this device on or off. If you don't explicitly tell SQL Server to treat a group of statements as a transaction, it implicitly puts each statement in its own transaction. For the purposes of an implicit transaction, the only statements that really count are the statements that interact with a database: SELECT, INSERT, UPDATE, and DELETE.

To explicitly put a group of statements into a transaction, you can use the BEGIN TRANSACTION command. This command tells SQL Server all commands that follow up until the end of the transaction, which is noted with a COMMIT

TRANSACTION. In the event of a problem with the data being manipulated, you can also call ROLLBACK TRANSACTION. If there is an error during the execution of the transaction, such as a server shutdown, a disk error of some type, or lock contention, then the transaction automatically rolls back.

Here's an example to help you understand why transactions need to be used. Let's say you have a bank database, and it has a Deposit table and a Withdrawal table. Somebody wants to transfer funds from one account, account number 42, into another account, account number 64. Here's how that would look:

```
INSERT INTO Deposit VALUES (64, 100.00)
INSERT INTO Withdrawal VALUES (42, 100.00)
```

That looks fine. However, there will be a significant issue if a failure occurs between the two INSERT statements. When the administrator brings the server back up, there has been a deposit for $100 into one account, but no withdrawal to match, so the SQL Server just invented $100. To handle this task correctly, these statements should be enclosed in an explicit transaction, like this:

```
BEGIN TRANSACTION
        INSERT INTO Deposit VALUES (64, 100.00)
        INSERT INTO Withdrawal VALUES (42, 100.00)
COMMIT TRANSACTION
```

SQL Server also has the capability to create nested transactions, in which transactions are inside other transactions. In that case, the global function @@TRANCOUNT contains the current nesting level of transactions, which is basically the number of times you've executed a BEGIN TRANSACTION statement.

➤ Several statements are not allowed inside an explicit transaction: CREATE DATABASE, ALTER DATABASE, DROP DATABASE, BACKUP DATABASE, RESTORE DATABASE, BACKUP LOG, RESTORE LOG, RECONFIGURE, and UPDATE STATISTICS.

➤ If you have nested transactions (transactions started within other transactions) and you call ROLLBACK TRANSACTION, it rolls back all the transactions currently pending.

➤ The COMMMIT WORK statement is functionally equivalent to the COMMIT TRANSACTION statement. The ROLLBACK WORK statement is functionally equivalent to the ROLLBACK TRANSACTION statement. These can all be abbreviated down to just COMMIT and ROLLBACK. You can also abbreviate the word TRANSACTION to TRAN, such as in COMMIT TRAN.

Two other complications need to be thrown into this already semiconfusing pile: naming transactions and savepoints. Anytime you execute a BEGIN TRANSACTION, you can tell SQL Server to assign a name to the transaction. The name for a BEGIN TRANSACTION is fairly superfluous, however, because any roll-back still rolls back all pending transactions. Here's an example:

```
BEGIN TRANSACTION OuterTransaction
        INSERT INTO Deposit VALUES (42, 100.00)
        BEGIN TRANSACTION InnerTransaction
        INSERT INTO Withdrawal VALUES (100, 37.50)
        ROLLBACK TRANSACTION
```

 You're almost guaranteed to find a question on your test relating to a rollback with a named transaction and how much it rolls back. Just remember: Unless a savepoint is involved, a rollback goes all the way back to the first **BEGIN TRANSACTION** that wasn't followed by a **COMMIT TRANSACTION**.

The final ROLLBACK TRANSACTION is still going to roll back all the way to OuterTransaction. As mentioned, this just adds to the complication. You can create a savepoint within a transaction and roll back to that savepoint without rolling back the entire transaction. To create a savepoint within a trans-action, use the SAVE TRANSACTION command and name the savepoint. Then when you want to roll back to the savepoint, you can use the savepoint name. The syntax is identical to that of a named transaction. Here's an example:

```
BEGIN TRANSACTION OuterTransaction
        INSERT INTO Deposit VALUES (42, 100.00)
        SAVE TRANSACTION SavePoint1
        INSERT INTO Withdrawal VALUES (100, 37.50)
        ROLLBACK TRANSACTION SavePoint1 --rolls back to the save point
```

If that ROLLBACK TRANSACTION didn't have the savepoint name out there, it would roll back to the beginning of the transaction, just as you'd expect. Although transactions can help control data access, their use within proce-dures can increase locking and they therefore have to be carefully designed.

Data Access Using Stored Procedures

Stored procedures are used extensively to encapsulate business logic, espe-cially by implementing transactions. Using stored procedures is an effective way to encapsulate an entire transaction into one line of execution: the stored procedure call. Using parameters to pass in data and resultsets to return out-put is a very common way to make sure that the data that comes in is vali-dated and correct and that the correlations between the data being returned conform to established business rules. There are several benefits to using stored procedures that far outweigh the costs.

In a multitier data architecture, SQL Server can provide both the bottom tier (data storage) and middle tier (business logic) parts of a large-scale, client/server application. With judicious use of stored procedures and triggers, data integrity and business rules can be enforced while also providing performance gains over other coding techniques.

Stored procedures can be faster than equivalent "dynamic" batches because SQL Server can cache the query plan and reuse the query plan. So the code is preparsed, preplanned, and ready to run, eliminating some of the startup time for running a batch, especially a significantly large batch. In this respect you get performance with control over the data access placed at the source.

Typically, programmers write programs and database administrators spend most of their time either writing queries for the programmers or fixing broken queries from the programmers. If the queries are encapsulated into stored procedures, the queries can be changed by the database administrator easily, and the database administrator just has to keep the incoming parameters and outgoing data formatted the same, but can make other changes inside the stored procedure without changing the application code.

Applications that do not use stored procedures for handling data make repeated trips to the database to get little pieces of information, which are then correlated and usually applied to the database. This involves data making several trips across the network, and sometimes involves making and breaking several database connections. This is a lot less efficient than simply telling SQL Server how to handle your data and letting the stored procedure process the data without it leaving the server.

Web Applications and Stored Procedures

If you've worked on web applications before, you've probably realized that most web programmers weren't hired to write good queries; they were hired to write good web pages. By encouraging, or perhaps mandating, the use of stored procedures, you can encapsulate all the queries that the web programmers write into one place with a consistent interface. Then, as the SQL guru you will be when you finish reading this book, you can go through and tweak their queries, make them more efficient, and leave the rowsets that get sent to their application and the parameter list the same. That way, you can rewrite the queries and leave the web pages completely alone.

But coding isn't everything. Optimization of data access begins from the outset. A good database design will go a long way toward achieving an efficient system that responds to user requests in a timely fashion.

Optimization Through Design

A lot of factors affect SQL Server and the applications that use its data resources. Gaining performance and response time from a server is a primary concern for database developers and administrators. One key element in obtaining the utmost from a database is an indexing strategy that helps to achieve the business needs of the enterprise, in part by returning data from queries in a responsive fashion.

The query optimizer in SQL Server reliably chooses the most effective index for use with any given query, which helps considerably if indexes have been created to choose from. In most cases the optimizer provides the best performance from the index choices provided. The overall index design strategy should provide a good selection of indexes for the optimizer to use.

You can't just start putting a lot of indexes throughout your table structures until you understand the implications of indexes. Although indexes provide good query performance, they can also take away from other processes. You can expect performance to degrade when performing updates against the data. Indexes consume hardware resources and processing cycles; memory overhead is associated with their use; regular maintenance is required to keep them at optimum levels; and many database processes have to work within the presence of the index.

SQL Server indexing strategies begin with the most basic elements of providing a primary index, but there are more advanced tuning and design considerations. The exam covers indexing in many categories, including index selection, tuning, maintenance, and specialty implementations.

Pointing an Index in the Right Direction

An indexing strategy involves your decisions on how to implement indexes, which columns you choose to index, and how you decide that one index is better than another. SQL Server supports two kinds of indexes: clustered and nonclustered. Creating additional indexes, including clustered and nonclustered, covering indexes, and indexed views, is imperative to optimize data access.

Choosing an indexing strategy can be an extremely hard decision. Know when to implement certain indexes and where to put them. Index choice is definitely going to be questioned on the exam. The Index Tuning Wizard can help improve and design accurate, efficient, and proficient indexes on the fly with fascinating results. The Index Tuning Wizard enables you to select and create powerful indexes and statistics for a Microsoft SQL Server 2000 database without prior knowledge of index and database structural designs. The Index Tuning Wizard simplifies one of the tasks that weigh on DBAs' backs: choosing the correct column to index.

Information concerning indexes can be viewed by using the `sp_helpindex` stored procedure. To rename or delete an index, use the `sp_rename` stored procedure and `DROP INDEX` statement, respectively. When information that affects data is modified, index information can go loose throughout the database.

Index statistics need to be up-to-date for the optimizer to decide on the fastest route of access. You can use the `UPDATE STATISTICS` command, which updates statistical information for an index. Rebuilding indexes helps in collecting the scattered information and bringing data back from its fragmented form. Use the `DBCC DBREINDEX` to re-index a single index or all indexes in a table.

SQL Server supports indexes defined on any column in a table, including computed columns. If a table is created with no clustered index, the data rows are not stored in any particular order. This structure is called a *heap*. If order is supplied by a clustered index, heap storage is not used. In this case, the data is stored in a given sequence based on the clustered index.

SQL Server supports indexing of two basic types, although there are many variations of those types. The two types of SQL Server indexes are *clustered* and *nonclustered* indexes. Clustered indexes are implemented so that the logical order of the key values determines the physical order of the corresponding rows in a table. Nonclustered indexes are indexes in which the logical order of the index is different than the physical, stored order of the rows on disk. The following sections examine them both.

Full-Text Indexing and Searches

Full-Text Search is a completely separate program that runs as a service, namely Microsoft Search Service, or MSSearch. Full-Text Search can be used in conjunction with all sorts of information from all the various MS BackOffice products. The Full-Text catalogs and indexes are not stored in a SQL Server database. They are stored in separate files managed by the Microsoft Search Service.

Full-Text indexes are special indexes that efficiently track the words you're looking for in a table. They help in enabling special searching functions that differ from regular indexes. Full-Text indexes are not automatically updated, and they reside in a storage space called the Full-Text catalog.

When a Full-Text index is created, you can perform wildcard searches (Full-Text search) that locate words in close proximity. All Full-Text indexes are by default placed in a single Full-Text catalog. Each SQL Server at its apex can store 256 Full-Text catalogs.

The Full-Text catalog files are not recovered during a SQL Server recovery. They also cannot be backed up and restored using the T-SQL BACKUP and RESTORE statements. The T catalogs must be resynchronized separately after a recovery or restore operation. The Full-Text catalog files are accessible only to the Microsoft Search Service and the Windows NT or Windows 2000 system administrator.

To enable Full-Text searches, you can run the Full-Text Indexing Wizard, which enables you to manage and create Full-Text indexes. Note that Full-Text indexes may be created only on columns that contain only text. Full-Text indexes are not automatically updated, thereby bringing up the need to automate the process of updating by setting a job or performing a manual administrative task.

Clustered Indexes

A clustered index is a type of index in which the logical order of the key values determines the physical order of the data stored on disk. Because a clustered index shows how the physical data of a table is stored, there can be only one clustered index per table.

The selection of appropriate column(s) on which to base a clustered index is particularly important. Columns should be chosen where range searches are frequently performed or based on the expected order of the majority of reports printed from the data. A range search occurs within a WHERE conditional operation, as in selecting the range of all authors who have an advance greater than $500 but less than $4,000. With this type of range search, the index, if present, first locates the smallest value (500), and then it locates the other values alongside that value until the last value is reached (4000).

Each index page holds a header that is followed by index rows. Each of these rows contains a pointer value to another subpage or a row of data. The lowest level of implementation in clustered indexes is known as the leaf page or node, and it contains data rows and pages. The first level of implementation is known as the root node. Anything between the root node and the leaf node is referred to as intermediate-level pages.

Candidates for clustered indexes have the following characteristics:

➤ A column queried using range operators such as BETWEEN, <, or >.

➤ Columns that are grouped using the GROUP BY clause or that involve joins or that represent the ORDER of displayed or printed output.

➤ Queries and reporting that access sequential data.

➤ Operations that result in large resultsets.

➤ Columns that don't have incremented values; for example, an ID column has incremented values.

➤ Columns with many duplicate values.

➤ Columns that don't have incremented values; for example, an ID column has incremented values.

➤ On the PK when there are many inserts causing all records to be inserted on the same page, which can remain in memory.

Defining clustered indexes on views enables you to store the resultsets of the view in the database, thereby reducing the overhead of dynamically building the resultset. Because you can create only one clustered index, the majority of indexes created are nonclustered indexes. A nonclustered index can operate over an existing clustered index or over a data heap.

Nonclustered Indexes

Nonclustered indexes are indexes in which the logical order of the key values in the index is different than the physical order of the rows in the indexed table. There are two major differences that distinguish them from clustered indexes. First, the leaf node of the nonclustered index does not contain the concrete data. It contains index rows having a nonclustered key value that point to a data row. Second, as already noted, nonclustered indexes do not physically rearrange the data.

When you query data on a column with a nonclustered index, SQL Server 2000 first tries to find a record containing your table object ID and a value in the indid column from the sysindexes table that is >= 1 and < 255, because a 0 implies there is no index at all, and 255 implies that the table has Text/Image pages. After it finds the record, SQL Server examines the root column to find the root page of the index. After SQL Server finds the root page, it can begin a search for your data.

The SQL Server 2000 optimizer chooses an index to use for the search. The Keys column in sysindexes lists which columns are involved in each index. If the optimizer knows this and knows which columns you are searching on, it can use index statistics to determine which index to use. In the simplest case, if you are searching on only one column, A, and only one index exists on column A, then it uses that index. When you are searching on multiple columns, and many or all of these columns are indexed, it uses statistical methods to determine the index.

It's important to understand the following guidelines before you create nonclustered indexes:

➤ Nonclustered indexes are good when queries don't return a large resultset.

➤ Columns that are used in a SELECT list or the WHERE clause are good candidates for nonclustered indexes.

➤ A nonclustered index is the default index in SQL Server.

➤ There can be up to 249 nonclustered indexes on a single table.

➤ Nonclustered indexes generally take more overhead than clustered indexes, so you should create them only when it is absolutely necessary.

➤ Nonclustered indexes make a good choice for use as a covering index.

 Be careful on the exam to pay close attention to **WHERE** and **ORDER** clause examples that don't have matching or covering indexes. Increased performance and decreased response time may be achieved by adding an index in these cases.

What to Index?

Column selectivity is a major step in the process of indexing. In general, columns that are frequently accessed by the WHERE or the ORDER BY clauses should be considered. When you build indexes, try to narrow indexes down to the minimum number of columns needed. Multicolumn indexes act negatively on performance. Columns with unique values serving as primary keys are also good candidates.

The challenge for the database designer is to build a physical data model that provides efficient data access. This can be done by minimizing I/O processing time. The following types of columns are good ones to index:

➤ A column that acts as the table's primary or foreign key.

➤ Columns that are regularly sorted by the ORDER BY clause.

➤ Columns that are filtered on an exact condition using the WHERE clause—for instance, WHERE state= 'Ca'.

➤ Columns that are queried on joins.

➤ Columns that hold integer values rather than character values.

➤ Searches for rows with search key values in a range of values—for example, WHERE Royalty BETWEEN 1000 and 4000.

➤ Queries that use the like clause, but only if they start with character data. Examine the following: WHERE au_fname LIKE 'sm%'.

The true test of any index strategy occurs when queries are processed during day-to-day operations. Strong guidelines also exist on things that should not be indexed.

What Not to Index?

You really can't and shouldn't index all the columns in your table. Doing so would significantly drop performance on inserts and deletes, even though most queries would run fast. When determining whether to index a small table, look to see whether it requires more page reads to scan the index than there are pages in the table. In this case an index will hurt performance, not help it. Therefore, a table with less than three pages is not helped by any index. Learn to use the SQL Server Query Analyzer tool as a guide for whether an index is useful. Recognize table scans; the process of reading all records from a table in sequence may take fewer cycles than accessing an index first—particularly on small tables.

Here are some conditions that would indicate you should not index a column:

➤ If the index is never used by the query optimizer

➤ If the column values exhibit low selectivity, often greater than 95% for nonclustered indexes

➤ If the columns to be indexed are very wide

➤ If the table is rarely queried

➤ If the columns are not used in WHERE clauses, aggregated, or used in sorting or in join operations.

Indexes provide many trade-offs. Although queries may show a performance improvement, INSERT, UPDATE, and DELETE operations could see a decline in performance. You may not know the power of indexes until you perform large searches on tables having tens of thousands of rows. Implementing an indexing strategy would not be proper for a small database with a few tables containing no more than 50 rows. Tables are benefited by indexing for the following reasons:

➤ As many as 249 nonclustered indexes can be created on a single table.

➤ Indexes help increase efficiency on complex searches on large tables.

➤ Indexes are easy to implement.

➤ Sixteen columns can compose the same composite index, as long as the total key length is less than 900 bytes.

➤ Indexes may be used to enforce uniqueness throughout rows in tables.

Creating indexes against a view is new to SQL Server 2000. With this functionality you can provide a few advanced implementations. Pay particular attention to restrictions and required settings, because they are sure to be needed on the exam.

Nonclustered Covering Indexes

A covering index is a nonclustered index that is built on all the columns needed to satisfy a SQL query, in both the selection criteria and the WHERE clause. Covering indexes save a huge amount of I/O and build a lot of efficiency in a query. For instance, if you query SQL Server with the statement

```
SELECT Au_FName, Au_LName FROM Authors WHERE State= 'ca'
```

you can run the following to create an index:

```
CREATE NONCLUSTERED INDEX MyIndex
ON Authors(State, Au_FName, Au_LName)
```

MyIndex would be considered a covering index because a composite index is built on all columns specified in the SELECT statement and WHERE clause. Covering indexes significantly boost performance because all the data needed for the query to base the search on is contained within the index; only the index pages, not the data pages, of the table must be referenced to resolve where to retrieve the data.

Indexing Strategies

One clustered index per table can be used and, if implemented, it determines the physical order of the data. Nonclustered indexes act like those in the back of a book—pointing out the physical location of the data. Nonclustered covering indexes can be created in cases in which the exact query content is known.

Keys, ranges, and unique values are strong selections for index candidates. Seldom-used data, binary data, and repeating values are poor index candidates. After index candidates have been selected, monitor application usage. Adjust the indexing strategy on a regular basis to provide reliably high performance.

Index Maintenance over Time

It is a little tricky, at best, to select an appropriate indexing strategy, and maintaining it in the face of ongoing changes inherent in a database life cycle is even more of a challenge. Index maintenance over time is the next consideration.

Index creation and alteration are two necessary mechanisms in any indexing strategy. A database goes through a life cycle and undergoes size changes, application uses, and other growth. Any database system is in a constant state of flux because data is always being added, changed, removed, or otherwise affected by change.

Sometimes indexes need to be rebuilt because of changes in data that occurred after it was built. Rebuilding indexes helps in collecting the scattered information and bringing index data back to its original form. This increases the overall performance by making it easier for SQL Server to read pages to get data. You can re-create an index in three ways:

➤ By deleting the original index and then re-creating it

➤ By specifying DROP_EXISTING in the CREATE INDEX clause

➤ By using the Database Console Command (DBCC), DBCC DBREINDEX

The first option is highly unfavorable for clustered indexes because other levels of indexes use the same index's cluster key as a pointer to data rows. When a clustered index is defined on a table, this dictates the physical order of the data. The clustered index key values are used as data pointers for all other nonclustered keys. Deleting a clustered index and then re-creating it means deleting and re-creating all nonclustered indexes.

The second option is rebuilding the index. This method reduces unnecessary work and is advantageous to both clustered and nonclustered indexes in that it significantly reduces the overhead of rebuilding the index.

The third option is the preferred out of the three choices, because it enables you to rebuild multiple indexes in a single shot, without rebuilding indexes individually. It also enables you to rebuild indexes on tables that use PRIMARY and UNIQUE constraints without requiring you to delete and rebuild each constraint.

SQL Server enables you to rebuild one or more indexes on a table by using the DBCC DBREINDEX statement, without having to rebuild each index separately. DBCC DBREINDEX is also useful if you want to rebuild indexes that enforce PRIMARY KEY or UNIQUE constraints without having to delete and re-create the constraints. If simple defragmentation of index space is desired, use the INDEXDEFRAG option. There are many uses of DBCC in database maintenance and in itself DBCC is a major topic; for that reason we will look at DBCC in depth later, in the section "Database Console Command (DBCC)."

Using the Index Tuning Wizard

The Index Tuning Wizard is a graphical tool that enables you to select and create powerful indexes and statistics for Microsoft SQL Server 2000 databases. The Index Tuning Wizard simplifies the task of choosing which indexes to create in a table. As you've seen previously, one of the most difficult tasks for a DBA is determining which columns get indexed. Fortunately, Microsoft has shipped a wizard that identifies the best clustered and nonclustered indexes for a table and the indexes that are most likely to improve query performance.

The Index Tuning Wizard is used to find the most efficient path of execution in a set of input. This input is a table or file, namely a workload. To make workloads, use the SQL Profiler to set a trace. The SQL Profiler enables you to monitor and record activity events in a file or table. SQL Profiler traces enable the Index Tuning Wizard to make accurate decisions. Traces of the different events that happen while work is performed can be recorded for hours or even days, depending on the period desired to be monitored. After the events are recorded, the Index Tuning Wizard works with the query processor to establish the viability of a configuration.

 Caution! Profiler can affect overall database performance, sometimes significantly, so use it sparingly and remember to turn it off as soon as you feel that the necessary information has been captured.

For the Index Tuning Wizard to really be useful, it must be executed during production use of the database, or at least under circumstances in which a sufficient query load will produce meaningful results.

Dropping Unwanted Indexes

If an index isn't in use any longer, you may want to delete it. Deleting an index means freeing all storage space the index was previously holding. It also results in more efficient INSERT, UPDATE, and DELETE operations. Only a table owner is granted permission to delete indexes. To delete an index or indexes, run the DROP INDEX statement.

Dropping an index may require the removal of constraints if those constraints are directly related to the index. In other instances, you may just want to remove an index that has outlived its usefulness. To help determine index validity, the Index Tuning Wizard is provided as an assistant in index analysis. You can't drop an index created with a PRIMARY KEY or UNIQUE constraint; the alter table command *must* be used.

Partitioned Views to Optimize Access

When a distributed partitioned view is used, the data resides on several servers that work together to maintain and display the data. These servers may be called federated database servers. This term is used to refer to these servers that share the data-hosting job but are independently administered.

With partitioned views, tables that store large amounts of data can be split up (using horizontal partitioning) into smaller member tables. This data in the member table holds the same number of columns as the original table; it is only the number of rows that is decreased. After the data is broken down into smaller member tables, a view defined with UNION ALL is used to bring all member tables together. This view looks like a single large resultset. When a SELECT query is run against the partitioned view, SQL Server uses CHECK constraints in determining which member table the data is from. The CHECK constraint is usually created on the primary key column.

A partitioned view combines horizontally partitioned data from member tables across one or more servers (distributed partitioned views). A member table can be thought of as a segment from a larger table. There are two types of partitioned views in SQL Server: a local partitioned view and a distributed partitioned view. A local partitioned view is a partitioned view in which all member tables reside on the local instance of SQL Server. Distributed partitioned views are new to SQL Server 2000 and are a bit more advanced than local partitioned views. The key difference between a distributed partitioned view and a local partitioned view is that in a local partitioned view, the data is collected from a single server alone. In contrast, a distributed partitioned view collects data from two or more instances of SQL Server, hence the name "distributed."

To decide whether you should create a partitioned view, you have to examine the data you will be working with, and consider how it is used. If you have a table that is used by many different department or regions (each with its own server), you can look at partitioning the database along those lines.

But, you say, the system has been in place for years and what used to perform well just doesn't seem to be doing so well anymore. A neglected system or just plain poor maintenance may be the cause, and there are several things you should look at before deciding that a redesign is necessary.

Optimizing Performance in the Partitions

To maximize performance in large applications, the design of partitioned views should be examined. Also, placing indexes on views will provide for faster searching and retrieval of data. In itself, a view generally provides for better performance because less data is involved. Always consider the use of views when tables have an extremely large number of columns, application design is left to the user, and tables contain sensitive information.

Indexing Views for Optimization

Indexed views are a new concept introduced in SQL Server 2000. They allow view resultsets to be stored in the database's physical storage after an index is created. In contrast to this, in a non-indexed view, the view is activated at runtime and the resultset is dynamically built based on logic needed to create output from the underlying base tables. Any computations, such as joins or aggregations, are done during query execution for each query referencing the view, ultimately leading in degraded performance.

Defining clustered indexes on views enables the resultsets of the view to be stored in the database, thereby reducing the overhead of dynamically building the resultset. This means that indexed views can be treated like any other table because additional nonclustered indexes can be added. An indexed view can be created using the CREATE INDEX or CREATE VIEW statements, which is done when data is occasionally updated. Some of the benefits of indexed views are listed here:

➤ They increase performance of queries that use joins and aggregates.

➤ Data in an indexed view is updated when a base table gets modified.

➤ Views that aggregate and join data are improved. When an index is created on a view, the view is executed and the resultset is stored in the database.

➤ The first time you create an index on a view, it has to be of type unique clustered.

Creating an indexed view is as simple as altering the CREATE INDEX statement. Use the same syntax used in creating table indexes except that the table name is replaced with the view name. Also, some session-level options must be toggled (see the preceding section). Keep in mind that only the view owner is allowed to execute a CREATE INDEX statement on a view.

All indexes on a view are dropped if the view is dropped. All nonclustered indexes on the view are dropped if the clustered index is dropped. Nonclustered indexes can be dropped individually. Dropping the clustered index on the view removes the stored resultset, and the optimizer returns to processing the view like a standard view.

Maintaining the System to Get Back Performance

Most post-implementation performance tuning falls under the job scope of the database administrator and for that reason will be found on the companion exam to this one, the administration exam. You will possibly have a few questions on general use and functionality of the tools, so in the sections that follow we will provide a short overview of some of the more important tools.

Stored Procedures Used for Maintenance

Many useful stored procedures are available for people who are a little more advanced with T-SQL and the design of system-level applications. Often a programmatic solution is desired over one that provides only visual feedback. In these instances the output from the stored procedures can be acted on in an automated manner.

The `sp_who` stored procedure reports snapshot information about current SQL Server users and processes. This is a T-SQL alternative to viewing user activity in the current activity window in SQL Server Enterprise Manager. Similarly, `sp_lock` reports snapshot information about locks, including the object ID, index ID, type of lock, and type or resource to which the lock applies. The `sp_lock` procedure is also a Transact-SQL alternative used to view lock activity in the current activity window in SQL Server Enterprise Manager.

Other procedures also present alternative mechanisms to query for results normally displayed. The `sp_spaceused` procedure displays an estimate of the current amount of disk space used by a table or database. This is a T-SQL alternative to viewing database usage in the Enterprise Manager.

Still further procedures provide specific information that can be immediately acted on. The `sp_monitor` statement displays statistics, including CPU usage, I/O usage, and the amount of time idle since last executed. This information can be used as an advanced mechanism for SQL Server monitoring.

Other information of interest to system developers is the availability of a wide variety of built-in system functions. Everything from the name of the server to the name of the user and beyond can be identified for a particular connection.

Various built-in SQL Server functions are available to find out information about the server. This information can be used as an aid in troubleshooting or determining SQL Server utilization, and/or to provide for optimization and performance tuning.

Statistics about SQL Server activity since the server was started are stored in predefined SQL Server counters. Other information pertaining to the server is also stored in similar variables. Functions are all categorized by the type of information provided.

Sometimes the answers won't be found in the system stored procedures, but over the life of a system, the user-defined procedures may have changed drastically. Conversely, the data under these stored procedures may have undergone significant development. In these cases maybe what is needed is a recompile.

Recompilation of Procedures

Adding or altering indexes or changing a stored procedure causes SQL Server to automatically recompile the procedure. This optimization occurs the next time the stored procedure is run, but only after SQL Server is restarted. In instances in which you want to force a recompilation, you can use the sp_recompile system-stored procedure.

Alternatively, you can use the WITH RECOMPILE option when you create or execute a stored procedure. Stored procedures are dealt with in depth in Chapter 9, "Designing a Database Security Plan."

Problem Analysis Through Statistical Functions

There are many statistical functions within the system that can help determine the status of the environment within which the DBMS is operating. For example, you can use the STATS_DATE function to test statistic update settings for any index. Often non-updated statistics cause a system to slow and become unresponsive over time. Periodic checking and UPDATE STATISTICS execution is warranted on most production systems.

What is probably one of the best function sets has been saved until last. Although all the functions mentioned in this unit are important and have their appropriate usage, the most useful set of functions for optimization purposes would be the system statistical functions. But there are many of these related functions, and I have summarized some of the more common-ly used ones in the following list:

➤ @@CONNECTIONS—Returns the number of connections, or attempted con-nections, the server last started.

➤ @@CPU_BUSY—Returns the time in milliseconds (based on the resolution of the system timer) that the CPU has spent working since the server was last started.

➤ @@IO_BUSY—Enables the database system team to see whether the current file and disk storage configuration is responding well to system stress or would benefit from the use of additional disk storage consideration.

➤ @@IDLE—Returns the time in milliseconds (based on the resolution of the system timer) that the server has been idle since last started.

➤ @@IO_BUSY—Returns the time in milliseconds (based on the resolution of the system timer) that the server has spent performing input and output operations since it was last started.

➤ @@PACK_RECEIVED—Returns the number of input packets read from the network by the server since it was last started.

➤ @@PACK_SENT—Returns the number of output packets written to the net-work by the server since it was last started.

➤ @@PACKET_ERRORS—Returns the number of network packet errors that have occurred on the server since it was last started.

➤ @@TOTAL_ERRORS—Returns the number of disk read/write errors encoun-tered by the server since it was last started.

➤ @@TOTAL_READ—Returns the number of noncache disk reads by the server since it was last started.

➤ @@TOTAL_WRITE—Returns the number of disk writes by the server since it was last started.

As you can see from the wide array of functions SQL Server provides, a lot of useful diagnostic information can be used to optimize throughput while providing maximum performance and user response time. One of the pri-mary database administration tools to begin on this arduous journey is DBCC. You can use DBCC to diagnose and act on some of the most fre-quent inadequacies of a server configuration.

@@CPU_BUSY enables the database system team to see whether the current configuration is responding well to system stress or whether it would benefit from the use
of additional processor consideration. See also "**@@IDLE**" in the preceding list for
related information.

Database Console Command (DBCC)

One of the most useful diagnostic/tuning tools available to the SQL Server
database developer and administrator is the DBCC command. The database
consistency checker allows you to diagnose and repair some common situations found on the server.

The Transact-SQL programming language provides DBCC statements that
act as Database Console Commands and also may be referred to as the
Database Consistency Checker. DBCC statements enable you to check performance statistics and the logical and physical consistency of a database system. Many DBCC statements can fix detected problems.

Some DBCC operations provide useful information about the processes that
have been performed most recently on the server. This type of information
can be quite useful in pinpointing the source of SQL activities. Each of the
options, presented in the following list, provides a small piece of a very large
puzzle, but collectively they can provide a useful picture of the current server activity:

➤ DBCC INPUTBUFFER—Provides the last statement sent from a client to the
server.

➤ DBCC OPENTRAN—Provides transaction information for the oldest active
transaction, distributed transaction, and nondistributed replicated
transaction.

➤ DBCC OUTPUTBUFFER—Returns the current output buffer in hexadecimal and
ASCII format for the specified system process ID.

➤ DBCC PROCCACHE—Displays information about the procedure cache.

➤ DBCC SHOWCONTIG—Displays fragmentation information for the data and
indexes.

One of the most frequently used DBCC status operations is the SHOWCONTIG.
Because it can display information specific to data and index fragmentation,
it is useful in determining when to carry out maintenance operations. Many
of the DBCC options can be effectively used in troubleshooting as in the following list:

➤ DBCC SHOW_STATISTICS—Displays the current distribution statistics for the specified target on the specified table.

➤ DBCC SQLPERF—Provides statistics about the use of transaction log space in all databases.

➤ DBCC TRACESTATUS—Displays the status of trace flags.

➤ DBCC USEROPTIONS—Returns the SET options active (set) for the current connection.

All these options can provide valuable data to help you determine how performance can be improved. After status information has been generated, the next task in information retrieval is obtaining validation data that can also give you insight into a server.

Use of DBCC CHECKDB and **DBCC CHECKALLOC** requires a little further clarification. Use of **CHECKALLOC** is unnecessary if **CHECKDB** is used first. **CHECKDB** contains a superset of options that includes all the functionality provided by **CHECKALLOC**.

Validation DBCC Operations

The validation options represent tools available that can reveal database storage problems and also provide the mechanisms to modify and fine-tune the environment. To validate various objects on the server, use the following:

➤ DBCC CHECKALLOC—Checks the consistency of disk space.

➤ DBCC CHECKCATALOG—Checks for consistency in system tables.

➤ DBCC CHECKCONSTRAINTS—Checks the integrity of constraints.

➤ DBCC CHECKDB—Checks the allocation and structural integrity of all the objects in the database.

➤ DBCC CHECKFILEGROUP—Checks the allocation and structural integrity of tables in a filegroup.

➤ DBCC CHECKIDENT—Checks the current identity value for a table and, if needed, corrects the value.

➤ DBCC CHECKTABLE—Checks the integrity of the data, index, text, ntext, and image pages.

➤ DBCC NEWALLOC—Checks the allocation of data and index pages. Equivalent to CHECKALLOC and used for backward compatibility only.

Some of these functions are very CPU- and disk-intensive. Caution should be exercised around the time of day a DBCC CHECKDB operation is performed. Other functions as well can impact the server and temporarily increase system overhead.

> The **DBCC DBDEPAIR** Compatibility is not used often. **DBCC DBREPAIR** is included for backward compatibility only. It is recommended that **DROP DATABASE** be used to drop damaged databases. **DBCC DBREPAIR** may not be supported in a future version of SQL Server.

Maintenance DBCC Operations

Regular maintenance is needed in all database environments. Data and index pages will become fragmented. Data may become corrupt, file sizes may need to be adjusted, and regular maintenance will help you optimize the server environment. The DBCC options that are used in maintenance processes are listed here:

➤ DBCC DBREINDEX—Rebuilds one or more indexes.

➤ DBCC DBREPAIR—Drops a damaged database.

➤ DBCC INDEXDEFRAG—Defragments clustered and secondary indexes of the specified table or view.

➤ DBCC SHRINKDATABASE—Shrinks the size of the data files in the specified database.

➤ DBCC SHRINKFILE—Shrinks a specified data file or log file.

➤ DBCC UPDATEUSAGE—Reports and corrects inaccuracies in the sysindexes table, which may result in incorrect space use reported by sp_spaceused.

Some DBCC options do not directly fit into any one of the aforementioned categories. Listed as miscellaneous options, these DBCC operations can provide assistance, help to free and better use resources, and provide some tracking mechanisms.

Miscellaneous Operations

Several of the DBCC options do not directly fall into any category. They have been included in the following list:

➤ DBCC dllname (FREE)—Unloads the specified extended stored procedure DLL from memory.

➤ DBCC HELP—Returns syntax information for the specified DBCC statement.

➤ DBCC PINTABLE—Marks a table to be pinned, and does not flush the pages for the table from memory.

➤ DBCC ROWLOCK—Is used for Microsoft SQL Server 6.5, enabling Insert Row Locking operations on tables.

➤ DBCC TRACEOFF—Disables trace flags. Trace flags are discussed in the next section.

➤ DBCC TRACEON—Enables trace flags. Trace flags are discussed completely in the next section.

➤ DBCC UNPINTABLE—Marks a table as unpinned. Table pages in the buffer cache can be flushed.

> The DBCC Row Lock Compatibility option is somewhat antiquated. Row-level locking is enabled by default in SQL Server version 2000. The locking strategy is row locking with possible promotion to page or table locking. **DBCC ROWLOCK** is included for backward compatibility. In a future version of SQL Server, **DBCC ROWLOCK** may not be supported.

Although DBCC represents one of the premier Microsoft tools available to a SQL Server administrator, there are other alternatives for troubleshooting. Trace flag usage has been a longstanding debugging tool that in the past has proven useful. However, with other graphic tools now available that are easier to use and decipher, the use of trace flags is decreasing. Microsoft has stated that behaviors available with these flags may not be supported in future releases of SQL Server.

Trace Flags

Trace flags display information about a specific activity within the server and are used to diagnose problems or performance issues. They are particularly useful in deadlock analysis. Trace flags temporarily set specific server characteristics or switch off a particular behavior. Trace flags are often used to diagnose and debug stored procedures and analyze complex system elements. Four common trace flags are used for troubleshooting different elements of SQL Server:

➤ 260—Determines DLL version information.

➤ 1204—Finds command affected by deadlock and type of locks partaking.

➤ 2528—Disables/enables parallel checking of objects during DBCC use.

➤ 3205—Disables/enables tape drive compression support.

To determine dynamic link library version information, see the support for GetXPVersion() in SQL Server Books Online, but other utilities are available without the use of a flag. Parallel DBCC checking should not usually be disabled, and tape dumps and backups should usually be compressed. SQL Server provides many tools to aid in the upkeep of the server. Although specific aspects of the use of these tools will be the role of the administrator, for this exam you will at least need to know what each of the tools does.

Exam Prep Questions

1. You are working for a small manufacturing company that has been operating well for some time. Lately the end users have been reporting that when performing queries against information on customers, the system is growing increasingly slow. After examining the system, you determine that the table definition has recently been altered. You want the response time to improve and be similar to what it was before the change. How would you fix the problem?

   ❑ A. Run a DBCC DBREINDEX.
   ❑ B. Drop and re-create the table's clustered index.
   ❑ C. Drop and re-create all indexes.
   ❑ D. Update the index statistics.
   ❑ E. Stop and restart the server.

   Answer: D. Because the table structure has recently been altered, it is a good possibility that this change has caused the indexing information to become unstable or that statistics affecting the index have not been updated. If you restart the service, SQL Server should then update the statistical information accordingly, but this may affect use of the server and may not be a possibility. After the restart, you may want to ensure that all statistics are intact. Also consider index fragmentation as a possible source to the problem. For more information, see the section "Pointing an Index in the Right Direction."

2. Your company has a table named Products that is dedicated to its goods. A month ago, you added three nonclustered indexes to the table named NC1_Pro, NC2_Pro, and NC3_Pro. You also added a clustered index named C1_Pro on the primary key named Prod_ID. You monitor the performance on the indexes and notice that the indexes are not as efficient as before. You decide to rebuild each index in the table. Which method should you use to rebuild all indexes in the fastest and most efficient way?

   ❑ A. Use DBCC DBREINDEX (Products).
   ❑ B. Create a clustered index with Drop-Existing; create a nonclustered index with Drop-Existing.
   ❑ C. Delete all indexes and then re-create them.
   ❑ D. Use DBCC DBREINDEX (NC1_Pro, NC2_Pro, NC3_Pro, C1_Pro).
   ❑ E. Update the index statistics.

   Answer: A. Use DBCC DBREINDEX. Answer B is wrong because this would be more time-consuming than DBCC DBREINDEX. You would have to individually rebuild all indexes. Answer C is not correct because deleting a clustered index and then re-creating it means deleting and re-creating all nonclustered indexes. Also, the process would have to involve two separate steps. For more details, refer to the section "Index Maintenance over Time."

3. You have a table named Products that holds information pertaining to the products your company trades. You need to perform quality searches on the Description column so that you can find products needed using diverse methods. You decide using full-text searches is the best method and so enable full-text indexing in your table. You want to keep performance consistent with the full-text indexes so that they do not degrade, and you want to minimize overhead associated with their maintenance. What should you do?

- ❑ A. Expand the database to accommodate future growth of the full-text indexes.
- ❑ B. Use the Index Tuning Wizard.
- ❑ C. Repopulate using the Full-Text Indexing Wizard and specify Keep Performance Consistency.
- ❑ D. Schedule regular repopulates of the full-text indexes.

Answer: D. Unlike regular SQL indexes, full-text indexes are not automatically kept up-to-date as data is modified in the associated tables. Full-text indexes should be frequently updated to maintain performance. For more information, see "Full-Text Indexing and Searches."

4. Which statements show the maximum number of clustered and nonclustered indexes allowed in a single table?

- ❑ A. Clustered 249 and nonclustered 149
- ❑ B. Clustered 249 and nonclustered 249
- ❑ C. Clustered 1 and nonclustered 249
- ❑ D. Clustered 1 and nonclustered unlimited

Answer: C. There can be only one clustered index per table and as many as 249 nonclustered indexes. For more details, refer to SQL Server Books Online.

5. Jauna is a DBA who has received complaints from many users concerning the data retrieval and modification times on the Sales table. She knows that you are a developer and asks you to figure out a way to resolve the problem she is facing. Because you are a new developer, you happen to know that indexes increase performance, and that's just about all you know about indexes. You imprudently index all 12 columns in the Sales table. Which of the following statements outlines the consequence of using the numerous indexes you have just done?

- ❑ A. Numerous indexes make modifying data slower.
- ❑ B. Numerous indexes are not allowed to be built; indexes can be used only in smaller quantities.
- ❑ C. Numerous indexes result in a very short index life span.
- ❑ D. Numerous indexes decrease performance on queries that select data with the SELECT clause.

Answer: A. Indexes used in larger quantities often degrade the rate at which insertions, deletions, and some modifications to data occur. Nevertheless, indexes generally speed up data access in cases in which the data in the table is sufficient to warrant indexing. For more information, see "Using the Index Tuning Wizard."

6. You are evaluating the database design given to you by another developer. This database was to be designed with an emphasis on query performance, and an attempt has been made to meet the design goal. Replying to this directive, the developer has sketched out a design for several indexes for the tables. These indexes have been put together with the highest expected query usage kept in mind. As you review his design, you notice that the new indexes provide varying degrees of benefit to various queries. Which of his indexes is likely to be the most effective?

- ❏ A. An index on gender for 134,000 registered voters.
- ❏ B. An index on the sales agent's last initial for 25,000 orders.
- ❏ C. An index for the StateCode primary key column in a US_States table.
- ❏ D. An index for the State column in a PacificTime_ZIP_Codes table.

Answer: C. Gender is never a good column to supply an index against because it has only two possible values. In general, a column with a high percentage of unique values is the best choice for indexing. An agent's last initial has 26 possibilities in a table of 25,000, which is still a rather poor choice. An index created on the state value would be a good choice in either C or D, but C provides the best ratio.

7. You have several procedures that will access existing indexed tables. Before you put the procedures into production, you want to ensure optimal performance. You also want to ensure that daily operations in the database are not adversely affected. What should you do?

- ❏ A. Create a covering index for each query in the procedures.
- ❏ B. Create an index that includes each column contained in every WHERE clause.
- ❏ C. Use the Index Tuning Wizard to identify whether indexes should be added.
- ❏ D. Create statistics on all columns in all the SELECT and WHERE clauses.

Answer: C. There are already indexes in place and you don't want to create additional indexes that are not needed and may adversely affect the current system. The first and second answers therefore are not suitable, at least until testing determines that the indexes will improve performance. Creating additional statistics may not be warranted. What is needed is an analysis of the system to determine the indexes needed.

8. Selects, inserts, and updates are taking too long against tables that are already indexed. Additional tables and stored procedures have been added since the original indexes were created, and many of the procedures are no longer used. What would you do to improve the response times as quickly as possible?

   ❏ A. Execute the DBCC UPDATEUSAGE statement.
   ❏ B. Execute the DBCC SHOW_STATISTICS to find high-density indexes to drop.
   ❏ C. Run the Index Tuning Wizard to find any missing or extra indexes.
   ❏ D. Use SQL profiler to find table problems.

   Answer: C. Although the profiler and DBCC operations are very good diagnostic tools, they will not provide the necessary improvements and overall quick analysis that the Index Tuning Wizard gives you. In this instance running the wizard will, in a single operation, provide the necessary information to both eliminate unwanted indexes and inform you of where additional indexes may be warranted.

9

Designing a Database Security Plan

Terms you'll need to understand:

✓ Login
✓ User
✓ Role
✓ Encryption
✓ Auditing
✓ C2 security
✓ Permissions

Techniques you'll need to master:

✓ Granting permissions
✓ Creating logins
✓ Assigning database access to users
✓ Creating database objects
✓ Creating roles and assigning users to roles
✓ Using application roles

Introduction

SQL Server has a built-in object security model that enables the system administrator to grant certain other individuals the rights to read and make changes to databases. Individuals are going to need a variety of access types to data, and this chapter looks at how to keep those folks from inadvertently or maliciously messing things up, while still providing the facilities needed.

There are various security issues that need to be taken at a larger scale. A database server needs to be secure at many levels before you even begin to talk about data security. To be secure, someone in the organization has gone about the task of securing the operating system on the computer your database is on—doing simple things, such as putting it behind a firewall and ensuring that the administrator account has a password. There are a lot of really great books on how to do this; see Appendix B, "Need to Know More?".

The SQL Server Login/User Model

You need to learn some very strict terminology before you'll understand what's really going on with security. This chapter uses terms such as *individual* or *person* to describe an actual bipedal carbon-based life-form. The term *login* describes a SQL Server login, whereas the term *NT login* describes an operating system login. Finally, the word *user* relates to how a specific login interacts inside a database.

In SQL Server, there are two security modes. In Integrated security mode, each NT login is mapped to exactly one SQL Server login. No passwords are stored in SQL Server in this case; instead, SQL Server accepts a token from the operating system, which basically says that the operating system trusts that the login is valid.

Mixed security mode includes Integrated security mode and what used to be called Standard security mode. With Standard mode, each login is created in SQL Server; SQL Server retains passwords for all the logins; and SQL Server is responsible for authenticating users. Microsoft warns against using Standard security, but it's the only way people using other operating systems or certain types of applications can use SQL Server.

Logins are stored in the Master database, complete with their passwords, which are stored encrypted. Each login is associated with one or more users. The user is associated with one database, and you must give each login access to each database it needs access to by creating a user in the database and linking it back to the login. The easiest method for interacting with logins and users is to use the Enterprise Manager, but it is possible to script this process utilizing a set of stored procedures.

To add a login for a SQL Server user who has a Windows NT account, you use the `sp_grantlogin` command, like this:

```
sp_grantlogin 'MYDOMAIN\Danny'
```

This creates a login for the NT user for integrated security. To add a user who doesn't have a user account, use this:

```
sp_addlogin 'Danny', 'DannysPassword'
```

After the login has been granted to the server, the user can be added to any of the databases. To add a user to a database, you can use the `sp_adduser` command or the newer `sp_grantdbaccess` command:

```
Use Northwind
sp_grantdbaccess 'Danny'
```

or

```
Use Northwind
sp_adduser 'Danny'
```

Both commands add a user linked to the login specified as the parameter to the current database. That's important: The user is added to the current database, so you need to make sure you know which database you are in before you execute those commands.

In looking at the security process used by SQL Server 2000, you may find yourself asking, "Where have the groups gone?" In particular, if you came up through an older version of SQL Server, such as SQL Server 7.0 or earlier, you might be used to using groups. Groups are now called roles. If you use one of the old-style group commands, such as `sp_changegroup`, you'll actually be changing the user's role. Roles have a lot more functionality than groups, such as enabling a user to belong to several roles.

Using Security Roles

To provide the capability to grant multiple users access to the same objects the same way, SQL Server provides a mechanism for creating collections of users, called *roles*. Roles are similar to groups found within a network security framework. There are sets of roles that have predetermined functionality on the server, but you also can define custom roles.

Two or three exam questions will deal with security-based roles. You will find permissions easier to control through the use of roles. There are various built-in roles that have predefined functionality, and application roles can be used to set the security for anyone performing a task through a common process.

SQL Server provides you with a set of roles you can use to assign different levels of permission to users. There are two types of fixed roles. Fixed server roles are server-wide permissions that can be used regardless of the database you are in. Then there are fixed database roles, which apply to only one database.

Fixed roles defined can be users assigned to pick up the associated administration permissions of the role. The permissions assigned represent server-wide privilege. The most important of these is the sysadmin role, whose members can perform any activity in SQL Server. You can get a list of the fixed server roles from `sp_helpsrvrole`, and get the specific permissions for each role from `sp_srvrolepermission`.

There is very little you need to know about the fixed roles for the exam; that is all relegated to the SQL Server Administration exam. For more information about the fixed server roles, you can look in SQL Server Books Online at the overview topic under "Roles."

Defining Your Own Roles

You can also define your own roles. To create a new role, use the `sp_addrole` system-stored procedure, like this:

```
sp_addrole 'rolename'
```

The `rolename` is the name of the role, which of course has to meet all the other restrictions for naming objects in SQL Server, except that roles cannot contain backslash characters. Backslash characters create an empty role with no permissions. To add users to a role, use the `sp_addrolemember` stored procedure:

```
sp_addrolemember 'rolename', 'security_account'
```

The `'security account'` parameter is the name of the security account that should be added to the role. A security account could include a user, a Windows NT account that has a user associated with it, or a Windows NT group. If a group is specified, all the members of the Windows NT group who have associated users in the current database are added to the role.

To give the role access to other objects, use the GRANT statement, as described earlier, and use the name of the role in place of the username.

Using Application Roles

One of the handy features of this security model is the *application role*. An application role is similar to other roles, but the role has no members associated with it. The GRANT and REVOKE statements work the same way with an application role as with any other role. To create an application role, use the sp_addapprole system-stored procedure:

```
sp_addapprole 'AppRoleName', 'Password'
```

Yes, there is a password. To activate the application role for a given connection, the connection must execute another stored procedure, sp_setapprole, this way:

```
sp_setapprole 'AppRoleName', 'Password'
```

This stored procedure causes the connection executing the stored procedure to acquire the permissions granted to the application. In other words, the application has to run that stored procedure and send the password to invoke the correct permissions. At the point at which sp_setapprole is used, any roles, permissions, or users associated with the connection are gone, and only the permissions assigned to the application role are valid.

An encryption option can be specified with the sp_addapprole command, which encrypts the password before it is sent across your network. To do this, use sp_setapprole as shown here:

```
sp_setapprole 'AppRoleName', {Encrypt N 'Password'}, 'odbc'
```

The little 'odbc' at the end specifies that the password should be encrypted using the standard ODBC encryption function. Otherwise, no encryption will be used.

There are two reasons you may want to use application roles. First of all, you can set up an application role for a user application, and give the role access to all the tables and other objects it needs to access, but users who try to log in to SQL Server with Query Analyzer do not necessarily have a valid password to use to get the same level of access, which prevents them from modifying data incorrectly or running queries that may impede overall server performance.

Encryption Can Secure Definitions

Data encryption is a mechanism that can be used to secure data, communications, procedures, and other sensitive information. When encryption techniques are applied, sensitive information is transformed into a nonreadable form that must be decrypted to be viewed. Encryption slows performance, regardless of the method implemented, because extra processing cycles are required whenever encryption or decryption occurs. SQL Server can use data encryption at several levels:

➤ Login information

➤ Application role passwords

➤ Stored procedures

➤ Views

➤ User-defined functions

➤ Triggers

➤ Defaults

➤ Rules

➤ Data sent over the network

 You are likely to see encryption settings within a couple of exam questions. Remember that you never want to mess around with the contents of the system tables. When securing the definition of objects, you should be using the built-in encryption command options.

Various encryption procedures can be performed by a developer or an administrator, depending on what level of encryption is desired. SQL Server always encrypts login and role passwords within the system tables stored on the server. This automatic encryption of the login information stored on the server can be overridden using sp_addlogin, but this is not recommended. By default, however, application role passwords are not encrypted if they are provided across the network to invoke a role. SQL Server can use SSL (Secure Sockets Layer) encryption across all network libraries, although multiprotocol encryption is still supported for backward-compatibility reasons. A consideration in any SQL Server installation that uses multiple instances installed on the same server is that multiprotocol encryption is not supported by named instances of SQL Server.

Process definition encryptions applied to stored procedures, defaults, rules, user-defined functions, triggers, and view definitions are all implemented in a similar fashion. The definition stored on the server is encrypted to prevent someone from viewing the details of the process. To encrypt these definitions, use the applicable CREATE statement, providing the WITH ENCRYPTION option as illustrated in the following VIEW definition:

```
CREATE VIEW SampleEncryptedView WITH ENCRYPTION AS
    SELECT FirstName, LastName, Wage FROM PayTable
```

Encryption can also serve the purpose of protecting the copyright that a developer might have over the processes created. In any case, before you encrypt a procedure, make sure you save a copy of the procedure to a file server or another backup mechanism, because future changes are difficult to implement if you do not have the original definition. To update any definition and remove encryption, simply supply the CREATE statement without the WITH ENCRYPTION option. This overwrites the encrypted process with a new version that is not encrypted.

Auditing User Activity

SQL Server provides an auditing facility as a way to trace and record activity. SQL Server 2000 also provides the SQL Profiler for performing more in-depth monitoring. Auditing can be enabled or modified only by system administrators, and every modification of an audit can also be audited to prevent administrative abuse. The capability to create, use, alter, and remove objects can also be tightly controlled through the use of statement and object permissions.

SQL Server can accommodate two types of auditing: standard auditing and C2 auditing. Standard auditing provides some level of auditing but does not require the same number of policies as C2 auditing. C2 auditing requires that you follow very specific security policies. C2 security is more than just a machine standard, but it has aspects to cover the whole computer facility. You can use SQL Profiler to perform both types of auditing.

C2 Security Auditing

Permission sets determine which network identifiers, groups, and roles can work with specific objects, and what degree of interaction is allowed. Permission sets in general are more an administrator concern at this level. For design purposes and more specifically the design exam, you only need to touch on a few considerations. If you are preparing for the companion exam, it is recommended that you learn more about this broad topic.

For more information about C2 certification, see the *C2 Administrator's and User's Security Guide*. This guide is in downloadable form from the Microsoft TechNet site. URL information is provided in Appendix B.

Security Audits

You use SQL Profiler for auditing events in several categories. A list of these categories and their descriptions is given here:

- *End user activity*—Login, SQL, and enabling of application roles.

- *DBA activity*—Includes configuration of database and server.

- *Security events*—Grant/revoke/deny, add/remove/configure.

- *Utility events*—Backup/restore/bulk insert/BCP/DBCC.

- *Server events*—Shutdown, pause, start.

- *Audit events*—Add audit, modify audit, stop audit.

With the SQL Profiler you can determine the date and time of an event, who caused the event to occur, the type of event, the success or failure of the event, the origin of the request, the name of the object accessed, and the text of the SQL statement.

Auditing can have a significant performance impact. Before you select any object for auditing, balance the trade-off between the likelihood of a security breach and the overhead of the audit. Carefully consider an audit strategy before merely turning on auditing for all objects. If SQL Server is started with the -f flag, auditing does not run.

Statement Permissions

Statement permissions are assigned to users to enable them to do things, such as create databases, define user-defined functions and stored procedures, and back up the database or transaction log. Statement permissions are assigned by using the GRANT statement, like this:

```
GRANT statement TO account list
```

The statement includes statements that create or destroy objects, such as CREATE DATABASE, DROP DATABASE, CREATE DEFAULT, DROP DEFAULT, and CREATE FUNCTION, along with statements that perform other tasks, such as BACKUP DATABASE and BACKUP LOG. The account list is a comma-delimited list of security accounts or roles you want to grant access to.

Object Permissions

Object permissions are permissions granted to access objects in certain ways. For tables and views, you can grant SELECT, DELETE, UPDATE, and INSERT permissions, and for stored procedure and function objects you can grant EXECUTE permissions. Permissions are granted to users, so the user must exist in the database before you grant permission. To give a user permission to access certain database objects, use the GRANT command, but with a different syntax:

```
GRANT permission ON object TO account list
```

So to grant a particular user permissions to read a table called MyTable, you'd execute this:

```
GRANT SELECT ON MyTable TO Danny
```

This grants Danny permission to select data from your table. If you wanted to give Danny permissions to do anything to your table short of dropping it, you could run either of these two statements:

```
GRANT ALL ON MyTable TO Danny
```

```
GRANT SELECT, INSERT, UPDATE, DELETE ON MyTable TO Danny
```

To allow a user the right to give other people permissions on the table, you can use the WITH GRANT option as in the following:

```
GRANT ALL ON MyTable TO Danny WITH GRANT OPTION
```

This enables Danny to grant permissions to other users on that object, up to the level of permissions that Danny has. So if you give Danny only SELECT permissions, he can grant only SELECT permissions.

 You may see questions dealing with the scripting of permissions through the use of **GRANT**, **DENY**, and **REVOKE**. Make sure you are confident with their use.

Now you've given Danny permission to change your table. That's probably not good given that Danny's boss fired him yesterday. Now what are you going to do? Good thing there's the REVOKE command. The following example rescinds any previous permissions given:

```
REVOKE ALL ON MyTable FROM Danny
```

The REVOKE command works for statement permissions and object permissions, and it looks just like the GRANT statement in that you can revoke SELECT, INSERT, UPDATE, DELETE, or any combination thereof. What about revoking just the ability to grant permissions to other users? The following code removes the capability to grant permissions:

```
REVOKE GRANT OPTION FOR ALL ON MyTable FROM Danny
```

That's necessary only if Danny still has permissions to access the table. But what if Danny had been giving people access to a bunch of tables he shouldn't have? You can revoke all the permissions that Danny ever granted on the table by using the CASCADE option like this:

```
REVOKE GRANT OPTION FOR ALL ON MyTable FROM Danny CASCADE
```

There are three basic commands to set permissions and five different actions they can control. The commands are GRANT, REVOKE, and DENY. The actions are SELECT, INSERT, UPDATE, DELETE, and DRI. GRANT and DENY allow or disallow access to the view, whereas REVOKE removes a previous GRANT or DENY. SELECT, INSERT, UPDATE, and DELETE should be self-explanatory, and DRI enables users to create references to the view, which would be required to create an object that refers to the view with the WITH SCHEMABINDING clause.

Using Statement and Object Permissions

Activities involved in creating a database or an item in a database, such as a table or stored procedure, require a class of permissions called statement permissions. Careful control over who can create and alter objects is very important. Essentially, statement permissions allow for the creation and alteration of objects. These are the statement permissions:

➤ BACKUP DATABASE

➤ BACKUP LOG

➤ CREATE DATABASE

➤ CREATE DEFAULT

➤ CREATE FUNCTION

➤ CREATE PROCEDURE

➤ CREATE RULE

➤ CREATE TABLE

➤ CREATE VIEW

Because object ownership is established upon creation of objects, and too many owners can add unnecessary overhead, you should ensure that anyone creating objects is doing so under dbo ownership. The dbo internal system user should own all objects regardless of who is actually doing the object creation.

Object permissions determine to what level data can be accessed or whether a procedure can be executed. The list of object permissions is given here:

➤ SELECT, INSERT, UPDATE, and DELETE permissions, which can be applied to data from a table and/or view

➤ SELECT and UPDATE statement permissions, which can be selectively applied to individual columns of a table or view

➤ SELECT permissions, which may be applied to user-defined functions

➤ INSERT and DELETE statement permissions, which affect the entire row, and therefore can be applied only to the table and view and not to individual columns

➤ EXECUTE statement permissions, which affect stored procedures and functions

Setting of permissions can allow audit processes to determine successful and failed attempts to use the permissions.

Using Views to Enhance Security

Views can be used to restrict what data is visible in a database. Because you can restrict what is visible in the view, you can restrict what data can be deleted. Views can also be created with the WITH CHECK OPTION. When the view is created using WITH CHECK OPTION, the view enables data to be added to the database only if the resulting data will be visible in the view.

If you compare views to triggers, triggers offer much greater flexibility in controlling what can be added, deleted, or modified in the database. Although views are very restricted in their power, they also have a very low processor cost. Views can restrict inserts into the database, but their main function is to restrict visibility of data.

Views resemble tables in concept, and many operations you execute against tables can also be executed against views. These include SELECT, INSERT, UPDATE, and DELETE statements. The one major difference between views and tables is that views refer to tables, and do not actually contain their own data. A view could be related to a television set, in that it doesn't actually store movies but makes it possible for you to view them remotely.

The CREATE VIEW statement defines the view based on a SELECT statement, with optional restrictions. The basic function of the statement is to define the range of data (columns and rows) that should be displayed from the table or tables used in the view. You also saw views in more detail in Chapter 3,

"Implementing the Physical Database," and Chapter 4, "Advanced Physical Database Implementation." Within views you can utilize many advanced features of the SELECT statement, such as joins and aggregates.

Data modification with views introduced several restrictions that prevent many types of modifications (INSERT, UPDATE, and DELETE) from happening. You were introduced to the WITH CHECK OPTION, which further restricts what you can do. These restrictions serve two purposes: They enable you to validate the data you enter and they enable you to make restrictions to prevent unwanted data modifications.

Displaying the definition of a view may need to be done at some time. To access the exact definition of the view you created, use the sp_helptext system stored procedure. The actual definition of a view is stored in the syscomments system table. The sp_helptext procedure queries the syscomments, organizes the information required, and displays the view definition.

As you've already seen, protecting a view definition is possible if you use the WITH ENCRYPTION option. sp_helptext lets you know what tables and views your view references. This information is helpful if you are having trouble figuring out why your view does not work because you will see what tables or views your malfunctioning view uses.

The syntax is relatively similar to CREATE VIEW. view_name is the name of the view being altered. The WITH ENCRYPTION clause protects the definition of your view. You encrypt the definition of your view because you may not want users to display it, to protect your design from duplication. Encrypting your view using WITH ENCRYPTION ensures that no one can display your view, whether using sp_helptext, viewing it through the Enterprise Manager, or generating it through a Database Creation Script.

Stored Procedures Security Implementations

Stored procedures can be used to modify data rather than allowing users to access data tables directly. When using stored procedures, you are able to write simple or complex logic that is performed when the stored procedure executes. Rather than the user issuing the statements manually, the stored procedure is used to make the modification based on parameters passed to the procedure. Stored procedures can impose rules and policies on the modification, and can perform complex procedures without the possibility of user-induced errors.

To hide the complexity of the logic and the tables being accessed, you can use stored procedures as an additional feature to an overall security plan. In addition, encrypting the procedure definition after it is working adds an additional level of security by keeping the contents of the procedure protected.

Using Defaults

Defaults do not restrict what data is put into a table, but rather they are used to provide values for columns into which you are not inserting data. An example of a default would be a company that is based in the United States with 80% of its client base in the United States. This company might decide to place a default on the Country field in its Customer table, because in most cases it will be correct. This default is used only if the INSERT statement does not provide a Country value.

Constraints to Control Input

There are five basic constraints that can be used to restrict inserts and updates: NOT NULL, CHECK, UNIQUE, PRIMARY KEY, and FOREIGN KEY. These constraints place restrictions on what data can be inserted or updated in the database. FOREIGN KEY constraints can also be used to restrict what data can be deleted from the database.

Constraints offer a fair amount of flexibility but do not possess the level of code or logic that is present in a trigger. Triggers can reference columns in other tables, and can evaluate the change in the data because they can examine the data both before and after modification. In general, constraints should be used when possible because they are more efficient and cost less on the CPU, and triggers should be used whenever constraints are not powerful enough to perform the job. Constraints are executed after INSTEAD OF triggers, but before AFTER triggers.

Controlling, Filtering, and Enforcing Data Access

The discussion of AFTER triggers earlier in this chapter included several examples that showed you when and how you might want to implement triggers. Triggers are capable of performing any action you want during their execution, and they execute based on data modification in a table. One task that can be given to triggers is controlling what modifications might be made to the data in a table. This could include restrictions like the following:

We would like only one customer/contact record for each company to exist. When a second customer/contact is added in the form of a new customer record, an INSERT trigger can check for the existence of that company in the Customer table. If the record exists, it can take the new contact and add it to an Alternate Contact column.

From the deletion perspective, you might allow multiple contact records to exist for each company in the Customer table. When a contact record is deleted, a DELETE trigger can confirm that this is not the last record for that company. If it is, you can have the deletion cancelled and simply remove the contact name from the record.

These are just two examples of how triggers can control what is done to the data in a table. Triggers can be used to restrict or log any and all data modifications made to a table in your database.

Troubleshooting Security Issues

There are inherent problems in trying to secure any environment. Two types of situations are bound to arise during the course of any implementation. You are likely to witness situations in which a user cannot access the data needed because of incorrectly applied restrictions, and conversely someone may be able to gain access to confidential information that he has no rights reading.

The SQL Profiler would be the tool of choice for troubleshooting most security issues because it has the capability to audit and review activity that occurred on an instance of SQL Server. This allows a security administrator to review any of the auditing events, including the success and failure of a login attempt and the success and failure of permissions in accessing statements and objects.

Dealing with Broken Ownership Chains

One problem that can arise when you are using views occurs when you have different owners for objects in your database. Whenever there is a change in ownership, the owner of each object has to grant permissions to the object. When the ownership of objects in a chain is changed, there is a break in ownership or you have a broken ownership chain.

When you're dealing with ownership chains, the single point that will reduce permission management for you is to have a single owner for the entire chain. The dbo makes a nice owner for all objects in the database. This means that you have to apply permissions only once—to the upper-level objects. If you have a broken ownership chain, you may have to apply permissions to objects along the entire chain, which makes it more difficult to implement permissions and provides reduced security. The reduced security is caused by the additional permissions granted to subsequent objects, which may create holes in your data security.

Ownership chains and the problems that can occur have been a favorite topic for SQL exams for a few years now. Expect to see at least one question dealing with objects that have multiple ownership.

If the same person owns a series of objects, such as views and the base tables, then he or she has to grant permissions to only the upper-layer objects or views. This is designed to make administration easier. If you don't own all the objects, permissions can falter in use of the objects.

In almost every database scenario, object ownership should be limited to a single user: dbo.

Ownership chains were designed to make it easier for you to assign permissions, and to enhance security by requiring users to have permissions to only the upper-level objects, such as views or stored procedures. As long as the same person owns all the objects in the chain, permission is only checked at the first object that she accesses. In this case, Mary was granted permission to the view (DBOPermsView) but was denied access to the table (DBOPermsTable). Because the dbo owns both objects, as access moves from the view to the table, the permissions are not checked, and Mary has access to the data. However, if Mary attempts to access the table directly, the permissions are checked at the table and she is denied access. The reasoning behind the ownership chain works like this: If I own a table and I own the view, then when I grant permissions to the view, I obviously want the user to have access to the table. By not granting specific permissions to the table, you also restrict access to the data because this data is accessible only through the view.

Exam Prep Questions

1. You are a senior developer working at a consulting firm. You have to make sure that a user does not enter an alphabetical character in the `Telephone`, `Date`, and `SSN` columns of the `Client` table. What is the best way to implement this type of validation?

   ❑ A. Create an `INSERT` trigger.
   ❑ B. Create an `INSTEAD OF` trigger.
   ❑ C. Use `CHECK` constraints.
   ❑ D. There is no way to implement this.

   Answer: C. Making sure that a user does not enter data of a different type is not best done with a trigger because the same can be done with a `CHECK` constraint, which processes faster and with less overhead than a trigger. For more information about different ways to constrain data input, see the "Constraints to Control Input" section of this chapter.

2. Harold has created an `Employee` table. The table contains confidential information, so he has granted `SELECT` permissions on the table only to the other developers. There is an HR role that contains all the employees in the personnel department. You create a view and grant `SELECT` permissions on the view to the HR role. When members of the HR role attempt to retrieve data from the view, they receive the following error message:

   ```
   SELECT permission denied on object
        'Employees', database 'Northwind', owner 'Harold'
   ```

   You as one of the developers must ensure that the HR role can use the view only to access the data. What should you do?

   ❑ A. Add the HR role to the sysadmin fixed server role.
   ❑ B. Transfer the ownership of the view to the HR role.
   ❑ C. Instruct Harold to transfer the ownership of the table to the HR role.
   ❑ D. Instruct Harold to grant the users `SELECT` permissions on the table.
   ❑ E. Drop the view. Instruct Harold to re-create the view and to grant `SELECT` permissions on the view to the HR role.

   Answer: E. Remember that in a proper system all the objects should belong to the same person to prevent a broken ownership chain, which could cause permission and performance problems. Never provide an individual with more power than the person needs, and in particular limit the members of the sysadmin role to a very few trusted and competent individuals.

3. You have an Employees table in the company database. A clerk requires access to the entire table. All clerks have been denied permissions on the employee salaries and pay codes but have been granted SELECT permissions on all the other data. What do you do to give the clerk access?

- ❏ A. Revoke SELECT permissions on the salaries and pay codes for the clerk.
- ❏ B. Add the clerk to the db_datareader database role.
- ❏ C. Add the clerk to the db_accessadmin database role.
- ❏ D. Grant SELECT permissions on the salaries and pay codes for the clerk.

Answer: D. The only thing that is necessary in this scenario is to change the permissions on the individual columns for the clerk. If you use the clerk's own account, you should not affect any of the other users. Assigning the user to any of the roles would not change the fact that the clerk has been denied permission to access some of the data.

4. You want to prevent a user from changing data but still allow him to create objects for other users. The user currently is a user in the database with no other permissions. No other permissions have yet to be set. What should you do? (Select two answers.)

- ❏ A. Deny SELECT, UPDATE, and DELETE permissions to the user.
- ❏ B. Deny SELECT permissions to the user.
- ❏ C. Deny UPDATE and DELETE permissions to the user.
- ❏ D. Add the user to the db_owner database role.
- ❏ E. Add the user to the db_ddladmin database role.
- ❏ F. Grant the user CREATE VIEW permissions.

Answer: C and E. Because the user is already in the database, you will have to deny UPDATE and DELETE permissions from the user; but because you still need the user to be able to read the data, you should leave him with SELECT permissions. To be able to create objects, the user will need to be a member of the db_ddladmin role. The db_owner role can create objects but has far more rights than what is needed.

5. You are designing a custom application to access secure data. The Public Relations department needs to be able to read and update the data. PR will also be inserting new data. The PR department will also use Microsoft Excel to retrieve and chart data. You want to allow the department access only while using the two applications. No users have been granted access to the server yet. What should you do?

❑ A. Create a database role. Grant SELECT, INSERT, and UPDATE to the role. Give the users server access. Assign the users to the role.

❑ B. Create an application role. Grant SELECT, INSERT, and UPDATE to the role. Have the two applications invoke the role.

❑ C. Give the users access to the server. Grant SELECT, INSERT, and UPDATE to each of the users. Deny DELETE to each of the users.

❑ D. Create a system role. Grant SELECT, INSERT, and UPDATE to the role.

Answer: B. To ensure that the users can make changes only from within the two applications, the applications will need to run under the context of an application role that handles the security. The other solutions do nothing to prevent access to the data using the permissions given through ODBC or other connectivity mechanisms. Also, it is not possible to create system roles.

6. Public Relations and Human Resources require SELECT, INSERT, and UPDATE permissions on all tables in the Company database. Public Relations employees belong to a Microsoft Windows 2000 group named PR, and Human Resources employees belong to a Windows 2000 group named HR. You want to ensure that only members of HR can remove data. Other permissions may already exist. What should you do?

❑ A. Create two database roles named HR and PR. Add the appropriate Windows 2000 groups to the user-defined database roles. Deny DELETE to PR.

❑ B. Create an HR database role. Grant DELETE permissions to the role. Grant SELECT, INSERT, and UPDATE permissions to the Windows 2000 PR group.

❑ C. Grant DELETE to HR. Revoke DELETE from Public. Grant SELECT, INSERT, and UPDATE to PR.

❑ D. Create two database roles named HR and PR. Add the appropriate Windows 2000 groups to the user-defined database roles. Revoke DELETE to PR.

Answer: C. Because some permissions have already been defined, you will need to revoke the DELETE permissions from the Public role to remove any permission previously defined. You do not want to deny DELETE to Public because every user in the database is a member of Public and this would effectively eliminate the possibility of anyone performing deletions. You then need to assign the permissions to the appropriate Windows 2000 groups. In this scenario it is not necessary to create roles.

Completing a Business System Design

Terms you'll need to understand:

✓ One-tier
✓ Two-tier
✓ N-tier
✓ ODBC
✓ OLE-DB
✓ Linked server
✓ Remote server
✓ Heterogeneous data
✓ Replication
✓ **OPENROWSET**
✓ **OPENQUERY**
✓ Automation
✓ Job
✓ Operator
✓ Alert
✓ SQL Server Agent

Techniques you'll need to master:

✓ Application architecture design
✓ ODBC and DSN creation
✓ Distributed data access
✓ Server connectivity
✓ Automating SQL Server processes

Introduction

This chapter attempts to tie together all the loose ends that may be remaining in your exam preparation. Although we have covered a lot in the course of this book, there are still a few nooks and crannies left to go into.

In finalizing a system design for a business project, there are many considerations outside of the traditional database design structure. These other areas include the interaction with other Microsoft back-office systems, integration with third-party elements (within the data-handling arena and other forms of technology), and building a framework that can expand into the extra-large enterprise systems.

Microsoft SQL Server 2000 handles well in a distributed environment. All offices can gain access to the data they need in virtually any size organization. There are many tools for interoperating in a heterogeneous environment. These tools help to integrate multiple vendors and database products. SQL Server uses ODBC and OLE-DB functionality to gain access to virtually any data stored anywhere.

SQL Server makes an excellent back-end database server for an Internet or intranet site. SQL Server and IIS integrate well to make data accessible over the Internet in a number of formats, including XML, HTML, ADO, and ADO.Net. SQL Server even has an HTML creation wizard, although it is limited to creating static HTML pages based on schedules or data changes.

With SQL Server replication, data can be transferred quickly and flexibly from one server to another. Options are available to maintain updatable copies at all locations if desired. It is a good fit for an organization looking for a centralized point in which to store data relating to all parts of the organization with distribution capabilities that can make that data quickly available throughout the globe.

In business application development you must select an appropriate model for your entire setup. These separate models are referred to as tier systems. At times the choice of the number of tiers is accomplished based on all requirements of the business application being implemented.

SQL Server Supporting Applications

Each tier of a business model represents the isolation of a process so that each individual tier performs a portion of the entire system's processing. The number of tiers is dependant on a lot of factors. In a full implementation each process delivers an important aspect of the system. In the following sections the different models are described so that an understanding of the choices can be reached.

One- and Two-Tier Systems

A one-tier system in a PC environment dates back 25 or more years to an environment in which the only way to share data was to use the "sneaker net" approach. In other words, copies of the data were made and distributed manually. This approach was adequate at best and caused many headaches for anyone trying to implement a multiple-user environment. Particularly difficult was the merging of updates from multiple copies of the data.

With a single-tier approach, one computer performs all the processing required to view, update, and store the data. Many products use this technique for small, single-user database systems, but this technique becomes overwhelming when the data is needed by multiple users sharing the same data. In this case, a two-tier system with a central data store on a proper server is a better approach.

A two-tier architecture places the user interface and data on separate machines. The client application sends queries across the network to be resolved by the data engine running on the server. The server resolves the query and sends the necessary data back across the network for the client application to display. There are two implementations of a two-tier system: "thin client" and "thick client."

In a thin approach the client application does little or no processing. A thin client just presents the data to the user and, when needed, communicates with the database engine on the server to work with the data. The thin client approach is best when the number of concurrent users accessing the data can be kept to a minimum. Because the server must perform the processing to validate the data as well as all other data manipulations, there is a lot of server overhead related to this approach. A thin client is a good approach for maintainability. If you need to upgrade software, for example, you do not have to do so on 1,000 clients. It also works well for Internet applications.

The thick client (sometimes referred to as a fat client) approach offloads some of the work needed to validate and process the data from the server machine to the client machine. In this approach the client may make some of the determinations as to whether data should be sent to the server based on validity checks coded in the client application. This approach enables many more users to access the same database concurrently. On the downside, though, application maintenance is more demanding, and higher performance is required from the client.

Although a two-tier architecture allows for more flexibility and a larger number of users, it is still quite a limited architecture that can serve only small environments. When a larger number of concurrent user accesses is needed, a better choice of architecture is a multiple "n-tier" architecture or possibly an Internet architecture.

Three- or More Tier Systems

In a three-tier system, the client system presents the interface and interacts with the user. The database server manipulates the data, but there also exists a middle tier to control some of the operations. The middle tier can be represented by one or more machines that offload some processing from the database server, which allows for a very large number of users. There is usually no differentiation between three or more tiers; instead they are all categorized as n-tier systems.

In an n-tier system, processing is divided into three categories. Each category represents one of the three main tiers in the three-tier system, which is also carried forward in an n-tier system regardless of the number of layers of processing.

The presentation, or client, tier contains the components of the system that interact directly with the user. The sole purpose of this tier is to focus on the end user and present data in an attractive, organized, and meaningful fashion.

The middle tier, or business tier, is responsible for communicating with the database server and also sets up the rules by which communication will be established. The idea behind the business tier is to provide mechanisms to implement the business rules that need to be applied to validate data and also perform intermediate processing that may be needed to prepare the data for presentation to the user. For this reason the business tier is often separated into two divisions: interactions with the user and interactions with the database server. With this approach business rules can be separated from data access processes.

The final tier is the data tier, which is responsible for the execution of the data engine to perform all manipulations of the data. Access to the data tier is made through the middle tier. The data tier doesn't directly interact with the presentation layer.

Internet Application Architecture

Internet applications can be said to fall under a two-, three-, or n-tier model, depending on the complexity and physical design. In an Internet application, the web server prepares the presentation elements to be displayed on the user's browser. If a middle tier server exists, the web server is configured to interact with that server. If no middle tier server exists, the web server interacts directly with the database server.

Depending on the implementation, the client's browser may also be considered a tier. If a set of records is sent to the browser by the web server to allow editing on the browser, the client is considered a tier. In this case, a disconnected recordset or XML data is used for the client's data manipulation. If a round-trip to the web server must take place to submit changes and interact with the data, the client is not considered a tier—it is more just a mechanism to display the HTML that is sent by the web server. In this case the user tier is the Internet server that acts as the user and prepares the HTML for display.

Internet applications have the best scalability of all application architecture types, meaning that they can support the largest number of concurrent users. The drawbacks to using Internet architecture are that there is a requirement for maintaining the state information of the client, a greater number of development skills are needed, and update conflict issues are inherent to the technology.

Although an Internet application is usually implemented so that the database can be accessed from anywhere in the world, it can also be used for internal purposes through a configured intranet. Under this principle, users can access the database from a corporate HTML or XML site.

Whatever model is chosen, many components must come together to complete the entire project. Database servers, email servers, Internet Information servers, and other hardware and software together make up the infrastructure of the system.

SQL Server 2000 Back Office Integration

SQL Server's capability to store data and handle scheduled procedures makes it an important portion of the Microsoft Server family. SQL Server can be used as the data support and back end of websites running on Internet Information Server (IIS). SQL Server stores the data gathered by Systems Management Server (SMS) in an enterprise infrastructure analysis. SQL Server can even supply information to the email system through Exchange.

SQL Server is quite at home hosting the databases that maintain the Internet's data. Through IIS and Microsoft's state-of-the-art development framework, IIS operates as a midpoint server between the web pages that expose the data to the Internet and the back-end storage of the data within SQL Server.

SMS provides change and configuration management as well as inventory over software and hardware within an organization. The information gathered by SQL is stored within databases on SQL Server, where it is updated as changes in the computer environment occur. SQL Server and SMS enable organizations to provide relevant software and updates to users quickly and cost-effectively while managing expensive assets.

The Exchange mail system, as well as other back-office systems, can utilize SQL Server capabilities for data storage and administration over related data activity. The many functionalities of the server provide flexibility when responding to the needs of diverse business systems.

SQL Server 2000 supports heterogeneous connectivity to any data source through the use of OLE-DB and ODBC drivers, which are available for most common databases. SQL Server can move data to and from these sources using Data Transformation Services (DTS), replication, and linked server operations. SQL Server can act as a gateway to any number of data sources and either handle a copy of the data itself or pass the processing to the third-party source.

Third-Party Database Interactions

The capability of SQL Server to act with almost any third-party source means that existing applications can continue to function in the environment undisturbed while SQL Server applications can also make use of the same data.

Replication, DTS, and linked servers are among the processes that can be set up among database servers other than SQL Server. SQL Server supports OLE-DB, which enables data to be replicated from SQL Server to any other database server, such as Sybase or Oracle. There is only a single requirement: The third-party server must provide a 32-bit ODBC or OLE-DB driver on any Microsoft Windows operating system. When the non–SQL Server database meets this requirement, it can be used in conjunction with SQL Server.

Data Replication

Replication is the process of carrying, modifying, and distributing data and database objects (stored procedures, extended properties, views, tables, user-defined functions, triggers, and indexes) from one source server to another, in a consistent fashion, independent of location. Replication is a huge topic.

Any implementation can use multiple types and an endless number of forms. This section describes just why replication is implemented.

Many corporations distribute information from remote sales locations to central order-processing locations. Other organizations operate distributed warehouses, with each individual location needing knowledge of the others' inventories. The problems are many. One of the potential solutions is the implementation of a replication strategy.

Replication can be performed across platforms, to and from virtually any data source. SQL Server provides for a very diverse strategy for implementing a replication strategy. After it is enabled, you can monitor the progress and quickly be alerted to any problem situations.

A push subscription in replication can send data to a third-party server. When you need to pull a subscription from SQL Server to a third-party database system such as Oracle, you need to create a custom program that accesses Distributed Management Objects (SQL-DMO).

Non–SQL Server database engines may also very well act as Publishers that replicate data and database objects to SQL Server Subscribers. ODBC or OLE-DB driver requirements must be met if you want to configure a publishing non–SQL Server database. SQL Server uses ODBC to make replication connections to other servers. That is, a foreign Subscriber must support transactions and be Level 1, ODBC compliant. When it meets this requirement, it can also receive data that is sent via a push subscription.

Of course, replication is only one mechanism that can be used to get data from another data source. DTS is equally capable of utilizing OLEDB or ODBC mechanisms to communicate with other systems.

Snapshot Replication

Snapshot replication is suited to situations in which data is likely to remain unchanged, it is acceptable to have a higher degree of latency, and replication involves small volumes of data. It is preferred over transactional replication when data changes are substantial but infrequent. Application of snapshots using native BCP or compression helps to improve performance.

Snapshot replication can be used alongside Immediate Updating Subscribers using two-phase commit (2PC). In this type of replication, the Subscriber needs to be in contact with the Publisher. Queued update, on the other hand, doesn't require constant connectivity. When you create a publication with queued updating, and a Subscriber performs INSERT, UPDATE, or DELETE statements on published data, the changes are stored in a queue. The queued transactions are applied at the Publisher when network connectivity is restored.

Transactional Replication

In transactional replication, as with snapshot replication, Updating Subscribers may be used with 2PC for the immediate update option. This enables the Subscriber to change the replica at his local server. Changes made to data at the Subscriber are applied to both the Subscriber and the Publisher databases at the same moment, proving high transactional consistency and less latency.

Merge Replication

Merge replication is well suited to scenarios in which conflicts are less likely to occur. For instance, a site might make changes to its internal records only, possibly needing data from all other locations, but not changing any of it. A conflict occurs when the two participants have *both* changed a record (or column within a record) since they last shared the same version.

Merge replication offers site autonomy at its apex—because sites are virtually independent—and low transactional consistency. These sites, or Subscribers, can freely make modifications to their local copies of the replicated data. These modifications and updates made to data are combined with modifications made at the other Subscribers and also with the modifications made at the Publisher. This process ultimately ensures that all Subscribers and Publishers receive modifications and updates from all other sites; it is better known as *convergence*.

Very Large Database Applications

SQL Server 2000 has high-speed optimizations that support very large database environments. Although previous versions lacked the capability to support larger systems, SQL Server 2000 and SQL Server 7.0 can effectively support terabyte-sized databases.

With the implementation of partitioned views in Enterprise Edition, servers can be scaled to meet the requirements of large websites and enterprise environments. Federated server implementations enable a large number of servers to assist in maintaining a complex large system.

Elements of the replication system can also help distribute data among a number of machines while providing mutual updatability and maintaining centralized control over the entire system.

Coding for Distributed Data

So far, all the data you've been able to access has been stored in databases on one SQL Server. This section talks about how to query data that's on other SQL Servers and in other systems without importing the data. Later sections in this chapter deal with how to import and export data with SQL Server.

You can use three types of syntax to access data; each one serves a different purpose. First, you're going to see OPENROWSET, which is the most flexible but hardest to use of the three. OPENQUERY is easier to use but requires a bit more setup. The third option is linked servers, which you will see how to set up and use in a multiserver relationship.

Each of the three methods—OPENROWSET, OPENQUERY, and linked servers—relies on having an operable OLE-DB driver for the system you're trying to talk to. SQL Server 2000 ships with OLE-DB drivers for SQL Server, text files, Oracle, IBM's DB/2, and others. To understand how to use each of these methods, you need to understand how to talk to an OLE-DB provider.

A Brief Discussion on OLE-DB

OLE-DB is a low-level database access protocol that is designed to enable a client to access different systems without having to understand how each system works. The foundation of OLE-DB is the OLE-DB provider, which has to implement certain methods. At this level, an OLE-DB provider needs to know certain things to make a connection to the system.

 NOTE You can find a list of the OLE-DB providers that you have installed in the Registry at **HKEY_LOCAL_MACHINE\Software_Microsoft\MSSQLServer\Providers\ _SQLOLEDB**.

In the case of another SQL Server, the OLE-DB provider needs to know the name of the server and how to log in to the server. In the case of a text file, the OLE-DB provider needs to know where the file is and what format the file is in, as well as other properties about the file, such as delimiters, whether the first row contains column names, and so on. The point here is that different providers have different requirements, but that after you get past those requirements they all work the same way as far as retrieving data.

The only way to understand how to use the provider is to consult the documentation for that provider and for that version of the provider and to actually work with it in a test or production environment.

Using **OPENROWSET**

The OPENROWSET function returns a rowset to SQL Server. It's used in a SELECT statement in the same place as a table. Here are the parameters for the OPENROWSET function with a short description of how to use each one:

➤ provider_name—This is the name of the provider, as specified in the Registry. It is not optional.

➤ datasource—This is the name of the file, server, or whatever the OLE-DB provider needs in order to figure out what it should be talking to.

➤ user_id—This is the username that the provider understands. Some providers may not need a username, so this could be blank.

➤ password—This is the password that the provider understands. Some providers may not need a password, so this could be blank also.

➤ provider_string—This is a free text field that has everything else that the provider needs in order to initiate the connection. Only the provider knows for sure what this is; you'll have to dig through piles of documentation.

➤ catalog—This is the name of the database, catalog, or whatever the provider understands. It's the top level of the hierarchy of object names. It's also likely to be blank if the provider doesn't use it.

➤ schema—This is the name of the owner of the object. It also may be blank if the provider doesn't use it.

➤ object—This is the name of the object being manipulated. Believe it or not, this may be blank if there's only one object in the data source, such as a text file.

➤ query—This is a string that's provider-specific, and it's passed directly to the provider as a query. It may be a SQL query; it may be something else. It's also not processed by SQL Server, so you should make sure that the syntax is valid before you send it; otherwise, you'll get a very incomprehensible error message.

Nearly every single argument in the entire OPENROWSET function is optional, and its use or lack thereof depends on the provider you are using. Experience dictates that the documentation and examples for how to use the particular provider in which you are interested will be either non-existent or inaccurate. In other words, good luck.

Actually, OPENROWSET is a very useful function; it's just complicated and difficult to set up. After you have it figured out for a particular provider, it works very well. You should plan on spending several hours with a new OLE-DB provider to figure out how it works. Here's an example of OPENROWSET in use:

```
SELECT * FROM openrowset('sqloledb',
       'SQLTest1';'sa';'', 'SELECT * FROM master.dbo.sysobjects')
```

This example is a fairly simple case; it just returns a rowset from another SQL Server—in this case a SQL Server running on a box named SQLTest1, which has a blank SA password. You can tell it's a request to another SQL Server because 'sqloledb' is the provider, and that's the name of the provider used to talk to other SQL Servers. It runs a simple SELECT statement and returns a simple rowset. Notice that it uses a full three-part name for the table. This isn't required, but it is good practice for doing remote queries. You can then use the results just as you would any other table: You can join them to other local tables, filter them, or whatever you like:

```
SELECT SQLTest1sysobjects.name FROM openrowset('sqloledb',
       'SQLTest1';'sa';'', 'SELECT * FROM sysobjects') SqlTest1sysobjects
INNER JOIN sysobjects
       ON sysobjects.name = SQLTest1sysobjects.name
WHERE SQLTest1sysobjects.type = 'u'
```

Notice that this uses a table alias to reference the OPENROWSET return values; it filters on the object type from the remote table and does a join. So it really does work as a table does. But the syntax is incredibly cumbersome. You're probably hoping there's some shortcut you can use to avoid all the complexity. Well, read ahead to see how that can happen.

Creating a Linked Server

You can think of a linked server as a prebuilt set of arguments for OPENROWSET stored in a database object. You can just create an object called a linked server, and create it with all the attributes you'd normally use in a call to OPENROWSET. Then, rather than having to type all those parameters over and over again, you can just use the linked server.

There are two ways to create a linked server: using the Query Analyzer and using Enterprise Manager. In Query Analyzer, you create the linked server using the sp_addlinkedserver system stored procedure as described in the next section. Using the Enterprise Manager, you can select the options needed through the graphical interface, shown in Figure 10.1.

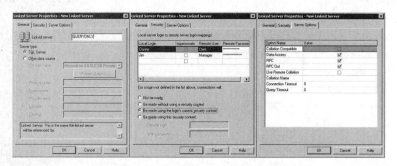

Figure 10.1 Linked Server options using the Enterprise Manager.

The Enterprise Manager interface is fairly straightforward. The only parameters that aren't part of the OPENROWSET you've already learned about are server and provider; the rest are just bad names on the same parameters. Server is the name of the linked server you are creating. Any SQL Server-approved object name works; it doesn't necessarily have to be the name of the server, but it probably should be. The srvproduct argument is the name of the OLE-DB data source. The provider argument specifies the same thing as the srvproduct, but does it with an OLE-DB PROGID, which is a long identifier. The rest of the options are from OPENROWSET. If you're linking to another Microsoft SQL Server, you can specify an @srvproduct of SQL Server only, and the @server argument must be the server's name. None of the other arguments is required or allowed. Here's a linked server definition for the server you saw used in the preceding section:

```
sp_addlinkedserver @Server = 'OpenRowsetTest',
        @SrvProduct = 'sqloledb',
        @Provider = 'sqloledb',
        @DataSrc = 'SQLTest1'
```

Then—and this is the really great part—you can query it like this:

```
SELECT * FROM openrowsettest.master.dbo.sysobjects
```

That's a four-part name. Four-part names are required when using linked servers. You can't shortcut the object owner part either; you have to fully specify the entire thing. You could, of course, alias it, join it, or whatever you want to do; it's going to act just like a normal table.

The Security tab needs a little more elaboration on a couple of fronts. First of all, in Figure 10.1 you'll notice that there are two parts to the window. In the top part you can specify local logins and map them to logins on the remote server. In the bottom part you can specify what happens to local logins that aren't in the list. You can specify that users who are not on the list will not be allowed to use the remote server by choosing the Not Be Made option. You can choose that the users not on the list be forced into "guest" status, if available, on the remote server by choosing the Be Made Without Using a Security Context option. You can choose to attempt to pass through the authentication that the user has on the local server by choosing the Be Made Using the Login's Current Security Context item, or you can force everyone who isn't on the list in the top part of the window to use a specific login and password with the Be Made Using This Security Context option.

Now that you know how to create linked servers, it's time to look at using them in a little more detail.

Using Linked Servers

There are two ways to use an established linked server. The first—and easiest to understand—method is to use the four-part name as shown previously. As you remember, a three-part name is `database.owner.object`, so for the `sysobjects` table in the Master database, you can reference it as `master.dbo.sysobjects`. For a linked server, you can use a four-part name, which is `server.database.owner.object`, or, in the preceding example, `sqltest1.master.dbo.sysobjects`.

The four-part name works great when you're using other SQL Servers as the remotes. What happens when you want to use something other than SQL Server on the other side? Then you need to use the OPENQUERY function. OPENQUERY looks suspiciously similar to OPENROWSET, but it takes only two arguments: the linked server name and a query. So you could run this:

```
SELECT * FROM  OPENROWSET test.master.dbo.sysobjects
```

Or you could run this:

```
SELECT * from OPENQUERY(OpenRowsetTest,
 'SELECT * FROM master.dbo.sysobjects')
```

Notice that the linked server name does not have quotation marks around it. SQL Server doesn't like quotation marks there. Both queries return the same resultset.

These linked servers are really great, but don't get any ideas about using them to import data. Although it works well for smaller datasets (less than a few hundred thousand rows), there are significantly more efficient ways to handle data imports.

Remote Servers

A remote server is a logical definition of an instance of SQL Server that can be used by remote stored procedure calls. Remote servers have been present in previous releases of SQL Server and are still supported in SQL Server 2000, but linked servers offer greater functionality.

 You may hit linked and remote servers on the exam as possible answers to connecting to other SQL Servers. When you do, remember that it is really the linked server that provides the most flexibility and can be applied in almost any circumstances.

A remote server configuration allows a client connected to one instance of SQL Server to execute a stored procedure on another instance without establishing another connection. The server to which the client is connected accepts the request and sends information to the remote server on behalf of the client. The remote server processes the request and returns any results to the original server.

SQL Server Automation of Processes

It is the role of the SQL Server Agent service running on the server to control a lot of mechanisms within an instance of SQL Server. The SQL Server Agent is responsible for running jobs and tasks scheduled to occur at specific times and/or intervals. The agent also helps detect conditions for which administrators have defined actions to be taken. The agent also runs replication tasks, and in general is responsible for handling repetitive tasks and exception-handling conditions defined through the other SQL Server components.

The statistical maintenance functionality introduced in SQL Server 7 and expanded on in SQL Server 2000 may generate unwanted overhead on a production system if it initiates statistical updates during heavy production periods or starts a high number of UPDATE STATISTICS processes. It may be worthwhile to schedule this type of maintenance to occur during idle time to prevent this behavior.

Using the SQL Server Agent to automate tasks involves scheduling periodic activities on the server. Jobs are defined for tasks that are to be scheduled. Jobs can also be defined to run on demand or during idle time on the server. Notification of completion, errors, or other defined conditions is performed through the definition of operators and the assignment of conditions under which the operator is to be contacted. The definition of alerts identifies circumstances that the agent will watch for and act on when they occur.

Job, Operator, Alert Integration

Jobs, alerts, and operators can be defined as a single step because the interface tools in the Enterprise Manager are linked together, and each portion of the definition allows for new entries.

An organized approach to automation, however, is recommended. Possibly the first step is to define the important individuals in the environment who could respond to potential problems. As you create the operators, you should also supply the operator definitions with short descriptions of the operator's purpose and function as it relates to the database system.

Any of the operators defined can be selected to receive notification by a number of SQL Server operations. Email and other message-sending capabilities have been built into most of the features in SQL Server 2000. For this example, the operators are going to receive notification of a new customer. After they have been contacted, they can potentially contact the customer and perform an initial sales call.

As well as performing operator notification, you may want to execute tasks based on an alert condition.

A lot of processes can be performed through automation, and this represents an area where development and process skills are important. In tuning and recognizing other performance factors, SQL Server Agent alerts can be set up based on performance criteria. The capability to monitor the server for this type of information can be a huge administrative benefit.

The SQL Server Agent, operators, jobs, and alerts provide for a mechanism whereby maintenance operations can be scheduled to occur on a regular basis. This facility can be in itself an application architecture to build around.

Jobs Perform Recurring Tasks

Using SQL Server Agent jobs, you can automate tasks. After jobs are created, they can be run manually, on schedule, or in response to alerts. Jobs can be written to run on the local server or on multiple servers. To run jobs on multiple servers, you must set up at least one master server and one or more target servers. Anyone can create a job, but a job can be edited only by its owner or members of the sysadmin role.

Jobs consist of one or more steps that need to be performed. The steps can be operating system commands, Java Script, Visual Basic Script, or, most commonly, T-SQL statements. These steps are controlled by the workflow defined within the structure of the job allowing for mandatory, optional, and conditional procedures.

Jobs can be placed into job categories to help you organize your jobs for easy filtering and grouping. You could organize all your database backup jobs in the Database Maintenance category. You can also create your own job categories.

Operators Can Respond to Events

Operators are individuals or groups of individuals who can be identified by a network account, email identifier, or computer identification, who can address problems with the database and other servers. An operator can be sent a message resulting from an alert, a job step, job completion, or other SQL Server processes. Messages can be sent through email, a pager, or a net send network command.

Operators are not solely used for problem reporting. In an application design they may be contacted as new records enter a table within the database. Operators could be a sales team that is sent information about new clients. In essence, if you would like to contact an individual or a group for any data or server event, operators can be set up to serve the purpose.

Alerts Inform Based on Events

Alerts are actions to be taken when specific events occur, such as an error on the server, an application process call, or any other definable event. A definable event is any process that places information into the Windows 2000 application event log. Specific errors, errors of certain severity, or performance criteria can all have a corresponding alert defined. The alert can be defined to take such actions as sending an email notification, paging an operator through a paging service, or running a job to respond to the situation.

A lot of options are available for the content of the alert message. Depending on how the message is being sent out, you can include data samples, text messages, and attachments along with the message. This is important because often when an alert occurs, the only information you have to help you understand what caused the alert and the appropriate action to take is contained in the alert message itself.

Alerts can be configured for essentially anything that happens on the database server. Whether the event occurs within the computer, its operating system, the application server, an application that is executing, or the data itself, events can be configured to react to the situation.

SQL Server Event Alert

Errors and messages, or events, are generated by SQL Server and entered into the Microsoft Windows application log. SQL Server Agent reads the log and fires an alert based on the conditions supplied in the alert definition. By default, the following SQL Server events are logged in the Windows application log:

➤ Severity 19 or higher sysmessages errors

➤ Any RAISERROR statement invoked by using the WITH LOG syntax

➤ Any application logged by using xp_logevent

In a design consideration you may want to have other elements reported on besides the defaults provided within the system. Events are a response to what is happening with the data and on the server in which the data is held. This could easily be turned into a reporting system for any application. When data is added, someone can be notified; as data values change, audit records may be recorded; if data is removed, archival data storage is possible.

Performance Counter Alerts

The SQL Server Agent can monitor performance conditions in a similar fashion to how the System Monitor is used. A System Monitor counter can be used as the basis for specifying a performance condition to monitor. The condition causes an alert to fire if the performance threshold is reached. You can define the area of SQL Server performance to be monitored by defining the object, counter, instance, and threshold condition just as you do with the system/performance monitor. The difference is that the monitoring can be performed on an ongoing basis without any additional overhead.

The counter selected represents the specific property to be monitored. Because the performance data is collected periodically, there is often a delay between the threshold being hit and the performance alert firing.

Performance alerts can be used to activate maintenance jobs, such as backing up and clearing a log file when it is close to becoming full. You may also want individuals to be contacted in the event of potential problems such as an inordinate number of deadlocks per second. It is easier to allow for proactive management and solve potential problems before they can affect the end user.

Exam Prep Questions

1. The master price list for the shoes your company has in stock is maintained in SQL Server in the corporate office that is updated constantly. You want all your outlets to receive the updated prices as quickly as possible from the corporate office. Which sort of replication is best suited for a situation like this?

   ❑ A. Transactional replication
   ❑ B. Snapshot replication
   ❑ C. Merge replication
   ❑ D. Immediate replication

   Answer: A. To receive updated prices as quickly as possible, use transactional replication. Merge replication is not appropriate because of the timing considerations, and snapshot replication would be too intensive, would slow down operations, and would produce a lot of latency (delay). Immediate replication does not exist, though immediate Updating Subscriptions are an option of transactional and snapshot replication types. Often exam answers attempt to fool you by using wording that is purposely confusing, so read carefully and make no assumptions. For more details, see the "Data Replication" section.

2. You need to query some data on a temporary remote server for a one-time report. Which of the following functions is the best to use?

   ❑ A. OPENQUERY()
   ❑ B. OPENROWSET()
   ❑ C. Linked servers
   ❑ D. OPENXML()

   Answer: B. Either option A or C would work, too, but they'd involve creating a linked server. For a one-time report it's more efficient to just use OPENROWSET. There's a whole section in this chapter on OPENROWSET called "Coding for Distributed Data."

3. Gordon is trying to get access to a server on the other side of the Black Mesa facility to complete his research. He just got access to the LambdaSQL server, and he is having problems running even simple queries. On the server, there is a database called BadThings with a table called Creepy. What's the problem with this query:

   ```
   select count(*) from LambdaSQL.BadThings.Creepy
   ```

   His colleagues seem to be having no problems.

   ❑ A. You can't run an aggregate function across a remote server.
   ❑ B. You should use OPENROWSET for this kind of an operation.
   ❑ C. You should use OPENXML for this.
   ❑ D. He left the owner name out of the object specification.

Answer: D. All cross-server activity has to be done with four-part names. The correct name is probably something like `LambdaSQL.BadThings.dbo.Creepy`. Cross-server joins were all covered in the section "Using Linked Servers."

4. You are designing a database that will be used for a small office. The client machines have minimal hard drive space and very little RAM. Other than the database server, no server-grade machines are available. You have chosen a SQL Server in a client/server architecture as the best implementation for this system. Which application architecture is best suited for this system?

❑ A. Single-tier

❑ B. Two-tier thin client

❑ C. Two-tier thick client

❑ D. N-tier

❑ E. Internet

Answer: B. With few resources on the clients, you have to make the clients as small as possible. N-tier or Internet could be potential solutions, but with the lack of sufficient processing power in the form of a server-grade machine, these would not suit this scenario. For more details, see the section "SQL Server Supporting Applications."

5. In a large office with hundreds of users, you have several servers that are centrally located in a secured room that only IT staff can access. One server is used as a security server and also acts as a DHCP server. A second dual-processor server is running SQL Server, and another machine runs an email system with IIS operational. The office does not permit any other user access to the Internet, nor does it expose any information to the Internet through a website. You must select an application architecture suitable to this configuration. No other software is available on the servers. What application architecture would be best suited?

❑ A. Single-tier

❑ B. Two-tier thin client

❑ C. Two-tier thick client

❑ D. N-tier

❑ E. Internet

Answer: E. This is a good candidate for an Internet solution because you already have an IIS server available. Whether or not you have Internet access is irrelevant because everything can be performed in-house using an HTML or XML solution across the network. For more information, see the "Internet Application Architecture" section.

6. In a large department store, an inventory database is maintained for all products sold. Data is updated frequently by multiple computer terminals. Four hundred computer terminals throughout the offices and store can access the database simultaneously to perform updates. You want to minimize conflict situations and reduce the load on the server as much as possible. The client systems have very little processing power of their own. What architecture would you select for this system?

❑ A. Single-tier

❑ B. Two-tier thin client

❑ C. Two-tier thick client

❑ D. N-tier

❑ E. Internet

Answer: D. To minimize the amount of processing performed on a server, you would need to offload the processing onto the client by way of the two-tier thick client approach, or use a middle tier component such as an n-tier model. Because the client machines don't have much processing capability, the only remaining choice is to use the n-tier approach. For more information, see the "One- and Two-Tier Systems" section.

7. You have prepared the logical design for a very large database system that will act as the back end for an Internet application, as well as being accessed from the corporate WAN. You need to support a large number of concurrent users who will be accessing the database at various bandwidth speeds. Which SQL Server technologies could assist in allowing the users access while providing good performance? (Choose all that apply.)

❑ A. Analysis services

❑ B. Replication

❑ C. Partitioned views

❑ D. English query

❑ E. Metadata services

Answer: B, C. Replication and partitioned views enable you to spread the load of a very large database system across several machines. The benefit of additional processing power and getting the data closer to the user could be recognized by both features, assuming that they were properly partitioned and configured. For more information, see the section "SQL Server Supporting Applications."

Practice Exam One

The actual certification exam is 50 questions. To best simulate exam circumstances, you should try to complete the 50 questions in 90 minutes.

1. You are a database developer for your company's SQL Server 2000. The database you are working with supports an Internet-based application to a busy website. The database is extremely large with many tables and indexes. Some of the tables and indexes are accessed frequently, whereas others have been created to support data of a historical nature and are used much less often. The server has two striped disk volumes and two other volumes that have been mirrored. You need to place objects in a location that will provide for the best performance. How would you place the objects?

- ❏ A. Create one filegroup on each of the striped volumes. Place tables that are frequently joined together on different filegroups. Place heavily accessed tables and the nonclustered indexes belonging to those tables on different filegroups.

- ❏ B. Create one filegroup on each of the striped volumes. Place tables that are frequently joined together on different filegroups. Place heavily accessed tables and the nonclustered indexes belonging to those tables on the same filegroup.

- ❏ C. Create one filegroup on each of the mirrored volumes. Place tables that are frequently joined together on different filegroups. Place heavily accessed tables and the nonclustered indexes belonging to those tables on different filegroups.

- ❏ D. Create one filegroup on each of the mirrored volumes. Place tables that are frequently joined together on the same filegroup. Place heavily accessed tables and the nonclustered indexes belonging to those tables on the same filegroup.

- ❏ E. Create one filegroup on each of the striped volumes. Place tables that are frequently joined together on the same filegroup. Place heavily accessed tables and all indexes belonging to those tables on different filegroups.

- ❏ F. Create one filegroup on each of the striped volumes. Place tables that are frequently joined together on the same filegroup. Place heavily accessed tables and the nonclustered indexes belonging to those tables on the same filegroup.

2. You are a database developer who works for a national company called Argo Alimentum. The company is responsible for database design and hosting for independent organizations. You are creating a database that will store statistical information for various amateur hockey teams. The project is being backed by one of the largest semi-pro hockey leagues in the nation. The information contained within the database will be used by the teams in the semi-pro league as they determine the value of the variety of players available to their draft system. Each of the professional teams uses the data internally. Each team has its own application that uses a variety of data structures and databases provided by many vendors. You would like to prepare the data in a singular framework that can be used by all concerned. How would you prepare the data?

❏ A. Use the `sp_makewebtask` system stored procedure to generate HTML data.

❏ B. Create DTS packages that export the data into tab-delimited text files.

❏ C. Back up the data, store the backup to CD, and distribute the CD to all teams.

❏ D. Extract the data using `SELECT` statements with the `FOR XML` clause.

❏ E. Configure replication. The hosted database publishes data to the subscribing teams.

3. You are creating a database that will store sales order information. Orders will be entered in a client/server application with your site and over the Internet via an ASP.NET application. Each time a new order is placed into the system, a unique order number must be assigned that is in ascending sequence. It is expected that the system will generate in excess of 100,000 orders weekly. You create a new table named `Orders` and a related table named `Order Details`. How should you create the Order Number to provide the required functionality?

❏ A. Use a `UniqueIdentifier` data type.

❏ B. Use an `Integer` data type, and set the `IDENTITY` property for the column.

❏ C. Use a `TimeStamp` data type. Create a user-defined function that sets the order number.

❏ D. Create a table to hold key values and assign order numbers from this table.

❏ E. Have the front-end application assign sequential integer order numbers.

4. You are creating a one-time report to supply the office staff with a revenue breakdown. The data source for the report contains cryptic column headings that cover several categories. You must provide the report in a manner the users can easily understand. Which of the following would be the best solution? Select 2; each answer represents half of the correct solution.

❑ A. Provide friendly aliases for the table names.
❑ B. Provide friendly aliases for the column names.
❑ C. Create a VIEW with corresponding definition.
❑ D. Create a corresponding DEFAULT definition.
❑ E. Execute a corresponding query from the Analyzer.
❑ F. Create a front-end program to execute the required query.

5. You have implemented a database for an international research organization and are performing some test queries against the tables within the database. You have some date fields within the database that store only date information. No time information is maintained within these columns. You would like to have a listing of the data from only the year 2000. Which of the following queries represents the best solution to the problem?

❑ A. `SELECT * FROM RTab`
`    WHERE RDate`
`    BETWEEN '01/01/2000' AND '01/01/2001'`

❑ B. `SELECT * FROM RTab`
`    WHERE RDate`
`    BETWEEN '12/31/1999' AND '12/31/2000'`

❑ C. `SELECT * FROM RTab`
`    WHERE RDate`
`    BETWEEN '12/31/1999' AND '01/01/2001'`

❑ D. `SELECT * FROM RTab`
`    WHERE RDate`
`    BETWEEN '01/01/2000' AND '12/31/2000'`

❑ E. `SELECT * FROM RTab`
`    WHERE RDate`
`    BETWEEN '12/31/2000' AND '01/01/2000'`

6. You have entered a query using a TOP function to limit the number of records being viewed to five. When you see the results of the query, the dates being viewed are not the first five in the data. What is the most likely source of the problem?

❏ A. The resultset has not been grouped.

❏ B. The data contains NULL values.

❏ C. There is an incorrect ORDER.

❏ D. Table aliases were used.

❏ E. Schema binding has been applied.

7. You have been chosen by your development team to provide a set of queries that will print various reports from the Customer table. After opening the Query Analyzer, you discover that the test database and table you just created do not appear. Which of the following is likely to solve the problem?

❏ A. There was an error in the script you used to create the objects, and you need to correct the error and rerun the scripts.

❏ B. The Query Analyzer needs to be refreshed, thus giving it access to all objects in the system.

❏ C. You need to create the database and table from the Enterprise Manager to ensure that temporary objects are not used.

❏ D. You must restart the SQL Server service so that it has access to all newly created objects.

8. You are developing a query that will look for invalid entries in a table before implementing a new check constraint. The constraint you are implementing will enforce data entry into the gender column of the table. Which of the following queries will seek out records that have no value or are not male or female? (Select all that apply.)

☐ A.
```
SELECT * FROM Employee
    WHERE Gndr = NULL
      or Gndr <> 'M' or Gndr <> 'F'
      or Gndr <> 'm' or Gndr <> 'f'
```

☐ B.
```
SELECT * FROM Employee
    WHERE Gndr = NULL
      and Gndr <> 'M' and Gndr <> 'F'
      and Gndr <> 'm' and Gndr <> 'f'
```

☐ C.
```
SELECT * FROM Employee
    WHERE Gndr IS NULL
      and Gndr <> 'M' and Gndr <> 'F'
      and Gndr <> 'm' and Gndr <> 'f'
```

☐ D.
```
SELECT * FROM Employee
    WHERE Gndr IS NULL
      or Gndr <> 'M' or Gndr <> 'F'
      or Gndr <> 'm' or Gndr <> 'f'
```

☐ E.
```
SELECT * FROM Employee
    WHERE Gndr IS NULL
      or (Gndr <> 'M' and Gndr <> 'F'
      and Gndr <> 'm' and Gndr <> 'f')
```

☐ F.
```
SELECT * FROM Employee
    WHERE Gndr IS NULL
      or Gndr NOT IN ('M', 'F', 'm', 'f')
```

9. A local manufacturing company uses a SQL Server to receive statistical information from various points on an assembly line. The information is gathered into a table called Production. Date information is maintained in a standard datetime column called Pdate. You would like to prepare a query that would list the production information from the preceding day. Which of the following queries solves the problem?

☐ A.
```
SELECT * FROM Production
    WHERE Pdate = GetDate() - 1
```

☐ B.
```
SELECT * FROM Production
    WHERE Pdate
    BETWEEN = GetDate() - 2 AND GetDate()
```

☐ C.
```
SELECT * FROM Production
    WHERE datediff(dd, PDate, getdate()) = 1
```

☐ D.
```
SELECT * FROM Production
    WHERE datediff(dd, getdate(), PDate) = 1
```

10. You are preparing to move a test database that you have been working on for the past several months over onto a production system. You are planning to go live with the new database sometime over the next few days. All the current data will be removed and replaced with production information when the system does go live. You are performing some final tests when you notice that the column that is going to be used as the ROWGUIDCOL does not have any values. The ID is to be generated by the system and afterward used as a permanent value. How can you ensure that values are placed into this column as data is entered in the production system?

❏ A. Correct the current data by providing the missing values and then add a constraint so that this doesn't happen again.

❏ B. Correct the current data by providing the missing values and then add a NEWID() as a default for the column.

❏ C. Correct the current data by providing the missing values and provide a formula to generate the value of the column.

❏ D. Correct the current values by using an UPDATE operation and the NEWID() function and then add a NEWID() as a default for the column.

❏ E. Empty the current table into a temporary table, add a default as NEWID(), and load the data back in using an INSERT INTO operation, omitting the ID column.

11. A local car dealership maintains a list of the current inventory on a single SQL Server. The machine also takes on some other networking roles for name resolution. Data is going to be moved off the existing machine to create a dedicated database server. You would like to execute a query that copies all the data to a test database. The test database has been created but no tables exist. Which of the following will solve the problem?

❏ A.
```
INSERT INTO Test.dbo.Automobiles
    SELECT * FROM Inventory.dbo.Automobiles
```

❏ B.
```
SELECT Test.dbo.Automobiles
    SELECT * FROM Inventory.dbo.Automobiles
```

❏ C.
```
INSERT Test.dbo.Automobiles
    SELECT * FROM Inventory.dbo.Automobiles
```

❏ D.
```
SELECT INTO Test.dbo.Automobiles
    SELECT * FROM Inventory.dbo.Automobiles
```

❏ E.
```
INSERT INTO Inventory.dbo.Automobiles
    SELECT * FROM Test.dbo.Automobiles
```

12. An accounting system that has been recording company financial information for the past three years is being upgraded and having some additional columns added to the structure of several of the existing tables. You need to ensure that all existing data remains intact during these operations. How is this best accommodated? (Select two.)

    ❑ A. Set the database files to read-only.
    ❑ B. Set the table properties to read-only.
    ❑ C. The addition of columns shouldn't affect the database.
    ❑ D. Set permissions on the database to prevent malicious updates.
    ❑ E. Set column-level permissions to prevent updates to existing data.

13. You administer the database server for a large lumber and building-materials supplier. You want to query the materials used by a single site. Which of the following queries would suit your needs?

    ❑ A. `SELECT Materials, Weight, Quantity`
            `FROM Inventory ORDER BY Site`

    ❑ B. `SELECT Materials, Weight, Quantity`
            `FROM Inventory WHERE Site = 4`

    ❑ C. `SELECT Materials, Weight, Quantity`
            `FROM Inventory ORDER BY Quantity`

    ❑ D. `SELECT Materials, Weight, Quantity`
            `FROM Inventory ORDER BY Site, Quantity`

    ❑ E. `SELECT Materials, Weight, Quantity`
            `FROM Inventory WHERE Materials = "Drywall"`

14. Which of the following provides the slowest data throughput for BCP?

    ❑ A. Native mode
    ❑ B. Native mode with Unicode support
    ❑ C. Wide native mode
    ❑ D. Comma-delimited text

15. In preparation for a major system upgrade, multiple data changes are going to be made on a system. You would like to implement various changes without disturbing any of the existing data. Which of the following operations do not affect any existing data values? (Select all that apply.)

    ❑ A. `INSERT`
    ❑ B. `UPDATE`
    ❑ C. Change column name
    ❑ D. Increase column length
    ❑ E. Decrease column length

16. You work for a large manufacturing organization that maintains a large production database system on a single SQL Server 2000 machine. In attempting to enter a query to add a record to a table, you find that it is not possible. Which of the following is not a likely cause for the error?

❏ A. Data doesn't meet constraint.

❏ B. Referential integrity.

❏ C. Database is read-only.

❏ D. Permissions.

❏ E. Other applications are locking data.

❏ F. SQL Server Agent is not started.

17. You are a database developer for a small private school. Currently the school maintains all records of students, instructors, courses, and class-room assignments on paper. The school would like to keep records by developing a database. You begin with the following table design:

```
Classroom
   ClassroomID
   ClassRoomNumber
   ClassTime

Student
   StudentID
   LastName
   FirstName
   HomePhone
   WorkPhone

Courses
   CourseID
   CourseNumber
   CourseTitle
   Description
   RequiredName
   InstructorName
   OfficePhone
```

You want to promote quick response times for queries and minimize redundant data. What should you do?

❏ A. Create a new table called `Instructors`. Include an `InstructorID` column, and the instructor's other information. Add an `InstructorID` column to the `Courses` table.

❏ B. Move all columns from the `Classroom` table to the `Courses` table.

❏ C. Base the PRIMARY KEY constraint for the `Courses` table on the `CourseID` and `CourseTitle`.

❏ D. Remove the `ClassroomID` column, and base the PRIMARY KEY constraint on the `ClassroomNumber` and `ClassTime` columns.

18. You are a database developer for a large international mail-order company called M and M and M. The company has two SQL Server 2000 computers named CANDY and CANDO. CANDY handles all the company's online transaction processing, and CANDO stores mostly historical sales data that is accessed only periodically. CANDO has been added as a linked server to CANDY. You are asked to create a list of customers who have purchased fudge bars. Lists will be generated on a recurring basis. Fudge bars are stored in the database with a category ID of 37. You must retrieve this information from a table named CandySalesHistory. This table is located in the PastSales database, which resides on CANDO. You need to execute this query from CANDY. Which script should you use?

❑ A. `EXEC sp_addlinkedserver`

```
      'CANDO', 'SQL Server'
   GO
   SELECT CustomerID
      FROM CANDO.Sales.dbo.CandySalesHistory
      WHERE CategoryID = 37
```

❑ B. `SELECT CusomerID`

```
      FROM OPENROWSET('SQLOLEDB','CANDO';' ',
      'SELECT CustomerID
      FROM Sales.dbo.CandySalesHistory
      WHERE CategoryID = 37')
```

❑ C. `SELECT CustomerID`

```
      FROM CANDO.Sales.dbo.CandySalesHistory
      WHERE CategoryID = 37
```

❑ D. `EXEC sp_addserver 'CANDO'`

```
      GO
   SELECT CustomerID
      FROM CANDO.Sales.dbo.CandySalesHistory
      WHERE CategoryID = 37
```

19. You are designing a database that will serve as a back end for several large websites. The websites themselves will communicate with each other and pass data back and forth using XML. You would like to control the data displayed on the user browser based on interactions with the user. In many cases columns and rows need to be eliminated based on the criteria supplied. You would like to minimize round-trips to the server for data exchange purposes. What technology is the best to apply?

- ❏ A. Use a user-defined function with SCHEMABINDING set to the XML recordsets.

- ❏ B. Create an indexed view of the XML recordset specifying only the columns needed, and supply a WHERE condition based on the rows selected.

- ❏ C. Create standard views of SQL Server data and export the requested data using XML.

- ❏ D. Send data requests and updates directly from the client machine to the SQL Server using FOR XML and OPENXML options.

- ❏ E. Use HTML and an XML schema to provide the necessary view of the data.

20. You have a SQL Server database implemented in a library that stores library-specific information. The description of each title that is present in the library is stored in the Titles table. The Description column is implemented as data type text. A full-text index exists for all columns in the Titles table. You want to search for a title that includes the phrase Programming SQL. Which query should you execute to return the required results?

- ❏ A.
```
SELECT * FROM Titles
     WHERE Description
     like '_Programming SQL_%'
```

- ❏ B.
```
SELECT * FROM Titles
     WHERE Description
     like '%Programming SQL%'
```

- ❏ C.
```
SELECT * FROM Titles
     WHERE CONTAINS(Titles,
     Description,'Programming SQL')
```

- ❏ D.
```
SELECT * FROM Titles
     WHERE FREETEXT(Description,
     'Programming SQL')
```

21. You are a database developer responsible for overseeing a CLIENT database system. The application currently in the design stage will be a multi-tier application with an Internet-facing front end. The application will also be used internally for employees to manage client accounts. The developer needs to retrieve client names from the CLIENT database to populate a list box in the application. You would like to limit the data retrieval to 10 rows at a time. Which technique is appropriate?

- ❑ A. Create a stored procedure to retrieve data called from the client.
- ❑ B. Use a server-side cursor initiated by the client to retrieve the data.
- ❑ C. Retrieve all the data at once and then load the data into the list box 10 at a time.
- ❑ D. Use a server-side cursor initiated by the server to retrieve the data.

22. You have 50,000 records in a database file, and you know you want to add 25,000 records in the next month. What FILLFACTOR should you specify to maximize performance? It should be mentioned that a new index is to be created and that you will change your FILLFACTOR; you also want fast INPUT into the tables.

- ❑ A. 0 (default setting)
- ❑ B. 100
- ❑ C. 70
- ❑ D. 50

23. Which of the following statements is true when full-text indexing is used? (Choose all that apply.)

- ❑ A. The column that you plan on indexing must not contain text if at all possible.
- ❑ B. The column that you index has to be made up of text data.
- ❑ C. Full-text indexes are not automatically updated and they reside in a storage space called a full-text catalog.
- ❑ D. There can be up to 200 catalogs and not more in a single server.
- ❑ E. Full-text searches are best performed on columns that hold integer values.

24. You are a database developer for a high-volume online transaction processing database. All tables are indexed. The heavily accessed tables have at least one index. Two RAID arrays on the database server will be used to contain the data. You want to place the tables and indexes to ensure optimal I/O performance. How should the files be configured?

❑ A. Place frequently joined tables on the same array. Place heavily accessed tables and all indexes belonging to those tables on different arrays.

❑ B. Place frequently joined tables on the same array. Place heavily accessed tables and the nonclustered indexes belonging to those tables on the same array.

❑ C. Place frequently joined tables on different arrays. Place heavily accessed tables and the nonclustered indexes belonging to those tables on different arrays.

❑ D. Place frequently joined tables on different arrays. Place heavily accessed tables and the nonclustered indexes belonging to those tables on the same array.

25. What is true about the WITH SCHEMABINDING argument of the CREATE INDEX statement? (Choose all that apply.)

❑ A. It must be specified to create an indexed view.

❑ B. It allows a view's name and other properties to be changed dynamically.

❑ C. It prevents the dropping and altering of tables participating in the view.

❑ D. It has to be specified only when you are creating a unique clustered index on text data.

26. On a low-volume application you have a few sporadic periods during which volume is high, and the system needs to be able to carry the spikes of volume and still provide reasonable response times. You must try to isolate the cause of data locking and slow query response times. How would this be done?

❑ A. Use the sp_lock and sp_who system stored procedures to find locked resources and to identify processes that are holding locks.

❑ B. Query the sysprocesses and sysobjects to find deadlocked resources.

❑ C. Set a shorter lock timeout for the processes that are accessing the deadlock resources.

❑ D. Add clustered indexes on the primary keys of all the tables.

❑ E. Use the sp_monitor system stored procedure to identify which processes are being affected by the increased query response times.

❑ F. Set a less restrictive transaction isolation level.

27. You are a database developer for a computer manufacturing company named Optima. For a limited time, Optima ships free software with the purchase of any desktop computer or notebook. The software titles, descriptions, values, and other information are located in the Software table. You configure full-text indexing on the Software_Description column that contains more than 2,000 rows and is located in the Software table. After executing a search using FREETEXT for the word Windows, you notice an empty resultset in the results pane. Why is this happening?

   ❑ A. The catalog is not populated.

   ❑ B. FREETEXT is not a valid keyword recognized by SQL Server 2000.

   ❑ C. FREETEXT is not allowed for columns that contain 2,000 or more rows.

   ❑ D. You didn't create a nonclustered index.

28. Which statements show the maximum number of clustered and non-clustered indexes allowed in a single table?

   ❑ A. Clustered 249 and nonclustered 149

   ❑ B. Clustered 249 and nonclustered 249

   ❑ C. Clustered 1 and nonclustered 249

   ❑ D. Clustered 1 and nonclustered unlimited

29. You are building a new database for a company with 10 departments. Each department contains multiple employees. In addition, each employee might work for several departments. How should you logically model the relationship between the department entity and the employee entity?

   ❑ A. Create a mandatory one-to-many relationship between department and employee.

   ❑ B. Create an optional one-to-many relationship between department and employee.

   ❑ C. Create a new entry; create a one-to-many relationship from the employee to the new entry; and create a one-to-many relationship from the department entry to the new entry.

   ❑ D. Create a new entry; create a one-to-many relationship from the new entry to the employee entry; and then create a one-to-many relationship from the entry to the department entry.

30. Peekaboo needs to write a query that will help her understand how many toys are in her toy box. Here's the table she created to track her toys:

```
create table woof (
ToyID int,
ToyType char(1), --B for ball, S for squeaky
ToyName varchar(15)
)
```

Which of the following queries will give Peekaboo a report complete with subtotals for each toy by type?

- ❏ A. ```
  select ToyType, Count(*)
        from woof
           compute count(*) by toytype
  ```

- ❏ B. ```
  select toytype
        from woof
           compute count(toytype) by toytype
  ```

- ❏ C. ```
  select toyname, toytype
        from woof order by toytype
           compute count(ToyName) by Toytype
  ```

- ❏ D. ```
  select toyname, toytype
        from woof with cube
  ```

31. Peekaboo is at it again. This time, she just wants a quick list of all her toy names and types, but she'd like the types to be spelled out with Ball for B and Squeaky for S. How can you make that happen? Here's the table again:

```
create table woof (
ToyID int,
ToyType char(1), --B for ball, S for squeaky
ToyName varchar(15)
)
```

- ❏ A. `select ToyType, ToyName from woof`

- ❏ B. ```
  select ToyName, case ToyType
           when 'B' then 'Ball'
           When 'S' then 'Squeaky'
           else 'broken'
        end
        from woof
  ```

- ❏ C. ```
  Select ToyName, case ToyType
             if 'B' then 'Ball'
             if 'S' then 'Squeaky'
             else 'broken'
        end
        from woof
  ```

- ❏ D. ```
  Select ToyName, case ToyType
             when 'B' then 'Ball'
             When 'S' then 'Squeaky'
             else 'broken'
        from woof
  ```
  ```

32. The people at the EconoVan Corporation are trying to figure out how many vans they have sold. They currently have a table that contains a sales record for each van by type that was created with this script:

```
create table
VanSales (VIN varchar(50),
          SalePrice float,
          Cost float,
          Type int,
          SaleDate datetime)
```

Which of the following queries will show them the number of vans they have sold?

- ❏ A. `SELECT * FROM vansales`
       `ORDER BY 1`

- ❏ B. `SELECT cnt(*) FROM VanSales`
       `ORDER BY 1`

- ❏ C. `SELECT COUNT(*) FROM VanSales`

- ❏ D. `SELECT COUNT(*) FROM VanSalesS`
       `WHERE Type = "YEAR"`

33. The people at the EconoVan Corporation are trying to figure out how many vans of each type they have sold. They currently have a table that contains a sales record for each van by type that was created with this script:

```
create table VanSales (
VIN varchar(50),
SalePrice float,
Cost float,
Type int,
SaleDate datetime
)
```

Which of the following queries will show them the number of vans they have sold by type?

- ❏ A. `SELECT COUNT(*)`
       `FROM VanSales ORDER BY Type`

- ❏ B. `SELECT Type, COUNT(*)`
       `FROM VanSales GROUP BY 1`

- ❏ C. `SELECT Type, COUNT(*)`
       `FROM VanSales GROUP BY Type ORDER BY Type`

- ❏ D. `SELECT COUNT(*)`
       `FROM VanSales GROUP_BY Type`

34. You're doing asset management for a small business. You need to figure out how many laptops, how many desktops, and the total number of computers there are in the company. Here's the table where the data is stored:

```
create table PCAsset (
AssetID int,
PCType char(1), -- L or D, Laptop or Desktop
AcquireDate datetime
)
```

Which of the following queries will do the job?

❑ A. `select AssetID, PCType`
`        from PCAsset group by AssetID`

❑ B. `select PCType, Count(*)`
`        from PCAsset group by PCType with rollup`

❑ C. `Select PCType, count(*)`
`        from PCAsset compute by PCType`

❑ D. `Select PCType, count(*)`
`        from PCAsset`
`        compute group by pctype`
`        with rollup`

35. Southwest Specialists is a firm dealing with the production of valuable ornamental goods. It is using merge replication to publish customer and order information to its infrequently connected sales representatives. The DBA does not, however, want sales representatives to see actual amounts paid, so it deselects the Amounts column and then replicates the data. This article is made so that it contains only selected columns from a table. What is this called?

❑ A. Horizontal partitioning
❑ B. Horizontal filtering
❑ C. Vertical partitioning
❑ D. Column Restriction Filtering (CRF)

36. What is the role of the Merge agent?

❑ A. Propagates updates, and monitors and resolves conflicts on Publishers and Subscribers.
❑ B. Stores records on the Distribution folder until needed, and then merges them with transactions.
❑ C. Enables records to be broken down into smaller subsets.
❑ D. Triggers when data modifications are made at the Subscriber after it has received a replica of data.

37. You have set up a replication process using the default locations for the agents. Your process involves data being replicated to 20 Subscribers using a transactional replication strategy. How are the replication agents configured in transactional replication that uses a push subscription?

 ❑ A. The Log Reader agent resides on the Subscriber and the Distribution agent is on the Subscriber.

 ❑ B. The Log Reader agent resides on the Distributor and the Distribution agent is on the Subscriber.

 ❑ C. The Log Reader agent resides on the Subscriber and the Distribution agent is on the Publisher.

 ❑ D. The Log Reader agent resides on the Distributor and the Distribution agent is also located on the Distributor.

38. Debra has just recently configured replication from the Products table to the Analysis table, located on the Headquarters and Research servers, respectively. Recently, Debra has noticed that replication failed for some unknown cause. Which of the following might be a likely cause of this problem? (Choose all that apply.)

 ❑ A. Replication requires three separate servers and Debra may not have implemented three servers.

 ❑ B. Replication cannot involve the Master, Msdb, Tempdb, and Model databases. Debra could have incorporated one of these databases with replication.

 ❑ C. Any replication process requires the use of at least two replication agents. Debra may have disabled one of the agents.

 ❑ D. Debra might have enabled Updating Subscribers, which is not allowed with any type of replication except for merge replication.

 ❑ E. The Transaction log of the Publisher may have been fully occupied, thus creating problem replication.

39. Which of the following statements describes the role of the Log Reader agent?

 ❑ A. The Log Reader agent moves transactions from the Transaction log of the published database on the Publisher to the Distribution database or server.

 ❑ B. The Log Reader agent moves transactions and snapshot jobs held in the Distribution database out to the Subscribers.

 ❑ C. The Log Reader agent gives you the ability to run transactions in a sequence.

 ❑ D. The Log Reader agent deletes transactions at the click of a button.

40. You are consulting for a manufacturing company that is running a single SQL Server 2000 computer. The server contains a database named Sales. The database has a group of tables that are used to examine sales trends. The database options are set to their default values.

Analysts who use the database are reporting that query performance has become slower. You analyze the clustered primary key on the Invoices table and receive the following results:

```
DBCC SHOWCONTIG
    scanning 'Invoices' table...
Table: 'Invoices' (21575115);
    index ID: 1, database ID: 6
TABLE level scan performed.
- Pages Scanned.....................: 200
- Extents Scanned...................: 50
- Extent Switches...................: 40
- Avg. Pages per Extent.............: 4.0
- Scan Density
    [Best Count:Actual Count]: 60.00% [3:5]
- Logical Scan_Fragmentation.......: 0.00%
- Extent Scan_Fragmentation.......: 40.00%
- Avg. Bytes Free per Page.........: 146.5
- Avg. Page Density (full)........: 98.19%
DBCC execution completed.
If DBCC printed error messages,
contact your system administrator.
```

You want to improve the performance of queries that join tables to the Invoices table. What are three possible T-SQL statements you can execute to achieve this goal? (Each correct answer represents a complete solution. Choose three.)

❑ A. DBCC UPDATEUSEAGE
         ('Sales','Invoices','PK_Invoices')

❑ B. CREATE UNIQUE CLUSTERED INDEX PK__Invoices
         On Invoices(InvoiceID) WITH DROP_EXISTING

❑ C. DBCC INDEXDEFRAG
         ('Sales','Invoices','PK_Invoices')

❑ D. DBCC DBREINDEX
         (Sales.dbo.Invoices, 'PK_Invoices')

❑ E. UPDATE STATISTICS 'Invoices'

❑ F. DBCC CHECKALLOC (Sales, REPAIR_FAST)

41. You are working on a SQL Server 2000 computer that contains a database that stores product data for your company. You need to execute an existing stored procedure that examines prices for your company's products and can modify them if necessary. You execute the stored procedure after business hours, but it does not complete. You execute the sp_lock stored procedure and receive the following output:

```
spid   dbid   ObjId         IndId    Type  Mode
------ ------ ------------- -------- ----  ----
61     7      0             0         DB    S
64     7      0             0         DB    S
72     7      0             0         DB    S
72     7      2145623952    1         PAG   IS
72     7      2145623952    0         TAB   IS
72     7      2145623952    1         KEY   S
78     7      0             0         DB    S
78     7      2145623952    1         PAG   IX
78     7      2145623952    0         TAB   IX
78     7      2145623952    1         KEY   X
```

You want the stored procedure to complete successfully. What should you do?

- ❏ A. Execute the stored procedure, and specify the WITH RECOMPILE option.
- ❏ B. Execute the DBCC FREEPROCCACHE statement.
- ❏ C. Release the locks that are held by connections 61 and 64.
- ❏ D. Release the locks that are held by connections 72 and 78.

42. You are working on a SQL Server 2000 computer that contains a database named Orders, which is used to record customer orders for the products your company sells. Your company's order volume exceeds one million orders per day. Each order uses approximately 100KB of space in the database. Users report that the database responds slowly when they enter new orders. You use SQL Profiler to monitor the activity on the database and receive the data shown in Figure 11.1.

StartTime	EventClass
2000-08-30 01:53:13.033	Data File Auto Grow
2000-08-30 01:53:15.147	Data File Auto Grow
2000-08-30 01:53:17.320	Data File Auto Grow
2000-08-30 01:53:19.323	Data File Auto Grow
2000-08-30 01:53:21.567	Data File Auto Grow
2000-08-30 01:53:23.470	Data File Auto Grow
2000-08-30 01:53:26.063	Data File Auto Grow
2000-08-30 01:53:28.157	Data File Auto Grow
2000-08-30 01:53:30.060	Data File Auto Grow
2000-08-30 01:53:32.150	Data File Auto Grow
2000-08-30 01:53:33.950	Data File Auto Grow

Figure 11.1 SQL Server Profiler output.

You need to modify the database to improve performance. What should you do?

❑ A. Double the size of the data file.

❑ B. Configure the database to automatically grow by 10%.

❑ C. Separate the database into two physical files.

❑ D. Increase the size of the transaction log file.

43. You are creating a database for a large government office. The primary key has already been established, but you need to supply another column that must have different values for each record. What data types could you use without creating additional constraints? (Choose all that apply.)

❑ A. timestamp

❑ B. bigint

❑ C. uniqueidentifier

❑ D. nvarchar

❑ E. sql_variant

44. You are creating a database for a large government office. The primary key has already been established, but you need to supply another column that must have different values for each record. What implementation techniques are available other than data type selection? (Choose all that apply.)

- ❑ A. Identity
- ❑ B. Foreign key
- ❑ C. Unique index
- ❑ D. Unique constraint
- ❑ E. Rule

45. You are putting together the logical design for a database. Tables to be included in the database are Employees, Customers, Supplies, Products, and Sales. The table used to store customer data has the following attributes: CustomerID (primary key), CustomerName, StreetAddress, City, State, ZipCode, BalanceOwing, SalesmanID, and SalesmanName. Which of the following rules of normalization are not being maintained? (Select all that apply.)

- ❑ A. First normal form
- ❑ B. Second normal form
- ❑ C. Third normal form
- ❑ D. Decomposable normal form
- ❑ E. Boyce-Codd normal form

46. You are working for an automobile dealership that tracks inventory in a SQL Server database. The database contains information on the autos in stock. A partial listing of attributes is as follows: VehicleIDNo(20 char), InvoiceNo_(bigint), Make(20 char), Model(15 char), Year(smalldate-time), Colorcode(int), PurchasePrice(smallmoney), StickerPrices_(small-money). Which of the columns would you choose as a primary key?

- ❑ A. Use a compound key with Make, Model, and Year.
- ❑ B. Create a surrogate identity key.
- ❑ C. Use the VehicleIDNo as the key.
- ❑ D. Use the InvoiceNo as the key.
- ❑ E. Use a compound key with InvoiceNo and VehicleIDNo.

47. You are working in a database that has an nchar(5) attribute used to store solely numeric data. You want to minimize the amount of disk space used for storage and need to select an alternative data type. Which of the following data types would you select?

- ❑ A. char(5)
- ❑ B. real
- ❑ C. smallint
- ❑ D. int
- ❑ E. bigint

48. You are creating a historical database that stores information about important dates in history. You need to be able to store dates from the beginning of the 14th century. You want to minimize the storage space used by the data. Which data type would you use?

- ❑ A. `datetime`
- ❑ B. `smalldatetime`
- ❑ C. `bigint`
- ❑ D. `int`
- ❑ E. `char(8)`

49. You are preparing a database structure for a large construction company. At any one time, the company is working on five or more job sites, and each site has between 25 and 200 homes. In charge of each site is a site supervisor who organizes the subcontractors at each phase of the building process (landscaping, framing, drywalling, electrical, plumbing, and so on). Any subcontractor who is planning on working on a given site must be found in a database of approved vendors. The company would like a structure that would allow for storage of the subcontractors' personal information and information about each site that includes the subcontractors assigned to the site. How would you set up this structure?

- ❑ A. A `Site` entity and a `Contractor` entity
- ❑ B. A `Site` entity, a `Contractor` entity, and a `Site/Contractor` entity
- ❑ C. A `Site` entity, a `Process` entity, and a `Contractor` entity
- ❑ D. A `Site` entity, a `Contractor` entity, and a `Site/Process` entity

50. A small scientific laboratory needs a powerful database server to perform analysis of complex measures performed on scientists' regular experiments. The lab requires exact accuracy with all calculations because the results determine the fracture points of various metals. Which data type offers the most accurate results?

- ❑ A. `smallmoney`
- ❑ B. `money`
- ❑ C. `float`
- ❑ D. `real`
- ❑ E. `decimal`

Answers to
Practice Exam One

1. A	18. C	35. C
2. D	19. E	36. A
3. B	20. D	37. D
4. B, E	21. B	38. B, C
5. D	22. D	39. A
6. C	23. B, C	40. B, C, D
7. B	24. C	41. D
8. E, F	25. A, C	42. B
9. C	26. A	43. A, C
10. E	27. A	44. A, C, D
11. D	28. C	45. A, C
12. C, D	29. C	46. B
13. B	30. C	47. D
14. D	31. B	48. D
15. A, C, D	32. C	49. B
16. F	33. C	50. C
17. A	34. B	

Remember that this is a Microsoft exam that must be answered in a Microsoft way. Here are the answers to the first practice exam. Each answer is accompanied by references to the applicable materials within SQL Server Books Online and on the Microsoft official websites.

1. **Answer: A.** By placing joined tables into separate filegroups on different arrays you can allow for the reading of both arrays at the same time during the join operation. For the same reason, when nonclustered indexes are separated from their data, both arrays can be best utilized simultaneously, allowing for sequential access through indexes that don't interfere with the random accesses of the data. Striped volumes will provide better performance than mirrored volumes.

   For more information see Chapter 3, "Implementing the Physical Database," and Chapter 8, "Designing for Optimized Data Access."

   Go to SQL Server Books Online, Creating and Maintaining Databases, Databases, Parts of a Database, Files and Filegroups, Using Files and Filegroups.

   Go to http://msdn.microsoft.com/library/default.asp?url=/library/en-us/dnpag/html/scalenetchapt14.asp, Chapter 14, "Improving SQL Server Performance," Deployment Considerations.

2. **Answer: D.** There are several keys to watch out for in this type of question. The first is the types of systems being distributed to. When you can't determine the design of the application that is going to use the data, more or less the data system that will store the data, you need a mechanism that provides for the most versatility for generic data distribution. This pretty well eliminates the backup/restore approach, which mandates the same versions and sort order of SQL Server–only database systems. Replication would require a different solution for each subscriber and would require some level of connectivity between the systems—in this instance, it's just too difficult a solution. XML, Text, and HTML files are all reasonable (or possible) solutions, but XML is preferred because it provides for descriptive data schema within the files themselves.

For more information see Chapter 6, "Programming Business Logic," and Chapter 10, "Completing a Business System Design."

Go to SQL Server Books Online, SQL Server Architecture, SQL Server and XML Support.

Go to http://msdn.microsoft.com/archive/default.asp?url=/archive/en-us/dnarxml/html/elxml.asp, XML and Web Services, Elementary XML (XML General Technical Articles).

3. **Answer: B.** An `integer` data type of one form or another would be the correct choice for the type for the order number. The size of integer used would be determined based on the total number of orders maintained in the table over time. By the looks of the volume being discussed, it may even be worth considering an `alphanumeric` data type in the future. `Small` and `tiny` integers would be out of the question because they don't provide for a size large enough to even hold a week's worth of data. An `IDENTITY` column is the best way to implement sequential numbering. It can be automated at the data store and thus guarantee uniqueness. The front-end application solution could easily produce duplicates between two different entry points. A `uniqueidentifier` is never a good choice for any field value that has the possibility of being placed within a key or an index. The space taken up by this type of field will hamper performance of data inserts and retrievals. A timestamp, though producing the necessary uniqueness, is cumbersome to work with as an order number.

For more information see Chapter 3, "Implementing the Physical Database."

Go to SQL Server Books Online, Transact-SQL Reference, Data Types.

Go to SQL Server Books Online, Using the SQL Server Tools, Using Interface Reference, Visual Database Tools, Developing Database Structure, Working with Keys, Defining Primary Keys.

Go to http://msdn.microsoft.com/library/default.asp?url=/library/en-us/vdbt7/html/dvcondatabasedesignerconsiderationssql.asp, Development Tools and Languages, Visual Studio.NET, Product

Documentation, Developing with Visual Studio.NET, Designing Distributed Applications, Visual Database Tools, Reference, Database Server Considerations, SQL Server Databases.

4. **Answer: B, E.** The key to this question is that this operation is going to be performed as a one-time thing, so the creation of data objects would likely be avoided and views would not be warranted. However, a script that performs the activity could easily be saved if needed in the future. Table aliases may help in your development, but in this scenario column aliases provide the end user with the necessary data definition.

For more information see Chapter 5, "Retrieving and Modifying Data."

Go to SQL Server Books Online, Data Transformation Services.

Go to SQL Server Books Online, Replication.

Go to SQL Server Books Online, Administering SQL Server, Importing and Exporting Data.

Go to http://msdn.microsoft.com/library/default.asp?url=/ library/en-us/adminsql/ad_impt_bcp_1njt.asp, MSDN Home, MSDN Library, Servers and Enterprise Development, SQL Server, SQL Server 2000, Importing and Exporting Data.

5. **Answer: D.** Dates are inclusive with the BETWEEN function. Be careful when using comparisons that may rely on the time elements of the data because improperly formulating a condition could exclude some desired data.

For more information see Chapter 5, "Retrieving and Modifying Data."

Go to SQL Server Books Online, Transact SQL Reference, BETWEEN.

Go to SQL Server Books Online, Transact SQL Reference, IN.

Go to http://msdn.microsoft.com/library/default.asp?url=/library/en-us/vdtsql/dvhowspecifyingmultiplesearchconditionsforonecolumn.asp,

MSDN Home, MSDN Library, Servers and Enterprise Development, SQL Server, SQL Server 2000, User Interface Reference, Designing Data Retrieval and Manipulation, Designing Queries.

6. **Answer: C.** You are probably not ordering the data to achieve the desired results. Grouping of the resultset doesn't seem to be warranted because the question is asking for five rows. NULL values should not affect this query, though in some instances NULL data can interfere with the results.

For more information see Chapter 5, "Retrieving and Modifying Data."

Go to SQL Server Books Online, Accessing and Changing Relational Data, Query Fundamentals, Filtering Rows with WHERE and HAVING, NULL Comparison Search Conditions.

Go to http://msdn.microsoft.com/library/default.asp?url=/library/en-us/vdbref/html/dvovrspecifyingsearchcriteria.asp, MSDN Home.

7. **Answer: B.** With all versions of SQL Server, the interface doesn't always show newly created objects. A periodic refresh in the Enterprise Manager and the object browser within the Query Analyzer is needed to ensure accuracy of the display.

For more information see Chapter 1, "Database Development on SQL Server 2000."

Go to SQL Server Books Online, SQL Server Architecture, Administration Architecture, Graphical Tools, SQL Query Analyzer.

Go to http://msdn.microsoft.com/library/default.asp?url=/library/en-us/qryanlzr/qryanlzr_1bad.asp, MSDN Home, MSDN Library, Servers and Enterprise Development, SQL Server, SQL Server 2000, User Interface Reference, SQL Query Analyzer Dialog Boxes and Windows.

8. **Answer: E, F.** Both E and F produce the desired results, though in this instance the IN may be easier to read and use and somewhat more efficient. The exam may ask you to choose the best of several working queries, in which case F would be the best answer.

For more information see Chapter 1, "Database Development on SQL Server 2000."

Go to SQL Server Books Online, SQL Server Architecture, Administration Architecture, Graphical Tools, SQL Query Analyzer.

Go to http://msdn.microsoft.com/library/default.asp?url=/library/en-us/qryanlzr/qryanlzr_1bad.asp, MSDN Home, MSDN Library, Servers and Enterprise Development, SQL Server, SQL Server 2000, User Interface Reference, SQL Query Analyzer Dialog Boxes and Windows.

9. **Answer: C.** Date data types also include information for time, which causes many comparisons to not provide the desired results. Use the DATEDIFF function to prevent this problem. In this case the current date would be greater than the production date on file, and therefore the first parameter must be PDate.

For more information see Chapter 3, "Implementing the Physical Database."

Go to SQL Server Books Online, Transact SQL Reference, DATEDIFF.

Go to SQL Server Books Online, Transact SQL Reference, Data Types.

Go to http://msdn.microsoft.com/library/default.asp?url=/library/en-us/spssdk/html/_where_clause.asp, MSDN Home, MSDN Library, Web Development, Server Technologies, SharePoint Products and Technologies, Reference, Search Programmability, SharePoint Portal Server Search SQL Syntax.

10. **Answer: E.** The most efficient and quickest way of performing this task would be to get the data out before you create the default. When the data is placed back without the ID, the default will generate the missing values.

For more information see Chapter 3, "Implementing the Physical Database."

Go to SQL Server Books Online, Creating and Maintaining Databases, Tables, Creating and Modifying a Table, Creating and Modifying Default Definitions.

Go to SQL Server Books Online, Transact SQL Reference, CREATE DEFAULT.

Go to http://msdn.microsoft.com/library/default.asp?url=/library/en-us/tsqlref/ts_create_3x4k.asp, MSDN Home, MSDN Library, Servers and Enterprise Development, SQL Server, SQL Server 2000, Create Default.

11. **Answer: D.** Both A and C essentially do the same thing and would provide the desired results if tables were already present. The INTO within the SELECT command is optional, which would allow for either syntax. SELECT INTO is the most appropriate when tables do not already exist.

For more information see Chapter 5, "Retrieving and Modifying Data."

Go to SQL Server Books Online, Using the SQL Server Tools, User Interface Reference, Visual Database Tools, Designing Data Retrieval and Manipulation, Manipulating Data, Creating INSERT INTO Queries.

Go to SQL Server Books Online, Transact SQL Reference, SELECT INTO.

Go to SQL Server Books Online, Transact SQL Reference, INSERT INTO.

Go to http://msdn.microsoft.com/library/default.asp?url=/library/en-us/tsqlref/ts_sa-ses_1l4j.asp, MSDN Home, MSDN Library, Servers and Enterprise Development, SQL Server, SQL Server 2000, SELECT.

12. **Answer: C, D.** You don't want to set unnecessary read-only properties that wouldn't permit any alterations to the database or the records contained therein.

For more information see Chapter 5, "Retrieving and Modifying Data."

Go to SQL Server Books Online, Creating and Maintaining Databases, Databases, Modifying a Database, Setting Database Options.

Go to SQL Server Books Online, Transact SQL Reference, System Stored Procedures, sp_dboption.

Go to http://msdn.microsoft.com/library/default.asp?url=/library/en-us/instsql/in_backcomp_2ke1.asp, MSDN Home.

13. **Answer: B.** The query needed is a simple SELECT query with a WHERE condition for the site.

For more information see Chapter 5, "Retrieving and Modifying Data."

Go to SQL Server Books Online, Transact SQL Reference, SELECT, SELECT Examples.

Go to http://msdn.microsoft.com/library/default.asp?url=/library/en-us/tsqlref/ts_sa-ses_9sfo.asp, MSDN Home, MSDN Library, Servers and Enterprise Development, SQL Server, SQL Server 2000, SELECT.

14. **Answer: D.** Option A is the fastest, and the options get slower as you go down the list.

For more information see Chapter 5, "Retrieving and Modifying Data."

Go to SQL Server Books Online, Using the SQL Server Tools, Command Prompt Utilities, Getting Started with Command Prompt Utilities, bcp Utility.

Go to http://msdn.microsoft.com/library/default.asp?url=/library/en-us/coprompt/cp_bcp_61et.asp, MSDN Home, MSDN Library, Servers and Enterprise Development, SQL Server, SQL Server 2000, Using the SQL Server Tools, BCP Utility.

15. **Answer: A, C, D.** In choosing UPDATE, you would be selecting an option whose purpose is exactly what you want to avoid. You should be able to increase the data storage size and alter a column name without affecting the internal data. However, decreasing the size for data storage results in data truncation or loss. INSERT, used appropriately, adds data but does not alter any existing values.

For more information see Chapter 5, "Retrieving and Modifying Data."

Go to SQL Server Books Online, Transact-SQL Reference, INSERT.

Go to SQL Server Books Online, Transact-SQL Reference, ALTER TABLE.

Go to http://msdn.microsoft.com/library/default.asp?url=/library/en-us/vdtsql/dvhowresizingpropertycolumns.asp, MSDN Home, MSDN Library, Servers and Enterprise Development, SQL Server, SQL Server 2000, User Interface Reference, Developing Database Structure, Working with Tables.

16. **Answer: F.** All the reasons, excluding the agent, are very possibly a cause of the symptoms being described. The SQL Server Agent handles nondata activity on the server related to operators, jobs, and events configured on the system. If the Agent is not running, only these particular processes are interrupted, not the entire database.

    For more information see Chapter 5, "Retrieving and Modifying Data."

    Go to SQL Server Books Online, Transact-SQL Reference, INSERT.

    Go to http://msdn.microsoft.com/library/default.asp?url=/library/en-us/dv_foxhelp9/html/f9d15b20-eb9d-4c37-8d4a-d9d02c01eb56.asp, MSDN Home, MSDN Library, Development Tools and Languages, Visual FoxPro, Reference, Language Reference, Commands, INSERT SQL Command.

17. **Answer: A.** Given the problem scenario, you will need an additional entity to maintain a normalized structure while still allowing for the instructor information to be attached to the course. Option B would cause significant redundant data and would be a poor design choice. Option C would create a far more complex key than is needed and would also cause the length of the key to be rather large. Option D is not necessarily a poor choice but would do nothing to sort out the data design issues.

For more information see Chapter 5, "Retrieving and Modifying Data."

Go to SQL Server Books Online, Creating and Maintaining Databases, Tables, Designing Tables.

Go to http://msdn.microsoft.com/library/default.asp?url=/library/en-us/vsent7/html/vxconDataNormalization.asp, MSDN Home, MSDN Library, Development Tools and Languages, Visual Studio .NET, Developing with Visual Studio .NET, Designing Distributed Applications, Data Design, Data Integrity, Data Normalization.

18. **Answer: C.** The communication configuration between the two servers has already been set up, so the only necessary element on the coding would be the use of a four-part name within the query. If the desire was to pass the query to the linked server, the OPENQUERY functionality could be utilized.

For more information see Chapter 5, "Retrieving and Modifying Data."

Go to SQL Server Books Online, Administering SQL Server, Managing Servers, Configuring Linked Servers.

Go to http://msdn.microsoft.com/library/default.asp?url=/library/en-us/olapdmpr/prsql_4vxv.asp, MSDN Home, MSDN Library, Servers and Enterprise Development, SQL Server, SQL Server 2000, Building SQL Server Applications, SQL in Analysis Services, Passing Queries from SQL Server to a Linked Analysis Server.

19. **Answer: E.** SCHEMABINDING refers only to SQL Server objects—specifically tables, views, and user-defined functions. An XML schema cannot be bound in this manner. XML resides in memory and is processed against its own internal set of rules, referred to as a schema. An XML schema interacts directly with the data to supply logic and display attributes on the user's browser. HTML does not have the required functionality.

For more information see Chapter 5, "Retrieving and Modifying Data."

Go to SQL Server Books Online, What's New, XML Integration of Relational Data.

Go to http://msdn.microsoft.com/library/default.asp?url=/library/en-us/adosql/adoprg03_2joz.asp, MSDN Home, MSDN Library, Servers and Enterprise Development, SQL Server, SQL Server 2000, Building SQL Server Applications, Programming ADO SQL Server Applications, ADO Support for SQL Server XML Features, Mapping an XML Schema to a Relational Schema Using Annotated Schemas.

20. **Answer: D.** Option A is incorrect because the LIKE keyword is not efficient in searching on text-based columns. Option B is wrong for the same reason. Option C is wrong because the syntax for CONTAINS is wrong. Option D is correct because it uses the correct method of searching, using FREETEXT. Where test searching is available, SQL Server will perform queries more efficiently with their use.

For more information see Chapter 5, "Retrieving and Modifying Data."

Go to SQL Server Books Online, Accessing and Changing Relational Data, Full-Text Search, Using the FREETEXT Predicate.

Go to http://msdn.microsoft.com/library/default.asp?url=/library/en-us/architec/8_ar_sa2_0ehx.asp, MSDN Home, MSDN Library, Servers and Enterprise Development, SQL Server, SQL Server 2000, Relational Database Engine Architecture, Full-Text Query Architecture.

21. **Answer: B.** What you are really looking at with this solution is to allow the client to have a 10-record window of data. The bulk of the data will be maintained on the server, with 10 records being sent to the client when the client requests the information. This is likely to be the best choice for the implementation of the process.

For more information see Chapter 6, "Programming Business Logic."

Go to SQL Server Books Online, Accessing and Changing Relational Data, Cursors, Cursor Implementations.

Go to http://msdn.microsoft.com/library/default.asp?url=/library/en-us/dnbda/html/daag.asp, MSDN Home, MSDN Library, Servers and Enterprise Development, Application Architecture, Microsoft Patterns and Practices for Application Architecture and Design, .NET Data Access Architecture Guide.

22. **Answer: D.** You know exactly how many new records are coming in. You know that 25,000 is 50% of 50,000, so filling the page by 50% and leaving 50% free space for the remaining 50,000 records seems logical. The default FILLFACTOR of 0 doesn't leave any room for additions; this will slow inserts. If you set the FILLFACTOR too big, searches slow down because any query processed has to cycle through a lot of empty space.

For more information see Chapter 3, "Implementing the Physical Database."

Go to SQL Server Books Online, Building SQL Server Applications, SQL-DMO, SQL-DMO Reference, Properties, F, FILLFACTOR.

Go to http://msdn.microsoft.com/library/default.asp?url=/library/en-us/createdb/cm_8_des_05_9ak5.asp, MSDN Home, MSDN Library, Servers and Enterprise Development, SQL Server, SQL Server 2000, Indexes, Designing an Index, Fill Factor.

23. **Answer: B, C.** The column that you plan to index has to be made up of text data. After you create a full-text index, it is not automatically updated and it resides in a storage space called a full-text catalog.

For more information see Chapter 4, "Advanced Physical Database Implementation."

Go to SQL Server Books Online, SQL Server Architecture, Relational Database Engine Architecture, Full-Text Query Architecture.

Go to http://msdn.microsoft.com/archive/default.asp?url=/archive/en-us/dnarexnt00/html/ewn0092.asp, MSDN Home, MSDN Library Archive, Exploring Windows NT (2000), Implementing the Full-Text Search Service in SQL Server.

24. **Answer: C.** To gain optimum performance, you want to get as many different physical devices into the fray as possible. By pulling data

simultaneously from different drive arrays and controllers, you can improve the speed at which data is read.

For more information see Chapter 3, "Implementing the Physical Database."

Go to SQL Server Books Online, Creating and Maintaining Databases, Databases, Parts of a Database, Files and Filegroups.

Go to http://msdn.microsoft.com/library/default.asp?url=/library/en-us/createdb/cm_8_des_02_2ak3.asp, MSDN Home, MSDN Library, Servers and Enterprise Development, SQL Server, SQL Server 2000, Databases, Parts of a Database, Files and Filegroups, Using Files and Filegroups.

25. **Answer: A, C.** The WITH SCHEMABINDING argument of the CREATE INDEX statement is needed when creating an indexed view. When WITH SCHEMABINDING is specified, tables participating in the indexed view are prevented from alteration and deletion.

For more information see Chapter 3, "Implementing the Physical Database."

Go to SQL Server Books Online, Creating and Maintaining Databases, Views, Creating a View, Creating an Indexed View.

Go to http://msdn.microsoft.com/library/default.asp?url=/library/en-us/dnsql2k/html/indexedviews1.asp, MSDN Home, MSDN Library, Servers and Enterprise Development, SQL Server, SQL Server 2000, Improving Performance with SQL Server 2000 Indexed Views.

26. **Answer: A.** You can use the stored procedures sp_who and sp_lock to find the locks that are currently in place and the owners of the processes. Similar information can be received by viewing the lock information in the Current Activity window of the SQL Server Enterprise manager.

For more information see Chapter 7, "Tuning and Optimizing Data Analysis."

Go to SQL Server Books Online, Transact-SQL Reference, Stored Procedures, sp_who.

Go to SQL Server Books Online, Transact-SQL Reference, Stored Procedures, `sp_lock`.

Go to http://msdn.microsoft.com/library/default.asp?url=/library/en-us/trblsql/tr_servdatabse_5xrn.asp, MSDN Home, MSDN Library, Servers and Enterprise Development, SQL Server, SQL Server 2000, Server and Database Troubleshooting, Troubleshooting Locking.

27. **Answer: A.** Before executing full-text searches, you must create and populate a full-text catalog. A full-text catalog is the basis of the storage used for the indexes. Periodically these catalogs should be repopulated to ensure usefulness. Repopulation can be done by schedule or by administrative task.

    For more information see Chapter 4, "Advanced Physical Database Implementation."

    Go to SQL Server Books Online, SQL Server Architecture, Relational Database Engine Architecture, Full-Text Query Architecture.

    Go to http://msdn.microsoft.com/archive/default.asp?url=/archive/en-us/dnarexnt00/html/ewn0092.asp, MSDN Home, MSDN Library Archive, Exploring Windows NT (2000), Implementing the Full-Text Search Service in SQL Server.

28. **Answer: C.** There can be only one clustered index per table and as many as 249 nonclustered indexes. This will become an issue only when you attempt to create a second clustered index or when you add an index to a table that has already been given a primary key with the default settings.

    For more information see Chapter 3, "Implementing the Physical Database," and Chapter 4, "Advanced Physical Database Implementation."

    Go to SQL Server Books Online, Using the SQL Server Tools, User Interface Reference, Visual Database Tools, Database Development and Visual Database Tools, Database Objects, Indexes.

    Go to http://msdn.microsoft.com/library/default.asp?url=/library/en-us/tsqlref/ts_create_64l4.asp, MSDN Home, MSDN Library, Servers and Enterprise Development, SQL Server, SQL Server 2000, Creating Indexes.

29. **Answer: C.** This is a many-to-many relationship scenario, which in SQL Server is implemented using three tables. The center table, often referred to as the connecting or joining table, is on the many side of both of the relationships to the other base table.

   For more information see Chapter 2, "Creating a Logical Data Model."

   Go to SQL Server Books Online, Using the SQL Server Tools, User Interface Reference, Visual Database Tools, Database Development, Database Objects, Table Relationships.

   Go to http://msdn.microsoft.com/library/default.asp?url=/library/en-us/vdbref/html/dvcontablerelationships.asp, MSDN Home, Table Relationships.

30. **Answer: C.** Option A is not correct because you can't use COUNT(*) with COMPUTE BY. Option B is not correct because it's missing the ORDER BY. The fourth choice is totally fictitious.

   For more information see Chapter 5, "Retrieving and Modifying Data."

   Go to SQL Server Books Online, Accessing and Changing Relational Data, Advanced Query Concepts, Summarizing Data, Summarizing Data Using COMPUTE and COMPUTE BY.

   Go to http://msdn.microsoft.com/library/default.asp?url=/library/en-us/acdata/ac_8_qd_08_4ego.asp, MSDN Home, MSDN Library, Servers and Enterprise Development, SQL Server, SQL Server 2000, Advanced Query Concepts, Summarizing Data, Summarizing Data Using COMPUTE and COMPUTE BY.

31. **Answer: B.** Option A doesn't fit the requirements, option C uses if rather than when, and option D is missing an end.

   For more information see Chapter 5, "Retrieving and Modifying Data."

Go to SQL Server Books Online, Accessing and Changing Relational Data, Accessing and Changing Data Fundamentals, Using Multiple Statements, Control-of-Flow, Using CASE.

Go to http://msdn.microsoft.com/library/default.asp?url=/library/en-us/tsqlref/ts_ca-co_5t9v.asp, MSDN Home, MSDN Library, Servers and Enterprise Development, SQL Server, SQL Server 2000, CASE.

32. **Answer: C.** The other close answer is A, but that shows you all the records, and not necessarily the count. Option B is wrong because CNT() is not an aggregate function. COUNT(*) is an aggregate function.

For more information see Chapter 5, "Retrieving and Modifying Data."

Go to SQL Server Books Online, Accessing and Changing Relational Data, Advanced Query Concepts, Using Aggregate Functions, Using COUNT(*).

Go to http://msdn.microsoft.com/library/default.asp?url=/library/en-us/tsqlref/ts_ca-co_5790.asp, MSDN Home, MSDN Library, Servers and Enterprise Development, SQL Server, SQL Server 2000, COUNT.

33. **Answer: C.** Option A would work if you could find someone who wanted to sit and count through the output. Options B and D are invalid syntax: B because you have to name fields in a GROUP BY, and D because the Type field isn't in the SELECT list.

For more information see Chapter 5, "Retrieving and Modifying Data."

Go to SQL Server Books Online, Accessing and Changing Relational Data, Advanced Query Concepts, Grouping Rows with GROUP BY.

Go to http://msdn.microsoft.com/library/default.asp?url=/library/en-us/tsqlref/ts_sa-ses_9sfo.asp, MSDN Home, MSDN Library, Servers and Enterprise Development, SQL Server, SQL Server 2000, SELECT, SELECT Examples.

34. **Answer: B.** Only option B uses correct syntax. Option A doesn't have everything in the select list it needs, and doesn't count anything.

Option C should read COMPUTE COUNT(*) BY PCType and it would work; but it still wouldn't be as efficient as option B. Option D is just a mess syntactically.

For more information see Chapter 5, "Retrieving and Modifying Data."

Go to SQL Server Books Online, Accessing and Changing Relational Data, Advanced Query Concepts, Summarizing Data, Summarizing Data with ROLLUP.

Go to http://msdn.microsoft.com/library/default.asp?url=/library/en-us/acdata/ac_8_qd_08_3ho3.asp, MSDN Home, MSDN Library, Servers and Enterprise Development, SQL Server, SQL Server 2000, Advanced Query Concepts, Summarizing Data, Summarizing Data with ROLLUP.

35. **Answer: C.** Vertical partitioning is the selection of some (but not all) columns in a table. Horizontal partitioning is the creation of an article based on some (but not all) rows in a table. Horizontal filtering is a term that is sometimes used as a synonym for horizontal partitioning.

For more information see Chapter 4, "Advanced Physical Database Implementation."

Go to SQL Server Books Online, Replication, Replication Options, Filtering Published Data.

Go to SQL Server Books Online, Optimizing Database Performance, Database Design, Physical Database Design, Partitioning.

Go to http://msdn.microsoft.com/library/default.asp?url=/library/en-us/replsql/reploptions_0jam.asp, MSDN Home, MSDN Library, Servers and Enterprise Development, SQL Server, SQL Server 2000, Replication Options, Filtering Published Data.

36. **Answer: A.** The Merge agent connects to the publishing server and the subscribing server and updates both as changes are made. The major role of the Merge agent is to propagate the updates, and then monitor for conflicts. The agent is also responsible for applying the initial snapshot at the subscriber.

For more information see Chapter 4, "Advanced Physical Database Implementation."

Go to SQL Server Books Online, Replication, Administering and Monitoring Replication, Replication Agents, Merge Agent.

Go to http://msdn.microsoft.com/library/default.asp?url=/library/en-us/replsql/repltypes_30z7.asp, MSDN Home, MSDN Library, Servers and Enterprise Development, SQL Server, SQL Server 2000, Types of Replication, Merge Replication.

37. **Answer: D.** In transactional replication, the Log Reader agent, by default, resides on the Distributor. Because you are using a push sub-scription, the Distribution agent is also located on the Distributor, by default. If you were to use a pull subscription, the Distribution agent would by default be located on the Subscriber. You can alter the loca-tion on which the agent is run by using remote agent activation if the load would be better distributed by not using defaults.

For more information see Chapter 4, "Advanced Physical Database Implementation."

Go to SQL Server Books Online, Replication, Administering and Monitoring Replication, Replication Agents, Merge Agent.

Go to http://msdn.microsoft.com/library/default.asp?url=/library/en-us/replsql/repltypes_30z7.asp, MSDN Home, MSDN Library, Servers and Enterprise Development, SQL Server, SQL Server 2000, Types of Replication, Merge Replication.

38. **Answer: B, C.** Out of the answer choices provided, only two were actually possible causes: The Model, Master, Msdb, and TempDB data-bases cannot be replicated, and a replication process must contain at least two agents, depending on the replication options chosen.

For more information see Chapter 4, "Advanced Physical Database Implementation."

Go to SQL Server Books Online, Replication, Replication Overview.

Go to SQL Server Books Online, Replication, Replication Data Considerations.

Go to http://msdn.microsoft.com/library/default.asp?url=/library/en-us/replsql/replover_694n.asp, MSDN Home, MSDN Library, Servers and Enterprise Development, SQL Server, SQL Server 2000, Replication Overview.

39. **Answer: A.** The Log Reader agent moves transactions from the transaction log of the published database on the Publisher to the distribution database or server.

    For more information see Chapter 4, "Advanced Physical Database Implementation."

    Go to SQL Server Books Online, Replication, Administering and Monitoring Replication, Replication Agents, Log Reader Agents.

    Go to http://msdn.microsoft.com/library/default.asp?url=/library/en-us/replsql/replmon_57xv.asp, MSDN Home, MSDN Library, Servers and Enterprise Development, SQL Server, SQL Server 2000, Administering and Monitoring Replication, Replication Agents, Log Reader Agent.

40. **Answer: B, C, D.** Because of index fragmentation, the reduction in performance in this database could be improved by rebuilding, re-creating, or defragmenting the current index.

    For more information see Chapter 7, "Tuning and Optimizing Analysis," and Chapter 8, "Designing for Optimized Data Access."

    Go to SQL Server Books Online, Transact-SQL Reference, DBCC.

    Go to http://msdn.microsoft.com/library/default.asp?url=/library/en-us/dnpag/html/scalenethowto03.asp, MSDN Home, MSDN Library, .NET Development, Improving .NET Application Performance and Scalability, How Tos, How To: Optimize SQL Indexes.

    Go to http://msdn.microsoft.com/library/default.asp?url=/library/en-us/tsqlref/ts_dbcc_46cn.asp, MSDN Home, MSDN Library, Servers and Enterprise Development, SQL Server, SQL Server 2000, DBCC, DBCC SHOWCONTIG.

41. **Answer: D.** Procedures 72 and 78 are holding locks against the database and preventing the stored procedure from executing.

For more information see Chapter 7, "Tuning and Optimizing Analysis."

Go to SQL Server Books Online, Accessing and Changing Relational Data, Locking, Displaying Locking Information.

Go to http://msdn.microsoft.com/library/default.asp?url=/library/en-us/acdata/ac_8_con_7a_0uni.asp, MSDN Home, MSDN Library, Servers and Enterprise Development, SQL Server, SQL Server 2000, Locking, Understanding Locking in SQL Server.

42. **Answer: B.** The data file is growing at too small an increment, which causes growth to occur in small, too-frequent increments. You may even want to set the growth rate higher than 10%, but of the available choices this is the best solution.

For more information see Chapter 3, "Implementing the Physical Database."

Go to SQL Server Books Online, Creating and Maintaining Databases, Databases, Parts of a Database, Database Files.

Go to SQL Server Books Online, SQL Server Architecture, Database Architecture, Physical Database Architecture, Physical Database Files.

Go to http://msdn.microsoft.com/library/default.asp?url=/library/en-us/architec/8_ar_da2_9sab.asp, MSDN Home, MSDN Library, Servers and Enterprise Development, SQL Server, SQL Server 2000, Database Architecture, Physical Database Architecture, Physical Database Files and Filegroups.

43. **Answer: A, C.** By definition, `timestamp` and `uniqueidentifier` data types are guaranteed to be unique. The `timestamp` is an automatically entered value. The `uniqueidentifier` is usually entered using a `NEWID()` function to generate the `uniqueidentifier`.

For more information see Chapter 2, "Creating a Logical Data Model," and Chapter 3, "Implementing the Physical Database."

Go to SQL Server Books Online, Accessing and Changing Relational Data, Transact-SQL Syntax Elements, Using Data Types.

Go to http://msdn.microsoft.com/library/default.asp?url=/library/en-us/tsqlref/ts_da-db_7msw.asp, MSDN Home, MSDN Library, Servers and Enterprise Development, SQL Server, SQL Server 2000, Data Types.

44. **Answer: A, C, D.** An Identity provides for uniqueness by increment-ing a value continually, and therefore it is a standard choice for a column that requires a unique value. Unique indexes and unique constraints enforce the uniqueness of entered values and do not let any entry come into the system that already exists.

For more information see Chapter 2, "Creating a Logical Data Model," and Chapter 3, "Implementing the Physical Database."

Go to SQL Server Books Online, Creating and Maintaining Databases, Tables, Designing Tables, Autonumbering and Identifier Columns.

Go to http://msdn.microsoft.com/library/default.asp?url=/library/en-us/createdb/cm_8_des_04_8kqb.asp, MSDN Home, MSDN Library, Servers and Enterprise Development, SQL Server, SQL Server 2000, Tables, Creating and Modifying a Table, Creating and Modifying Identity Columns.

45. **Answer: A, C.** The name fields can be broken down into `firstname` and `lastname` and therefore are not in their most decomposed form. This breaks the first normal form rule of normalization. The salesman name should not be stored in this entity because it depends on the `SalesmanID` and not the `CustomerID`. This breaks the third normal form rule of nor-malization.

For more information see Chapter 2, "Creating a Logical Data Model."

Go to SQL Server Books Online, Creating and Maintaining Databases, Databases, Database Design Considerations, Normalization.

Go to http://msdn.microsoft.com/library/default.asp?url=/library/en-us/vsent7/html/vxconDataNormalization.asp, MSDN Home, MSDN

Library, Development Tools and Languages, Visual Studio .NET, Developing with Visual Studio .NET, Designing Distributed Applications, Data Design, Data Integrity, Data Normalization.

46. **Answer: B.** An automobile's VIN (Vehicle Identification Number), though unique, is character data and is much too large to use as a primary key. This is a perfect situation for an automatically incremented numeric surrogate key that will take up a lot less storage space.

For more information see Chapter 2, "Creating a Logical Data Model."

Go to SQL Server Books Online, Creating and Maintaining Databases, Tables, Designing Tables, Using Constraints, Defaults and NULL Values, PRIMARY KEY Constraints.

Go to http://msdn.microsoft.com/library/default.asp?url=/library/en-us/createdb/cm_8_des_02_3bsp.asp, MSDN Home, MSDN Library, Servers and Enterprise Development, SQL Server, SQL Server 2000, Databases, Database Design Considerations, Data Integrity.

47. **Answer: D.** According to byte sizes, int would take considerably less space compared against the current nchar(5) setting. Smallint would even be better, but it has an upper limit of 32,767. char(5) would cut the space used in half but is not as good as using actual numeric storage. Whenever a variable is going to contain only numbers, numeric storage is always more efficient.

For more information see Chapter 2, "Creating a Logical Data Model."

Go to SQL Server Books Online, Transact-SQL Reference, Data Types.

Go to http://msdn.microsoft.com/library/default.asp?url=/library/en-us/tsqlref/ts_da-db_7msw.asp, MSDN Home, MSDN Library, Servers and Enterprise Development, SQL Server, SQL Server 2000, Data Types.

Go to http://msdn.microsoft.com/library/default.asp?url=/library/en-us/dblibc/dbc_pdcapb_7dr6.asp, MSDN Home, MSDN Library,

Servers and Enterprise Development, SQL Server, SQL Server 2000, Building SQL Server Applications, DB-Library and C Reference, Using DB-Library and C Datatypes.

48. **Answer: D.** This is a tricky question to resolve, and if it were not for the space restriction, there would be a temptation to use characters for the storage. At 8 bytes each (double that of int) the easier technique would be to track days from the beginning of recorded time in an integer. $(2001-1300)\infty 365\frac{1}{4}$ requires six digits, and therefore int is the closest to the size required. Datetime allows dates only in the 1700s; small-datetime, in the 1900s.

For more information see Chapter 2, "Creating a Logical Data Model."

Go to SQL Server Books Online, Transact-SQL Reference, Data Types.

Go to http://msdn.microsoft.com/library/default.asp?url=/library/en-us/tsqlref/ts_da-db_7msw.asp, MSDN Home, MSDN Library, Servers and Enterprise Development, SQL Server, SQL Server 2000, Data Types.

49. **Answer: B.** The many-to-many relationship in this scenario occurs because many contractors can work on a single site, and a single contractor can work at many sites. The connection needs to involve both sites and contractors for an appropriate relationship to be drawn.

For more information see Chapter 2, "Creating a Logical Data Model."

Go to SQL Server Books Online, Optimizing Database Performance, Database Design, Logical Database Design.

Go to http://msdn.microsoft.com/library/default.asp?url=/library/en-us/createdb/cm_8_des_02_2oby.asp, MSDN Home, MSDN Library, Servers and Enterprise Development, SQL Server, SQL Server 2000, Databases, Database Design Considerations, Normalization.

50. **Answer: C.** Float gives accuracy up to 308 decimal places, which is almost 10 times better than can be achieved with any of the other

types. Real and decimal data types provide only 38 decimal places of accuracy at, whereas money and smallmoney have accuracy to only the ten-thousandths.

For more information see Chapter 2, "Creating a Logical Data Model."

Go to SQL Server Books Online, Transact-SQL Reference, Data Types.

Go to http://msdn.microsoft.com/library/default.asp?url=/library/en-us/tsqlref/ts_da-db_7msw.asp, MSDN Home, MSDN Library, Servers and Enterprise Development, SQL Server, SQL Server 2000, Data Types.

Practice Exam Two

The actual certification exam is 50 questions. To best simulate exam circumstances, you should try to complete the 50 questions in 90 minutes.

1. John has just been impressed with the amount of power that full-text searches can provide and how easy they are to implement. Before John actually upgrades to a full-text search, he wants to try out the full-text searching "dream" capabilities by testing them on the Products table of his company's database. John would like to perform flexible searches on a text column in the Products table. Which tool will help him accomplish his task?

   ❑ A. Index Tuning Wizard
   ❑ B. Full-Text Searching Wizard
   ❑ C. Full-Text Indexing Wizard
   ❑ D. MSSearch Index Wizard

2. David is a database implementer who works for a major car retailer that tracks information on the latest car models available by the various car manufacturers. The company currently searches for the latest car model description using a regular search engine that is not capable of performing the complex searches that full-text searches can perform. David needs to upgrade the company's searches to full-text searches. What must he do before creating a full-text index?

   ❑ A. End all wizards and programs using the MSSearch utility.
   ❑ B. Create an index using the Index Tuning Wizard.
   ❑ C. Run a custom setup to install Microsoft Full-Text Search Engine.
   ❑ D. He doesn't have to do anything.

3. You are designing a database that will contain customer orders. Customers will be able to order multiple products each time they place an order. You review the database design, which is show here:

```
Customers
  CustomerID
  CompanyName
  Address
  City
  State

Orders
  OrderID
  ProductID
  OrderDate
  Quantity
  CustomerID

Product
  ProductID
  Description
  UnitPrice
```

What can you do to achieve quick response times with minimal redundant data? (Each correct answer presents part of the solution. Choose two.)

❏ A. Create a new order table named OrdersDetail. Add OrderID, ProductID, and Quantity columns to this table.

❏ B. Create a composite PRIMARY KEY constraint on the OrderID and ProductID columns of the Orders table.

❏ C. Remove the ProductID and Quantity columns from the Orders table.

❏ D. Create a UNIQUE constraint on the OrderID column of the Orders table.

❏ E. Move the UnitPrice column from the Products table to the Orders table.

4. You are a database developer for an IT consulting company. You are designing a database to record information about potential employees. You create a table named ApplicantAttributes for the database. The table is shown here:

```
ApplicantAttributes
  ApplicantID
  AttributeID
  YearsExperience
  Proficiency
```

How should you uniquely identify the skills for each consultant?

❏ A. Create a PRIMARY KEY constraint on the ApplicantID column.

❏ B. Create a PRIMARY KEY constraint on the ApplicantID and YearsExperience columns.

❏ C. Create a PRIMARY KEY constraint on the ApplicantID and AttributeID columns.

❏ D. Create a PRIMARY KEY constraint on the ApplicantID, AttributeID, and YearsExperience columns.

5. Users inform you that recently they have been receiving error messages frequently as query volume has steadily increased. The following message was captured by one of the users:

```
Transaction was deadlocked on resources with another
process and has been chosen as the deadlock victim.
Rerun the transaction.
```

What is your next step?

❏ A. Use a different transaction isolation level.

❏ B. Use SQL Profiler to capture deadlock events.

❏ C. Use System Monitor to monitor locks.

❏ D. Add more client access licenses to the server.

6. Lately the end users have been reporting that when performing queries against information on customers, the system has been growing increasingly slow. After examining the system, you determine that the table definition has recently been altered. You want the response time to improve and be similar to what it was before the change. How would you fix the problem?

❏ A. Run a DBCC DBREINDEX.

❏ B. Drop and re-create the table's clustered index.

❏ C. Drop and re-create all indexes.

❏ D. Update the index statistics.

❏ E. Reboot the server.

7. Your company has a table named Products. Some time ago you added three nonclustered indexes to the table. You also added a clustered index on the primary key. You monitor the performance on the indexes and notice that the indexes are not as efficient as they were when they were originally created. You decide to rebuild each index in the table. Which method should you use to rebuild all indexes in the fastest and most efficient way?

❏ A. Use DBCC DBREINDEX.

❏ B. Create a clustered index with Drop-Existing; create a nonclustered index with Drop-Existing.

❏ C. Delete all indexes and then re-create them.

❏ D. Update the index statistics.

8. You are building a database and you want to eliminate duplicate entries and minimize data storage wherever possible. You want to track the following information for employees and managers: first name, middle name, last name, employee identification number, address, date of hire, department, salary, and name of manager. Which table design should you use?

   ❑ A. Table1: `EmpID, MgrID, Firstname, Middlename, Lastname, Address, Hiredate, Dept, Salary.` Table2: `MgrID, Firstname, Middlename, Lastname.`

   ❑ B. Table1: `EmpID, Firstname, Middlename, Lastname, Address, Hiredate, Dept, Salary.` Table2: `MgrID, Firstname, Middlename, Lastname.` Table3: `EmpID, MgrID.`

   ❑ C. Table1: `EmpID, MgrID, Firstname, Middlename, Lastname, Address, Hiredate, Dept, Salary.`

   ❑ D. Table1: `EmpID, Firstname, Middlename, Lastname, Address, Hiredate, Dept, Salary.` Table2: `EmpID, MgrID` Table3: `MgrID.`

9. You have a table that is defined this way:

   ```
   CREATE TABLE Books ( Book_ID char, Description Text,
       Price Integer, Author char(32))
   ```

   You write the following:

   ```
   SELECT * FROM Books WHERE CONTAINS (Description, 'Server')
   ```

   You know for a fact that there are matching rows, but you receive an empty resultset when you try to execute the query. What should you do?

   ❑ A. Ensure that there is a non-unique index on `Description` column.

   ❑ B. Create a unique clustered index on the `Description` column.

   ❑ C. Populate the `FULLTEXT` catalog for the `Books` table.

   ❑ D. Use the `sp_fulltext_populate` stored procedure.

10. You are the database developer for a leasing company. Your database includes a table that is defined like this:

    ```
    CREATE TABLE Lease
    (Id Int IDENTITY NOT NULL
       CONSTRAINT pk_lesse_id PRIMARY KEY NONCLUSTERED,
    Lastname varchar(50) NOT NULL,
    FirstName varchar(50) NOT NULL,
    SSNo char(9) NOT NULL,
    Rating char(10) NULL,
    Limit money NULL)
    ```

    Each `SSNo` must be unique. You want the data to be physically stored in `SSNo` sequence. Which constraint should you add to the `SSNo` column on the `Lease` table?

    ❑ A. `UNIQUE CLUSTERED` constraint

    ❑ B. `UNIQUE UNCLUSTERED` constraint

    ❑ C. `PRIMARY KEY CLUSTERED` constraint

    ❑ D. `PRIMARY KEY UNCLUSTERED` constraint

11. After receiving complaints from many users concerning the data retrieval and modification times, an administrator creates a set of 10 indexes. Performance has increased in some processes but decreased in others. Which of the following statements outlines the consequence of using the numerous indexes you have just done?

 - ❑ A. Numerous indexes decrease performance when modifying data.
 - ❑ B. Numerous indexes are not permitted; you can create only one clustered and one nonclustered index.
 - ❑ C. Numerous indexes result in a very short index life span.
 - ❑ D. Numerous indexes decrease performance on queries that select data with the SELECT clause.

12. You are designing a database that will serve as a back end for several large websites. The websites themselves will communicate with each other and pass data back and forth using XML. You would like to control the data displayed on the user browser based on interactions with the user. In many cases columns and rows need to be eliminated based on the criteria supplied. You would like to minimize round-trips to the server for data-exchange purposes. What technology is the best to apply?

 - ❑ A. Use a user-defined function with SCHEMABINDING set to the XML recordsets.
 - ❑ B. Create an indexed view of the XML recordset, specifying only the columns needed, and supply a WHERE condition based on the rows selected.
 - ❑ C. Create standard views of SQL Server data and export the requested data using XML.
 - ❑ D. Send data requests and updates directly from the client machine to the SQL Server using FOR XML and OPENXML options.
 - ❑ E. Use HTML and an XML schema to provide the necessary view of the data.

13. You are creating a set of queries to produce reports for a Human Resources database. Based on the queries, you design and create the indexes. You want to ensure that you have created sufficient indexes. What would you do next?

 - ❑ A. Run a SQL Profiler trace.
 - ❑ B. Run the Index Tuning Wizard against a workload file.
 - ❑ C. Run System Monitor.
 - ❑ D. In SQL Query Analyzer use the SHOWPLAN_TEXT option.

14. You create two transactions to support the data entry of employee information. One transaction inserts the compulsory employee name and address information, and the other inserts optional employee demographics. The server occasionally encounters errors during the process and randomly terminates one of the transactions. You must ensure that the server never terminates the more important transaction. Which of the following is the best solution?

   ❏ A. Set the DEADLOCK_PRIORITY to LOW for the insert of the name and address.

   ❏ B. Set the DEADLOCK_PRIORITY to LOW for the insert of the demographics.

   ❏ C. Add error checking on the insert of the name and address. If terminated, restart the transaction.

   ❏ D. Add the ROWLOCK optimizer to the transaction that inserts the name and address.

   ❏ E. Set the isolation to SERIALIZABLE for the insert of the name and address.

15. You are setting up a new snapshot replication environment for five large tables. To save disk space, you want to delete the data objects that are generated by snapshot replication. Where can you find these objects?

   ❏ A. Inside the MSSQL2000\Replication\Data directory on the Publisher

   ❏ B. In the sysArticles table in the database that is being published

   ❏ C. In the Mssql\Repldata directory in the Distributor

   ❏ D. In the Mssql\Repldata directory on the Subscriber

16. Eric is working on setting up a new product application and runs the following:

```
SELECT * FROM Sales1
UPDATE Products SET price= price * 2
GO
```

When Eric runs the batch, he receives an error message stating that the table Sales1 was not found. He also notices that the UPDATE statement didn't run. How could the batch be written so that the UPDATE statement runs even in the event of an error?

- ❑ A. GO
    ```
    SELECT * FROM Sales1
    UPDATE Products SET price= price * 2
    GO
    ```

- ❑ B. SELECT * FROM Sales1
    ```
    UPDATE Products
    SET price= price * 2 AS INDEPENDENT
    GO
    ```

- ❑ C. SELECT * FROM Sales1
    ```
    GO
    UPDATE Products SET price= price * 2
    GO
    ```

- ❑ D. SELECT * FROM Sales1
    ```
    UPDATE Products SET price= price * 2
    ```

17. You work for a small web development shop. Your new apprentice has been trying to write SQL Scripts. He has given you this script to run, but you want to make sure that it doesn't block all the users out of the server and set all the pricing information to zero, like last time. So, given the script

```
DECLARE @Var int
SET @var = 1
GO

WHILE @Var < 11
BEGIN
PRINT @Var * 2
SET @Var= @Var + 1
END
```

what will be printed on the output screen?

- ❑ A. A line of zeros.
- ❑ B. A line of ones.
- ❑ C. The multiples of two.
- ❑ D. An error will occur.

18. You are a SQL Developer working on an Internet application in SQL Server 2000. You need to write a batch that prints the first 10 multiples of 5. Which of the following gets the job done?

❑ A.
```
DECLARE @MyVar int
    SET @MyVar =1
    WHILE @MyVar < 11
    BEGIN
    PRINT @MyVar *5
    SET @MyVar = @MyVar +1
    END
```

❑ B.
```
DECLARE @MyVar int
    SET @MyVar =1
    WHILE @MyVar < 10
    BEGIN
    PRINT @MyVar *5
    SET @MyVar = @MyVar +1
    END
```

❑ C.
```
DECLARE @MyVar int
    SET @MyVar =1
    WHILE @MyVar < 11
    BEGIN
    PRINT @MyVar *5
    SET @MyVar = 5
    END
```

❑ D.
```
DECLARE @MyVar int
    SET @MyVar =1
    GO
    WHILE @MyVar < 11
    BEGIN
    PRINT @MyVar *5
    SET @MyVar = @MyVar +1
    END
```

19. You are writing a procedure that requires the use of a cursor to return data. You need a statement to retrieve the first record to initiate a loop. Which of the following statements would you use?

❑ A. DECLARE

❑ B. OPEN

❑ C. RETRIEVE

❑ D. FETCH

20. You are hearing complaints from users about their applications hanging, occasionally receiving error messages. You've found a couple of batches that are being run at the time that appear to be causing the errors:

Batch 1:

```
Set Transaction Isolation Level Serializable
Begin Transaction
Declare @ProductID int
Select @ProductID = ProdCode
     From Product
     where ProductName like 'Deluxe Widget'
Update SalesTracker
     Set ProdCode = @ProductID
     where SalesID = 19
Commit Transaction
```

Batch 2:

```
Set Transaction Isolation Level Serializable
Begin Transaction
Declare @SalesID int
Select @SalesID from SalesTracker
     where ProductCode = 42
Update Product
     Set SalesCode = @SalesID
     where ProductCode = 42
Commit Transaction
```

What's a likely cause of the problem?

- ❏ A. Data corruption in the Product table due to dirty reads
- ❏ B. Data corruption in the SalesTracker table due to dirty reads
- ❏ C. A deadlock between the Product table and the SalesTracker table
- ❏ D. Invalid use of isolation levels

21. You are performing some scripting for a database system that requires you to monitor the transaction nesting levels. What is the value of the @@TRANCOUNT function when this code is finished executing?

```
declare @Counter int
begin transaction
        update mytable set value = 42
        save transaction Point1
        while @Counter < 19
        begin
                begin transaction
                insert into MyTable
                  values(2, 3, 42, 'hello')
                set @Counter = 1
                commit transaction
        end
        rollback Point1
        begin transaction Point2
                insert into mytable (2, 3,42, 'goodbye')
        rollback
```

- ❑ A. -1
- ❑ B. 0
- ❑ C. 1
- ❑ D. 2

22. Carl needs to write a SQL Script that will change everyone's pay status from part-time to full-time. Which of the following is the best way to accomplish the task?

❏ A.
```
declare cursor FixStatus for
        SELECT ID, Status from employees
        for update of status
    declare @ID int, @Status varchar(4)
    fetch next from FixStatus into @ID, @Status
    while @@FETCH_STATUS = 0
    begin
            update Employees set Status = 'Full'
                    where current of FixStatus
            fetch next from FixStatus
                into @ID,@Status
    end
```

❏ B.
```
declare cursor FixStatus for
        SELECT ID, Status from employees
        for update of status
    declare @ID int, @Status varchar(4)
    fetch next from FixStatus into @ID,@Status
    while @@FETCH_STATUS = 0
            begin
                    update Employees
                    set Status = 'Full'
                    where current of FixStatus
                    fetch next from FixStatus
                        into @ID, @Status
            end
    close FixStatus
    Deallocate FixStatus
```

❏ C.
```
begin transaction
    declare cursor FixStatus for
        SELECT ID,Status from employees
        for update of status
    declare @ID int, @Status varchar(4)
    fetch next from FixStatus into @ID, @Status
    while @@FETCH_STATUS = 0
            begin
                    update Employees
                    set Status = 'Full'
                        where current of FixStatus
                    fetch next from FixStatus
                        into @ID, @Status
            end
    close FixStatus
    Deallocate FixStatus
    commit transaction
```

❏ D.
```
update employee set status = 'full'
```

23. You are a database administrator at a small corporation. You've just been asked to run a stored procedure, but you're wary because the last time someone did this, it caused massive lock contention and forced a system shutdown. What is printed by the following stored procedure?

```
begin transaction
        declare @foo int
        select @foo = id from mytable
  print @foo
rollback transaction
```

❑ A. Nothing.

❑ B. There are no database changes to the database, so this causes an error.

❑ C. It prints the value of @Foo.

❑ D. It prints the value of @Foo twice because of the rollback.

24. You are developing a database that will be using some advanced trigger functionality in combination with other methods of controlling data. In some instances you believe that triggers are not firing because of other conditions within the design. In what order do these events happen?

❑ A. Constraints, BEFORE triggers, INSTEAD OF triggers

❑ B. INSTEAD OF triggers, constraints, BEFORE triggers, AFTER triggers

❑ C. INSTEAD OF triggers, constraints, AFTER triggers

❑ D. Constraints, INSTEAD OF triggers, AFTER triggers

25. You are attempting to create a trigger that will run transactional information within a database. The code you are attempting to use is as follows:

```
EXEC sp_configure 'remote proc trans', '1'
RECONFIGURE
CREATE TABLE #MyTempTable (cola INT PRIMARY KEY)
BEGIN TRANSACTION
    UPDATE Server2.dbo.Jolly.CCola Set Bottle = 3
    UPDATE Server2.dbo.Jolly.CCola Set Can = 2
COMMIT TRANSACTION
...
```

Which of the following statements cannot be used within a trigger? (Select all that apply.)

❑ A. CREATE TABLE

❑ B. COMMIT TRANSACTION

❑ C. sp_configure

❑ D. RECONFIGURE

❑ E. UPDATE

26. You plan on implementing a simple triggering strategy for a large college located in the heart of New York. The college has planned a 30-day trip to Paris for those interested. The college enters the names of those desiring to go and then checks to see whether they have paid the fees. If they have not paid the required fees, their names should not get entered; otherwise, they should be entered. Which type of trigger should the school implement?

    ❏ A. Indirect recursion trigger (IRT)
    ❏ B. Direct recursion trigger (DRT)
    ❏ C. INSERT trigger
    ❏ D. UPDATE trigger

27. You need to develop a database that will be using triggers to assist in the control of the data being entered. Which of the following statements are not true for all types of triggers?

    ❏ A. Triggers can fire on all three events—UPDATE, DELETE, and INSERT.
    ❏ B. Only one trigger per table is allowed.
    ❏ C. Triggers can execute stored procedures.
    ❏ D. Triggers can be used to validate the data being entered into a table.

28. Which of the following methods can be used to create a trigger and then later modify its definition?

    ❏ A. sp_createtrigger and sp_altertrigger
    ❏ B. CREATE TRIGGER and MODIFY TRIGGER
    ❏ C. CREATE TRIGGER and ALTER TRIGGER
    ❏ D. CREATE TABLE and ALTER TABLE

29. You are updating the table structure within a production database on your corporate server. You need to drop a trigger that is no longer desired on one of the tables. What should you do before renaming or dropping a trigger?

    ❏ A. Use sp_freename to ensure that the name of your trigger can be reused.
    ❏ B. Use sp_helpdependants to check for dependent objects.
    ❏ C. Use sp_depends to examine dependencies.
    ❏ D. No additional steps are required.

30. You are working on a database that has several views designed and configured so that updates cannot be made through the views. You need to implement functionality that will allow for some updates to be performed. You don't want to affect the current functionality that is implemented. How would you implement the update functionality?

    ❏ A. Execute sp_makeupdatableview.
    ❏ B. Create an AFTER trigger.
    ❏ C. Create a DELETE trigger.
    ❏ D. Create an INSTEAD OF trigger.

31. You have been assigned to investigate the actions of a trigger on one of the tables in the Products database. Which of the following commands would enable you to read a trigger definition?

   ❏ A. sp_helptext
   ❏ B. sp_helptrigger
   ❏ C. sp_displaydef
   ❏ D. sp_help

32. You are attempting to explain to an apprentice the different types of situations in which user-defined functions might provide necessary functionality. Which of the following problems would be appropriately implemented with a scalar user-defined function?

   ❏ A. Returning a list of customer names
   ❏ B. Updating a customer name to upper case
   ❏ C. Getting the absolute value of a number
   ❏ D. Calculating a customer's outstanding account balance

33. You are again trying to explain to an apprentice the appropriate use of user-defined functions. Which of the following is not a valid reason to use a view rather than an inline user-defined function?

   ❏ A. Need to update the recordset directly
   ❏ B. Need to return a recordset with a consistent set of parameters
   ❏ C. Need to combine data from several tables into one resultset
   ❏ D. Need to be able to change the filter on the recordset

34. Eric is having a problem getting his stored procedure to run with acceptable performance with all the different parameters he can use. Basically, the parameters specify whether a search should be done on last name, first name, or address, or some other parameter in his customer table. What can Eric do that may improve performance?

   ❏ A. Use views rather than stored procedures.
   ❏ B. Create the procedure using WITH RECOMPILE to avoid using the cached plan.
   ❏ C. Create the procedure in Enterprise Manager rather than Query Analyzer.
   ❏ D. Use more user-defined functions to handle the parameter input.

35. Kyle is writing a system that will monitor the number of customer accounts in the database and, when an account representative has exceeded the number of accounts he is allowed to manage, send an email to the sales manager. He's going to use the SQL Server Agent to schedule the job to run nightly. Which of the following tools can he use to send the email?

   ❏ A. A stored procedure
   ❏ B. A table-valued user-defined function
   ❏ C. A scalar user-defined function
   ❏ D. An inline user-defined function

36. Stan is trying to figure out why his user-defined function isn't working properly. He keeps getting an incorrect syntax near the keyword 'return' error. What's wrong?

```
create FUNCTION distance (
        @x1 int = 0,
        @y1 int = 0,
        @x2 int = 0,
        @y2 int = 0  )
return float
as
begin
        declare @distance float
         set @distance =
          sqrt(power(@y1-@y2,2)+power(@x1-@x2,2))
         return @distance
end
```

- ❑ A. Side effects are caused by returning a value of type float.
- ❑ B. A comma is missing after the @y2 parameter.
- ❑ C. The return float should be returns float.
- ❑ D. A parenthesis is missing on the SET @distance statement.

37. Kenny is trying to pass values into a stored procedure. Here's what the CREATE PROCEDURE statement looks like:

```
create Procedure CalculateSalesTax
        @ItemPrice float,
        @Qty int,
        @TaxRate float,
        @SalesTax float OUTPUT
```

Which of the following EXEC statements returns the sales tax into the @SalesTax variable?

- ❑ A. EXEC CalculateSalesTax 2.39, 1, 4, @SalesTax

- ❑ B. EXEC @SalesTax =
        CalculateSalesTax 2.39, 1, 4, 0

- ❑ C. EXEC CalculateSalesTax @ItemPrice =
        2.39, 1, 4, @SalesTax OUTPUT

- ❑ D. EXEC CalculateSalesTax @ItemPrice =
        2.39, @Qty = 1, @TaxRate = .04,
        @SalesTax = @SalesTax OUTPUT

38. Wendy has created a stored procedure to insert new values into her database:

```
create procedure InsertPlayer
    @PlayerID int, @Comment varchar(2000) as
begin
      insert into CommentTracker
        values (@PlayerID, @Comment)
      exec xp_sendmail @message =
       @Comment, @recipients = _'WendyT',
        @subject = 'Comment Activity'
end
```

The problem is that sometimes the insert fails with a constraint violation, and Wendy would like an email when those fail also. Which of the following approaches would enable this to happen?

- ❏ A. Capture the value of @@ERROR and use an IF statement to send an email if the INSERT statement fails.
- ❏ B. Capture the value of @@ERROR and use a WHILE loop to retry the insert in the event of an error.
- ❏ C. Combine the INSERT and the xp_sendmail into a transaction.
- ❏ D. Capture the value of @@LAST_ERROR and use an IF statement to send an email if the INSERT statement fails.

39. You are responsible for designing a function that will be used to categorize player information for a local sports franchise. You design a user-defined function with the following:

```
create function InsertPlayer
        (@PlayerID int,
         @Comment varchar(2000))
returns int
begin
        insert into CommentTracker
             values (@PlayerID, @Comment)
        return 1
end
```

What's wrong with this user-defined function?

- ❏ A. The function is correct as is.
- ❏ B. It's missing the keyword AS before the BEGIN.
- ❏ C. The functionality is not valid.
- ❏ D. It is a table-valued function.

40. Bette is trying to write a stored procedure that will return a subset of a table back to her script. Which of the following methods will not work?

- ❏ A. Use a temporary table defined inside the stored procedure.
- ❏ B. Use a static cursor as an output parameter.
- ❏ C. Insert data into a temporary table that's defined before calling the stored procedure.
- ❏ D. Use a variable of type table as an output parameter.

41. Consider the following stored procedure declaration:

```
CREATE PROC Test2
        @I int,
        @J float,
        @K varchar(2000)
```

Which of the following EXEC statements will work?

- ❏ A. EXEC Test2 4.3, 19, 27
- ❏ B. EXEC Test2 @J=4.3, @I = 20, @K = 'value'
- ❏ C. EXEC Test2 20, @J=4.3, 'value'
- ❏ D. EXEC Test2 20, @J=4.3, @K = 'value' OUTPUT

42. To properly process an insurance claim, Esther has to have a client ID number and a claim amount. On claims over a certain amount of money, she has to have the name of the adjuster. Which of the following would be the best way to make sure that Esther had entered all the information properly before trying to process the claim?

- ❏ A. A multiline table-valued stored procedure
- ❏ B. An inline function
- ❏ C. A cursor
- ❏ D. A stored procedure

43. You are writing a procedure that needs to send a return value back from the call. Which of the following accepts the return value from the stored procedure CheckInsuranceClaim?

- ❏ A. declare @RetVal float =
      CheckInsuranceClaim @ClaimID = 41400

- ❏ B. declare @RetVal int exec
          CheckInsuranceClaim
          @ClaimID = 41400, @RetVal OUTPUT

- ❏ C. declare @RetVal int exec
          CheckInsuranceClaim @ClaimID = 41400

- ❏ D. declare @RetVal int exec
          @RetVal = CheckInsuranceClaim
          @ClaimID = 41400

44. Which of the following inline function definitions would correctly return the information for the customer with CustomerID 42?

☐ A. Create Function GetCustomerInfo
```
    @CustomerID int = 42 returns
    select * from customer
    where customerid = @CustomerID
```

☐ B. Create Function GetCustomerInfo
```
    (@CustomerID int = 42) returns
    table as return (select * from customer
    where customerid = 42)
```

☐ C. Create Inline Function GetCustomerInfo
```
    (@CustomerID int = 42 ) returns
    (select * from customer
    where customerid = 42)
```

☐ D. Create Function GetCustomerInfo
```
    (@CustomerID int = 42) returns
    @ReturnTable table (CustomerID int,
    CustomerName varchar(50)) as
    begin
        insert into @ReturnTable
            select * from customer
            where customerid =
            @CustomerID return
    end
```

45. After examining his stored procedure that runs one statement, an INSERT, Larry determines that he's going to have a problem with users passing in bad data, which will cause inserts to fail because of constraints. Which of the following is the best approach to handling the situation?

☐ A. Use an inline function to check the constraint first.

☐ B. Check all the applicable constraints with SELECT statements before performing the insert.

☐ C. Attempt the insert and check the @@ERROR variable after the insert.

☐ D. Remove the constraints.

46. You are working for a large international organization that supplies packaging materials for companies that require custom commercial designs. The number of products is becoming too large for the current computer system to handle, and you need to provide a solution that will spread the load over the current server and a new machine coming into the system. Queries need to be performed over a wide variety of products, and there is no predictable pattern to the queries. Which of the following is the most appropriate technique to implement the changes?

   ❑ A. Configure replication using the new machine as a Subscriber and the original machine as the Publisher/Distributor to balance the workload.

   ❑ B. Separate the table into two smaller tables and place one table on each server. Configure a partitioned view and appropriate constraints on each of the machines.

   ❑ C. Implement multiserver clustering so that each of the two servers can respond to data activities, thus achieving a balanced workload.

   ❑ D. Configure log shipping on both servers to have a copy of the data on each of the servers and propagate all changes to the alternate machine.

47. As a developer for a large healthcare provider, you are assigned the task of developing a process for updating a patient database. When a patient is transferred from one floor to another, an internal identifier, CurrentRoomID, which is used as the primary key, needs to be altered, while the original key, AdmittanceRoomID, is still maintained. If a patient is moved more than once, only the original key and the current key need to be maintained. Several underlying tables have been configured for referential integrity against the patient table. These underlying tables must change in an appropriate manner to match with one or the other of the room keys in the patient table. These relationships will be altered based on different situations in other tables. What method would you use to accommodate the update?

   ❑ A. Use the Cascade Update Related Fields option to have changes in the primary key automatically update the keys in all referenced tables.

   ❑ B. Use an indexed view to enable the user to make changes to multiple tables concurrently.

   ❑ C. Disable the Enforce Relationship for INSERTs and DELETEs option to enable an AFTER TRIGGER to handle the necessary changes.

   ❑ D. Define an INSTEAD OF UPDATE TRIGGER to perform the necessary updates to all related tables.

48. A large organization needs to maintain IMAGE data on a database server. The data is scanned in from documents received from the federal government. Updates to the images are infrequent. When a change occurs, usually the old row of data is archived out of the system and the new document takes its place. Other column information that contains key identifiers about the nature of the document is frequently queried by an OLAP system. Statistical information on how the data was queried is also stored in additional columns. The actual document itself is rarely needed except in processes that print the image. Which of the following represents an appropriate storage configuration?

   - ❏ A. Place the IMAGE data into a filegroup of its own, but on the same volume as the remainder of the data. Place the log onto a volume of its own.

   - ❏ B. Place all the data onto one volume in a single file. Configure the volume as a RAID parity set, and place the log into a volume of its own.

   - ❏ C. Place the IMAGE onto one volume in a file of its own, and place the data and log files together on a second volume.

   - ❏ D. Place the IMAGE into a separate filegroup with the log on one volume and the remainder of the data on a second volume.

49. You are the administrator of a SQL Server 2000 computer. The server contains your company's Accounts database. Thousands of users access the database each day. You have been experiencing power interruptions, and you want to protect the physical integrity of the Accounts database. You do not want to slow down server operations. What should you do?

   - ❏ A. Enable the torn page detection database option for each database.

   - ❏ B. Disable write caching on all disk controllers.

   - ❏ C. Create a database maintenance plan to check database integrity and make repairs nightly.

   - ❏ D. Ensure that the write caching disk controllers have battery backups.

50. An Internet company sells outdoor hardware online to more than
    100,000 clients in various areas of the globe. Servicing the website is a
    SQL Server whose performance is barely adequate to meet the needs
    of the site. You would like to apply a business rule to the existing sys-
    tem that will limit the outstanding balance of each customer. The out-
    standing balance is maintained as a denormalized column within the
    customer table. Orders are collected in a second table containing a
    trigger that updates the customer balance based on INSERT, UPDATE, and
    DELETE activity. Up to this point, care has been taken to remove any
    data from the table if the client balance is too high, so all data should
    meet the requirements of your new process. How would you apply the
    new data check?

    ❑ A. Modify the existing trigger so that an order that allows the balance to
          exceed the limit is not permitted.

    ❑ B. Create a check constraint with the No Check option enabled on the
          customer table so that any inappropriate order is refused.

    ❑ C. Create a rule that doesn't permit an order that exceeds the limit, and
          bind the rule to the Orders table.

    ❑ D. Create a new trigger on the Orders table that refuses an order that
          causes the balance to exceed the maximum. Apply the new trigger to
          only INSERT and UPDATE operations.

Answers to
Practice Exam Two

1. C	18. A	35. A
2. A	19. D	36. C
3. A, C	20. C	37. D
4. C	21. B	38. A
5. B	22. D	39. C
6. D	23. C	40. A
7. A	24. C	41. B
8. C	25. A, D	42. D
9. C	26. C	43. D
10. A	27. B	44. B
11. A	28. C	45. C
12. C	29. C	46. B
13. B	30. D	47. D
14. B	31. A	48. D
15. C	32. D	49. D
16. C	33. D	50. A
17. D	34. B	

Remember that this is a Microsoft exam that must be answered in a Microsoft way. Here are the answers to the second practice exam. Each answer is accompanied by references to the applicable materials within SQL Server Books Online and on the Microsoft official websites.

1. **Answer: C.** The Full-Text Indexing Wizard is a graphical tool that enables full-text searches on columns by easily and quickly creating full-text indexes and full-text catalogs.

   For more information see Chapter 4, "Advanced Physical Database Implementation."

   Go to SQL Server Books Online, SQL Server Architecture, Database Architecture, Logical Database Components, SQL Indexes, Full-Text Catalog and Indexes.

   Go to http://msdn.microsoft.com/archive/default.asp?url=/archive/en-us/dnarexnt00/html/ewn0092.asp, MSDN, MSDN Library Archive, Exploring Windows NT (2000).

2. **Answer: A.** Before creating a full-text index, it is required that you close all applications and wizards running or using the MSSearch utility.

   For more information see Chapter 4, "Advanced Physical Database Implementation."

   Go to SQL Server Books Online, SQL Server Architecture, Database Architecture, Logical Database Components, SQL Indexes, Full-Text Catalog and Indexes.

   Go to http://msdn.microsoft.com/archive/default.asp?url=/archive/en-us/dnarexnt00/html/ewn0092.asp, MSDN, MSDN Library Archive, Exploring Windows NT (2000).

3. **Answer: A, C.** The question is really asking you to normalize the data. In the current design the general information within an order will be repeated for each line item in the order. To eliminate the redundant data, an OrdersDetail table could be used in a one-to-many relationship with orders. By creating a more efficient relationship structure, you will promote fast responses from queries.

   For more information see Chapter 2, "Creating a Logical Data Model."

   Go to SQL Server Books Online, Creating and Maintaining Databases, Databases, Database Design Considerations, Normalization.

Go to http://support.microsoft.com/default.aspx?scid=kb;en-us;100139, Database Normalization Basics.

4. **Answer: C.** First off, you must assume that this is not the only table in the system. The indicators present in the table for AttributeID and ApplicantID indicate at least two other related tables. This table will represent a connection to those tables. The final thing to determine is the relationship between the tables, and because each applicant could have many attributes with each attribute belonging to several applicants, you have a traditional many-to-many relationship.

For more information see Chapter 2, "Creating a Logical Data Model."

Go to SQL Server Books Online, Using the SQL Server Tools, User Interface Reference, Visual Database Tools, Database Development and Visual Database Tools, Database Objects, Table Relationships.

Go to http://support.microsoft.com/kb/234208/EN-US/, Understanding Relational Database Design.

5. **Answer: B.** Recognize that deadlock scenarios in most instances are caused by poor application design. Numerous types of design flaws can cause deadlock scenarios, including accessing of objects in an inconsistent order or setting unnecessary locks, to name a couple. To isolate the part of the application causing the problem, you will need to test the program within its production environment. Although the System Monitor will be able to provide you with information on the numbers of deadlocks, it does not provide much specific information about where they are occurring. The SQL Profiler is specifically designed to closely monitor what is going on within the DBMS and provide detailed information.

For more information see Chapter 8, "Designing for Optimized Data Access."

Go to SQL Server Books Online, Accessing and Changing Relational Data, Locking.

Go to SQL Server Books Online, Administering SQL Server, Monitoring Server Performance, Monitoring with SQL Profiler.

Go to http://msdn.microsoft.com/library/default.asp?url=/library/en-us/optimsql/odp_tun_1a_4uav.asp, MSDN Home, MSDN Library, Servers and Enterprise Development, SQL Server, SQL Server 2000, Application Design.

6. **Answer: D.** Because the table structure has recently been altered, it is a good possibility that this change has caused the indexing information to become unstable or that statistics affecting the index have not been updated. If you restart the service, SQL Server should then update the statistical information accordingly. After the restart, you may want to ensure that all statistics are intact. Restarting the service is a far more reasonable solution than rebooting the server, though potentially both would serve the same purpose. Also consider index fragmentation as a possible source of the problem.

For more information see Chapter 7, "Tuning and Optimizing Analysis."

Go to SQL Server Books Online, Creating and Maintaining Databases, Indexes, Creating an Index, Statistical Information.

Go to http://msdn.microsoft.com/library/default.asp?url=/library/en-us/dnpag/html/scalenethowto03.asp, MSDN Home, MSDN Library, .NET Development, Improving .NET Application Performance and Scalability, How Tos, Optimizing SQL Indexes.

7. **Answer: A.** Answer B is wrong because this would be more time-consuming than DBCC DBREINDEX. You would have to individually rebuild all indexes. Answer C is not correct because deleting a clustered index and then re-creating it means deleting and re-creating all nonclustered indexes. Also, the process would have to involve two separate steps.

For more information see Chapter 7, "Tuning and Optimizing Analysis."

Go to SQL Server Books Online, Transact SQL Reference, DBCC.

Go to http://msdn.microsoft.com/library/default.asp?url=/library/en-us/dnpag/html/scalenetchapt14.asp, MSDN Home, MSDN Library, .NET Development, Improving .NET Application Performance and Scalability, Improving SQL Server Performance.

8. **Answer: C.** A single table could provide all the necessary information with no redundancy. The table could easily be represented using a self-join operation to provide the desired reporting.

For more information see Chapter 2, "Creating a Logical Data Model."

Go to SQL Server Books Online, English Query, English Query Fundamentals, SQL Database Normalization Rules.

Go to http://msdn.microsoft.com/library/default.asp?url=/library/en-us/createdb/cm_8_des_02_2oby.asp, MSDN Home, MSDN Library, Servers and Enterprise Development, SQL Server, SQL Server 2000, Databases, Database Design Considerations.

9. **Answer: C.** To enable full-text searching, you must create a catalog for a table and then populate manually or schedule a job. Answer A is incorrect because creating a non-unique index does not help in any way. B is incorrect because creating a unique clustered index does not enable full-text searching. D is incorrect because there is no such procedure as `sp_fulltext_populate` (but there is a stored procedure named `sp_fulltext_catalog`).

For more information see Chapter 4, "Advanced Physical Database Implementation."

Go to SQL Server Books Online, SQL Server Architecture, Database Architecture, Logical Database Components, SQL Indexes, Full-Text Catalogs and Indexes.

Go to http://msdn.microsoft.com/library/default.asp?url=/library/en-us/architec/8_ar_sa2_0ehx.asp, MSDN Home, MSDN Library, Servers and Enterprise Development, SQL Server, SQL Server 2000, Relational Database Engine Architecture, Full-Text Query Architecture.

10. **Answer: A.** To obtain the physical storage sequence of the data, you must use a clustered constraint or index. Although a primary key would also provide for the level of uniqueness, it is not the desired key for this table.

For more information see Chapter 2, "Creating a Logical Data Model," and Chapter 3, "Implementing the Physical Database."

Go to SQL Server Books Online, SQL Server Architecture, Database Architecture, Logical Database Components, SQL Indexes, Table Indexes.

Go to http://msdn.microsoft.com/library/default.asp?url=/library/en-us/architec/8_ar_da_5b1v.asp, MSDN Home, MSDN Library, Servers and Enterprise Development, SQL Server, SQL Server 2000, Database Architecture, Logical Database Components, SQL Indexes, Table Indexes.

11. **Answer: A.** Indexes used in larger quantities often degrade the rate at which insertions, deletions, and some modifications to data occur. Nevertheless, indexes generally speed up data access in cases in which the data in the table is sufficient to warrant indexing.

For more information see Chapter 3, "Implementing the Physical Database," and Chapter 7, "Tuning and Optimizing Analysis."

Go to SQL Server Books Online, Optimizing Database Performance, Database Design, Physical Database Design, Index Tuning Recommendations.

Go to http://msdn.microsoft.com/library/default.asp?url=/library/en-us/dnpag/html/scalenethowto03.asp, MSDN Home, MSDN Library, .NET Development, Improving .NET Application Performance and Scalability, How Tos, Optimizing SQL Indexes.

12. **Answer: C.** This is a perfect situation for sending a recordset to the client machine that can then be used by the front-end application to show only the data needed. XML provides a mechanism by which the data is shipped to the client, resides in the background of the client machine, and is present by the front end in any manner desired. SCHEMABINDING refers only to SQL Server objects—specifically tables, views, and user-defined functions. An XML schema cannot be bound in this manner. XML resides in memory and is processed against its own internal set of rules, referred to as a schema. An XML schema interacts directly with the data to supply logic and display attributes on the user's browser. HTML does not have the required functionality.

For more information see Chapter 3, "Implementing the Physical Database," and Chapter 5, "Retrieving and Modifying Data."

Go to SQL Server Books Online, XML and Internet Support, XML and Internet Support Overview.

Go to http://msdn.microsoft.com/library/default.asp?url=/library/en-us/dnexxml/html/xml07162001.asp, MSDN Home, MSDN Library, .NET Development, A Survey of Microsoft SQL Server 2000 XML Features.

13. **Answer: B.** For index analysis, the Index Tuning Wizard will help determine whether indexing is sufficient for the queries used within a workload file. The workload file should be created using the queries that are going to make up the reporting. A profiler trace would not provide the complete analysis of the indexes requested. The Query Analyzer is more for fine-tuning queries, as opposed to the table and index structures. The System Monitor is used more for an overview of the application server, the operating system, and the interactions with the server hardware.

For more information see Chapter 3, "Implementing the Physical Database," and Chapter 5, "Retrieving and Modifying Data."

Go to SQL Server Books Online, Using the SQL Server Tools.

Go to http://msdn.microsoft.com/library/default.asp?url=/library/en-us/dnpag/html/scalenetchapt14.asp, MSDN Home, MSDN Library, .NET Development, Improving .NET Application Performance and Scalability, Improving SQL Server Performance.

14. **Answer: B.** You want to set the priority to LOW for the less important transaction. This will cause the transaction to be the victim of choice should a deadlock scenario occur. It is a simple matter of having this setting whenever deadlocks are possible and the transaction is not a critical part of the process. Error checking is not a suitable solution to this particular problem. In a sound application there will be error checking of some type, but in this instance the priority setting will take care of the situation.

For more information see Chapter 6, "Programming Business Logic."

Go to SQL Server Books Online, Accessing and Changing Relational Data, Transactions, Controlling Transactions.

Go to http://msdn.microsoft.com/library/default.asp?url=/library/en-us/acdata/ac_8_con_7a_3hdf.asp, MSDN Home, MSDN Library, Servers and Enterprise Development, SQL Server, SQL Server 2000, Locking, Customizing Locking with SQL Server, Deadlocking, Minimizing Deadlocks.

15. **Answer: C.** The default location for the snapshot information is in the Distributor in the Mssql\Repldata folder. Using the publication properties, this location can be altered to a newly desired position. Be sure to enable FTP access to this new location if FTP is being used to transfer the snapshots.

For more information see Chapter 4, "Advanced Physical Database Implementation."

Go to SQL Server Books Online, Replication, Implementing Replication, Applying the Initial Snapshot.

Go to http://msdn.microsoft.com/library/default.asp?url=/library/en-us/replsql/replplan_271q.asp, MSDN Home, MSDN Library, Servers and Enterprise Development, SQL Server, SQL Server 2000, Planning for Replication, Planning for Each Type of Replication, Planning Snapshot Replication.

16. **Answer: C.** The GO delimiter separates one batch from another. The error in the batch prevented the entire batch from running, so to make the UPDATE statement run, put it into a different batch.

    For more information see Chapter 6, "Programming Business Logic."

    Go to SQL Server Books Online, Transact-SQL Reference, GO.

    Go to SQL Server Books Online, Accessing and Changing Relational Data, Accessing and Changing Data Fundamentals, Using Multiple Statements, Batches.

    Go to http://msdn.microsoft.com/library/default.asp?url=/library/en-us/acdata/ac_8_con_04_9elv.asp, MSDN Home, MSDN Library, Servers and Enterprise Development, SQL Server, SQL Server 2000, Accessing and Changing Data Fundamentals, Using Multiple Statements, Batches.

17. **Answer: D.** An error will occur because the variable @var does not exist when the second batch of the script runs. A variable exists only within the batch that it was created in. This script contains two batches separated by the GO statement. Because the variable was declared in the first batch, it falls out of scope upon execution of the GO operation and thus does not exist when attempted to be used within the second batch.

    For more information see Chapter 6, "Programming Business Logic."

    Go to SQL Server Books Online, Transact-SQL Reference, GO.

    Go to SQL Server Books Online, Accessing and Changing Relational Data, Accessing and Changing Data Fundamentals, Using Multiple Statements, Batches.

    Go to http://msdn.microsoft.com/library/default.asp?url=/library/en-us/acdata/ac_8_con_04_9elv.asp, MSDN Home, MSDN Library, Servers and Enterprise Development, SQL Server, SQL Server 2000, Accessing and Changing Data Fundamentals, Using Multiple Statements, Batches.

18. **Answer: A.** Batch A works correctly and prints the multiples of 5 from 5 to 50. Batch B prints the multiples of 5 from 5 to 45, so it prints only nine of them. Batch C is an infinite loop because it doesn't increment its loop counter, and Batch D has a GO in the middle of it, so the variables aren't defined when they're being used.

    For more information see Chapter 6, "Programming Business Logic."

    Go to SQL Server Books Online, Transact-SQL Reference, GO.

Go to SQL Server Books Online, Transact-SQL Reference, WHILE.

Go to http://msdn.microsoft.com/library/default.asp?url=/library/en-us/acdata/ac_8_con_04_9elv.asp, MSDN Home, MSDN Library, Servers and Enterprise Development, SQL Server, SQL Server 2000, Accessing and Changing Data Fundamentals, Using Multiple Statements, Batches.

19. **Answer: D.** The FETCH statement is used to retrieve data from a cursor. To start the process, you would normally use a FETCH FIRST before entering a loop. At the tail end of the loop, you would implement a FETCH NEXT. DECLARE and OPEN are used to initialize the cursor but do not retrieve any data. RETRIEVE isn't a T-SQL command.

For more information see Chapter 6, "Programming Business Logic."

Go to SQL Server Books Online, Transact-SQL Reference, FETCH.

Go to SQL Server Books Online, Accessing and Changing Relational Data, Cursors, Fetching and Scrolling.

Go to http://msdn.microsoft.com/library/default.asp?url=/library/en-us/acdata/ac_8_con_07_9bzn.asp, MSDN Home, MSDN Library, Servers and Enterprise Development, SQL Server, SQL Server 2000, Cursors, Cursor Implementations, Accessing and Changing Relational Data.

20. **Answer: C.** A deadlock is probably the best explanation. With that high a transaction isolation level, you're going to have lock contention in any busy database. You should likely reexamine the isolation level being used and consider eliminating this part of both batches. Data corruption would not occur from the result of the batches because dirty reads are not occurring at this isolation level. Although the isolation level is questionable, it is not invalid.

For more information see Chapter 6, "Programming Business Logic," and Chapter 7, "Tuning and Optimizing Analysis."

Go to SQL Server Books Online, Accessing and Changing Relational Data, Locking, Isolation Levels.

Go to http://msdn.microsoft.com/library/default.asp?url=/library/en-us/odbc/htm/odbctransaction_isolation_levels.asp, MSDN Home, MSDN Library, Data Access, Microsoft Open Database Connectivity (ODBC), ODBC Programmer's Reference, Developing Applications and Drivers, Transactions, Transaction Isolation.

21. Answer: B. The value of the `@@TRANCOUNT` variable increases by one when a `BEGIN TRANSACTION` statement is encountered, and it decreases to `0` when the `ROLLBACK` happens. The last transaction statement run was a `ROLLBACK`, which leaves `@@TRANCOUNT` set to `0`.

For more information see Chapter 6, "Programming Business Logic."

Go to SQL Server Books Online, Transact-SQL Reference, `BEGIN TRANSACTION`.

Go to SQL Server Books Online, Building SQL Server Applications, Meta Data Services Programming, Programming Information Models, Managing Transactions and Threads, Transaction Management Overview.

Go to http://msdn.microsoft.com/library/default,asp?url=/library/en-us/acdata/ac_8_md_06_66nq.asp, MSDN Home, MSDN Library, Servers and Enterprise Development, SQL Server, SQL Server 2000, Transactions, Advanced Topics.

22. Answer: D. To some extent, all the answers work. The only differences between the first three are minor tweaks to the cursor operation. The best answer, though, is to not use a cursor, which is usually the right answer anyway. When an operation can be performed without a cursor, there is far less overhead and performance will improve.

For more information see Chapter 6, "Programming Business Logic."

Go to SQL Server Books Online, Accessing and Changing Relational Data, Cursors.

Go to http://msdn.microsoft.com/library/default.asp?url=/library/en-us/optimsql/odp_tun_1a_71nw.asp, MSDN Home, MSDN Library, Servers and Enterprise Development, SQL Server, SQL Server 2000, Application Design.

23. Answer: C. It will print the value of `@Foo`. Rollbacks do not change how print statements work. A print happens immediately. Also, it's not an error to have an empty transaction or a transaction that just doesn't do any database updates. It's unwise, but not an error.

For more information see Chapter 6, "Programming Business Logic."

Go to SQL Server Books Online, Transact-SQL Reference, Print.

Go to SQL Server Books Online, Transact-SQL Reference, `ROLLBACK TRANSACTION`.

Go to http://msdn.microsoft.com/library/default.asp?url=/library/en-us/acdata/ac_8_md_06_2it2.asp, MSDN Home, MSDN Library, Servers and Enterprise Development, SQL Server, SQL Server 2000, Transactions, Controlling Transactions.

24. **Answer: C.** The correct order for the events are INSTEAD OF triggers, constraints, AFTER triggers. Constraints will not prevent the execution of code for INSTEAD OF triggers but will prevent the code for an AFTER trigger from executing when the data does not conform to the restrictions of the constraint.

    For more information see Chapter 4, "Advanced Physical Database Implementation."

    Go to SQL Server Books Online, Transact-SQL Reference, SQL Server Architecture, Database Architecture, Logical Database Components, Constraints Rules Defaults and Triggers.

    Go to SQL Server Books Online, Creating and Maintaining Databases, Enforcing Business Rules with Triggers.

    Go to http://msdn.microsoft.com/library/default.asp?url=/library/en-us/createdb/cm_8_des_08_37zi.asp, MSDN Home, MSDN Library, Servers and Enterprise Development, SQL Server, SQL Server 2000, Enforcing Business Rules with Triggers, Designing Triggers, Trigger Execution.

25. **Answer: A, D.** CREATE TABLE, DROP TABLE, ALTER TABLE, GRANT, REVOKE, DISK, ALTER DATABASE, LOAD DATABASE, RESTORE DATABASE, UPDATE STATISTICS, SELECT INTO, LOAD TRANSACTION, and RECONFIGURE are all commands that cannot be used within a trigger.

    For more information see Chapter 4, "Advanced Physical Database Implementation."

    Go to SQL Server Books Online, Creating and Maintaining Databases, Enforcing Business Rules with Triggers.

    Go to http://msdn.microsoft.com/library/default.asp?url=/library/en-us/createdb/cm_8_des_08_4xmb.asp, MSDN Home, MSDN Library, Servers and Enterprise Development, SQL Server, SQL Server 2000, Enforcing Business Rules with Triggers, Creating a Trigger.

26. **Answer: C.** An INSERT trigger is the best choice because data is validated as it is inserted. Second, there are no such things as direct and indirect recursion triggers; recursion is something the triggers might do.

For more information see Chapter 4, "Advanced Physical Database Implementation."

Go to SQL Server Books Online, Creating and Maintaining Databases, Enforcing Business Rules with Triggers.

Go to http://msdn.microsoft.com/library/default.asp?url=/library/en-us/createdb/cm_8_des_08_4xmb.asp, MSDN Home, MSDN Library, Servers and Enterprise Development, SQL Server, SQL Server 2000, Enforcing Business Rules with Triggers, Creating a Trigger.

27. **Answer: B.** More than one trigger may be placed on a table; however, only one INSTEAD OF trigger, per trigger action, may be placed on a table.

For more information see Chapter 4, "Advanced Physical Database Implementation."

Go to SQL Server Books Online, Creating and Maintaining Databases, Enforcing Business Rules with Triggers.

Go to http://msdn.microsoft.com/library/default.asp?url=/library/en-us/createdb/cm_8_des_08_4xmb.asp, MSDN Home, MSDN Library, Servers and Enterprise Development, SQL Server, SQL Server 2000, Enforcing Business Rules with Triggers, Creating a Trigger.

28. **Answer: C.** The CREATE TRIGGER statement is used to create a trigger, and the ALTER TRIGGER statement is used to later modify the trigger. Although many objects can be created within the context of a CREATE TABLE statement, triggers are not one of them.

For more information see Chapter 4, "Advanced Physical Database Implementation."

Go to SQL Server Books Online, Creating and Maintaining Databases, Enforcing Business Rules with Triggers.

Go to http://msdn.microsoft.com/library/default.asp?url=/library/en-us/createdb/cm_8_des_08_4xmb.asp, MSDN Home, MSDN Library, Servers and Enterprise Development, SQL Server, SQL Server 2000, Enforcing Business Rules with Triggers, Creating a Trigger.

29. **Answer: C.** Dropping a trigger could have ramifications elsewhere in the environment. Before dropping any object you should also find out what other objects may be effected. You should check for dependent objects when renaming or deleting a trigger. You can also use the Enterprise Manager to visually check object dependencies.

For more information see Chapter 6, "Programming Business Logic."

Go to SQL Server Books Online, Creating and Maintaining Databases, Enforcing Business Rules with Triggers, Deleting a Trigger.

Go to SQL Server Books Online, Transact-SQL Reference, System Stored Procedures, sp_depends.

Go to SQL Server Books Online, Transact-SQL Reference, System Stored Procedures, DROP TRIGGER.

Go to http://msdn.microsoft.com/library/default.asp?url=/library/en-us/tsqlref/ts_de-dz_8wj6.asp, MSDN Home, MSDN Library, Servers and Enterprise Development, SQL Server, SQL Server 2000, DROP TRIGGER.

30. **Answer: D.** INSTEAD OF triggers can be used to make non-updatable views capable of supporting updates. The process would not affect the views themselves and would allow for updates to be performed through the code within the trigger.

For more information see Chapter 6, "Programming Business Logic."

Go to SQL Server Books Online, Creating and Maintaining Databases, Enforcing Business Rules with Triggers, Designing Triggers, Designing INSTEAD OF Triggers.

Go to http://msdn.microsoft.com/library/default.asp?url=/library/en-us/vdbt7/html/dvconusinginsteadoftriggersonviews.asp, MSDN Home, MSDN Library, Development Tools and Languages, Visual Studio .NET, Developing with Visual Studio .NET, Designing Distributed Applications, Visual Database Tools, Developing Database Structure, Working with Triggers, Using INSTEAD OF Triggers on Views.

31. **Answer: A.** The sp_helptext stored procedure can be used to read the trigger definition. sp_helptrigger is used to find the type or types of triggers defined for a database. sp_displaydef is not a valid system stored procedure. sp_help provides name and type information about various database objects. If a procedure is encrypted, you can not use sp_helptext to obtain the trigger definition.

For more information see Chapter 6, "Programming Business Logic."

Go to SQL Server Books Online, Transact-SQL Reference, System Stored Procedures.

Go to http://msdn.microsoft.com/library/default.asp?url=/library/en-us/tsqlref/ts_sp_help_7c38.asp, MSDN Home, MSDN Library, Servers and Enterprise Development, SQL Server, SQL Server 2000, System Stored Procedures.

32. **Answer: D.** A scalar user-defined function will return a single value. Option A needs to return a list, not a single value; option B would change data, which is not allowed within the context of a scalar UDF; option C is already implemented through a system-defined function. Option D needs to return only a single number, the value of the bill, so it's the best answer.

For more information see Chapter 6, "Programming Business Logic."

Go to SQL Server Books Online, SQL Server Architecture, Database Architecture, Logical Database Components, SQL User-Defined Functions.

Go to http://msdn.microsoft.com/library/default.asp?url=/library/en-us/acdata/ac_8_con_11_5spx.asp, MSDN Home, MSDN Library, Servers and Enterprise Development, SQL Server, SQL Server 2000, Transact-SQL Syntax Elements, Using Functions, Invoking User-Defined Functions, Invoking User-Defined Functions That Return Scalar Values.

33. **Answer: D.** Options A, B, and C are all possible using a view. Option A is not possible with a user-defined function. Option D is not possible with a view; a view has a static filter on the output with no recordset.

For more information see Chapter 6, "Programming Business Logic."

Go to SQL Server Books Online, SQL Server Architecture, Database Architecture, Logical Database Components, SQL User-Defined Functions.

Go to http://msdn.microsoft.com/library/default.asp?url=/library/en-us/createdb/cm_8_des_08_73lf.asp, MSDN Home, MSDN Library, Servers and Enterprise Development, SQL Server, SQL Server 2000, User-Defined Functions, Inline User-Defined Functions.

34. **Answer: B.** Because you are using a parameter that drastically affects the output, you want to avoid using the cached plan. Option A doesn't allow enough flexibility in the resultset; option C is simply a developer's preference for the creation of the procedure and would make no difference to the end result. Option D would make minimal difference and adds unnecessary complexity to the process.

For more information see Chapter 6, "Programming Business Logic."

Go to SQL Server Books Online, Creating and Maintaining Databases, Stored Procedures, Creating a Stored Procedure.

Go to http://msdn.microsoft.com/library/default.asp?url=/library/en-us/createdb/cm_8_des_07_6cmd.asp, MSDN Home, MSDN Library, Servers and Enterprise Development, SQL Server, SQL Server 2000, Stored Procedures, Recompiling a Stored Procedure.

35. **Answer: A.** User-defined functions cannot send email; sending email is a side effect, and user-defined functions are not allowed to have side effects. Depending on how the system process is desired, the functionality can be provided with a trigger, an alert, or a stored procedure. Often the three objects work together to provide this type of capability.

For more information see Chapter 6, "Programming Business Logic."

Go to SQL Server Books Online, SQL Server Architecture, Relational Database Engine Architecture, SQL Server and e-mail Integration.

Go to http://msdn.microsoft.com/library/default.asp?url=/library/en-us/adminsql/ad_1_server_8xf0.asp, MSDN Home, MSDN Library, Servers and Enterprise Development, SQL Server, SQL Server 2000, Managing Servers, SQL Mail.

36. **Answer: C.** This is a very common typographical error to make. return will cause a stored procedure to immediately exit, and statements following the return will not be executed. returns, however, specifies the type of value returned by a function. Such errors are spotted more easily as you do more development. It is common on Microsoft development exams to be faced with questions that will involve analyzing these types of errors.

For more information see Chapter 6, "Programming Business Logic."

Go to SQL Server Books Online, Transact-SQL Reference, RETURN.

Go to SQL Server Books Online, Transact-SQL Reference, CREATE FUNCTION.

Go to SQL Server Books Online, Accessing and Changing Relational Data, Accessing and Changing Data Fundamentals, Using Multiple Statements, Control of Flow, Using RETURN.

Go to http://msdn.microsoft.com/library/default.asp?url=/library/en-us/createdb/cm_8_des_08_361x.asp, MSDN Home, MSDN Library, Servers and Enterprise Development, SQL Server, SQL Server 2000, User-Defined Functions.

Go to http://msdn.microsoft.com/library/default.asp?url=/library/en-us/adosql/adoprg02_525v.asp, MSDN Home, MSDN Library, Servers and Enterprise Development, SQL Server, SQL Server 2000, Building

SQL Server Applications, Programming ADO SQL Server Applications, Executing Queries, Executing Stored Procedures, Using Return Code and Output Parameters for Stored Procedures.

37. **Answer: D.** Option A will run without an error, and won't return the result. Option B will run without an error, and capture the return code into the @SalesTax variable, which can't handle the floating-point number that is the @SalesTax. Option C won't work because the first parameter is specified by name, but the rest are specified by position, which is a syntax error.

For more information see Chapter 6, "Programming Business Logic."

Go to SQL Server Books Online, Accessing and Changing Relational Data, Accessing and Changing Data Fundamentals, Using Multiple Statements, Using Variables and Parameters.

Go to http://msdn.microsoft.com/library/default.asp?url=/library/en-us/acdata/ac_8_con_04_6e5v.asp, MSDN Home, MSDN Library, Servers and Enterprise Development, SQL Server, SQL Server 2000, Accessing and Changing Data Fundamentals, Using Multiple Statements, Using Variables and Parameters.

38. **Answer: A.** Using an IF statement with @@ERROR sends the email. Option B won't send an email and will probably result in a particularly nasty infinite loop; option C won't work because it doesn't send the email on failure, and option D won't work because @@LAST_ERROR isn't a valid system function.

For more information see Chapter 6, "Programming Business Logic."

Go to SQL Server Books Online, Accessing and Changing Relational Data, Advanced Query Concepts, Error Handling, Using @@ERROR.

Go to http://msdn.microsoft.com/library/default.asp?url=/library/en-us/dnsqlpro2k/html/sql00f15.asp, MSDN Home, MSDN Library, Servers and Enterprise Development, SQL Server, Error Handling in T-SQL: From Casual to Religious.

39. **Answer: C.** INSERT statements are not allowed within functions because they have the side effect of changing data in a table somewhere. Formatting is not relevant to how well the function operates; the keyword AS is optional in a CREATE FUNCTION statement (but required in a CREATE PROCEDURE); and the function is scalar, not table valued, but that doesn't even matter.

For more information see Chapter 6, "Programming Business Logic."

Go to SQL Server Books Online, SQL Server Architecture, Database Architecture, Logical Database Components, SQL User-Defined Functions.

Go to http://msdn.microsoft.com/library/default.asp?url=/library/en-us/architec/8_ar_da_50mr.asp, MSDN Home, MSDN Library, Servers and Enterprise Development, SQL Server, SQL Server 2000, Database Architecture, Logical Database Components, SQL User-Defined Functions.

40. **Answer: A.** If a temporary table is created inside a stored procedure, it is dropped when the stored procedure terminates, so this won't work to get tabular data outside the stored procedure.

For more information see Chapter 6, "Programming Business Logic."

Go to SQL Server Books Online, Transact-SQL Reference, CREATE TABLE.

Go to SQL Server Books Online, Creating and Maintaining Databases, Tables, Creating and Modifying a Table.

Go to http://msdn.microsoft.com/library/default.asp?url=/library/en-us/createdb/cm_8_des_04_8jtx.asp, MSDN Home, MSDN Library, Servers and Enterprise Development, SQL Server, SQL Server 2000, Tables, Creating and Modifying a Table.

41. **Answer: B.** Option A is a type mismatch because trying to put the value 4.3 into an integer doesn't work. Option C has a positional parameter after a named parameter, which won't work, and option D has something as OUTPUT which isn't declared that way.

For more information see Chapter 6, "Programming Business Logic."

Go to SQL Server Books Online, Transact-SQL Reference, CREATE PROCEDURE.

Go to SQL Server Books Online, SQL Server Architecture, Database Architecture, Logical Database Components, SQL Stored Procedures.

Go to http://msdn.microsoft.com/library/default.asp?url=/library/en-us/architec/8_ar_da_0nxv.asp, MSDN Home, MSDN Library, Servers and Enterprise Development, SQL Server, SQL Server 2000, Database Architecture, Logical Database Components, SQL Stored Procedures.

42. **Answer: D.** Option A is nonsense. Option B won't work because functions can't actually record anything. Option C won't work because cursors aren't used to validate data.

For more information see Chapter 6, "Programming Business Logic."

Go to SQL Server Books Online, SQL Server Architecture, Database Architecture, Logical Database Components, SQL Stored Procedures.

Go to http://msdn.microsoft.com/library/default.asp?url=/library/en-us/architec/8_ar_da_0nxv.asp, MSDN Home, MSDN Library, Servers and Enterprise Development, SQL Server, SQL Server 2000, Database Architecture, Logical Database Components, SQL Stored Procedures.

43. Answer: D. Option A is an incorrect `declare` statement; option B would be valid for an output parameter, but not a return value; and option C just ignores the whole return-value issue altogether.

For more information see Chapter 6, "Programming Business Logic."

Go to SQL Server Books Online, SQL Server Architecture, Database Architecture, Logical Database Components, SQL Stored Procedures.

Go to http://msdn.microsoft.com/library/default.asp?url=/library/en-us/architec/8_ar_da_0nxv.asp, MSDN Home, MSDN Library, Servers and Enterprise Development, SQL Server, SQL Server 2000, Database Architecture, Logical Database Components, SQL Stored Procedures.

44. Answer: B. Option A is missing a lot of parentheses; option C is wrong because there isn't a `CREATE INLINE FUNCTION` statement; and option D is a multiline table-valued function, not an inline.

For more information see Chapter 6, "Programming Business Logic."

Go to SQL Server Books Online, Creating and Maintaining Databases, User-Defined Functions, Inline User Defined Functions.

Go to http://msdn.microsoft.com/library/default.asp?url=/library/en-us/createdb/cm_8_des_08_73lf.asp, MSDN Home, MSDN Library, Servers and Enterprise Development, SQL Server, SQL Server 2000, User-Defined Functions, Inline User-Defined Functions.

45. Answer: C. Options A and B have the same problem: If the constraints on the tables change, the user-defined function or the stored procedure will need to be rewritten. Option D would be nice; but the constraints are probably there for a reason, and removing them just so that an `INSERT` can put suspect data into a table is not the correct approach.

For more information see Chapter 6, "Programming Business Logic."

Go to SQL Server Books Online, Accessing and Changing Relational Data, Advanced Query Concepts, Error Handling, Using `@@ERROR`.

Go to http://msdn.microsoft.com/library/default.asp?url=/library/en-us/acdata/ac_8_con_05_8oc2.asp, MSDN Home, MSDN Library, Servers and Enterprise Development, SQL Server, SQL Server 2000, Advanced Query Concepts, Error Handling.

46. **Answer: B.** This is a perfect example of how partitioning a table into two smaller objects enables you to use two machines to help reduce the load on the overall application. Remember that failover clustering is the only form of clustering supported by SQL and therefore does not actually reduce the load; it only assists in obtaining an around-the-clock operation. Log shipping assists in offloading query load, but does little to reduce update load because it leaves the second server in a read-only state. Merge replication may enable updates to span many servers, but the associated overhead and data latency makes it a less-than-desirable alternative.

For more information see Chapter 4, "Advanced Physical Database Implementation."

Go to SQL Server Books Online, Creating and Maintaining Databases, Views, Creating a View, Creating a Partitioned View.

Go to http://msdn.microsoft.com/library/default.asp?url=/library/en-us/acdata/ac_8_qd_10_2z4x.asp, MSDN Home, MSDN Library, Servers and Enterprise Development, SQL Server, SQL Server 2000, Advanced Query Concepts, Using Partitioned Views.

47. **Answer: D.** The INSTEAD OF trigger was designed specifically for this type of situation and also to handle complicated updates where columns are defined as Timestamp, Calculated, or Identity. Cascade operations are inappropriate because the updated key is not always stored. Indexed views by themselves do not allow for the type of alteration desired and would have to be complemented with the actions of a trigger. Disabling referential integrity is a poor solution to any problem, especially considering the medical nature of this application and the possible ramifications.

For more information see Chapter 6, "Programming Business Logic."

Go to SQL Server Books Online, Creating and Maintaining Databases, Enforcing Business Rules with Triggers, Creating a Trigger, Using INSTEAD OF Triggers.

Go to http://msdn.microsoft.com/library/default.asp?url=/library/en-us/dnsqlmag2k/html/INSTEADOF.asp, MSDN Home, MSDN Library, Servers and Enterprise Development, SQL Server, INSTEAD OF Triggers.

48. **Answer: D.** Because the IMAGE data will seldom be accessed, it makes sense to get the remainder of the data away from the images while moving the log away from the data. This will help to improve performance while providing optimum recoverability in the event of a failure.

    For more information see Chapter 3, "Implementing the Physical Database."

    Go to SQL Server Books Online, Optimizing Database Performance, Database Design, Physical Database Design, Data Placement Using Filegroups.

    Go to http://msdn.microsoft.com/library/default.asp?url=/library/en-us/optimsql/odp_tun_1_4cj7.asp, MSDN Home, MSDN Library, Servers and Enterprise Development, SQL Server, SQL Server 2000, Database Design, Physical Database Design, Data Placement Using Filegroups, Placing Tables on Filegroups.

49. **Answer: D.** Good controllers suitable for database use will have a battery backup. The battery should be regularly tested under controlled circumstances. Disabling caching, if currently in place, is likely to affect performance, as will enabling torn page detection. Torn page detection might help point out whether data is being corrupted because of failures. A maintenance plan is recommended, although it is not an entire solution in its own right.

    For more information see Chapter 3, "Implementing the Physical Database."

    Go to SQL Server Books Online, Creating and Maintaining Databases, Databases, Modifying a Database, Setting Database Options.

    Go to http://msdn.microsoft.com/library/default.asp?url=/library/en-us/dnsql7/html/msdn_sql7perftune.asp, MSDN Home, MSDN Library, Servers and Enterprise Development, SQL Server.

50. **Answer: A.** Because a trigger is already in place, it can easily be altered to perform the additional data check. A rule cannot provide the required functionality because you cannot compare the data. The CHECK constraint may be a viable solution, but you would have to alter the trigger to check for an error and provide for nested operations. The number of triggers firing should be kept to a minimum. To accommodate additional triggers, you would have to check the order in which they are being fired and again set properties of the server and database accordingly.

For more information see Chapter 3, "Implementing the Physical Database," and Chapter 6, "Programming Business Logic."

Go to SQL Server Books Online, Creating and Maintaining Databases, Enforcing Business Rules with Triggers.

Go to http://msdn.microsoft.com/library/default.asp?url=/library/en-us/createdb/cm_8_des_08_116g.asp, MSDN Home, MSDN Library, Servers and Enterprise Development, SQL Server, SQL Server 2000, Enforcing Business Rules with Triggers.

What's on the CD-ROM?

The CD features an innovative practice test engine powered by MeasureUp™, giving you yet another effective tool to assess your readiness for the exam.

Multiple Test Modes

MeasureUp practice tests are available in Study, Certification, Custom, Missed Question, and Non-Duplicate question modes.

Study Mode

Tests administered in Study Mode allow you to request the correct answer(s) and explanation to each question during the test. These tests are not timed. You can modify the testing environment *during* the test by clicking the Options button.

Certification Mode

Tests administered in Certification Mode closely simulate the actual testing environment you will encounter when taking a certification exam. These tests do not allow you to request the answer(s) and/or explanation to each question until after the exam.

Custom Mode

Custom Mode allows you to specify your preferred testing environment. Use this mode to specify the objectives you want to include in your test, the timer length, and other test properties. You can also modify the testing environment *during* the test by selecting the Options button.

Missed Question Mode

Missed Question Mode allows you to take a test containing only the questions you missed previously.

Non-Duplicate Mode

Non-Duplicate Mode allows you to take a test containing only questions not displayed previously.

Question Types

The practice question types simulate the real exam experience. For a complete description of each question type, visit http://www.microsoft.com/learning/mcpexams/faq/innovations.asp.

The following list represents some of the common question types you can expect to see on the exam:

➤ Create a Tree Type

➤ Select and Place

➤ Drop and Connect

➤ Build List

➤ Reorder List

➤ Build and Reorder List

➤ Single Hotspot

➤ Multiple Hotspots

➤ Live Screen

➤ Command-Line

➤ Hot Area

Random Questions and Order of Answers

This feature helps you learn the material without memorizing questions and answers. Each time you take a practice test, the questions and answers appear in a different randomized order.

Detailed Explanations of Correct and Incorrect Answers

You'll receive automatic feedback on all correct and incorrect answers. The detailed answer explanations are a superb learning tool in their own right.

Attention to Exam Objectives

MeasureUp practice tests are designed to appropriately balance the questions over each technical area covered by a specific exam.

Installing the CD

These are the minimum system requirements for the CD-ROM:

➤ Windows 95, 98, ME, NT4, 2000, or XP

➤ 7MB disk space for testing engine

➤ An average of 1MB disk space for each test

To install the CD-ROM, follow these instructions:

NOTE   If you need technical support, you can contact MeasureUp by calling 678-356-5050 or emailing support@measureup.com. Additionally, you'll find Frequently Asked Questions (FAQs) at www.measureup.com.

1. Close all applications before beginning this installation.

2. Insert the CD into your CD-ROM drive. If the setup starts automatically, go to step 6. If the setup does not start automatically, continue with step 3.

3. From the Start menu, select Run.

4. Click Browse to locate the MeasureUp CD. In the Browse dialog box, from the Look In drop-down list, select the CD-ROM drive.

5. In the Browse dialog box, double-click on setup.exe. In the Run dialog box, click OK to begin the installation.

6. On the welcome screen, click MeasureUp Practice Questions to begin installation.

7. Follow the Certification Prep Wizard by clicking Next.

8. To agree to the Software License Agreement, click Yes.

9. On the Choose Destination Location screen, click Next to install the software to `C:\Program Files\Certification Preparation`.

 If you cannot locate MeasureUp Practice Tests through the Start menu, see the section "Creating a Shortcut to the MeasureUp Practice Tests" later in this appendix.

10. On the Setup Type screen, select Typical Setup. Click Next to continue.

11. In the Select Program Folder screen you can name the program folder your tests will be in. To select the default, simply click Next and the installation will continue.

12. After the installation is complete, verify that Yes, I Want to Restart My Computer Now is selected. If you select No, I Will Restart My Computer Later, you will not be able to use the program until you restart your computer.

13. Click Finish.

14. After restarting your computer, choose Start, Programs, MeasureUp, MeasureUp Practice Tests.

15. On the MeasureUp Welcome Screen, click Create User Profile.

16. In the User Profile dialog box, complete the mandatory fields and click Create Profile.

17. Select the practice test you want to access, and click Start Test.

Creating a Shortcut to the MeasureUp Practice Tests

To create a shortcut to the MeasureUp Practice Tests, follow these steps:

1. Right-click on your desktop.

2. From the shortcut menu select New, Shortcut.

3. Browse to `C:\Program Files\MeasureUp Practice Tests` and select the `MeasureUpCertification.exe` or `Localware.exe` file.

4. Click OK.

5. Click Next.

6. Rename the shortcut MeasureUp.

7. Click Finish.

After you have completed step 7, use the MeasureUp shortcut on your desktop to access the MeasureUp products you ordered.

Technical Support

If you encounter problems with the MeasureUp test engine on the CD-ROM, you can contact MeasureUp by calling 678-356-5050 or emailing support@measureup.com. Technical support hours are from 8 a.m. to 5 p.m. EST Monday through Friday. Additionally, you'll find Frequently Asked Questions (FAQs) at www.measureup.com.

If you'd like to purchase additional MeasureUp products, phone 678-356-5050 or 800-649-1MUP (1687) or visit www.measureup.com.

Need to Know More?

Chapter 1

SQL Server Features:

 Holzner, Steven. *Inside XML*. New Riders Publishing, 2001.

 SQL Server Books Online:

➤ Getting Started with SQL Server Books Online

➤ What's New in Microsoft SQL Server 2000

➤ SQL Server Architecture Overview

➤ XML and Internet Support Overview

 MSDN Online Internet Reference (http://msdn.microsoft.com):

➤ XML Online Developer Center (/xml/default.asp)

➤ Developer Resources for SQL Server (/sqlserver)

 TechNet Online Internet Reference: IT Resources for SQL Server (http://www.microsoft.com/technet/sql/default.asp)

 MS Press Online Internet Reference: Learning and Training Resources for IT Professionals/SQL Server 2000 (http://mspress. microsoft.com/it/feature/100500.htm)

Chapter 2

Data Modeling:

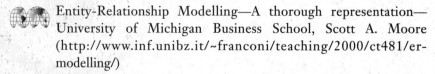 Entity-Relationship Modelling—A thorough representation—University of Michigan Business School, Scott A. Moore (http://www.inf.unibz.it/~franconi/teaching/2000/ct481/er-modelling/)

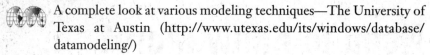 A complete look at various modeling techniques—The University of Texas at Austin (http://www.utexas.edu/its/windows/database/datamodeling/)

Normalization/Denormalization:

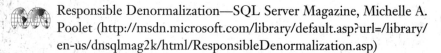 Responsible Denormalization—SQL Server Magazine, Michelle A. Poolet (http://msdn.microsoft.com/library/default.asp?url=/library/en-us/dnsqlmag2k/html/ResponsibleDenormalization.asp)

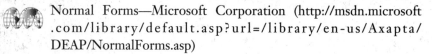 Normal Forms—Microsoft Corporation (http://msdn.microsoft.com/library/default.asp?url=/library/en-us/Axapta/DEAP/NormalForms.asp)

Chapter 3

SQL Server on the Physical Side:

 Delaney, Kalen. *Inside SQL Server 2000*. Microsoft Press, 2001. www.insidesqlserver.com.

Not a beginner book, but it fills in many of the gaps left out of the SQL Server Books Online documentation. Explains fully how SQL Server stores and processes data internally.

 SQL Server Books Online:

➤ Creating and Maintaining Databases. (Look particularly at the sections on indexes, views, and triggers.)

➤ Transact-SQL Reference. (Use this as a resource for the specific syntax requirements of each statement, as well as some code examples.)

➤ Optimizing Database Performance. (Focus on database and application design.)

➤ Troubleshooting: Server and Database Troubleshooting.

MSDN Online Internet Reference (http://msdn.microsoft.com):

➤ Transact SQL Overview (/library/psdk/sql/ts_tsqlcon_6lyk.htm)

➤ Transact SQL Syntax Conventions (/library/psdk/sql/ts_syntaxc_9kvn.htm)

➤ Transact SQL Tips (/library/psdk/sql/ac_8_qd_14_2kc3.htm)

Chapter 4

SQL Server on the Physical Side:

 Delaney, Kalen. *Inside SQL Server 2000*. Microsoft Press, 2001. www.insidesqlserver.com.

 SQL Server Books Online:

➤ SQL Server Architecture, Database Architecture, Logical Database Components, SQL Views. This contains basic information about the creation and definition of views.

➤ Creating and Maintaining Databases, Views, Creating a View, Creating a Partitioned View. This document introduces you to partitioned views.

➤ Introducing Replication, Types of Replication, Implementing Replication, Replication Options. These many titles cover replication thoroughly.

 MSDN Online Internet Reference (http://msdn.microsoft.com):

➤ SQL Server Replication (/library/officedev/odeopg/_deovrsqlserverreplication.htm)

➤ Replication Between Different Versions of SQL Server (/library/psdk/sql/replimpl_4joy.htm)

Chapter 5

ANSI SQL-92:

 SQL Server Books Online:

➤ Accessing and Changing Relational Data

Michael Reilly, Michelle Poolet, SQL Server 2000 Design and TSQL Programming, Osborne (December 2000).

Robin Dewson, Beginning SQL Server Programming, Wrox Press (June 2001).

BCP:

 SQL Server Books Online:

➤ Getting Started with Command Prompt Utilities

XML:

 Griffin, John. *XML and SQL Server 2000*. New Riders, 1995–2005.

Chapter 6

Programming and T-SQL:

 Henderson, Ken. *The Guru's Guide to Transact-SQL*. Addison-Wesley, 2000.

 Vieira, Robert. *Professional SQL Server 2000 Programming*. WROX Press, 2003.

 SQL Server Books Online:

➤ Building SQL Server Applications

Specific Function Reference:

 For information about standard deviation and variance, try the Internet Statistics Glossary, located at http://www.animatedsoftware.com/_statglos/statglos.htm.

Chapter 7

 SQL Server Books Online:

➤ Transact-SQL Reference DBCC

➤ Administering SQL Server—Automating Administrative Tasks

➤ Optimizing Database Performance

 Internet Web Links:

➤ C2 Administrator's Guide:

http://www.microsoft.com/technet/prodtechnol/sql/2000/maintain/sqlc2.mspx

➤ SQL Server Performance Tuning and Optimization:

http://www.sql-server-performance.com/

An excellent site for looking further into any of the topics covered in this chapter and then some.

Chapter 8

 Delaney, Kalen. *Inside SQL Server 2000*. Microsoft Press, 2001. www.insidesqlserver.com.

Not a beginner book, but it fills in many of the gaps left out of the SQL Server Books Online documentation. Explains fully how SQL Server stores and processes data internally.

 SQL Server Books Online:

➤ Index Tuning Recommendations

➤ Placing Indexes on Filegroups

➤ Database Design Considerations

➤ Creating and Maintaining Databases: Indexes

Chapter 9

 SQL Server Books Online:

➤ Managing Permissions

➤ Transact SQL Reference: GRANT, DENY, REVOKE

➤ Administering SQL Server: Managing Security

 Internet Web Links:

➤ C2 Administrator's Guide:

http://www.microsoft.com/technet/_prodtechnol/sql/
maintain/security/_sqlc2.asp

➤ Online tutorial for database security:

http://www.microsoft.com/seminar/shared/asp/view.asp?url=/
Seminar/en/20020918TNT1-55/manifest.xml

➤ Online tutorial for Baseline Security Analyzer:

http://www.microsoft.com/seminar/shared/asp/view.asp?url=
Seminar/en/20020918TNT1-55/manifest.xml

➤ Online reference for coding as related to this exam:

http://www.codeclinic.com/70-229skills.htm

Chapter 10

Programming and T-SQL:

 SQL Server Books Online:

➤ Building SQL Server Applications

Heterogeneous Data Access:

 SQL Server Books Online:

➤ Replication—Replicating and Heterogeneous Data

➤ Data Transformation

 MSDN   Website—http://msdn.microsoft.com/library/default.
asp?url=/library/en-us/adsi/adsi/joining_heterogeneous_data.asp

Glossary

A

ADO (ActiveX Data Objects) An easy-to-use application programming interface (API) that wraps OLE DB for use in languages, such as Visual Basic, Visual Basic for Applications, Active Server Pages, and Microsoft Internet Explorer Visual Basic Scripting.

aggregate functions Functions that provide summary data over sets returning a singular value.

alert A user-defined response to a SQL Server event. Alerts can either execute a defined task or send an email and/or pager message to a specified operator.

ALTER A command used to change a database object, such as a function or procedure. Using ALTER allows the object to be changed without losing permissions and other database settings.

ALTER TRIGGER The ALTER TRIGGER statement is used to change the definition of a trigger. Its syntax and arguments are similar to CREATE TRIGGER.

ALTER VIEW The ALTER VIEW statement is used to easily reshape the definition of a view without affecting permissions granted. Its syntax is similar to the CREATE VIEW statement's syntax.

analysis server The server component of Analysis Services that is specifically designed to create and maintain multidimensional data structures and provide multidimensional data in response to client queries.

articles Data structures made from selected columns from a table, or an entire table, that need to be bundled into a publication to be used for replication. A publication is composed of one or more articles. An article represents some or all columns, and some or all rows in a single table.

attributes The characteristics given to an entity, such as PhoneNumber and State; they are usually represented as rows inside an entity. An attribute in data modeling can be thought of as the columns of a table implemented in SQL Server.

B

batch Multiple batches can be combined in a single script or procedure using the GO Keyword to separate the batches. A collection of zero, one, or more T-SQL statements sent to SQL Server to be run together.

BCP A command prompt bulk copy utility that copies SQL Server data to or from an operating system file in a user-specified format.

binding In SQL application programming interfaces (APIs), binding is associating a resultset column or a parameter with a program variable, so that data is moved automatically into or out of a program variable when a row is fetched or updated.

blocked process A process that cannot continue until a lock that another process holds is released.

Books Online A comprehensive help facility and electronic reference manual.

built-in function A group of predefined functions provided as part of the T-SQL and Multidimensional Expressions (MDX) languages.

C

cascading actions Cascading delete or cascading update operations that either delete a row containing a Primary Key or updates a Primary Key value referenced by Foreign Key columns in existing rows in other tables. On a cascading delete, all the rows whose Foreign Key values reference the deleted Primary Key value are also deleted. On a cascading update, all the Foreign Key values are updated to match the new Primary Key value.

CASE expression A complex expression that handles multiple-branch conditional logic.

CAST The CAST function converts data from one type to another and is based on the ANSI SQL-92 standard as opposed to the CONVERT function.

CHECK constraint Defines what values are acceptable in a column. You can apply CHECK constraints to multiple columns, and you can apply multiple CHECK constraints to a single column. When a table is dropped, CHECK constraints are also dropped.

Client Network utility   The Client Network utility is used to manage the client net-libraries and define server alias names. It can also be used to set the default options used by DB-Library applications.

client/server   A physically or logically implemented system where a device or application called the server requests services or data from another device or application and the server fulfills the request.

clustered index   A clustered index in SQL Server is a type of index in which the logical order of key values determines the actual data rows; thereby the data rows are kept sorted. Using a clustered index causes the actual data rows to move into the leaf level of the index.

collation (sequence)   A set of rules that determines how data is compared, ordered, and presented. Character data is sorted using collation information, including locale, sort order, and case sensitivity.

column list   The column list, or select list, is the part of the SELECT statement that specifies the columns being accessed.

comment   Inline documentation used to explain what a set of T-SQL statements is doing. This is also a technique used to temporarily prevent statements from running for diagnostic and troubleshooting reasons; usually used in the sense "comment out."

constraint   A property assigned to a table column that prevents certain types of invalid data values from being placed in the column. For example, a UNIQUE or PRIMARY KEY constraint prevents you from inserting a value that is a duplicate of an existing value; a CHECK constraint prevents you from inserting a value that does not match a search condition; and NOT NULL prevents you from inserting a NULL value.

CREATE   A command used to create a database object, such as a view or stored procedure.

CREATE TRIGGER   Using the CREATE TRIGGER statement is the T-SQL way to create a trigger, but they can also be created using the Enterprise Manager. As with CREATE VIEW, you can specify useful arguments, such as WITH ENCRYPTION.

Current Activity window   The window view in the Enterprise Manager that enables you to see current processes, objects, and locks held by SQL Server.

cursor   A construct that holds a rowset from a SELECT statement, which can then be stepped through row by row for various operations.

D

data warehouse   A database specifically structured for query and analysis. A data warehouse typically contains data representing the business history of an organization.

database lock The largest of locking increments affecting the entire database.

DBRE DBREINDEX A Database Console Command used to rebuild indexes. Out of the different ways of rebuilding an index, the preferred is DBREINDEX because it does not require that you rebuild indexes individually, but it enables you to rebuild multiple indexes in a single shot.

deadlock A state in which two users or processes cannot continue processing because they each have a resource that the other needs.

DELETE The DELETE T-SQL statement can be used to delete data from a table. A fast way to delete all rows is TRUNCATE TABLE.

DELETE trigger DELETE triggers are FOR or AFTER triggers that can restrict data from being deleted from a table, or to perform any other action with the deleted data—such as logging the deletion or generating an alert. They fire automatically when a DELETE statement is executed against the table.

denormalization The process of adding planned redundancy to an already fully normalized data model.

derived table In a FROM clause, you can use a SELECT statement in parentheses as one of the tables you are selecting from. This is called a derived table.

deterministic A function is deterministic if it always returns the same output when presented with the same input. Mathematical functions, such as SQRT, are deterministic because they always return the same output given the same input.

distributed partitioned view A distributed partitioned view collects data from two or more instances of SQL Server; a new feature to SQL Server 2000.

distributor In SQL Server terminology, the Distributor is the server that contains the distribution database, data history, and transactions; as its name implies, its job is to distribute data to Subscribers.

DROP A command used to drop a database object, such as a view or stored procedure. Using DROP removes all the permissions for the object, as well as the object itself. For example, the DROP VIEW statement is used to remove a view or indexed view from the database. Dropping a view removes the definition of a view from the database and an entry in the sysobjects while not affecting the underlying tables and views.

E

encryption A method for keeping sensitive information confidential by changing data into an unreadable form.

English Query   Refers to a Microsoft application development product that enables users to ask questions in English, rather than in a computer language, such as SQL. For example, you might ask, "How many customers bought products last year?" rather than prepare an equivalent SQL statement.

entity   The main object in an entity-relationship model, which can be deduced by case study examination. Entities represent the things, places, people, concepts, and things involved in a real-world situation, and contain within them properties or attributes that relate to them.

entity decomposition   The breaking down of attributes so that they are made into a more basic form. Entity decomposition needs to be undertaken before applying attributes into the final data model.

execution plan   The method in which the query optimizer has chosen to execute a SQL operation.

extent lock   A lock covering eight contiguous data or index pages.

F

filegroups   In SQL Server, a named collection of one or more files that forms a single unit of allocation. Also for administration of a database.

FILLFACTOR   An attribute of an index that defines the amount of free space allotted to each page of the index. FILLFACTOR can be used to allocate space for future expansion. FILLFACTOR is a value from 1 through 100 that specifies the percentage of the index page to be left empty.

filter   A set of criteria that controls the set of records returned as a resultset. Filters can also define the sequence in which rows are returned.

Foreign Key   A column or multiple columns whose values match the Primary Key of another table. Foreign Keys help in the relational process between two entities by connecting the foreign attribute in the child entity to a Primary Key in a parent entity.

fragmentation   Occurs when data modifications are made. You can reduce fragmentation and improve read-ahead performance by dropping and re-creating a clustered index.

FROM   The FROM part of the SELECT statement specifies the tables being accessed. Specifying what tables are being accessed is compulsory for any SELECT data retrieval statement.

Full-Text catalog   A Full-Text catalog is a special storage space used to house Full-Text indexes. By default, all Full-Text indexes are housed in a single catalog.

Full-Text index   A special index that efficiently tracks the words you're looking for in a table. They help in enabling special searching functions that differ from those used in regular indexes.

G

GROUP BY operator   The operator that creates aggregated sets from a single `select` statement.

H

HTML (Hypertext Markup Language)   A system of marking up, or tagging, a document so that it can be published on the World Wide Web. Documents prepared in HTML include reference graphics and formatting tags. You use a web browser (such as Microsoft Internet Explorer) to view these documents.

I

identity   A column in a table that has been assigned the `identity` property. The `identity` property generates unique numbers.

IIS   Microsoft Internet Information Server.

IN operator   The operator that compares a single value to a set, and returns true if the single value occurs within the set.

index   In a relational database, a database object that provides fast access to data in the rows of a table, based on key values. Indexes can also enforce uniqueness on the rows in a table. SQL Server supports clustered and non-clustered indexes. The `primary key/unique` constraint automatically causes an index to be built. In full-text searches, a full-text index stores information about significant words and their location within a given column.

Index Tuning wizard   A graphical tool that enables you to select and create powerful indexes and statistics for a Microsoft SQL Server 2000 database without prior knowledge of index and database internal structural designs.

indexed view   A view that has an index defined onto it. Indexes on views enable view resultsets to be stored in the database's physical storage after an index is created. In contrast to this, in a non-indexed view, the view is activated at runtime and the resultset is dynamically built.

INSERT   T-SQL command used to add one or more records to a table.

INSERT INTO   The INSERT INTO T-SQL statement can be used to insert rows of data into a table when needed.

INSERT trigger   FOR or AFTER triggers that can be used to verify the data being inserted or to perform any other action with the data. They fire automatically when an INSERT statement is made against the underlying table.

INSTEAD OF trigger   A trigger new to SQL Server 2000, which replaces the action that an INSERT, DELETE, or UPDATE trigger might take.

Internet host name (DNS name) Fully qualified name that is associated with the computer on the Internet (for example, mycomputer.mydomain.com).

J

job   A specified series of operations, called steps, performed sequentially by a SQL Server agent.

join   The act of combining the data in two tables based on values found in each of the tables.

K-L

LIKE   The LIKE predicate is used to search through character strings by specifying a search string. A LIKE search is primarily used for searches based on wildcard characters, such as the percent sign (%).

linked server   A database object that represents a particular data source and the attributes, including security and collation attributes, necessary to access the data source.

local partitioned view   A partitioned view where all member tables reside on the local instance of SQL Server.

lock   A method of ensuring concurrency. Locking enables users to temporarily "check out" an object, preventing other users from changing the object, for the purpose of ensuring consistency.

log file   A file or set of files containing a record of the modifications made in a database.

M

many-to-many relationship   This type of relationship occurs when many rows or things in an entity (many instances of an entity) are associated with many rows or things in another entity. This type of relationship is not uncommon in the real world. SQL Server doesn't actually allow direct implementation of many-to-many relationships; nevertheless, you can do so by creating two one-to-many relationships to a new entity.

Master database   The database that controls the operation of each instance of SQL Server. It is installed automatically with each instance of SQL Server and keeps track of user accounts, remote user accounts, and remote servers that each instance can interact with. It also tracks ongoing processes, configurable environment variables, system error messages, tapes and disks available on the system, and active locks.

merge replication The process of transferring data from the Publisher to the Subscriber, allowing the Publisher and Subscriber to update data while connected or disconnected and then merging the updates after they both are connected. Merge replication begins with a snapshot. Thereafter, no data is replicated until the Publisher and Subscriber do a "merge." The merge can be scheduled or done via an ad-hoc request. Merge replication's main benefit is that it supports subscribers who are not on the network much of the time. Transactions, which are committed, however, may be rolled back as the result of conflict resolution.

meta data Information about the properties of data, such as the type of data in a column (numeric, text, and so on) or the length of a column. It can also be information about the structure of data or information that specifies the design of objects, such as cubes or dimensions.

MIB (Management Information Base) The SNMP protocol used to define a hierarchical list of objects.

MMC (Microsoft Management Console) A common console framework for server and network management applications known as snap-ins.

Model database A database installed with SQL Server that provides the template for new user databases. SQL Server 2000 creates a new database by copying the contents of the Model database and then expanding it to the size requested.

msdb database The msdb database is used by the SQL Server agent for scheduling alerts and jobs and for recording server operator information.

N

NetBIOS computer name The Windows network name associated with the computer.

non-clustered index An index in which the logical order of the index is different than the physical, stored order of the rows on disk. In contrast to clustered indexes, non-clustered indexes are totally separated from the actual data rows, causing an unsorted order of data based on non-clustered keys. Non-clustered indexes differ from the clustered indexes at the leaf level. The leaf level of a non-clustered index contains the key value and the row locator. The row locator is either the physical row address (if there is no clustered index) or the clustered index key value (if a clustered index exists).

non-deterministic   A function is non-deterministic if it can return different results when provided with the same input. The RAND function is non-deterministic because it returns a different randomly generated number each time it is called.

normalization   Developed by Dr. E. F. Codd in 1970, database normalization is the process of simplifying data and database design to achieve maximum performance and simplicity. This process involves the removing of useless and redundant data.

O

ODBC (Open Database Connectivity)   A data access application programming interface (API) that supports access to any data source for which an ODBC driver is available. ODBC is aligned with the American National Standards Institute (ANSI) and International Standards Organization for (ISO) standards for a database Call Level Interface (CLI).

OLE-DB   A COM-based application programming interface (API) for accessing data. OLE-DB supports accessing data stored in any format (databases, spreadsheets, text files, and so on) for which an OLE-DB provider is available.

one-to-many relationships   These relationships exist when a single instance of an entity (the parent entity) relates to many instances of another entity (the child entity). One-to-many relationships are the most common relationships in the real world.

one-to-one relationship   Occurs when one row or thing of an entity is associated with only one row or thing of another. One-to-one relationships are uncommon in the real world.

Online Analytical Processing (OLAP)   A technology that uses multidimensional structures to provide rapid access to data for analysis. The source data for OLAP is commonly stored in data warehouses in a relational database.

Online Transaction Processing (OLTP)   A data processing system designed to record all the business transactions of an organization as they occur. An OLTP system is characterized by many concurrent users actively adding and modifying data.

operator   An individual that can potentially receive messages from SQL Server via email, pager, or Net send.

ORDER BY   A sub-statement found in the SELECT statement used to order the rows in the resultset in either descending or ascending order: DESC and ASC, respectively.

OSQL (ODBC Structured Query Language) An interactive command prompt utility provided with SQL Server that enables users to execute T-SQL statements or batches from a server or workstation and view the results returned.

P

page lock A lock that covers 8KB of data.

partitioned view A table that has been replaced with multiple, smaller tables. Each smaller table has the same format as the original table, but with a subset of the data. Each partitioned table has rows allocated to it based on some characteristic of the data, such as specific key ranges. The rules that define into which table the rows go must be unambiguous. For example, a table is partitioned into two tables. All rows with Primary Key values lower than a specified value are allocated to one table, and all rows equal to or greater than the value are allocated to the other. Partitioning can improve application processing speeds and reduce the potential for conflicts in multi-site update replication. You can improve the usability of partitioned tables by creating a view. The view, created by a union of select operations on all the partitioned tables, presents the data as if it all resided in a single table.

performance monitor The NT implementation of system monitor.

Primary Key A column or set of columns that uniquely identify all the rows in a table. Primary Keys do not allow null values. No two rows can have the same Primary Key value; therefore, a Primary Key value always uniquely identifies a single row. More than one key can uniquely identify rows in a table; each of these keys is called a candidate key. Only one candidate can be chosen as the Primary Key of a table; all other candidate keys are known as alternate keys. Although tables are not required to have Primary Keys, it is good practice to define them. In a normalized table, all the data values in each row are fully dependent on the Primary Key. For example, in a normalized employee table that has EmployeeID as the Primary Key, all the columns should contain data related to a specific employee. This table does not have the column DepartmentName because the name of the department is dependent on a department ID, not on an employee ID.

Profiler SQL Profiler is a tool that captures SQL Server 2000 events from a server. The events are saved in a trace file that can later be analyzed or used to replay a specific series of steps when you want to diagnose a problem.

publication   A container for articles that is capable of being replicated. A publication, which may include one or more articles, is the basic unit of replication. A publication has a single, specific replication type: either snapshot, transactional, or merge. When a subscriber chooses a publication, all the articles contained within the publication are part of the subscription.

Publisher   In respect with replication, the Publisher is the server that produces data so that it can be replicated to Subscribers.

Q

Query Analyzer   SQL Query Analyzer is an interactive, graphical tool that enables a database administrator or developer to write queries, execute multiple queries simultaneously, view results, analyze the query plan, and receive assistance to improve the query performance.

query optimizer   The SQL Server database engine component responsible for generating efficient execution plans for SQL statements.

R

RAID (redundant array of independent disks)
A disk system that comprises multiple disk drives (an array) to provide higher performance, reliability, storage capacity, and lower cost. Fault-tolerant arrays are categorized in six RAID levels: 0 through 5. Each level uses a different algorithm to implement fault tolerance.

rebuilding indexes   Helps in collecting the defragmented pages of information and bringing index data back to its original form. This increases the overall performance by making it easier for SQL Server to read pages to get data.

recompile   The queries used by stored procedures and triggers are optimized only when they are compiled. As indexes or other changes that affect statistics are made to the database, compiled stored procedures and triggers may lose efficiency. By recompiling stored procedures and triggers that act on a table, you can reoptimize the queries.

reconfigure   Command used to update the currently configured value of a configuration option changed with the sp_configure system stored procedure.

recursive trigger   A recursive trigger is a trigger that updates, deletes, or inserts data into its own table or another table, which houses a trigger, and then fires another trigger.

relational database A collection of information organized in tables. Each table models a class of objects of interest to the organization (for example, Customers, Parts, Suppliers). Each column in a table models an attribute of the object (for example, LastName, Price, Color). Each row in a table represents one entity in the class of objects modeled by the table (for example, the customer name John Smith or the part number 1346). Queries can use data from one table to find related data in other tables.

Relational Database Management System The controlling software for databases in which data is organized into related objects within a database rather than tied to a file. Each of these objects is related to another in some way.

relationship A connection between entities ties a parent entity to a child entity through the Primary Key in one entity to a Foreign Key in another.

replication A process that copies and distributes data and database objects from one database to another and then synchronizes information between databases for consistency.

Replication agent Tool that enables SQL Server to perform the different types of replication processes when distributing data.

replication configurations Different physical scenarios in which replication is set up; these provide specific benefits and uses that are relevant to the configuration you use. Replication models, which include Single Publisher/Multiple Subscriber, Single Subscriber/Multiple Publishers, and Multiple Publishers/Multiple Subscribers, are the physical implementation. Each of the replication types may be implemented using any of the these models.

roles A SQL Server security account is a collection of other security accounts that can be treated as a single unit when managing permissions. A role can contain SQL Server logins, other roles, and Windows logins or groups.

row lock The finest granularity of locking available on SQL Server allowing for a single data record to be locked.

rules A database object that is bound to columns or user-defined data types, and specifies what data values are acceptable in a column. CHECK constraints provide the same functionality and are preferred because they are in the SQL-92 standard.

S

schema In the SQL-92 standard, a collection of database objects that are owned by a single user and form a single namespace. A namespace is a set of objects that cannot have duplicate names. For example, two tables can have the same name only if they are in separate schemas; no two tables in the same schema can have the same name. In T-SQL, much of the functionality associated with schemas is implemented by database user IDs. In database tools, schema also refers to the catalog information that describes the objects in a schema or database. In analysis services, a schema is a description of multidimensional objects, such as cubes and dimensions.

SCHEMABINDING An option for a user-defined function or a view that prevents changes to the objects referenced by the function or view unless you first drop the view. This makes the views and functions more reliable, because they can rely on their database objects always being present.

scope The lifetime of an object. Specifically, a variable has a scope within a single batch, which means it ceases to exist outside the batch.

script A collection of batches, usually stored in a text file.

SELECT The T-SQL statement used to return data to an application or another T-SQL statement, or to populate a cursor. The SELECT statement returns a tabular result set consisting of data that is typically extracted from one or more tables. The result set contains data from only those rows that match the search conditions specified in the WHERE or HAVING clauses.

Server Network utility The Server Network utility is used to manage the server net-libraries.

Service Manager SQL Server Service Manager is used to start, stop, and pause the SQL Server 2000 components on the server. These components run as services on Microsoft Windows NT or Microsoft Windows 2000 and as separate executable programs on Microsoft Windows 95 and Microsoft Windows 98.

SET The statement used to alter environment settings for a session.

snapshot replication A type of replication wherein data and database objects are distributed by copying published items via the Distributor and on to the Subscriber exactly as they appear at a specific moment in time. Snapshot replication provides the distribution of both data and structure (tables, indexes, and so on) on a scheduled basis. It may be thought of as a "whole table refresh." No updates to the source table are replicated until the next scheduled snapshot.

SNMP (Simple Network Management Protocol) Used for troubleshooting and querying TCP/IP servers.

SQL Profiler A tool used to trace SQL Server activity.

statement permissions An attribute that controls whether a user can execute CREATE or BACKUP statements.

statistics SQL Server keeps statistics about the distribution of the key values in each index and uses these statistics to determine what index(es) to use in query processing.

stored procedure A collection of T-SQL statements with a well-defined set of inputs, called input parameters, and a well-defined set of outputs, which may be output parameters, return values, or cursors. Stored procedures allow the encapsulation of various database operations.

string concatenation Combining of two strings, such as the results of the first name and last name columns. String concatenation can be performed using the plus (+) operator.

Structured Query Language (SQL) A language used to insert, retrieve, modify, and delete data in a relational database. SQL also contains statements for defining and administering the objects in a database. SQL is the language supported by most relational databases, and is the subject of standards published by the International Standards Organization (ISO) and the American National Standards Institute (ANSI). SQL Server 2000 uses a version of the SQL language called T-SQL.

Subscriber The server that receives replicated data (in the form of publications) from the Publisher.

System Monitor The performance monitoring tool available in Windows 2000 operating systems.

T

table A two-dimensional object, consisting of rows and columns, used to store data in a relational database. Each table stores information about one of the types of objects modeled by the database.

table lock A lock on a table, including all data and indexes.

TCP/IP (Transmission Control Protocol/Internet Protocol) An industry standard network protocol used by most companies for inter-networking computer equipment.

tempdb   The database that provides a storage area for temporary tables, temporary stored procedures, and other temporary working storage needs.

TOP   The TOP keyword can be used in conjunction with the SELECT statement to select the top *n* rows or a percentage of the resultset rows.

trace   The SQL Profiler method for recording server events.

trace flags   Flags that can be enabled to aid in troubleshooting.

transactional replication   A type of replication where data and database objects are distributed by first applying an initial snapshot at the Subscriber and then later capturing transactions made at the Publisher and propagating them to individual Subscribers. Transactional replication, as with all replication types, begins with a synchronizing snapshot. After the initial synchronization, transactions, which are committed at the Publisher, are automatically replicated to the Subscribers.

Transact-SQL (T-SQL)   The language containing the commands used to administer instances of SQL Server, create and manage all objects in an instance of SQL Server, and to insert, retrieve, modify, and delete all data in SQL Server tables. T-SQL is an extension of the language defined in the SQL standards published by the International Standards Organization (ISO) and the American National Standards Institute (ANSI).

trigger   A trigger is a stored procedure that is fired when data is modified from a table using any of the three modification statements: DELETE, INSERT, or UPDATE. FOR and AFTER are synonymous, and are usually implied when referring to triggers, rather than INSTEAD OF triggers. Triggers are often created to enforce referential integrity or consistency among logically related data in different tables.

T-SQL   See *Transact-SQL*.

U

UNION operator   An operator that can combine two SELECT statements into one large rowset.

UNIQUE constraint   Constraints that enforce entity integrity on a non-Primary Key. UNIQUE constraints ensure that no duplicate values are entered and that an index is created to enhance performance.

UNIQUE index   An index in which no two rows are permitted to have the same index value, thus prohibiting duplicate index or key values. The system checks for duplicate key values when the index is created and checks each time data is added with an INSERT or UPDATE statement.

UPDATE The act of modifying one or more data values in an existing row or rows, typically by using the UPDATE statement. Sometimes, the term *update* refers to any data modification, including INSERT, UPDATE, and DELETE operations.

UPDATE STATISTICS A command that updates statistical information for an index. Index statistics need to be up to date for the optimizer to decide upon the fastest route of access.

UPDATE trigger UPDATE triggers are FOR or AFTER triggers that can be used to evaluate UPDATE statements issued against a table to modify existing data. They can be used to allow or reject data modification attempts, to log the attempt, or to generate an alert. They fire automatically when an UPDATE statement is executed against the table.

updateable Subscribers Subscribers that are capable of updating and modifying data when it is replicated. This option can be used with snapshot replication and transactional replication. A transactional or snapshot publication may allow updateable Subscribers. Changes made on the Subscriber's replica are propagated to the Publisher either in real time via DTC, or near real time via a queue.

user A user is a database-wide security context.

user-defined function A collection of T-SQL statements with a well-defined set of input parameters, but only one output—which can be a scalar value or a table. User-defined functions allow the encapsulation of various logical and database operations, but cannot be used to affect changes to a database.

V

variable A construct that can temporarily hold values for use in a Transact-SQL batch.

view A view is a relational database object that can be referenced and built by using SELECT statements to join data from one or more base tables. Views are similar to tables in that data can be retrieved and modified and indexes can be built.

W

WHERE A sub-statement found in the SELECT statement that uses any of various filter conditions, such as BETWEEN, IN, and LIKE, to limit the number of rows retrieved.

Windows application log The operating system event log used to record application events sent by SQL Server services.

WITH ENCRYPTION The WITH
ENCRYPTION clause protects the definition of your view. If you specify
this, you encrypt the definition of
your view because you may not
want users to display it. Encrypting
using WITH ENCRYPTION disallows
anyone from using
sp_heptext to display your view or
viewing it via the Enterprise
Manager.

WITH SCHEMABINDING The WITH
SCHEMABINDING option specifies that
the view be bound to the schema.
This has to be specified when you
want to create views with indexes.
Also, when WITH SCHEMABINDING is
specified, you have to adhere to the
owner.object syntax when referencing tables or views in the creation of
your view.

X-Z

**XML (Extensible Markup
Language)** A hypertext programming language used to describe the
contents of a set of data and how the
data should be output to a device or
displayed in a web page. Used to
move data between systems.

Index

How can we make this index more useful? Email us at indexes@quepublishing.com

indexed views, 274
nonclustered, 85-86, 267-268
Pad Index setting, 87
rebuilding, 86, 270-271
strategies, 270
unique indexes, 86
what not to index, 269-270
what to index, 268-269
INFORMATION_SCHEMA views, 200
INNER JOIN statement, 166-167
inner joins, 166-167
INSERT statement, 171-172
inserting data, 171-172
instances, 36
INSTEAD OF triggers, 5, 220, 223-224
Integrated security mode, 288
integrity of data, 37, 82
Internet application architecture, 308-309
INTO clause (SELECT statement),
 153-154
@@IO_BUSY function, 277
IS NOT NULL statement, 160
IS NULL statement, 160
Is RowGuid descriptor (columns), 80
ISNULL() function, 199
isolation (transactions), 258-260

J-K

jobs, 18, 89, 319-320
join entities, 49
join hints, 248
joining multiple sets of data, 165-166
 cross joins, 169
 inner joins, 166-167
 outer joins, 167-169
 unions, 169-171

kernel entities, 33
key attributes, 38-39
keys
 definitions of, 80
 FOREIGN KEY, 82
 foreign keys, 40-41
 PRIMARY KEY, 81-82
 primary keys, 39-41
 surrogate keys, 40
KEYSET cursors, 213

L

latency, 136
LEN() function, 197
Length descriptor (columns), 79
Lightweight Pooling option (server
 properties), 117
linked servers, 19, 315-317
LOCAL cursors, 213
Lock:Acquired event, 240
Lock:Cancel event, 240
Lock:Deadlock Chain event, 240
Lock:Deadlock event, 240
Lock:Escalation event, 240
Lock:Released event, 240
Lock:Timeout event, 240
locks
 contentions, 257-258
 controlling lock behavior, 258-260
 diagnosing with Profiler traces, 239-241
 exclusive locks, 257
 events, 240-241
 granularity, 259
 locks by object, 18
 locks by process ID, 18
 shared locks, 257
 transaction isolation levels, 258-259
Locks option (server properties), 117
log files, 18, 64-65, 236
logical data modeling, 30-32
 attributes
 decomposing, 37-38
 defining, 35-37
 definition of, 32
 foreign keys, 40-41
 identifiers, 39
 key attributes, 38-39
 primary keys, 39-41
 surrogate keys, 40
 dependencies, 46-48
 entities
 associate entities, 49
 associative entities, 33
 characteristic entities, 34
 definition of, 32
 kernel entities, 33
 selecting, 33-35
 unary entities, 49

T

U